Coaching Practiced

BPS Textbooks in Psychology

BPS Wiley presents a comprehensive and authoritative series covering everything a student needs in order to obtain an academic qualification in psychology. Refreshingly written to consider more than North American research, this series is the first to give a truly international perspective. Written by the very best names in the field, the series offers an extensive range of titles suited to undergraduate through to postgraduate and doctoral programmes, and every text fully complies with the BPS syllabus on the topic. No other series bears the BPS seal of approval.

Many of the books are supported by a companion website, featuring additional resource materials for both instructors and students, designed to encourage critical thinking, and providing for all your course lecturing and testing needs.

For other titles in this series, please go to **http://psychsource.bps.org.uk**

Coaching Practiced

EDITED BY

DAVID TEE

&

JONATHAN PASSMORE

The British
Psychological Society

WILEY

Registered Offices
John Wiley & Sons, Inc., 111 River Street, Hoboken, NJ 07030, USA
John Wiley & Sons Ltd, The Atrium, Southern Gate, Chichester, West Sussex, PO19 8SQ, UK

Editorial Office
The Atrium, Southern Gate, Chichester, West Sussex, PO19 8SQ, UK

For details of our global editorial offices, customer services, and more information about Wiley products visit us at www.wiley.com.

Wiley also publishes its books in a variety of electronic formats and by print-on-demand. Some content that appears in standard print versions of this book may not be available in other formats.

Library of Congress Cataloging-in-Publication Data
Names: Passmore, Jonathan, editor. | Tee, David, editor.
Title: Coaching practiced / edited by Jonathan Passmore, David Tee.
Description: First Edition. | Hoboken, NJ : John Wiley & Sons, [2022] | Series: BPS Textbooks in Psychology | Includes bibliographical references and index. | Contents: The Psychology of Coaching: Coaching Psychology - Eclectic Approaches and Diversity in Practice -- Coaching Frameworks: The Role of Frameworks, Models and Approaches in Coaching -- Reflective Practice and Professional Development: Introduction -- Well-being Coaching: Introduction--Workplace Coaching: Introduction--Cognitive Approaches -- Motivational Interviewing: Introduction -- Solution-Focused Coaching: Introduction -- Mindfulness: Introduction -- Narrative Coaching: Introduction -- Positive Psychology: Introduction -- Part 4. Narrative Coaching - Redesigning the GROW Model as the Fourth-Generation Coaching for People and the Planet.
Identifiers: LCCN 2021043982 (print) | LCCN 2021043983 (ebook) | ISBN 9781119835691 (Paperback) | ISBN 9781119835707 (ePub) | ISBN 9781119835714 (eBook)
Subjects: LCSH: Personal coaching. | Counseling.
Classification: LCC BF637.P36 C6345 2022 (print) | LCC BF637.P36 (ebook) | DDC 158.3--dc23/eng/20211207
LC record available at https://lccn.loc.gov/2021043982
LC ebook record available at https://lccn.loc.gov/2021043983

Cover image: © Rajeev Sreedharan/Getty Images
Cover design by Wiley

Set in 10/12 and DanteMTStd-Regular by Integra Software Services, Pondicherry, India

SKY55C3C9FA-E3CC-4468-A974-4C0317F3BB02_033122

All of the royalty proceeds from this title have been gifted to the British Psychological Society by the contributors, authors and editors.

This book is dedicated to Sir John Whitmore, a true pioneer of contemporary coaching, whose teachings exalted the importance of awareness, responsibility and self-belief and who encouraged us – individually and collectively – to embrace our higher values and human potential.

Contents

About the Editors

David Tee

David is the editor of *The Coaching Psychologist*, published by BPS. He is a chartered psychologist and practising coach and coach supervisor. David is the Global Director of Science at CoachHuB, a visiting lecturer for University of Worcester and programme director of coaching at the University of South Wales, where he is a visiting fellow. He has published widely, including papers in *International Journal of Evidence-Based Coaching and Mentoring*, *International Coaching Psychology Review* and *Action Learning: Research and Practice*.

Jonathan Passmore

Jonathan is editor-in-chief of the *International Coaching Psychology Review* and chair of the BPS Division of Coaching Psychology (2021–2022). He is senior vice president at CoachHub, and professor of coaching and behavioural change at Henley Business School. He has published widely, with over 100 scientific papers and 30 books. His latest titles include *The Coaches Handbook*, *Becoming a Coach: The Essential ICF Guide* and *CoachMe: My Personal Board of Directors*. He is one of the most cited coaching researchers worldwide, has won multiple awards for his work and is listed in the Coaching Global Gurus Top 20 Coaches (2021).

Section 1

The Psychology of Coaching

Coaching Psychology – Eclectic Approaches and Diversity in Practice

David Tee & Jonathan Passmore

The first two decades of the third millennium have witnessed a proliferation of coaching psychology approaches. These approaches have extended the original modules developed in the 1980s and 1990s such as GROW and co-active coaching into new territories. Many of these new approaches have been drawn from the therapeutic and counselling domain; these initially included cognitive-behavioural coaching, solution-focused coaching and psychodynamic coaching during the 2000–2010 period. This was followed by a more diverse range of models including motivational interviewing, acceptance and commitment coaching, compassion-based coaching and Gestalt, which have each been developed for use in coaching. In the period post-2020, other models are also now being considered as possible frameworks for use with coaching clients in non-clinical relationships, such as dialectical behavioural therapy and meta-cognitive therapy (for a wider discussion of third wave cognitive-behavioural coaching (CBC), see Passmore & Leach, 2022). In addition to the influences from therapy, psychological models have also been translated for use in coaching psychology practice, such as positive psychology and mindfulness. This flow of models from therapy and psychology contrasts with the relative sparse influence from change management and organisational development, with appreciative coaching being a rare exception drawing on appreciative inquiry as a structure to frame positive-focused conversations.

Coaching Practiced, First Edition. Edited by David Tee and Jonathan Passmore.
© 2022 John Wiley & Sons Ltd. Published 2022 by John Wiley & Sons Ltd.
DOI: 10.1002/9781119835714.s01

This multiplicity of available frameworks can be confusing for the coach. Some have responded by focusing on a single model or framework as a way to structure all conversations. However, the evidence suggests the majority of coaches have adopted a more eclectic approach and have sought to integrate a range of different models into their work with clients. This follows suggestions from writers in the emerging years of coaching, such as Alison Hardingham (2006) and Jonathan Passmore (2006), who advocated for a more eclectic approach, by which the coach should draw from a number of different streams and, in doing so, would be best able to respond to the unique individual and their specific presenting issue, as opposed to forcing each client to become the round peg required to fit the shape and size of 'hole' offered by the coach. These ideas of eclectic approaches have been further developed (Hardingham, 2021; Passmore, 2021), with an emphasis on each coach developing their own distinctive evidence-based approach informed by the cultural context, types of clients and their own personal style to build an approach which is informed by science but which can also be flexed and adapted to meet the client where they are.

Where does this leave coaching? Are coaching and coaching psychology essentially the same, or are there differences? For many clients, and even for practitioners, this is an academic debate. But it matters for three reasons: Firstly, it is important to define something to be able to provide it. If the label on the tin says 'tomato soup', but it is crab soup when you open it, you may well be disappointed. A failure to clearly define and manage boundaries can also lead the coach into difficulties and risk causing harm to the client if the coach is not qualified and trained to work with an issue. Secondly, definitions matter for research. If we have not clearly defined our intervention, it is hard to measure the effect. We might be assessing if lunch poisoned the individual; however, if we cannot differentiate between the wholemeal bread and the crab soup, we do not know if the problem is a wheat intolerance or shellfish poisoning. Finally, and possibly most important for practitioners, if it is not clearly defined, we cannot teach it. Knowing the crucial ingredients – and the boundaries – allows for a syllabus and criteria for assessment to be developed: definitions matter.

This is not the place for a deep discussion of definitions, but practitioners should know what they are doing and be able to define, with precision, their intervention. In doing so they may reference one of the many definitions available: John Whitmore's classic definition of coaching: 'unlocking a person's potential to maximise their own performance. It is helping them to learn rather than teaching them – a facilitation approach' (Whitmore, 1992, p. 8), Laura Whitworth's definition of co-active coaching, 'a relationship of possibilities … based on trust, confidentiality' (Kimsey-House et al., 2011, p. 19), Passmore and Fillery-Travis's (2011) more process-focused definition '… a Socratic-based dialogue between a facilitator (coach) and a participant (client) where the majority of interventions used by the facilitator are open questions which are aimed at stimulating the self-awareness and personal responsibility of the participant', or one of the professional bodies' definitions, such as that of the International Coaching Federation.

For us, coaching psychology has a distinctive role to play. "Coaching psychology is 'the well' which refreshes the wider coaching profession" (Passmore & Yi-Ling, 2019, p. 79). Coaching psychologists draw on their deeper understanding of research to actively contribute new theories, models, frameworks and, most importantly, evidence, to take forward evidence-based practice. While their practices may be consistent with many other evidence-based practitioners, their understanding of the wider psychological frameworks and the evidence underpinning their approach mark them out as distinctive. The client may witness little of this deeper knowledge in an individual session, but the wider body of coaching will benefit from their contribution, as they challenge and push the boundaries of practice through scientific-led enquiry, engaging in research and sharing their work through journals and other publications. In essence, the coaching psychologist is a scholar-practitioner, constantly crossing and re-crossing the bridge between practice and academia.

The British Psychological Society defines *coaching psychology* as "the scientific study and application of behaviour, cognition and emotion to deepen our understanding of individuals' and groups' performance, achievement and wellbeing, and to enhance practice within coaching" (BPS, 2021).

As we continue to move forward, the definition of coaching and the areas of work in which coaching psychologists engage is likely to continue to change. It is twenty years since this journey of encouraging a focus on evidence-based coaching practice started, marked by the formation of the 'Coaching Psychology Network' within the British Psychological Society. Two decades on, that group has evolved into the Division of Coaching Psychology with pathways for accredited training and the pace of change for coaching is quickening. While evidence will continue to grow in importance, digital platforms, artificial intelligence (AI) coaching apps and the blurring of the boundaries between coaching and counselling are likely to continue. The world of coaching in 2050 will be a fascinating place but, whatever changes, psychology, understanding human behaviour, emotion and cognition will be at its heart.

REFERENCES

BPS (2021). BPS Division of Coaching Psychology – Definition of Coaching Psychology. Retrieved on 1 November 2021 from https://www.bps.org.uk/member-microsites/division-coaching-psychology

Hardingham, A. (2006). The British Eclectic model of coaching, *International Journal of Mentoring and Coaching* IV(1).

Hardingham, A. (2021). The Universal Eclectic model of executive coaching. In J. Passmore (ed.), *The Coaches Handbook: The Complete Practitioners Guide for Professional Coaches* (pp. 167–175). Routledge.

Kimsey-House, H., Kimsey-House, K., Sandahl, P., & Whitworth, L. (2011). *Co-Active Coaching: Changing Business, Transforming Lives* (3rd ed.). Boston: Nicholas Brealey.

Passmore, J. (2006). Integrated coaching model. In J. Passmore (ed.), *Excellence in Coaching: The Industry Guide* (1st ed.). Kogan Page.

Passmore, J. (2021). Developing an integrated approach to coaching. In J. Passmore (ed.), *The Coaches Handbook: The Complete Practitioners Guide for Professional Coaches* (pp. 322–330). Routledge.

Passmore, J. & Fillery-Travis, A. (2011). A critical review of executive coaching research: A decade of progress and what's to come. *Coaching: An International Journal of Theory, Research and Practice*, 4(2), 70–88.

Passmore, J. & Leach, S. (2022). Third Wave Cognitive Behavioural coaching: Contextual, Behavioural and neuroscience Approaches for Evidence-Based Coaches. Shoreham-by-Sea: Pavilion Publishing.

Passmore, J., & Yi-Ling, Y. (2019). Coaching psychology: Exploring definitions and research contribution to practice? *International Coaching Psychology Review*, 14(2), 69–83.

Whitmore, J. (1992). Coaching for Performance. London: Nicholas Brealey.

Section 2
Coaching Frameworks

The Role of Frameworks, Models and Approaches in Coaching

David Tee & Jonathan Passmore

While coaching is similar to other helping-by-talking interventions such as counselling and therapy in the range of 'approaches' available (many of these coaching approaches indeed having their conceptual roots within therapy), the ever-growing number of 'models' is something that sets coaching apart from related practices. Given this, it is of interest that the term 'model' is rarely defined and variously applied in the coaching literature.

Within the context of counselling supervision, Reeves (2013) uses the term 'models' to refer to frameworks which bring "…a particular perspective to how the supervisory process might be negotiated and understood" (p. 387). Within the coaching practitioner literature, 'models' can be used to refer to any theory, theoretical framework or tool deemed of potential use to coaches in their client work (Bates, 2015). More commonly, however, the term applies to frameworks or structures, often producing acronyms, which suggest a sequence of linear stages to follow within a coaching conversation. As an example, the RADAR model has the steps Rapport, Analyse, Demonstrate, Activity, Review (Giangregorio, 2016) or alternatively Relationship, Awareness, Dream, Action, Results/Review (Hilliard, 2012).

A general point can be made before specific models are considered. Coaching models are often positioned as how coaching practitioners cut their teeth, whether it be through introductory training programmes or texts (e.g., Gilbert & Whittleworth, 2009; van Niewerburgh, 2014) or as a dominant framework for practice: The Work Foundation (2002, as cited in Dembkowski & Eldridge, 2003) found over a third of respondent coaches reported a reliance on the GROW model, while a survey of practitioners within England suggests almost 70% use goal-focused models such as GROW in their work (Tee et al., 2019).

Coaching Practiced, First Edition. Edited by David Tee and Jonathan Passmore.
© 2022 John Wiley & Sons Ltd. Published 2022 by John Wiley & Sons Ltd.
DOI: 10.1002/9781119835714.s02

Such coaching models do provide benefits. As Adams (2016) explains, they act as an aide-memoire to the coach using them, as well as providing structure and momentum to the conversation itself. In addition, they can provide a reassurance to neophyte practitioners that they are 'doing it right': that, by using a published framework that is providing a route map through a conversation, stating the function of each step and, often, helpfully providing a set of questions to use at each stage, the coach is providing something of value to the client.

However, there are risks and limitations, too. A practitioner using a structured model, such as COACH (Webb, 2019), may take false reassurance that the structure is all-encompassing, covering every element and consideration required of an ethical and effective coach. A coach may also adhere to the model or technique too rigidly, rather than using it as a baseline from which to improvise or deviate (Clutterbuck, 2010). Finally, even if used lightly, the overlaying of one or two familiar models onto a coach's work with their clients may become repetitive and mechanistic, diminishing the opportunity to maximise insight and learning.

Mindful of these limitations, Clutterbuck (2010) states more experienced practitioners move beyond this mechanistic approach towards a more eclectic drawing upon a range of techniques, and from this to operating within a specific theoretical framework, such as 'Gestalt', before finally reaching a stage of 'liberation'. At this point in the practitioner's role maturity, their craft is typified more by a way of being than a way of doing. If this is accurate, then it echoes the distinction that the professional body EMCC (2015) makes between foundation and master practitioners, with the latter expected to formulate their own tools, adapt from moment to moment in response to client information and to have a unique approach based upon their own critical evaluation of existing models.

We argue here that there may be a distinction between coaching models and coaching psychology models. While many of the caveats indicated above apply in the use of either category of model, coaching psychology models have a theoretical and conceptual rooting within a psychological approach, drawing upon its associated body of theory and research evidence. While there may be some coaching models for which this is also the case, Passmore (2007) argues that such roots are typically not made overt – or possibly even known – by the authors of such models.

Coaching psychology models, such as those detailed in this volume, explicitly embed specific aspects of evidence-based practice from their respective approaches within their stages. The ENABLE model (Adams, 2016), for example, incorporates the solution-focused practices of scaling questions, working with exceptions and the building of client self-efficacy. The SPACE model includes the cognitive-behavioural focus on cognitions, emotions and behaviours (or 'A'ctions in the model's acronym). It could be argued that the transparency of the theoretical roots of coaching psychology models allows a coach to make an informed decision as to whether to integrate it into their way of being with clients and the extent to which it fits in with their own values, preferences and assumptions about what constitutes 'good' practice.

This section opens with three coaching psychology models. The first is Nick Edgerton and Stephen Palmer's (2005) cognitive-behavioural SPACE model. Initially developed in 2002, this model is intended to raise client awareness of the interactions involved in their own or other people's psychological processes. As such, SPACE is less linear than many other models, with the ACE and PACE variants offered within the paper as options for the coaching psychologist, dependent on the needs of the client at that time.

Garret O'Moore (2012) details the integrative model PEAK, intended for performance coaching and designed to focus coaching session attention on three key performance factors: ability, effort and difficulty. Anthony M. Grant (2011) then offers a variation on GROW: the RE-GROW model. Grant identifies the risk of coaching, as a series of structured conversations, becoming disjointed. This would reduce the focus, momentum and progress towards goal attainment that the client (and their sponsor organisation) may desire. By building in an initial Review and Evaluate (the 'RE' in 'RE-GROW') at the opening of each session, Grant suggests goal-directed self-regulation should increase.

The section finishes with Zsófia Anna Utry and colleagues (2015) offering a coaching psychology variant of pluralistic counselling and psychotherapy. The paper offers a number of practical steps that coaching psychologists may take in building up the collaborative capacity of their clients, as well as checking their own capacity and alignment to pluralistic principles.

REFERENCES

Adams, M. (2016) ENABLE: A solution-focused coaching model for individual and team coaching. *The Coaching Psychologist*, 12(1), 17–23

Bates, B. (2015). *The little book of big coaching models*. Pearson Education Ltd.

Clutterbuck, D. (2010). Coaching reflection: The liberated coach. *Coaching: An International Journal of Theory, Research and Practice*, 3(1), 73–81.

Dembkowski, S., & Eldridge, F. (2003). Beyond GROW: A new coaching model. *The International Journal of Mentoring and Coaching*, 1(1), 21–26.

Edgerton, N., & Palmer, S. (2005). SPACE: A psychological model for use within cognitive-behavioural coaching, therapy and stress management. *The Coaching Psychologist 2*(2), 25–31.

EMCC (2015). *EMCC Competence Framework v2*. EMCC UK. https://emccuk.org/Public/Accreditation/Competence_Framework.aspx. Last accessed on 8 December 2021.

Giangregorio, E. (2016, March 8). *RADAR Instructional Coaching Model. Emanuela Giangregorio*. https://www.aikaizen.com/radar-instructional-coaching-model. Last accessed on 8 December 2021.

Gilbert, A., & Whittleworth, K. (2009). *The OSCAR Coaching Model*. Worth Consulting.

Hilliard, P. (2012, June 4). Coaching Model: The RADAR. *International Coach Academy*. https://coachcampus.com/coach-portfolios/coaching-models/pearl-hilliard-the-radar. Last accessed on 8 December 2021.

Passmore, J. (2007). Behavioural Coaching. In S. Palmer and A. Whybrow (Eds.), *Handbook of coaching psychology*. Routledge.

Reeves, A. (2013). *An introduction to counselling and psychotherapy*. SAGE.

Tee, D., Passmore, J., & Brown, H. (2019). Distinctions in coaching practice between England and the rest of Europe. *The Coaching Psychologist*, *15*(2), 30–37.

van Niewerburgh, C. (2014). *An Introduction to Coaching Skills*. SAGE.

Webb, K. (2019). *The COACH Model for Christian Leaders*. Morgan James Publishing.

O'Moore, G. (2012). PEAK: A model for use within performance coaching. *The Coaching Psychologist*, *8*(1), 39–45.

Grant, A. M. (2011). Is it time to REGROW the GROW model? Issues related to teaching coaching session structures. *The Coaching Psychologist*, *7*(2), 118–126.

Utry, Z. A., Palmer, S., McLeod, J., & Cooper, M. (2015). A pluralistic approach to coaching. *The Coaching Psychologist*, *11*(1), 47.

1 SPACE: A psychological model for use within cognitive behavioural coaching, therapy and stress management

Nick Edgerton & Stephen Palmer

Abstract

This paper introduces 'SPACE', a comprehensive psychological model that can be used within cognitive behavioural coaching, therapy and stress management to aid assessment, explain the cognitive model to the client, and assist in the development of a coaching, therapeutic or training programme. Other models, coaching processes and acronyms will be briefly covered to put 'SPACE' into a coaching context. For illustrative purposes this paper will focus on coaching.

Over the past couple of decades a number of different coaching models, processes and associated acronyms have been developed by coaching practitioners to enhance and inform their practice, and provide a useful framework. These models are usually shared with the client in a transparent manner and help to facilitate the change and goal-focused process. The next section will highlight a number of the different models including the cognitive model. Then the SPACE model will be illustrated.

Original publication details: Edgerton, N., & Palmer, S. (2005, November). SPACE: A psychological model for use within cognitive behavioural coaching, therapy and stress management. *The Coaching Psychologist, 2*(2), 25–31. Reproduced with permission of The British Psychological Society.

GROW MODEL

The GROW model of coaching has been popularised by Sir John Whitmore (e.g. 1996) although according to the literature (see Boyle et al., 2005) it was developed by Graham Alexander. It is probably one of the most well used models of coaching.

Whitmore (2004, p.54) describes the sequence for GROW as follows:

- GOAL setting for the session as well as short and long term;
- REALITY checking to explore the current situation;
- OPTIONS and alterative strategies or courses of action;
- WHAT is to be done, WHEN, by WHOM and the WILL to do it.

The last stage is also known as WRAP-UP by some practitioners. The GROW model appears to be taught by many coaching training centres throughout the UK. It is relatively straight forward and would be at the behavioural end of the coaching spectrum.

ACHIEVE MODEL

The ACHIEVE model was developed by Sabine Dembkowski and Fiona Elridge (2003). They believe that it is a logical progression from the GROW model and follows the development of a coaching relationship in a systematic manner:

- Assess current situation;
- Creative brainstorming of alternative to current situation;
- Hone goals;
- Initiate options;
- Evaluative options;
- Valid action programme design;
- Encourage momentum.

The ACHIEVE model does allow for flexibility and individuality.

LASER: A COACHING PROCESS

Graham Lee (2003) describes LASER, a five-stage coaching process which provides a frame of reference for moving a manager through the journey of leadership coaching. According to Lee it is a flexible framework that indicates the core activities. The five stages are:

- Learning;
- Assessing;
- Story-making;

- Enabling;
- Reframing.

Unlike some of the other coaching models Lee does not conceive LASER as a rigid linear journey.

POSITIVE MODEL

Vincenzo Libri (2004) suggested the POSITIVE model developed from the GROW and ACHIEVE and influenced by psychological contributions that produce 'an optimum coaching relationship'. Examples of key questions in each phase are provided below:

- Purpose, e.g. what is it you want to achieve?
- Observations, e.g. what have you tried so far?
- Strategy, e.g. what does success look like for you?
- Insight, e.g. how committed are you in achieving this goal on a scale of 1 – 10?
- Team, e.g. who will you share your goal with?
- Initiate, e.g. when will you start to act on this?
- Value, e.g. how will you celebrate your success?
- Encourage, e.g. how are you going with your goals?

Libri (2004) provides a useful list of key questions at each stage.

TRADITIONAL PROBLEM-SOLVING MODELS

Wasik (1984) proposed a seven-step problem-solving sequence and accompanying questions that practitioners and more importantly their clients can ask themselves at each step of the process as below.

Steps	Questions/Actions
1. Problem identification	What is the concern?
2. Goal selection	What do I want?
3. Generation of alternatives	What can I do?
4. Consideration of consequences	What might happen?
5. Decision making	What is my decision?
6. Implementation	Now do it!
7. Evaluation	Did it work?

Even though it does not have a convenient acronym, this seven-step model has been adapted to coaching, therapy, training and stress management (Palmer & Burton, 1996; Palmer, 1997a, b; Neenan & Palmer, 2001a, b). Once the client becomes adept at using the seven-step model, Neenan and Palmer (2001a, b) suggest that the client may want to use a shorter model to quicken the problem-solving process. For example, STIR and PIE:

Select a problem
Target a solution
Implement a solution
Review outcome
Problem definition
Implement a solution
Evaluate outcome

They assert that shorter models of problem-solving are usually used for rapid processing of a problem in order to deal with a crisis or make a quick decision. However, with these shorter models, deliberation is exchanged for speed, so a less satisfactory outcome may be experienced by the client.

ABCDE COGNITIVE MODEL

The problem-solving models or frameworks described above form an integrated part of the cognitive or cognitive behavioural coaching approach. If the issue or problem can be addressed by focusing on the practical aspects of the problem then the problem solving models are sufficient. However, if the client experiences a psychological or emotional block largely caused by unhelpful, goal-blocking or performance interfering thoughts (PITs), then the practitioner uses the well known ABCDE model (Ellis *et al.*, 1997). Often this need becomes apparent when the client cannot successfully complete Step 5 of the seven-step problem-solving model:

A – Activating event – stops working on the solution chosen at step 5.
B – Beliefs or PITs, e.g. 'I can't stand all this hard work. I'll never reach the deadline.'
C – Consequences: emotion – anxiety; behaviour – procrastinates; physiological palpitations.
D – Disputing – 'I don't like it but in reality I can stand it. If I start work NOW then I'm more likely to reach the deadline.
E – Effective new approach – reduction in of anxiety. Starts to focus on the tasks involved which would assist in reaching the project deadline with the proposed solution at step 5. Cognitive Coaching or Cognitive Behavioural Coaching or Rational Emotive Behavioural Coaching can all be considered as dual systems approaches focusing on the practical and/or psychological aspects of a client's problem or issue as and when required. Palmer (1997a, b) described the integration of the ABCDE and problem-solving models as 'an intrinsically brief integrative approach'.

INTRODUCING THE SPACE MODEL – AN OVERVIEW

The SPACE model was developed in 2002 and is an attempt to portray the interactions involved in psychological process in a manner that is more graphical than the two or five column worksheets that are commonly used in cognitive behavioural approaches. It is also an easy to remember acronym:

Social context
Physiology
Action
Cognition
Emotion

The model has two further components which are also referred to when in use with clients:

Action	Physiology
Cognition	Action
Emotion	Cognition
	Emotion

The literature relating to cognitive behaviour coaching and therapy deals largely with the importance of the Cognitions as determinates of Emotional states and the resultant Behaviours or Actions (see Beck, 1995; Ellis *et al.*, 1997; Neenan & Palmer, 2001a, b). The 'ABCDE' model is one of the most widely used in cognitive behavioural approaches. Implicit in the model is the belief that Cognitions largely determine Emotions.

This can be depicted as:

C ⟶ E

As cognitions can lead to an emotional response, a person with anger provoking thoughts is likely to experience anger as an emotion. Cognitions include images or pictures a person may also experiences in their mind's eye. An example is provided below of a teacher in a specific situation:

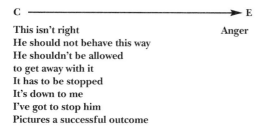

C ⟶ E

This isn't right   Anger
He should not behave this way
He shouldn't be allowed
to get away with it
It has to be stopped
It's down to me
I've got to stop him
Pictures a successful outcome

However, if someone is already in an angry mood, a mood being a longer lasting emotional state, then the mood is likely to result in a tendency to have further angry cognitions in the next situation.

Since the angry cognitions will again result in anger as an emotion we could depict it better:

There is clearly an interaction between cognitions and emotions and this is indicated by the two-way arrow.

In the example above, the thought, 'I've got to stop him' clearly relates to potential Actions. Adding an A to the diagram would give us:

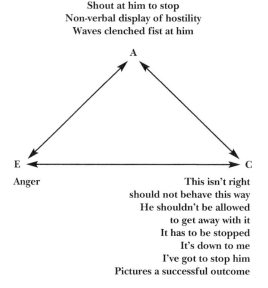

This **ACE** model can be seen as a basic psychological model depicting a three way interaction between Actions Cognitions and Emotions. A similar model ACE has also been described by Lee (2003). Taking our example a step further we can see that a person in this Emotional state with these Cognitions and Action tendencies would also experience sensations in their bodies relating to **P**hysiological arousal.

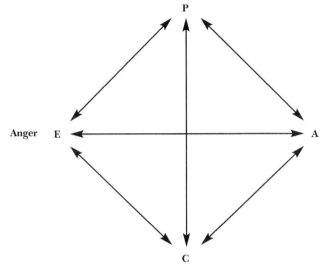

PACE Model

Red face
Heart rate up
Respiration rate up
Adrenaline flow

P

Shout at him to stop
Hostile non-verbal
display
Restrain him

Anger   E ← → A

C

This isn't right
He should not behave this way
He shouldn't be allowed to get away with it
It has to be stopped
It's down to me
I've got to stop him
Pictures a successful outcome

Adding a 'P' for Physiological would give us a **PACE** model that (see below) would depict Biological/Psychological interactions for an individual.

To further understand a person's reaction to a situation it is often helpful to understand the Social Context that the person is operating in. This can be displayed as a circle surrounding the PACE model.

With the addition of the Social Context to our model it becomes a Bio – Psycho – Social model that will help practitioners and their clients to understand a person's reaction in a Social Context. The Social Context can include sets of beliefs about social roles, customs and rules.

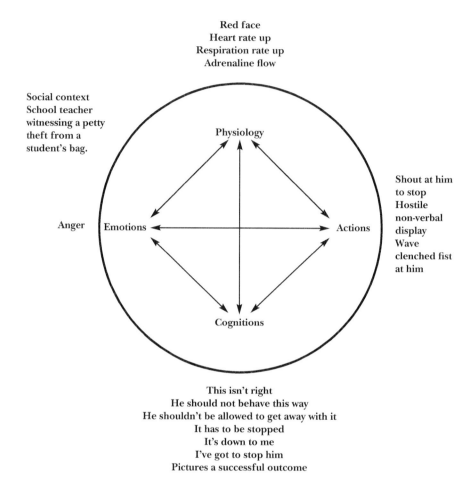

SPACE: FROM ASSESSMENT TO INTERVENTION

In the first or later session with a client, a particular situation, problem or mood can be analysed using the ACE, PACE and finally the SPACE models. This helps provide a quick assessment, illustrates to the client the interaction between the five key modalities, and provides an opening for possible interventions. For example, a client who experiences presentation nerves could consider modifying cognitions such as, 'I must perform well. It will be awful if I make a mistake', replacing catastrophic imagery with helpful coping imagery (C), stopping procrastinating behaviour and learning new presentation behavioural skills (A), using techniques such as relaxation to reduce stress and anxiety (P), feeling identification to help the client identify anxiety (E), and increase the awareness of the social context and others' expectations of the client's performance e.g. they may want an acceptable performance, not 'perfect' performance (S). These possible interventions can also be inserted onto the SPACE diagram using a different colour ink. (Or a new SPACE diagram can be used instead.) Thus the SPACE diagram shifts from assessment tool into the coaching programme. SPACE is used in a similar way in counselling, psychotherapy and training settings.

USE OF TIME

Some clients experience difficulties remembering the very nature of cognitions. When using cognitive models including SPACE it is important that clients can recall what the 'C' stands for. Another aide memoire, TIME, can assist:

Thoughts
Images
Memories
Expectations

This helps clients complete the 'C' part of the SPACE diagram outside of the coaching session.

CONCLUSION

This article highlighted a number of different coaching models and introduced the comprehensive SPACE model that can be used within cognitive behavioural approaches. SPACE can also be used in parallel the other models such as GROW or POSITIVE described above, to aid clients understand how to overcome the psychological blocks that are sometimes associated with their problems or issues. So often with performance-related issues, cognitions, imagery, emotions and physiological reactions need to be addressed in coaching and SPACE provides the framework for both assessment and the subsequent development of an individual coaching programme.

REFERENCES

Beck, J.S. (1995). *Cognitive therapy: Basics and beyond*. New York: Guilford Press.

Boyle, C., Callaghan, A. & Stokes, C. (2005). Coaching, commitment and collaboration. Downloaded on 9 October 2005. http://www.uk.hudson.com/documents/uk_article coaching.pdf First published in the *Law Society Gazette*, December, 2004.

Dembkowski, S. & Eldridge, F. (2003). Beyond GROW: A new coaching model. *The International Journal of Mentoring and Coaching*, 1(1), November.

Ellis, A., Gordon, J., Neenan, M. & Palmer, S. (1997). *Stress counselling: A rational emotive behaviour approach*. London: Cassell.

Lee, G. (2003). *Leadership coaching: From personal insight to organisational performance*. London: CIPD.

Libri, V. (2004). Beyond GROW: In search of acronyms and coaching models. *The International Journal of Mentoring and Coaching*, 2(1), July.

Neenan, M. & Palmer, S. (2001a). Cognitive behavioural coaching. *Stress News*, 13(3), 15–18.

Neenan, M. & Palmer, S. (2001b). Rational emotive behaviour coaching. *Rational Emotive Behaviour Therapist*, 9(1), 34–41.

Palmer, S. & Burton, T. (1996). *Dealing with people problems at work*. Maidenhead: McGraw-Hill.

Palmer, S. (1997a). Problem-focused stress counselling and stress management: An intrinsically brief integrative approach. Part 1. *Stress News*, 9(2), 7–12.

Palmer, S. (1997b). Problem-focused stress counselling and stress management training: An intrinsically brief integrative approach. Part 2. *Stress News*, 9(3), 6–10.

Wasik, B. (1984). *Teaching parents effective problem-solving: A handbook for professionals*. Unpublished manuscript. Chapel Hill: University of North Carolina.

Whitmore, J. (1996). *Coaching for performance* (2nd ed.). London: Nicholas Brealey Publishing.

Whitmore, J. (2004). *Coaching for performance: GROWing people, performance and purpose* (3rd ed.). London: Nicholas Brealey Publishing.

2 PEAK: A model for use within performance coaching

Garret O'Moore

Abstract

This paper introduces 'PEAK', a model suitable for use within performance coaching. PEAK is an acronym formed from the four interacting domains that are considered to underpin performance: Purpose, Engagement, Ability, and Know-how. The aim is to present an overview of the model and the theory that underpins it as well as providing a brief example of the model in practise.

Keywords

PEAK; performance coaching; coaching model

Over the years a number of general purpose coaching models have been developed (see Grant, 2011, p.120, and Edgerton & Palmer, 2005, p.21, for useful overviews), to aid practitioners working across a range of coaching topics. With the London 2012 Olympic Games fast approaching it seemed fitting to introduce 'PEAK', a model developed for performance coaching. The paper will provide a brief overview of what is meant by performance. It will then seek to outline the model and theory that underpins it before illustrating it in practise with a coaching example.

Original publication details: O'Moore, G. (2012, June). PEAK: A model for use within performance coaching. *The Coaching Psychologist*, 8(1), 39–45. Reproduced with permission of The British Psychological Society.

OVERVIEW OF PERFORMANCE

Performance in a coaching context is usually understood 'as a task or operation seen in terms of how successfully it is performed' (Oxford Dictionaries, 2012). For concision it has been conceptualised as comprising three interconnected factors: (1) ability, the extent to which an individual can successfully undertake the task; (2) effort, the degree of physical and mental power directed to the task; and (3) difficulty, the degree of challenge inherent in the task. Visualised as an equation (see Figure 1) performance is considered as the sum of the multiplication of task ability and task effort divided by task difficulty.

$$\text{Task Performance} = \frac{\text{Task Ability x Task Effort}}{\text{Task Difficulty}}$$

Figure 1 *Performance equation.*

Simply put, to increase performance one should strive to enhance ability and effort whilst, reducing difficulty. In situations where the level of difficulty is inextricably linked with the performance goal (e.g. running a sub four-minute mile) it may be more useful to consider difficulty as the factor/s that are increasing the challenge, for example, poor training facilities or an uninspiring coach. Attention will now turn to providing an overview of PEAK.

INTRODUCING THE PEAK MODEL – AN OVERVIEW

PEAK is an integrative model that draws on concepts from a number of established coaching paradigms; cognitive behavioural coaching (CBC; Palmer & Szymanska, 2007), solution focused coaching (SFC; O'Connell & Palmer, 2007) and motivational interviewing (MI; Passmore & Whybrow, 2007; Passmore, 2011). The model is intended to be clear and accessible and its conceptualisation was influenced by the interrelated phases of earlier models such as GROW (Alexander, 2010) and models with reciprocal interactivity between domains such as SPACE (Edgerton & Palmer, 2005). Whilst influenced by existing coaching paradigms and coaching frameworks, PEAK also draws on a body of interrelated theory and field research that has identified psychological factors that underpin performance and wellbeing. In particular: self-efficacy theory (Bandura, 1997), goal setting theory (Locke & Latham, 1990, Locke & Latham 2002), The transtheoretical model of behavior change (TTM; Di Clemente & Prochaska, 1998), the self-determination theory of motivation (SDT; Deci & Ryan, 1985, Ryan & Deci, 2000) and the self-concordance

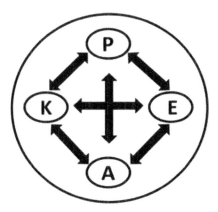

Figure 2   *The interacting domains of the PEAK model.*

model of healthy goal striving (Sheldon & Eliot, 1999). Within the model performance is conceptualised (see Figure 2) as resulting from the reciprocal inter-action of four domains that are considered to underpin performance within a given environment: Purpose, Engagement, Ability, and Know-how, together forming an easy to remember acronym: PEAK. Each of the four domains can be visualised on a continuum that ranges from low to high and which has a bearing on overall performance. The domains are understood to act synergistically so if the coachee considers the purpose to be clear and meaningful, is actively engaged, utilises their ability and has the know-how to succeed then performance is likely to occur.

PEAK is considered a collaborative model whereby the coach strives to facilitate attainment of the coachee's goals through increasing the coachee's self-directed moti-vation as well as their actual and perceived task ability.

PURPOSE

Purpose refers to understanding what it is that the coachee wishes to achieve and why they want to achieve it. Whilst the 'what' is an explicit focus of many coaching models, the 'why' that underpins the goal, known as the locus of motivation (type of motivation) is often assumed. It is useful to recognise that the locus of motiva-tion can be distinct from the level of motivation. For instance, two people may be equally motivated to succeed at an exam but for differing reasons, for example, enjoying the challenge of the exam versus requiring the necessary grades to get into a desired course.

Within SDT (Ryan & Deci, 2000) intrinsic goals (goals that are internally moti-vating) and extrinsic goals (goals pursued because of external motives) are considered to exist on a spectrum model of self-regulation in which behaviour is guided by intrinsic motivation and several types of extrinsic motivation that exist on a continuum of internalisation from external motives that are passively or reluctantly accepted to external motives that have been integrated as personally meaningful.

Gaining insight into the coachee's locus of motivation is considered significant given the findings that intrinsic goals are more likely to be attained than extrinsic goals (Sheldon, 2002) and have also been associated with enhanced well-being (Sheldon & Kasser, 1998). The benefits of goal setting have also been found to depend on a person's commitment and determination (Hollenbeck, Williams & Kline, 1989) with difficult goals having been found to lead to higher performance than simple goals provided they have been accepted (Locke & Latham, 2002). Finally ensuring goal clarity and a degree of challenge is important given the strong relationship between goal specificity, difficulty and high performance (Locke & Latham, 1990).

ENGAGEMENT

Engagement refers to how invested the coachee is in realising their goal. The TTM (DiClemente & Prochaska, 1998) which strongly influences MI (Miller & Rollnick, 2002) conceptualises change as a cyclical process involving a number of stages from pre-contemplation through contemplation, planning, action and change maintenance. Within PEAK the TTM stages can be used to gauge 'how bought in' the coachee is to realising their goal. For instance, a client who is still weighing up the pros and cons of committing to a performance goal would be considered to be less engaged than a client who was already planning how to increase their performance.

The TTM also usefully recognises the difficulty in sustaining change and recognises that relapses to earlier stages and spiralling through stages can occur. Gaining insight into the stages of change is useful as a smooth transition through stages (e.g. moving from goal planning to action) would suggest that engagement is likely to be high with corresponding levels of goal oriented motivation and effort. In contrast a coachee who does not appear to be progressing through the stages or has become stuck in a particular stage may experience a reduction in engagement with the consequence that motivation and effort may decrease. In such instances a number of causal factors could be involved such as: problems inherent in the performance goal, competing demands for resources, efficacy beliefs or tangible barriers such as skill deficits or time constraints.

ABILITY

Ability is a broad concept and refers to the interplay of knowledge (what you have to do and how you do it) and skill (your proficiency at doing it). Ability within PEAK considers both objective and subjective ability, namely the coachee's perception of their capacity to achieve their goal, known as their self-efficacy (Bandura, 1997).

Identifying a coachee's self-efficacy which can be both general and domain specific is considered to be crucial to performance improvement as motivation to change will be undermined unless there is a corresponding belief that one has the ability to change. Individuals possessing high self-efficacy have been shown to increase goal directed effort and to persist longer than those with low self-efficacy who may be prone to overestimating task difficulty (Bandura, 1977).

KNOW-HOW

Within PEAK Know-how can be conceptualised as the strategy or approach that is required to realise the performance goal. It is within this domain that a plan of action is generated so that the coachee's skills and knowledge can be harnessed and enhanced to initiate and maintain goal striving towards their performance goal. The focus will vary according to the degree and complexity of the challenge, how motivated the coachee is, how engaged they are in the change process, their objective ability and their subjective sense of it.

COACHING EXAMPLE

Attention will now turn to providing a straightforward coaching example of PEAK involving a fictitious coachee, Chris, who works in sales. Suggested steps and example questions for each domain are outlined in Table 1.

PURPOSE

The session should start with a focus on understanding what the coachee wishes to achieve and the context in which it would occur. The coach should then seek to explore the coachee's motives to better understand the degree to which the performance increase has been accepted and is valued.

Coach: What is it that you'd like to achieve?
Chris: I'd be keen to increase my sales targets by 20 per cent.
Coach: Can you give me a sense of why increasing your sales by 20 per cent is important to you?
Chris: Sure, I'm really keen to get the end of year bonus. It's a lot of money!
Coach: You said earlier that you earn a good salary so I'm wondering if there's anything apart from the extra money that's motivating you?
Chris: The money is great but there's also the enjoyment I feel when I'm making sales, I relish the challenge and it reminds me that I'm good at what I do.

Table 1 *Domain specific steps and example questions for use within PEAK.*

Useful steps within each domain	Example questions
Purpose	
Have a broad discussion about the goal	What would you like to achieve?
Explore type of motivation	What's important to you about achieving that?
Increase self-directed motivation	Have you considered how achieving X may help you realise Y?
Clarify the goal (e.g. SMART)	Do you consider your goal to be achievable/realistic?
Engagement	
Check commitment level	How committed are you feeling? Rating: 0 – 10/ What makes it a 7?
Identify stage of change	Are you still considering or already working towards your goal?
Increase engagement	What are the pros/cons of achieving X?
Ability	
Identify challenge	What has to change to move from your current to your desired performance?
Identify relevant skills and knowledge	What skills or knowledge do you have that could help you do that?
Identify self-efficacy beliefs	How confident are you in your ability to use what we've identified?
Leverage skills and knowledge/strengths	Can you think of ways you could develop that?
Know-how	
Develop actionable strategy	Let's consider the best way to realise X
Encourage solution finding	Imagine you're already performing at your desired level, now describe it?

In instances where a coachee's motivation is extrinsic but the goal has been accepted as being important (e.g. having to carry out a challenging presentation for one's manager) the coach should support their coachee in identifying how achieving the goal could help them to realise other personally valued goals. As Chris's motivation appears to be intrinsic the coach and Chris move to focusing on clarifying his goal.

ENGAGEMENT

Once the type of motivation has been identified and an initial goal has been developed the focus should shift to determining the coachee's current level of engagement towards their goal.

Coach: It might be useful now that you've clarified your goal to consider how committed you are to achieving it on a scale of 0 to 10, with 0=No commitment; 10=Very high commitment.

Chris: I'd say it's a 9.

Coach: A 9, so there appears to be a high level of commitment. I know we've clarified your goal today but I'm wondering if it's a recent aim or something that you've put some thought into?

Chris: Yeah I've been thinking about it for a few weeks, I was hoping you could help me figure out how to realise it.

If engagement is low it can prove useful to utilise the MI techniques of open questioning and reflective listening to identify possible reasons why. Furthermore facilitating positive change talk to support the coachee in increasing their engagement can be accomplished through asking what they consider the benefits of realising their goal to be. This is particularly useful as uncertainty or ambivalence may suggest that the goal has not been accepted or indicate a possible gap between desire to change and ability to do so. As Chris appears to be highly motivated and at the planning stage of the change process he and his coach can move to identify abilities relevant to his goal.

ABILITY

After gaining a sense of the level of engagement attention should turn to considering what is required to move from current to desired performance. The coach and coachee should then collaborate on identifying relevant skills and knowledge and consider how they can be harnessed and developed to facilitate goal attainment, for example, through identifying and harnessing coachee strengths (Linley & Harrington, 2006). Importantly the coach should also seek to gauge the coachee's level of goal specific and general self-efficacy.

Coach: How confident are you in leveraging the skills we've identified, on a scale of 0 to 10, with 0=No confidence; 10=High confidence?

Chris: I'd say a 7.

Coach: What would make it a 9?

Chris: Having some initial successes.

Coach: Talk me through what those successes would look like.

If the coachee's self-efficacy is low the coach can attempt to facilitate an increase in self-efficacy through drawing on strategies from a range of coaching paradigms, for example, through helping the coachee to reappraise any performance interfering thoughts (CBC) or through focusing on previous instances where the coachee has increased their performance or by building on exceptions (SFC). As Chris has goal relevant ability and a high level of self-efficacy his coach moves the focus to identifying the steps to realise his goal.

KNOW-HOW

After identifying the relevant skills and knowledge attention should turn to developing an actionable strategy that incorporates the steps required to realise the goal. Ideally the coach would encourage a solution finding approach (SFC) whereby the coach encourages problem-free talk, focuses on what can be learnt from earlier successes and builds on any exceptions to problems. The coach may also consider techniques such as the miracle question (De Shazer, 1988) to help the coachee to identify what they would be doing if they were performing at the requisite level.

> *Coach*: Imagine if you were already performing at your desired level, now describe it for me, what would be different?
>
> *Chris*: For a start I'd be much more focused, I wouldn't waste so much time surfing the web and constantly checking for new emails, also I'd make a weekly plan with daily targets to aim for…

Over the following sessions the coach and Chris cycled through the four domains, refining his goal, reviewing and enhancing engagement and adapting the strategy based on feedback. It is important to recognise that PEAK is not a strictly linear model and sessions usually cycle back and forth between different domains as per coaching requirements.

APPLICATIONS

PEAK is a flexible framework that can be applied to a range of performance coaching topics such as performance development, improvement, enhancement and management. If used judiciously PEAK can also be used in team coaching and as an aid in identifying possible reasons for underperformance.

CONCLUSION

This article introduced PEAK a coaching model that is influenced by established coaching paradigms and a broad body of research that has identified the psychological factors that underpin sustainable performance and well-being. It is designed to be flexible and adaptable and can be used within a number of coaching paradigms. As with other coaching models positive outcomes are predicated on PEAK being used in a collaborative manner, in the service of the coachee and not as a means of coercion.

REFERENCES

Alexander, G. (2010). Behavioural coaching – the GROW model. In J. Passmore (Ed.), *Excellence in coaching: The industry guide* (pp.83–93). London: Kogan Page.

Bandura, A. (1977). Self-efficacy: Toward a unifying theory of behavioural change. *Psychological Review*, 84(2) 191–215.

Bandura, A. (1997). *Self-efficacy: The exercise of control.* Stanford: W.H. Freeman.

Deci, E.L. & Ryan, R.M. (1985). *Intrinsic motivation and self-determination in human behaviour.* New York: Plenum Press.

De Shazer, S. (1988). *Clues: Investigating solutions in brief therapy.* New York: W.W. Norton.

DiClemente, C.C. & Prochaska, J.O. (1998). Toward a comprehensive, transtheoretical model of change: Stages of change and addictive behaviours. In W.R. Miller & N. Heather (Eds.), *Treating addictive behaviours* (2nd ed., pp.3–24).

Edgerton, N. & Palmer. S. (2005). SPACE: A psychological model for use within cognitive behavioural coaching, therapy and stress management. *The Coaching Psychologist*, 2(2), 21–27.

Grant, A.M. (2011). Is it time to REGROW the GROW model? Issues related to teaching coaching session structures. *The Coaching Psychologist*, 7(2), 118–125.

Hollenbeck, J.R., Williams, C.R. & Klein, H.J. (1989). An empirical examination of the antecedents of commitment to difficult goals. *Journal of Applied Psychology*, 74, 18–23.

Linley, P.A. & Harrington, S. (2006). Playing to your strengths. *The Psychologist*, 19(2), 86–89.

Locke, E.A. & Latham, G.P. (1990). *A theory of goalsetting and task performance.* Englewood Cliffs, NJ: Prentice Hall.

Locke, E.A. & Latham, G.P. (2002). Building a practically useful theory of goal setting and task motivation: A 35-year odyssey. *American Psychologist*, 57, 705-717.

Miller, W.R. & Rollnick, S. (2002). *Motivational Interviewing: Preparing people for change* (2nd ed.). New York: Guilford Press.

O'Connell, B. & Palmer, S. (2007). Solution-focused coaching. In S. Palmer & Whybrow, A. (Eds.), *Handbook of coaching psychology* (pp.278–292). London: Routledge.

Palmer, S. & Szymanska, K. (2007). Cognitive behavioural coaching: An integrative approach. In S. Palmer & Whybrow, A. (Eds.), *Handbook of coaching psychology* (pp.86–117). London: Routledge.

Passmore, J. & Whybrow, A. (2007). Motivational Interviewing: A specific approach for coaching psychologists. In S. Palmer & Whybrow, A. (Eds.), *Handbook of coaching psychology* (pp.160–173). London: Routledge.

Passmore, J. (2011). Motivational Interviewing – a model for coaching psychology practice. *The Coaching Psychologist*, 7(1), 36–41.

Ryan, R.M. & Deci, E.L. (2000). Self-determination theory and the facilitation of intrinsic, motivation, social development, and well-being. *American Psychologist*, 55, 68–78.

Sheldon, K.M. (2002). The self-concordance model of healthy goal striving: When personal goals correctly represent the person. In E.L. Deci & R.M. Ryan (Eds.), *Handbook of self determination research* (pp.65–86). Rochester, NY: University of Rochester Press.

Sheldon, K.M. & Elliot, A.J. (1999). Goal striving, need-satisfaction, and longitudinal well-being: The Self-Concordance Model. *Journal of Personality and Social Psychology*, 76, 482–497.

Sheldon, K.M. & Kasser, T. (1998). Pursuing personal goals: Skills enable progress, but not all progress is beneficial. *Personality and Social Psychology Bulletin*, 24, 1319–1331.

3 Is it time to REGROW the GROW model?

Issues related to teaching coaching session structures

Anthony M. Grant

Abstract

Although models of how to structure coaching sessions are widely taught in coach training programmes there has been little or no debate in the literature about the use of session structures, the teaching of them, or the relative advantages or disadvantage of different specific session structure frameworks, and there have been few links drawn between the theoretical underpinnings of coaching and session structures. This paper explores these issues, giving examples of session structures and presents some frameworks that may help guide the categorisation and teaching of these structures. A variation of the well-known GROW model is presented; the RE-GROW model which explicitly links coaching session structure to self-regulation theory.

Keywords

GROW; RE-GROW; coaching psychology; teaching coaching; session structure.

Original publication details: Grant, A. M. (2011, December). Is it time to REGROW the GROW model? Issues related to teaching coaching session structures. *The Coaching Psychologist*, 7(2), 118–126. Reproduced with permission of The British Psychological Society.

Virtually all programmes that teach coaching and coaching psychology include material about how to structure coaching sessions. But to date there has been little or no debate in the literature about the use of session structures, the teaching of them, or the relative advantages or disadvantage of different specific session structure frameworks. This is surprising because, for many coaches, session structures are seen to be a vital part of their coaching methodology. Further, there has been little or no attempts to draw explicit links between theoretical underpinnings of coaching and session structures. This paper explores these issues, giving examples of session structures and presents some frameworks that may help guide the categorisation and teaching of these structures. Finally, and somewhat tongue-in-check, a new 'improved' version of the well-known GROW model is presented – the RE-GROW model.

WHAT ARE COACHING SESSION STRUCTURES?

Coaching session structures are models that are designed to help provide a framework for the coaching session. They are primarily designed to act as a guide for the coach, helping the coach and coachee to stay focused on relevant issues and preventing the coaching session drifting off into a conversation that has no clear purpose or goal. A wide range of session structure models have been developed over the years, often developed and promoted by a specific coach training organisation or consultants as unique intellectual property.

A key purpose of such models is to delineate specific phases of the coaching conversations (for example, the beginning, middle or ending phases of the session), as well as acting as a memory aid to remind the coach, for example, to check levels of motivation (e.g. Mackintosh, 2005), or to ensure that any barriers to change have been addressed (e.g. Smith, 1998).

MINIMAL EXISTING RESEARCH ON SESSION STRUCTURE MODELS

It is worth reflecting that within the coaching domain, there has been very little scholarship or empirical research into the use of session structure models in terms of the possible comparative effectiveness of various models, nor indeed if the use of such models *per se* produces better outcomes for clients.

There is some survey data on coaches' use of models such as GROW (GROW will be discussed in some detail in following sections of this article). For example, a 2002 study conducted by the Work Foundation and the School of Coaching reported that about one-third of respondents used the GROW model, one-third said that they used a number of different models and the remaining third were not able to say what model or process was used in their coaching activities (Dembkowski & Eldridge, 2003). In a survey conducted by Palmer and Whybrow in 2006–2007, GROW was used by 53.2 per cent of the coaching psychologists surveyed. In a 2008–2009 survey, again conducted by Palmer and Whybrow, GROW was used by 40.6 per cent of the coaching psychologists surveyed and 9.4 per cent of coaching psychologists in the 2008–2009 study reported using RE-GROW (Palmer, 2011).

There is also some empirical research in the area of clinical psychology which has looked at the effect of structured or manualised treatment programmes compared with non-manualised treatments, although typically no firm conclusions can be drawn about the relative efficacy of manualised treatment programmes compared with nonmanualised treatments due the multitude of factors that impact on therapy outcome (e.g. Shirk & Karver, 2003).

A search of the database PsycINFO in August 2011 using the keywords 'session structure' found only 31 citations, most of which referred to the use of sessions structures as being a central part of the cognitive-behavioural therapeutic paradigm (e.g. Fairburn, et al., 2008; Friedberg & Brelsford, 2011; Wenzel, Brown & Beck, 2009), but which did not present data regarding the relative efficacy of session structures.

ASSOCIATED RESEARCH ON SESSION STRUCTURES FROM THE THERAPY DOMAIN

Only one somewhat relevant paper emerged from this literature search: Stiles et al. (1996) evaluated a total of 2305 therapy sessions of either cognitive-behavioural or psychodynamic-interpersonal therapy, and identified session structure as a key and conceptually coherent facet of treatment. Session structure here was exemplified by two characteristics: Clarification and Focus. Clarification was defined as 'to provide or solicit more elaboration, emphasis or specification when client was being vague, incomplete or confusing…' and Focus was defined as 'to help get the client back on track, to change subject or structure the discussion if he/she was unable to begin or was being diffuse or rambling' (Stiles et al., 1996, p.404). Session structure was used to '…draw participants' attention to the matter at hand – the 'here and now' – when it has wandered elsewhere' (p.408); the same purpose for which session structures are typically used in coaching (Wilson, 2011).

Of relevance to the present discussion on the use of session structure in coaching, given the diversity of coaching methodologies, was the reported Stiles et al. (1996) finding that the use of session structure was the same in both cognitive-behavioural or psychodynamic-interpersonal therapy, and that session structure was particularly used when sessions were difficult or slow moving. Interestingly this study found that there was a decrease in focus on session structure towards the end of treatment (treatment was between eight and 16 sessions in length) – that is session structure was strongly used in the initial sessions, but over time this emphasise tended to dissipate somewhat.

Because Stiles et al. (1996) was concerned only with processes of therapy, unfortunately no outcome measures were reported. Clearly further empirical research is needed here.

IMPLICATIONS FOR TEACHING EVIDENCE-BASED COACHING

Regardless of the apparent lack of empirical research on this topic in relation to coaching, a vast range of anecdotal reports over some considerable time, as well as this author's own personal experience, testifies to the usefulness of such structures, although as will be discussed, the effective use of these structures may not be as straightforward as is sometimes thought.

This situation has implications for those engaged in teaching evidence-based approaches to coaching and coaching psychology. We need to emphasise to students that the evidence about the effectiveness of coaching session structures is, at this point in time, primarily anecdotal and teachers and supervisors might do well to encourage new research in this area so that the foundational knowledge base of coaching and coaching psychology can be further developed.

OVERVIEW OF COACHING SESSION STRUCTURES

The GROW model is probably the best known session structure model. Initially developed by Graham Alexander (for discussion on the origins of the GROW model see Alexander, 2010) and popularised by Sir John Whitmore (Whitmore, 1992) the GROW model breaks a coaching session into four interrelated phases: Goals; Reality; Options; and Wrap-up (sometimes called Will or Way forward). See Table 1 for further details.

Over time a wide range of variations of the GROW model have emerged. These have included the T-GROW model (Topic; Goal; Reality; Options; Wrap-up; Downey, 2003); the I-GROW model (Issue; Goal; Reality; Options; Wrap-up; Wilson, 2011). Other variations include McKinsey's SO*I*GROW (Situation; Opportunities; Implications; Goal; Reality; Options: and Will) and the Mount Eliza School of Business 4-A model (Agenda; Analysis; Agreement; Action). The CLEAR coaching model (Contracting; Listening; Exploring; Action; Review; for details see Hawkins & Smith, 2007) developed by Peter Hawkins in the early 1980s is also similar to GROW, and there are also a range of solution-focused session structures which present variations on the GROW model, most notably the OSKAR model (Outcome; Scaling; Knowhow and resources; Affirm and action; Review; Jackson & McKergow, 2002)

Some models present quite detailed steps. The ACHIEVE model (Dembkowski & Eldridge, 2003) has seven steps: (1) Assess current situation; (2) Creative brainstorming of alternatives to current situation; (3) Hone goals; (4) Initiate options; (5) Evaluate options; (6) Valid action programme design;(7) Encourage momentum.

The PRACTICE model (Palmer, 2007) has seven detailed steps or sections: (1) Problem identification; (2) Realistic, relevant goals developed; (3) Alternative solutions generated; (4) Consideration of consequences; (5) Target most feasible solution/s; (6) Implementation of Chosen solutions; (7) Evaluation.

The OUTCOMES model (Mackintosh, 2005) is even more complex with eight highly detailed steps: (1) Objectives for the session; (2) Understanding – the coach should understand why the coachee wants to reach the objective; (3) Take stock; (4) Clarify; (5) Option generation; (6) Motivate to action; (7) Enthuse and encourage; (8) Support.

GAP ANALYSIS MODELS

Some models take a gap analysis approach, where the current or existing situation is initially discussed before moving on to detailing the preferred outcome or goal and then, through a gap analysis process, developing action steps or strategies to facilitate goal attainment. Perhaps the oldest model of this type, and one well-used in the counselling domain primarily to structure whole interventions rather than individual

Table 1   *The GROW Model.*

Acronym	*Description*	*Example Questions*
G – Goal	Coachee is asked to clarify what they want to achieve from each session. Determines the focus of coaching.	What do you want to achieve this session? How would you like to feel afterwards? What would be the best use of this time?
R – Reality	Raise awareness of present realities. Examine how current situation is impacting coachee's goals.	How have things gone in the past week? How have you handled any problems? What worked? What didn't work?
O – Options	Identify and assess available options. Encourage solution-focused thinking and brainstorming.	What possible options do you have? What has worked for you in the past? What haven't you tried yet that might work?
W -Wrap-Up	Assists the coachee determine next steps. Develops an action plan and builds motivation.	What is the most important thing to do next? What might get in the way? Who might be able to support you? How will you feel when this is done?

Sources: Grant & Greene, 2004;Landsberg, 1997; Spence & Grant, 2007; Whitmore, 1992.

sessions, is Egan's (1974) Skilled Helper Model. This has three key stages: (1) Current scenario; (2) Preferred scenario; and (3) Strategies to get there. Each of these three stages has itself three sub stages which are: (1) story; blind spots; leverage; (2) possibilities; agenda; commitment; (3) strategies; best fit; plan.

A simplified version of Egan's work is represented by Greene and Grant's (2003) CIGAR model (Current situation; Ideal outcome; Gap analysis; Action plan; Review). The Coach U five-step coaching conversation model (Smith, 1998) aims to move clients 'from where they are to where they want to be' (CoachWorks, 1998, pp.2–3) – from their current reality to their goal – and takes a similar 'coaching through the gap' approach. The five stages are: (1) establish focus; (2) discover possibilities; (3) plan the action; (4) remove barriers; (5) recap.

KEEPING IT SIMPLE!

However, every aspect of a coaching session cannot be notarised and codified. It is clear that some of these models are quite complex and many coaches would consider these to be too detailed – a cynic might argue that the only person that could remember what some of these acronyms mean is the person who invented the model!

Nevertheless, the more detailed models may still serve a very useful function in teaching about session structure, because they can give the novice coach some insight into different aspects that may need to be addressed within a specific coaching session. However, in terms of practice applicability within a real-life coaching session I would argue that the strength of some of these models lies in their simplicity. This simplicity allows for great flexibility in responding to the demands of any specific session. This is a key point and one that should probably be emphasised when teaching students who are new to coaching about session structures.

A BIPARTITE TYPOLOGY FOR UNDERSTANDING MODELS

From the above it can be seen that approaches to session structures tend to broadly fall into one of two categories: (1) models that ask the client to identify the preferred outcome or broad presenting issues before exploring the current situation or reality, and then developing options and action steps; and (2) models that explore the current situation before moving on to goal setting and developing options and action steps.

In addition, coaching sessions themselves can be seen to lie on a dimension from those sessions that are very tightly structured to those that are much less structured. Which end of this dimension could be considered the 'correct' approach for any specific session depends on a wide range of factors. These could include issues such as the coach's preferred theoretical framework; the client's readiness to change; the issue or goal under discussion; client's levels of emotionality; and the complexity of the goal and contextual factors (see Figure 1).

The key point here for the teaching of session structures is that the coach needs informed flexibility. Coaches need to be comfortable in moving from a highly structured approach to a less tightly structured approach as the situation demands. The primary driver should be the needs of the coachee and how the coach can be flexible in best serving the needs of the coachee, not how attached the coach is to any specific model. GROW (and other session structures) are methodologies to be used, not ideologies to be rigidly adhered to!

THE NON-LINEAR NATURE OF COACHING SESSIONS: THE NOVICE TO EXPERT SHIFT

Many session models give the impression that coaching is a linear process and that coaches work through the steps in a straightforward fashion. This notion may especially appeal to novice coaches who are looking for clear and simple rules to follow as they begin to master their craft. But coaching is frequently an oscillating, non-linear process as the coach helps the coachee untangle their convoluted thinking.

This kind of oscillating process is well-exemplified using the GROW model. When using GROW the coaching session typically starts with goal setting. Even if the client is not clear about what they want to achieve, the coach asks them to state in broad terms what they want to get out of the session. Having set a direction, the conversation moves on to discussing the reality, what is really happening. Frequently, in this section ideas are uncovered which lead to the goal being redefined, and so the coach will cycle back to the goal and help the client to redefine their goal. Having redefined the goal, and explored the reality again, the coach will then guide the conversation to the discussion of options. In this section a wide range of client-generated options are explored, and there will probably some cycling back and forth between different sections of the model until a range of action steps emerge. Sometimes at this point the goal will be revisited again to make sure that the options meet the goal, or alternatively the options may have to be redefined. Finally the coach can move the conversation into the wrap-up stage and start to help the client detail specific action steps. Bearing this process in mind the GROW model might be more accurately represented as GRGROGROOGROWOGORW!

Of course, it is never obvious at the start of any coaching session how the session will actually evolve, and coaches need to work with an emergent, iterative process. Indeed, for experienced coaches the uncertainty of the session and the unexpected discoveries made along the way are a large part of the joy of coaching. For the novice however, this uncertainty is often a source of anxiety and frustration and novice coaches tend to react to these feelings by to clinging too tightly to the model.

Less Tightly Structured   More Tightly Structured

More about telling the story   Early SMART goal setting
Focus on micro-skill use   More task-focus
May have more emotional content   Faster paced session
Possibly client less ready to change   Client ready to change
Rapport may need building   Good initial rapport

Figure 1   *Dimensions of session structure.*

IDEAS TO HELP TEACH THE USE OF SESSION STRUCTURE

A key point to get across is that models such as GROW provide a simple map to help guide the coaching session – the map here is most definitely not the territory (Korzybski, 1933) – and clinging tightly to the map will not aid the journey. A useful teaching technique during skills-based coaching session practice is to randomly ask the student whereabouts in the coaching session model they are at any point in time (i.e. the student then states if they are in the goal setting, reality exploration, option generation phase, etc.), and also states which phase they were previously in, and where they are taking the conversation to next. These kind of in-the-moment reflective techniques can really help the student engage in double and triple loop learning (Argyris, 2002) and help them develop more sophisticated meta-cognitive skills in relation to the coaching process.

Teachers and trainers can also help beginners make the novice-expert shift in the use of session structures by helping students set realistic expectations for themselves. Doing so requires that they can benchmark their level of existing expertise and thus set appropriate learning goals. David Peterson (2011) presents an adaptation of Dreyfus and Dreyfus's (1986) work on the novice-expert shift in developing coaching skills, and this can provide a valuable framework for helping student coaches gauge their existing level of expertise. Table 2 presents this typology.

Table 2   *Novice to expert delineations as applied to the use of coaching session structures.*

Level of Expertise	*Characteristics*
Novices	Focus on immediate tasks. Need to follow clear rules and can't deal with complex coaching issues that arise in the coaching situation. Rigidly follows session model step-by-step
Advanced beginners	Tends to use rules as guidelines rather than prescriptions, but still finds it hard to handle exceptions to 'normal' coaching practice issues. Relies on model, but not always rigidly. Reverts to basic rules when feels under pressure in a coaching session.

Competent performers	Are at the stage where they can begin to create their own conceptual models of what they do, and can handle more complex situations. More flexible in use of session models. Able to move from one model to another to suit different coaching issues that arise within one coaching session.
Proficient performers:	Have experienced wide range of coaching situations, are able to see the big picture, and can interpret underlying principles and adjust their behaviours to suit relatively novel coaching situations. Very flexible use of models. Can develop own conceptually coherent and meaningful models to suit novel situations. Enjoys the challenge of coaching difficult issues.
Experts:	Have significant face-to-face coaching experience. Their high level of experience allows them to identify and solve problems with little explicit analysis. Can extrapolate solutions from principles even in very complex or highly novel situations.

For further reading see: Peterson, D.B. (2011). Good to great coaching. In G. Hernez-Broome & L. A. Boyce (Eds.), *Advancing executive coaching: Setting the course of successful leadership coaching* (pp.83–102). San Francisco: Jossey-Bass.

FROM GROW TO RE-GROW!

The kind of goal-directed self-regulation that sits at the heart of the coaching process is a series of processes in which an individual sets a goal, develops a plan of action, begins action, monitors his or her performance, evaluates his or her performance by comparison to a standard, and based on this evaluation changes his or her actions to better reach his or her goals. The coach's role is to facilitate the coachee's movement through the self-regulatory cycle (see Figure 2). This process requires that each coaching session takes stock of the outcomes of the previous session, and a coaching engagement is thus typically an iterative process in which the action steps from one session provide information and learning points for the following session (Kemp, 2008).

Without a clear and explicit link from one session to the next, the coaching engagement runs the risk of becoming a series of disjointed conversations. Yet most coaching session structures focus on structuring a single coaching session. We need coaching session models that recognise the iterative nature of the coaching engagement and explicitly provide a framework for incorporating the learning from the prior session into the current session.

The RE-GROW model is one way that this can be achieved (Greene & Grant, 2003). The initial stages of this model are Review and Evaluate. Thus each coaching session should start with a process of reviewing and evaluating the learnings and actions completed since the last session (see Figure 3). The trap here for the novice is to spend too much time in the review and evaluate process – with the possibility of de-railing the main coaching session. Thus it is important to make sure that only a short amount of time is spent in the review and evaluate section (approximately five to 10 minutes).

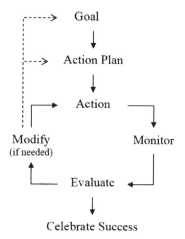

Figure 2 *Generic model of self-regulation.*
Adapted from Grant (2003).

Figure 3 *The RE-GROW Model.*

Personal experience and anecdotal evidence indicates that the use of RE-GROW can help maintain focus on the goals of coaching over the course of a coaching engagement, but more scholarship is needed in this area.

WRAP-UP AND WAY FORWARD

In wrapping-up this article, as in a coaching session, it might be useful to think about the next steps and the way forward. It is clear that coaching session structures are here to stay and are an integral part of coaching practice, and hence coaching-related teaching and training. But there has been little scholarship in this area of coaching practice on which to base our teaching and training. Research and scholarship into this area has the potential to further develop the evidence-base for coaching and also inform the broader psychological enterprise, particularly in relation to the further development of psychological theories of self-regulation and goal attainment. In order to keep the evidence-based coaching endeavour moving forward we need to pay attention to the this issue – we need to revitalise our approach to session structures. Maybe it is indeed time to re-grow the GROW model.

REFERENCES

Alexander, G. (2010). Behavioural coaching – the GROW model. In J. Passmore (Ed.), *Excellence in coaching: The industry guide* (pp.83–93). London: Kogan Page.

Argyris, C. (2002). Double-loop learning, teaching and research. *Academy of Management Learning and Education*, 1(2), 206–218.

CoachWorks (1998). *Module 2: The coaching conversation*. Dallas, TX: CoachWorks International.

Dembkowski, S. & Eldridge, F. (2003). Beyond GROW: A new coaching model. *The International Journal of Mentoring and Coaching*, 1(1).

Downey, M. (2003). *Effective coaching: Lessons from the coach's coach*. London: Texere.

Dreyfus, H.L. & Dreyfus, S.E. (1986). *Mind over machine: The power of human intuition and expertise in the era of the computer*. New York: The Free Press.

Egan, G. (1974). *The skilled helper*. Pacific Grove, CA: Brooks/Cole Publishing Co.

Fairburn, C.G., Cooper, Z., Shafran, R., Bohn, K., Hawker, D.M., Murphy, R. et al. (2008). *Cognitive behaviour therapy and eating disorders* (pp.183–193). New York: The Guilford Press.

Friedberg, R.D. & Brelsford, G.M. (2011). Core principles in cognitive therapy with youth. *Child and Adolescent Psychiatric Clinics of North America*, 20(2), 369–378.

Grant, A.M. (2003). The impact of life coaching on goal attainment, metacognition and mental health. *Social Behaviour and Personality: An International Journal*, 31(3), 253–264.

Grant, A.M. & Greene, J. (2004). *Coach yourself: Make real change in your life* (2nd ed.). London: Momentum Press.

Greene, J. & Grant, A.M. (2003). *Solution-focused coaching: Managing people in a complex world*. London: Momentum Press.

Hawkins, P. & Smith, N. (2007). *Coaching, mentoring and organisational consultancy: Supervision and development*. London: Open University Press.

Jackson, P.Z. & McKergow, M. (2002). *The solutions focus: The SIMPLE way to positive change*. London: Nicholas Brealey.

Kemp, T. (2008). Searching for the elusive model of coaching: Could the 'Holy Grail' be right in front of us? *International Coaching Psychology Review*, 3(3), 219–226.

Korzybski, A. (1933). A non-Aristotelian system and its necessity for rigour in mathematics and physics. *Science and Sanity*, 747–761.

Landsberg, M. (1997). *The Tao of coaching*. London: HarperCollins.

Mackintosh, A. (2005). *Growing on GROW – a more specific coaching model for busy managers; OUTCOMES*. ezinearticles Retrieved 15 August 2011, from: http://ezinearticles.com/?Growing-On G.R.O.W-A-More-Specific-Coaching-Model For–Busy-Managers&id=27766.

Palmer, S. (2007). PRACTICE: A model suitable for coaching, counselling, psychotherapy and stress management. *The Coaching Psychologist*, 3(2), 71–77.

Palmer, S. (2010). An international perspective on the development of coaching psychology: From Socrates to the present and where do we go from here? Keynote paper given on the 26 May 2010, at the 1st International Congress of Coaching Psychology, South Africa.

Peterson, D.B. (2011). Good to great coaching. In G. Hernez-Broome & L.A. Boyce (Eds.), *Advancing executive coaching: Setting the course of successful leadership coaching* (pp.83–102). San Francisco: Jossey-Bass.

Shirk, S.R. & Karver, M. (2003). Prediction of treatment outcome from relationship variables in child and adolescent therapy: A meta-analytic review. *Journal of Consulting and Clinical Psychology*, 71(3), 452–464.

Smith, L. (1998). *The five-step coaching model*. Dallas, TX: Corporate Coach U International.

Spence, G.B. & Grant, A.M. (2007). Professional and peer life coaching and the enhancement of goal striving and well-being: An exploratory study. *Journal of Positive Psychology*, 2(3), 185–194.

Stiles, W.B., Startup, M., Hardy, G.E., Barkham, M., Rees, A., Shapiro, D.A. et al. (1996). Therapist session intentions in cognitive-behavioural and psychodynamic-interpersonal psychotherapy. *Journal of Counseling Psychology*, 43(4), 402–414.

Wenzel, A., Brown, G.K. & Beck, A.T. (2009). *Cognitive therapy: General principles*. Washington, DC: American Psychological Association.

Whitmore, J. (1992). *Coaching for performance*. London: Nicholas Brealey.

Wilson, C. (2011). Solution-focused coaching and the GROW model. In L. Wildflower & D. Brennan (Eds.), *The handbook of knowledge-based coaching* (pp.279–285). San Francisco: Wiley and Sons.

4 A pluralistic approach to coaching

Zsófia Anna Utry, Stephen Palmer,
John McLeod & Mick Cooper

Abstract

A pluralistic approach to coaching and coaching psychology is proposed, based on Cooper and McLeod's (2011) pluralistic counselling and psychotherapy. Since we live in increasing complexity, it can be assumed that there are many right ways to coaching. The pluralistic approach suggests that instead of leaving the coach responsible for choosing the right interventions for their coachees it might be better not just to trust the coachee with the-content but to actively encourage them to co-determine the process. Setting up a feedback culture and regular metacommunication may make it more likely that high quality decision-making will be realised in practice. Such an approach also helps to develop the coachee's collaborative capacity, which is in high demand in work and business. A pluralistic coaching approach resonates with the current zeitgeist's values of desiring both autonomy and belonging.

Keywords

coaching; pluralistic coaching; pluralism; shared decision-making; coachee-centred attitude; collaborative capacity; feedback culture; diversity.

Original publication details: Utry, Z. A., Palmer, S., McLeod, J., & Cooper, M. (2015, June). A pluralistic approach to coaching. *The Coaching Psychologist*, 11(1), 46–52. Reproduced with permission of The British Psychological Society.

LIVING IN A DIGIMODERN SOCIETY

Coaching theory has shifted its focus in recent years from the specific and measurable to values and reflective capacity. This is a response to rapid changes and increasing uncertainty in business and life.

Emerging new theories (e.g. Clutterbuck & David, 2013; Stelter, 2014; Western, 2012) have challenged the late 20th century's most popular coaching models (e.g. Alexander, 2010; Joseph & Bryant-Jefferies; O'Connell & Palmer, 2008; Whitmore, 2002). What is common about these theories is that they all argue for the necessity of a paradigm shift in coaching and coaching psychology, and they base their claims on the needs of a rapidly changing and super-connected globalised world. This change has been attributed to our postmodern living conditions: the decline of traditional religions and a dramatic increase in economic and technological developments (Spencer, 2001).

Postmodernism is variably interpreted but generally brings together those thinkers who share a preference for scepticism, antifoundational bias and a dislike of authority (Sim, 2001).

Gergen (1991) as a social psychologist, argues that the individual in postmodern times is overwhelmed by information, by the diversity of values, and by the multiplicity of their relationships. These have been generated by the development of communication technology, globalisation and multiculturalism. Going beyond postmodernism, Kirby (2009, 2010) argues for a new cultural paradigm, *digimodernism*, which stands for the emergence of a different logic in (digital) culture, mainly dictated by the popularisation of the internet and the digital technology revolution. Digimodernism shares many similarities with postmodernism (Kirby, 2010). However, one of the distinct characteristics of digimodernism is the change in understandings of authorship of cultural products or 'texts' (Kirby, 2009). On the web, it is not entirely clear now who is the author and who is the reader anymore, or who is the producer and who is the consumer (Kirby, 2009; Mulady, 2010). Even if people only just sequence the content they want to see, that can leave the marketer out of control when they want to advertise.

With the advent of Web 2.0 people have become technologically empowered to participate actively in marketing processes now, by sharing, commenting, liking or blogging about products, news and ideas on the internet. Consequently, some refer to this approach to marketing as 'collaborative marketing' (Cova & Cova, 2009, as cited in Mulady, 2010). People co-create, take part and not just consume (digital) media anymore (Mulady, 2010).

A specific example is content marketing. This field experienced rapid growth in the past few years (NewsCred, 2014). It is now recognised that people want authentic, relevant and personalised content from the marketers. NewsCred (2014), 'thought leaders' in this area, quote Doug Kessler in their online white paper on content marketing strategy: 'Traditional marketing talks at people. Content marketing talks with them.'

THE WORLD OF WORK

Another area which has been highly affected by the rapidly changing conditions and digital revolution is the world of work. By now, cloud technology and social media platforms enable organisations to think beyond their traditional boundaries in terms of recruiting their workforce, and this makes diversity and adaptability highly valued both in the individual and in the organisation (Institute for the Future, 2011).

The Global Talent 2021 Survey (Oxford Economics, 2012) found four main categories as key areas for development for successful future human capital outcomes. These are digital skills, agile thinking skills, interpersonal and communication skills, and global operating skills.

Another large scale survey, *The Future Work Skills 2020* (Institute for the Future, 2011) also draws attention to the ability of sense making and being critical to decision making (agile thinking skills) and social intelligence to ensure effective collaboration through trusting relationships (interpersonal and communication skills). Moreover, situational adaptivity, cross-cultural competency, using technology for communication, collaboration and managing workload (global operating skills and digital skills) were found to be very important. In the end, this survey also adds trans-disciplinarity to the list of skills in demand which is about the ability to understand other disciplines and the ability to communicate effectively across several departments.

Hawkins (2012), a leading advocate of coaching cultures in organisations, argues that companies for the future should practise high critique and high support at work and at business. This means it is necessary to develop people's ability to challenge and collaborate, and this will help to deal with economic and environmental challenges they possibly face when aiming towards continuous development and sustainability in their organisations.

A PLURALISTIC APPROACH TO COACHING

A new approach to coaching that may suit this postmodern, digimodern era is a pluralistic one. This is not a set of techniques but a commitment in practice to deeply value the coachee's needs, which can be achieved by encouraging him or her to actively participate in the management of the coaching process. Through this, the coachee is not only working towards their goals, but also stretching his or her collaborative and challenging capacity. These are skills they potentially can transfer to other areas of work and life.

Pluralism in terms of religion and culture is more than diversity, tolerance, relativism and listening of the other. Eck (2006), who is the head of The Pluralism Project at Harvard University, describes pluralism as:

- …the energetic engagement with diversity…
- …the active seeking of understanding across lines of difference…
- …the encounter of commitments…
- …based on dialogue…

Transferring these principles into coaching could certainly be useful if we consider the skills, discussed above, that are currently in demand in the workplace, and for the future. But how can we bring them into practice?

Pluralistic psychotherapy and counselling, developed by Cooper and McLeod (2011) in the UK, is based on a postmodern and poststructuralist philosophy. At its heart is also an ethical perspective which builds on humanistic and existential philosophy, where the 'Other' is deeply valued and respected.

Two basic principles of the pluralistic approach to counselling and psychotherapy have been articulated as follows:

1. Lots of different things can be helpful to clients.
2. If we want to know what is most likely to help clients, we should talk to them about it. (Cooper & McLeod, 2011, p.24)

Pluralistic practice draws on a wide variety of approaches, but moves beyond eclectic and integrative practices. It is centred around a collaborative dialogue between client and practitioner. In this respect, it does not simply rely on what the practitioner intuitively assumes will or might be good for a client (Cooper & McLeod, 2011).

In pluralistic counselling and psychotherapy, clients are actively encouraged to be involved in the decision making process about what kind of interventions they think would do the best for them. The practitioner is not expected to deliver whatever the client says but rather expected to be ready to discuss and negotiate with their client about what would be most likely to serve them.

Metatherapeutic communication is the process of communication about the therapeutic process itself, through which a feedback culture and collaborative practice can be realised (Cooper & McLeod, 2011). Cooper et al. (2016) also argue that metatherapeutic communication can serve a therapeutic function: increasing the client's interpersonal relating, ability to dialogue, assertiveness, and reflective functioning.

It has the capacity, they argue, to build self-confidence by involving the client in decisions as an equal person in the room.

Is there a case, then, for 'metacoaching communication', when coach and coachee would communicate about what is happening in the coaching session? Currently, Ely et al. (2010) found that executive coaches tend to ask for feedback on an ad hoc, rather than systematic, basis. This might suggest that client satisfaction and process is not monitored well at the moment in coaching, and coaches may not engage regularly in metacoaching communication with their clients.

A PLURALISTIC FRAMEWORK FOR COACHING

Cooper and McLeod's (2011) framework for pluralistic therapy might fit coaching well. In this framework, the client's own *goals* are considered to anchor the process (both goals for the therapeutic process and goals for life). This provides the basis to talk about the *tasks* to be undertaken (i.e. what macro-level areas of thinking or behaviour to focus on to achieve the coachee's goals). The *methods* of completing the tasks are then considered (i.e. the specific activities of coach and coachee at the micro level). Figure 1 shows a possible way to adapt the pluralistic framework to coaching.

Talking through the goals, methods and tasks with the coachee can help the coach to practice in a coachee-centred way, enhance the supervisory alliance, and encourage metacommunication such that coach and coachee can reach high quality decisions.

PRACTICAL STEPS TO DEVELOP THE COACHEE'S COLLABORATIVE CAPACITY

Based on Cooper and McLeod's (2011) work, the following steps can be suggested in pluralistic coaching practice:

- Provide information about coaching prior to the first meeting, so the coachee will know what to expect in the session. This can be supported by a brochure, telephone call, or email about the approach.
- Establish a feedback culture from the beginning by reminders to the coachee that the coach is interested in his or her ideas, preferences and feedback.
- Explain the different options that are available to coachees, and what these would actually mean in practice. Provide evidence, where available, on the typical outcomes of particular ways of working.
- Engage in metacoaching communication with the coachee about the process of coaching itself. Review goals, methods and tasks on an ongoing basis. This may be particularly helpful if coach or coachee are uncertain about what is going on in the coaching, or if there is a rupture in the coaching relationship.
- Actively invite discussion on all aspects of the coaching work, from duration, through payment, to possible involvement in research. This discussion can prove particularly interesting as the digital age offers a range of non-traditional ways for interaction, such as instant messaging or even communicating with pictures.
- Adapt the style of relating to the coachee's needs and preferences. Different people have different needs and this can mean to adapt to at what level a coachee wants to collaborate.
- Use outcome forms (for instance, a goal assessment form) to monitor progress in a way that fits the coachee. This can help to keep the process of coaching on track.
- Use process measures to facilitate conversation about preferences and the process itself. The pluralistic therapy personalisation form can be a helpful guide, though it still needs to be tested for coaching. (The therapy and supervision versions can be found at www.pluralistictherapy.com.)

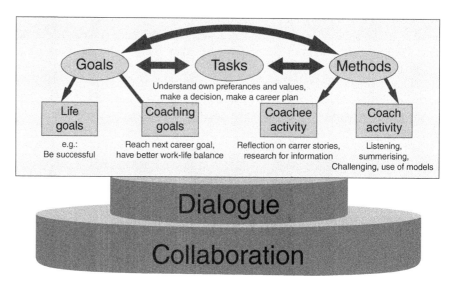

Figure 1 *A pluralistic framework for coaching.*

EARLY RESEARCH INTO COACHES' PERCEPTIONS OF PLURALISM

In a qualitative study with six experienced female coaches, Pendle (2014) explored the potential of the pluralistic approach in coaching. It was found that the participants saw pluralism as offering benefits to coaches mainly in terms of providing a greater structure to organise their knowledge and practice and an enriched sense of professional identity. Participants seemed to have few issues with blending different coaching approaches in their practices. However, it was evident that most of them found it more difficult to grasp, and apply, the philosophical foundation of the pluralistic approach. They also struggled to realise close collaboration during the coaching process with their coachees. In this respect, they found it easy to think about pluralism (for instance, 'I love the idea of the collaborative approach, it's very much the ethos of how I see coaching', Pendle, 2014, p.16); but tended to think differently in practice.

CONCLUSION

Are you talking *at*, or talking *with*, your coachees? Do you think coaches intuitively know what is good for their coachees? How far are you willing to go to share responsibility with your coachee in designing the coaching process?

This article invited the readers to think critically about coaching practice: global economy, super-connectedness and digital revolutions that transform everyday and working life. The coaching profession has already started questioning the traditional approaches to coaching, which tend to offer easy and quick problem solving or solution finding with measurable and predictable outcomes.

While there are many good ways to practise coaching, coaches tend to be expected to take responsibility for selecting interventions and managing the process (Passmore, 2014). By contrast, the counselling and wider health care field has started to consider – and apply – shared decision-making, which involves the client actively in figuring out how to approach his or her issues.

While all coaches say they 'collaborate' or work in a 'partnership' with their clients or coaches and there is a 'feedback culture' in the sessions, there is little evidence that they really have one (Ely et al., 2010). Preliminary research about a pluralistic approach indicates that coaches found the idea of collaboration inspiring, but struggled to practice in a truly collaborative manner (Pendle, 2014).

The pluralistic approach, and its strategies, may be helpful for coaches for this reason. With the pluralistic framework, they can organise their practice and work with coachees in a more collaborative way.

Cooper and McLeod (2011) differentiate between a pluralistic perspective and pluralistic practice. In this respect, practitioners with a specific coaching approach still can have a pluralistic view. This means they adapt their work to individual needs as much as possible, recognise their limitations, and strive to make informed referrals where appropriate.

Many work skills, in demand for the foreseeable future, could be developed by a collaborative type of coaching. For the development of interpersonal and communication skills – such as co-creativity and brainstorming, relationship building, teaming and collaboration – pluralistic coaching might be especially able to contribute.

From the global operating skills, a pluralistic approach to coaching has the potential to support the development of cultural sensitivity, and the ability to manage diverse employees through the promotion of its humanistic and progressive values.

Using a pluralistic framework can also help to identify micro practices in coaching and help to design research into coaching effectiveness. Future research, for instance, could look into how satisfied coachees really are with coaching and whether a pluralistic approach would be useful. It would be also interesting to explore whether coachees feel comfortable to give feedback to their coaches, and what might inhibit or facilitate this process. Comparative and observational studies could also examine whether those who participated in pluralistic coaching develop better collaborative skills.

People have access to information on the internet, and they can take control of what is happening with them in the digital world. However, the line between the digital and real world is increasingly blurred. It will be interesting to see whether coaching will be able to meet the needs of those people: who both want to experience agency in their lives, but also a sense of belongingness.

REFERENCES

Alexander, G. (2010). Behavioural coaching – GROW model. In J. Passmore (Ed.), *Excellence in coaching: The industry guide* (pp.83–93). London: Kogan Page Limited.

Clutterbuck, D. & David, S. (2013). Goals in coaching and mentoring: The current state of play. In S. David, D. Clutterbuck & D. Megginson (Eds.), *Beyond goals – effective strategies for coaching and mentoring* (pp.21–36). Farnham, Surrey: Gower.

Cooper, M., Dryden, W., Martin, K. & Papayianni, F. (2016). Metatherapeutic communication and shared decision-making. In M. Cooper & W. Dryden (Eds.), *Handbook of pluralistic counselling and psychotherapy* (Ch. 1). London: Sage.

Cooper, M. & McLeod, J. (2011). *Pluralistic counselling and psychotherapy*. London: Sage.

Eck, D. L. (2006). *What is pluralism?* Retrieved 11 March 2015, from: http://www.pluralism.org/pluralism/what_is_pluralism

Ely, K., Boyce, L.A., Nelson, J.K., Zaccaro, S.J., Hernez-Broome, G. & Whyman, W. (2010). Evaluating leadership coaching: A review and integrated framework. *The Leadership Quarterly*, 21, 585–599.

Gergen, K.J. (1991). *The saturated self: Dilemmas of identity in contemporary life*. New York: Basic Books.

Hawkins, P. (2012). *Creating a coaching culture: Developing a coaching strategy for your organisation*. Maidenhead: Open University Press.

Institute for the Future (2011). *Future work skills 2020*. Palo Alto, CA: Institute for the Future. Retrieved 11 March 2015, from: http://www.iftf.org/uploads/media/SR-1382A_UPRI_future_work_skills_sm.pdf

Joseph, S. & Bryant-Jefferies, R. (2008). Person-centred coaching psychology. In S. Palmer & A. Whybrow (Eds.), *Handbook of coaching psychology: A guide for practitioners* (pp.211–228). Hove: Routledge.

Kirby, A. (2009). *Digimodernism: How new technologies dismantle the postmodern and reconfigure our culture*. New York: Continuum.

Kirby, A. (2010). Successor states to an empire in free fall. The Times Higher Education, 27 May. Retrieved 11 March 2015, from: http://www.timeshighereducation.co.uk/411731.article

Mulady, L. (2010). *Digimodernism; the future is now!* (Master's dissertation). Retrieved 11 March 2015, from: http://pure.au.dk/portal/files/13871/Final_Paper_for_Upload.pdf

NewsCred (2014). *NewsCred white paper on content marketing* [White paper]. Retrieved 11 March 2015, from: http://newscred.com/theacademy/learn/content-marketing-playbook-nine-strategies

Zsófia Anna Utry, Stephen Palmer, John McLeod & Mick Cooper

O'Connell, B. & Palmer, S. (2008). Solution-focused coaching. In S. Palmer & A. Whybrow (Eds.), *Handbook of coaching psychology: A guide for practitioners* (pp.278–292). Hove: Routledge.

Oxford Economics (2012). *Global Talent 2021: How the new geography of talent will transform human resource strategies*. Oxford: Oxford Economics. Retrieved from: https://www.oxfordeconomics.com/Media/Default/Thought%20Leadership/global-talent-2021.pdf

Passmore, J. (2014). *Mastery in coaching*. London: Kogan Page Ltd.

Pendle, A.P. (2014). *Pluralistic coaching? An exploration of the potential for pluralistic approach to coaching* (Unpublished Master's dissertation). University of East London, London.

Sim, S. (2001). Postmodernism and philosophy. In S. Sim (Ed.), *The Routledge companion to postmodernism* (pp.3–11). London: Routledge.

Spencer, L. (2001). Postmodernism, modernity and the tradition of dissent. In S. Sim (Ed.), *The Rout-ledge companion to postmodernism* (pp.125–134). London: Routledge.

Stelter, R. (2014). *A guide to third generation coaching*. London: Springer.

Western, S. (2012). *Coaching and mentoring: A critical text*. London: Sage.

Whitmore, J. (2002). *Coaching for performance GROWing people performance, and purpose* (3rd ed.). London: Nicholas Brealey Publishing.

Section 3

Reflective Practice and Professional Development

Introduction

David Tee & Jonathan Passmore

Reflective practice is widely accepted as a critical component in the development of most practitioners, from master chefs to master coaches (Passmore, 2014). Yet, surprisingly, reflective practice is not widely covered in the coaching literature; only a relatively few papers have engaged with the why, what and how of reflective practice, and, as such, many coach education programmes focus on the skills or competencies and count the hours of practice, while ignoring the importance of reflection as a tool for learning. Taking time to reflect provides a means for the coach to examine themselves, their presence and the quality of their coaching practice. Once learnt, the reflective process can become an integral part of the coach's practice, enabling the coach to engage in a journey of continuous professional development based on insights, evidence and feedback from clients, supervisors and their own judgements; all to be subsequently tested and retested in the furnace of practice with the next client.

In other domains, reflection has been more highly regarded and has attracted the interest of theorists. Donald Schon (1991, p. 145) distinguishes between two kinds of reflection: 'reflection in action' and 'reflection on action'. Reflection in action takes place during the 'doing' stage. This means the coach is required to be both fully present with their client, and fully aware of themselves as the agent and their actions. In this state, the coach is reflecting on the conversation as it happens, adapting and flexing their interventions in best service of their client. This is the state advocated in one of the papers below (Grant, 2016). Schon's second reflective style is 'reflection on action'. This takes place later, with the coach looking back at the conversation and seeking to develop an insight either alone, for example, through a reflective journal, or in

Coaching Practiced, First Edition. Edited by David Tee and Jonathan Passmore.
© 2022 John Wiley & Sons Ltd. Published 2022 by John Wiley & Sons Ltd.
DOI: 10.1002/9781119835714.s03

discussion with a peer or supervisor. We argue that high-level reflective practice requires both. Reflection in the moment, flexing and adapting, and reflecting in depth later outside of the cut and thrust of the session, to go deeper and explore what might have been going on, initially through a reflective journal, using a model such as the Henley 8 (Passmore & Sinclair, 2020, Table 1), but also explored in more depth later in discussions with a supervisor.

In this section, writers explore the different aspects of reflective practice and its different forms. In the first paper in this series, Sarah Corrie and David Lane (2009) explore the topic of the scientist-practitioner model. The model was originally conceived in 1949 for the then emerging profession of clinical psychology. The model advocates psychologists should be trained as both scientists and practitioners but, as the authors note, the idea has been hotly contested over the decades, with the question whether it is reasonable for psychologists to achieve both a high standard in research and a comparable standard in practice. The authors acknowledge much of the criticism and call for a new framework which recognises the complexity of coaching work with clients, and the changing nature of what is evidence. The debate is one which is ongoing but, as we suggested in our introduction, the coaching psychologist's training means they are able to develop a deeper understanding of both compared with most coaching practitioners.

In the second paper, Manfusa Sham and Ho Law (2012) explore the role of peer coaching in supporting the development of coaches. The writers offer a model for peer practice based on the open system model. These ideas were influencing in the British Psychological Society's subsequent work which has led to the development of peer mentoring groups supporting the ongoing reflective practice of coaching psychologists.

In the third paper in this section, Anthony Grant explores the role of note-taking in coaching. He argues that capturing notes can enhance, rather than detract, from reflective practice. He notes, "levels of self-insight can be developed by mindfully engaging in exercises designed to raise in-the-moment awareness during the actual coaching process. Structured note-taking is one such approach that has been shown to be effective" (Grant, 2016, p. 51). What is critical in all such activities is that the reflective exercise does not interfere with the client relationship, for example with the coach

Table 1   *Henley 8: Eight questions to guide a reflective journaling process*

What did I notice?

How did I respond?

What does this tell me about me?

What does this tell me about me as a coach?

What strengths does this offer me?

What pitfalls should I watch out for?

What did I learn?

What should I do differently next time?

(Adapted from Passmore & Sinclair, 2020, p. 251)

spending long periods capturing content and, in so doing, avoiding eye contact and thus potentially missing out on a deeper level of listening which comes through combining the words and the body. However, by engaging in the moment, the coach can capture both the essence of the content and also their response in the moment to the client's communication, forming hypotheses and developing ideas as to how and in which direction to move forward both within the session and across the assignment, as well as personal insights to explore in supervision.

In the final paper in this section, Louise Kovacs and Sarah Corrie (2017) explore the role of reflection as a tool to enhance practice. The writers note the centrality of reflection within learning and offer ways for coaching psychologists to further develop their reflective practice.

REFERENCES

Corrie, S., & Lane, D. A. (2009). The scientist-practitioner model as a framework for coaching psychologists. *The Coaching Psychologist*, *5*(2), 61–68

Grant, A. M. (2016) Reflection, note-taking and coaching. *The Coaching Psychologist*, *12*(2), 49–58.

Kovacs, L., & Corrie, S. (2017) Building reflective capability to enhance coaching practice, *The Coaching Psychologists*, *13*(1), 4–14.

Passmore, J. (2014). Mastery in coaching. In J. Passmore (ed.). *Mastery in Coaching: A complete psychological toolkit for advanced coaching* (pp 1–14). Kogan Page.

Passmore, J., & Sinclair, T. (2020). *Becoming a coach: The Essential ICF guide*. Pavilion Press.

Schon, D. A. (1991). *The Reflective Practitioner: How Professionals Think in Action*. Aldershot: Ashgate Publishing Ltd.

Shams, M., & Law, H. (2012) Peer coaching framework. *The Coaching Psychologist*, *8*(1), 46–49.

5 The scientist-practitioner model as a framework for coaching psychology

Sarah Corrie & David A. Lane

Abstract

The scientist-practitioner model has been proposed as a viable basis for the development of coaching psychology, despite proving to be a controversial ideal in other forms of applied psychology. This article examines what is meant by this term and how it can contribute to the development of coaching psychology and proposes a redefinition of the model that is fit for the purposes of contemporary coaching practice.

Keywords

scientist-practitioner model, coaching psychology, science, identity, applied psychology.

The Scientist-Practitioner model has long been heralded as the authorised model of training and practice in professional psychology (Barlow et al., 1984; British Psychological Society, 2005; Lane & Corrie, 2006; Trierweiler & Stricker, 1998). In consequence, it is not surprising that it has also been proposed as an appropriate framework for the emerging profession of coaching psychology (Cavanagh & Grant, 2006; Short & Blumberg, 2009). However, within the wider spectrum of applied psychology, the scientist-practitioner model has proved to be a controversial, and some would

Original publication details: Corrie, S., & Lane, D. A. (2009, December). The scientist-practitioner model as a framework for coaching psychology. *The Coaching Psychologist*, *5*(2), 61–67. Reproduced with permission of The British Psychological Society.

argue a misplaced, ideal. Coaching psychologists must, therefore, consider carefully what they mean when they describe themselves as scientist-practitioners and in particular, avoid any overly-simplistic notions of how science informs practice. In this article we consider the role of the scientist-practitioner model in coaching psychology and make the case for elevating the model to the heart of coaching psychology identity and practice. However, we argue that to do so in any meaningful way requires a fundamental revisioning of its aims and purpose. This article provides one such 'revisioning' which we believe can accommodate both the need to develop a systematic evidence-base and enhance the credibility of coaching psychology's offer in the wider market place.

THE SCIENTIST-PRACTITIONER MODEL AND PSYCHOLOGY: A BRIEF HISTORY

The scientist-practitioner model was originally conceived in 1949, for the then emerging profession of clinical psychology. Since that time, it has received wide official endorsement as the basis for a distinctive professional 'brand' (British Psychological Society, 2005; Kennedy & Llewellyn, 2001; Woolfe & Dryden, 1996).

In simple terms, the scientist-practitioner model proposed that psychologists should be trained as both scientists and practitioners. In their historical review, Lane and Corrie (2006) highlight that there were compelling political reasons for endorsing this emerging profession with the hallmark of scientific respectability. However, implementation of the ideal has proved problematic and the scientist-practitioner model has been hotly debated and subject to severe criticism. The debates have spanned whether it is feasible – and indeed possible – to train psychologists to operate as both scientists and practitioners, whether the model equips practitioners with the prerequisite skills for responding effectively to social need and whether the scientist-practitioner model can truly promote the systematic development of psychological knowledge more broadly.

Some have argued that the scientific identity of the practitioner is 'fraudulent' (Jones, 1998) and that the divergent priorities of scientist and practitioner lead to an inevitable and irreconcilable rift in purpose and activity (Rennie, 1994; Williams & Irving, 1996). Others have claimed that a significant proportion of research conducted in academic settings lacks relevance to the needs of practitioners (see Bergin & Strupp, 1972), with doubts about the extent to which the model equips trainees with the necessary competences for effective clinical practice (Sheehan, 1994). Evidence in support of these claims has come from a number of sources. Nathan (2000) and Head and Harmon (1990), for example, have observed that at post-qualification, relatively few psychologists conduct research whilst Allen (1985) found that professional psychologists rank research as a lower priority than service-related commitments.

As Shapiro (2002) observes, the original definition gave relatively little consideration to how science and practice would be integrated in routine clinical practice, thus fuelling an underlying tension between science and practice that persists today. However, despite the difficulties associated with its implementation, support for the scientist-practitioner model has remained. Stoltenberg et al. (2000), for example, argue that psychologists cannot be competent in the delivery of their practice unless they possess the skills to evaluate it. The ability to conduct research is an essential starting point for understanding and making use of the published research literature in an informed way.

Belar and Perry (1992) have also proposed that the scientist-practitioner model provides an important framework for theory-building whereby, through a systematic approach to enquiry, random observations can be shaped into hypotheses that presage the development of new theories and interventions. A similar argument was made by Stricker (1992) who advocates that the impact of research on practice often occurs through an indirect 'meta effect' whereby the research questions of one generation tend to presage the professional developments of the next.

The issue of definition would also appear to be critical to the debate. Milne et al. (1990), for example, found that when a wider definition of scientific activity is adopted – one that encompasses publishing in non-refereed journals, compiling service evaluation reports and undertaking small-scale research projects – a closer approximation to the ideal begins to emerge.

Corrie and Callanan (2001) found marked variations amongst practitioners in terms of how the scientist-practitioner model is defined and also observed that idiosyncratic definitions were related to perceptions of its value. Different interpretations could be placed on a continuum of closed to open definitions, where: (1) the most 'closed' related to a model of science that was essentially concerned with traditional experimental testing; and (2) the most 'open' definition conceptualised the scientist-practitioner model as a spirit of enquiry whereby psychological evidence could be used in a more holistic way according to the needs of a particular practice-based enquiry. These findings led Corrie and Callanan (2001) to conclude that it is no longer justifiable to define the scientist-practitioner model as a single way of working, but rather to interpret it as a framework that encompasses a broad range of more idiosyncratic models of practice and systems of values which should become a focus of enquiry in their own right.

These debates have important implications for coaching psychology which are considered next.

THE COACHING PSYCHOLOGIST AS SCIENTIST-PRACTITIONER

Short and Blumberg (2009) highlight that one of the central aims of the SGCP is to encourage research that can inform the development of coaching psychology in the variety of contexts in which it occurs. The fact that a section of *The Coaching Psychologist* is now devoted to sharing ideas about, and facilitating the undertaking of, research attests to the central importance of underpinning coaching psychology with a strong evidence-base and developing its knowledge through recourse to science. The scientist-practitioner model is promoted as a viable and valuable framework in this context. However, if the discipline is to avoid the pitfalls faced by other forms of applied psychology, then it will be necessary to consider what this terms means and how we conceptualise its aims and function, as well as the definition of science contained within it.

In their examination of how the scientist-practitioner model can add value to coaching psychology, Cavanagh and Grant (2006) point out that there is not, as yet, a robust coaching-specific scientific literature that can systematically guide the development of its knowledge base. This is a particular challenge given both the rapid growth of interest in coaching and its applications within a highly diverse range of settings. As coaching psychology is distinguished from other forms of applied psychology by the breadth of its knowledge base rather than by its uniqueness (Cavanagh & Grant, 2006), it has inevitably drawn upon theories and techniques from across the spectrum of psychological sciences. But which model of science and which forms of scientific activity best fit the range of investigative questions with which coaching psychologists are most concerned?

Kwiatkowski and Winter (2006) argue that to intervene effectively, scientist-practitioners must be able to navigate the worlds of industry and commerce, in addition to the world of science. They make the important distinction between sophistication and impact and how, when it comes to producing impactful research, the small scale project may be preferable to an elegantly designed and rigorously controlled study. Indeed, Kwiatkowski and Winter (2006) suggest that an over-attachment to sophistication and rigour may actually hinder the 'take up' of psychological science.

Any redefinition of the scientist-practitioner model must, then, be considered in relation to what we hope that our science will achieve for us. Science is a marketable product (Corrie, 2010). We must consider carefully who gets to define what counts as 'evidence', the most appropriate way to use the results obtained and their potential impact – for good and ill (Sturdee, 2001). Appreciating the more contextual positioning of our science is what we believe lies at the heart of a more sophisticated interpretation of the scientist-practitioner model. As Miller and Frederickson (2006) comment, we do not become scientist-practitioners solely by conducting large numbers of measurements, but through being able to examine our epistemologies, science and practice in the context of the multiple social systems in which we operate. Coaching interventions are embedded within domains that require non-linear thinking and creative solutions.

Psychology's traditional allegiance to the empiricist model as the epitome of scientific credibility, and the hypothetico-deductive method that has dominated much of its research, may not prove adequate to address the majority of questions with which coaching psychologists are faced. Cavanagh and Grant (2006) propose that in order to achieve a robust scientific basis for the development of coaching psychology, a preferable model is one that draws on complexity theory in which human systems are seen as open systems that interact in non-linear and adaptive ways. The coaching relationship is part of a complex system that exists within, and forms part of, a network of other complex systems. As the interactions and responses governing a coaching session are determined by an almost infinite and unpredictable causal field, they cannot be predicted or controlled in the way that the experimental method favours.

However, this is not seen as a reason to abandon the quest for a scientific foundation. Indeed, Cavanagh and Grant (2006) propose that it is precisely in such contexts that the scientist-practitioner model makes its most significant contribution. Specifically, they propose that the nature of the coaching intervention needs to be continually renegotiated as each party comes to better understand the critical issues involved. This ability to work towards a shared case conceptualisation depends upon the coach's knowledge of, and ability to use, a wide range of evidence to meet the needs of the enquiry at hand. It is precisely the training in the production and interpretation of research that they argue enables the coach to operate effectively within the wide spectrum of psychological knowledge and which enables them to develop the skills to collect data, form and test hypotheses, evaluate the findings and infer conclusions that are relevant to the individual client. As they suggest:

> 'The strength of the scientist-practitioner model is not in developing prescriptive models of psychological intervention which can be applied with unquestioning confidence in their scientific veracity. Rather, its strength is that it provides both information and methodological rigour that the practitioner can use to negotiate the ever-changing waters of psychological intervention' (p.157).

'REVISIONING' THE SCIENTIST-PRACTITIONER MODEL FOR THE FUTURE

The skills required of the psychologist operating in today's complex world are sophisticated and diverse and the contexts in which coaching psychologists operate will entail a wide range of approaches to research and enquiry. In a previous volume (Lane & Corrie, 2006), we proposed that the prerequisite skills for effective practice fall within four main domains which can provide an overarching framework for exploring what it means to be a modern scientist-practitioner. These are: (1) the ability to think (judge, reason, make decisions and problem-solve); (2) the ability to weave data from different sources into a coherent formulation or case conceptualisation; (3) the ability to act effectively (that is, to devise and implement specific interventions strategies, design solutions and innovate creatively on a case-by-case basis); and (4) the skills to evaluate and critique our work (including the use of psychological science and evidence in addition to relevant reading, personal audits and use of supervision and training).

However, the scientist-practitioner model may also represent a distinct type of professional identity. Abrahamson and Pearlman (1993) have observed an emerging consensus that the scientist-practitioner model is a distinctive inner professional 'compass' which carries with it a moral injunction to distinguish between sources of knowledge on the basis of their origins. This echoes Singer's (1980) earlier argument that the relationship between research and practice should be elevated to the realms of ethical responsibility.

Aspenson et al. (1993) also found this to be an important feature of psychology trainees' attitudes towards the scientist-practitioner model. In particular, those with positive attitudes towards the model also held a belief that ethical and effective practice was dependent upon practitioners keeping themselves informed about theoretical and empirical advancements within the field. Over time, these attitudes appeared to become internalised suggesting that for some, commitment to the scientist-practitioner identity is consistent with the commitment to a particular set of values.

Of further relevance here, is Crane and Hafen's (2002) developmental perspective. They propose that practitioners travel through a series of scientist-practitioner stages. In the earliest stages, as fundamental competencies are acquired, the focus is on becoming an evidence-based practitioner (that is, implementing the knowledge and methods established by others). In the next stage, practitioners can be taught how to use research through evaluating the contribution of different studies, which enables them to determine what has meaning in an applied domain. Practitioners then learn to collect data from clients which introduces them to specific scientific methods they need to conduct their own research. Finally, they become 'translators' of research for other practitioners in the field.

Thus, novice practitioners may prefer a more concrete definition of what it means to be a scientist-practitioner as this offers a clear framework in which specific skills can be systematically developed. In contrast, highly experienced practitioners may favour the flexibility to determine how they define and implement the model. This would appear to be consistent with the literature on professional development more broadly, whereby it is recognised that practitioners' relationship with diverse sources of knowledge, both formal and informal, acquires different meanings at different stages in their careers (Skovholt & Rønnestad, 1995).

Elsewhere (Lane & Corrie, 2006) we summarised a vision of the scientist-practitioner model as a distinct approach to enquiry rather than the undertaking of any specific activity. We proposed that the scientist-practitioner model can no longer be defined as the application of psychological science to practice in any simplistic fashion, but is rather a framework in which the discipline of psychology becomes personalised so that we can: (1) respond optimally to the dilemmas experienced by the clients who seek out our services; and (2) reflect upon and enhance our practice in systematic ways. As we view it, the coaching psychologist as scientist-practitioner is someone who has embarked upon a never-ending search for new approaches that facilitate increasingly helpful ways of working with clients to make sense of the puzzles that we, and they, are attempting to solve. In addition to identifying these approaches we search for ways through which they might be validated and refined.

In choosing the identity of the scientist-practitioner, coaching psychologists will be committed to holding in mind a framework for distinguishing between different forms of knowledge and a general set of psychological principles for informing the creation of a systematic approach to professional decision-making. Likewise, when investigating their own practice or when examining or conducting research, we would expect the scientist-practitioner to be able to justify their decision to rely on one model of science rather than another. In this way, the scientist-practitioner model becomes a system through which coaching psychologists can both evaluate the limitations of their chosen model and be clear about the functions it can fulfil (Lane & Corrie, 2006).

Ultimately, there are many ways of being a scientist and multiple ways in which being a scientist-practitioner might manifest itself. As coaching psychologists and scientist-practitioners, we are not solely interested in how effective our interventions are, but also concerned with the process of enquiry itself. In this sense, we concur with Stoltenberg et al.'s (2000) view that the scientist-practitioner model is essentially an integrated approach to knowledge. A new vision is viable but will necessitate the promotion of multiple narratives, representing a broad approach to enquiry that embraces a multitude of purposes, myriad perspectives and a wide variety of processes.

CONCLUSION

Coaching takes place alongside other offers in the marketplace and so we need to consider what we offer that adds value and how our position as scientist-practitioners contributes to that value. In this paper we have argued that the scientist-practitioner model does indeed add value, but only if we look beyond a 60-year-old definition of what it means to be a professional psychologist. The scientist-practitioner model conceived of in 1949 had key advantages for the embryonic profession of clinical psychology but does not meet the needs of the emerging discipline of coaching psychology.

We concur with Short and Blumberg's (2009) view that we need to '…increase the credibility of our profession through the sharing of scientific- and enquiry-based practice' (p.44) and strongly endorse the view that our practice must indeed have a scientific foundation. However, the wide range of activities, professional contexts and interest in positive and constructivist approaches that coaching psychology embodies has major implications for our understanding of ourselves as scientists. We must remain open to exploring, questioning and critiquing the versions of science to which we subscribe if we are to avoid what Salkovskis (2002) has termed the '…unthinking application of scientism' (p.4).

The challenge facing coaching psychology is how to look beyond the authorised version of the scientist-practitioner model in order to engage with a sophisticated consideration of the range of models of science and practice encompassed within it. This article is one response to what we would see as a pressing need and an area in which we would welcome further discussion and debate.

REFERENCES

Abrahamson, D.J. & Pearlman, L.A. (1993). The need for scientist-practitioner employment settings. *American Psychologist*, 48, 59–60.

Allen, C. (1985). *Training for what? Clinical psychologists' perceptions of their roles*. Unpublished MSc Thesis, University of Newcastle-upon-Tyne.

Aspenson, D.O., Gersh, T.L., Perot, A.R., Galassi, J.P., Schroeder, R., Kerick, S., Bulger, J. & Brooks, L. (1993). Graduate psychology students' perceptions of the scientist-practitioner model. *Counselling Psychology Quarterly*, 6(3), 201–215.

Barlow, D.H., Hayes, S.C. & Nelson, R.O. (1984). *The scientist-practitioner: Research and accountability in clinical and educational settings*. Needham Heights, MA: Allyn & Bacon.

Belar, C.D. & Perry, N.W. (1992). National conference on scientist-practitioner education and training for professional practice of psychology. *American Psychologist*, 47, 71–75.

Bergin, A. & Strupp, H. (1972). *Changing frontiers in the science of psychotherapy*. Chicago: Aldine.

British Psychological Society (2005). *Subject benchmarks for applied psychology*. Leicester: British Psychological Society.

Cavanagh, M.J. & Grant, A.M. (2006). Coaching psychology and the scientist-practitioner model. In D.A. Lane & S. Corrie (Eds.), *The modern scientist-practitioner: A guide to practice in psychology* (pp.146–157). Hove, East Sussex: Routledge.

Corrie, S. (2010). What is evidence? In R. Woolfe, S. Strawbridge, B. Douglas & W. Dryden (Eds), *Handbook of counselling psychology* (3rd ed., pp.44–61). London: Sage.

Corrie & Callanan, M.M. (2001). Therapists' beliefs about research and the scientist-practitioner model in an evidence-based health care climate: a qualitative study. *British Journal of Medical Psychology*, 74, 135–149.

Crane, D.R. & Hafen, M. (2002). Meeting the needs of evidence-based practice in family therapy: Developing the scientist-practitioner model. *Journal of Family Therapy*, 24, 113–124.

Head, D. & Harmon, G.A. (1990). The scientist-practitioner in practice: A short reply. *Clinical Psychology Forum*, 33, 33.

Jones, A. (1998). 'What's the bloody point?' More thoughts on fraudulent identity. *Clinical Psychology Forum*, 112, 3–9.

Kennedy, P. & Llewelyn, S. (2001). Does the future belong to the scientist-practitioner? *The Psychologist*, 14(2), 74–78.

Kwiatkowski, R. & Winter, B. (2006). Roots, relativity and realism: the occupational psychologist as scientist-practitioner. In D.A. Lane & S. Corrie (Eds.), *The modern scientist-practitioner: A guide to practice in psychology* (pp.158–172). Hove, East Sussex: Routledge.

Lane, D.A. & Corrie, S. (2006). *The modern scientist-practitioner. A guide to practice in psychology*. Hove, East Sussex: Routledge.

Miller, A. & Frederickson, N. (2006). Generalisable findings and idiographic problems: struggles and successes for educational psychologists as scientist-practitioners. In D.A. Lane & S. Corrie (Eds.), *The modern scientist-practitioner: A guide to practice in psychology* (pp.103–118). Hove, East Sussex: Routledge.

Milne, D., Britton, P. & Wilkinson, I. (1990). The scientist-practitioner in practice. *Clinical Psychology Forum*, 30, 27–30.

Nathan, P.E. (2000). The Boulder model: A dream deferred – or lost? *American Psychologist*, 55, 250–252.

Rennie, D.L. (1994). Human science and counselling psychology: Closing the gap between research and practice. *Counselling Psychology Quarterly*, 7(3), 235–251.

Salkovskis, P.M. (2002). Empirically grounded clinical interventions: Cognitive-behavioural therapy progresses through a multi-dimensional approach to clinical science. *Behavioural and Cognitive Psychotherapy*, 30, 3–9.

Shapiro, D. (2002). Renewing the scientist-practitioner model. *The Psychologist*, 15(5), 232–234.

Sheehan, P.W. (1994). Psychology as a science and as a profession. An Australian perspective. *Australian Psychologist*, 29, 174–177.

Short, E. & Blumberg, M. (2009). Coaching psychology in action. *The Coaching Psychologist*, 5(1), 43–44.

Singer, J.L. (1980). The scientific basis of psychotherapeutic practice: A question of values and ethics. *Psychotherapy. Theory, Research and Practice*, 17, 372–383.

Skovholt, T.M. & Rønnestad, M.H. (1995). *The evolving professional self. Stages and themes in therapist and counsellor development*. Chichester, West Sussex: Wiley.

Stoltenberg, C.D., Pace, T.M. & Kashubeck-West, S. (2000). Counselling psychology and the scientist-practitioner model: An identity and logical match, not an option. In C.D. Stoltenberg, T.M. Pace, S. Kashubeck-West, J.L. Biever, T. Patterson & I.D. Welch, Training models in counseling psychology: scientist-practitioner versus practitioner-scholar. *The Counselling Psychologist*, 28(5), 622–640.

Stricker, G. (1992). The relationship of research to clinical practice. *American Psychologist*, 47(4), 543–549.

Sturdee, P. (2001). Evidence, influence or evaluation? Fact and value in clinical science. In C. Mace, S. Moorey & B. Roberts (Eds.), *Evidence in the psychological therapies: A critical guide for practitioners* (pp.61–79). Hove: Brunner-Routledge.

Trierweiler, S.J. & Stricker, G. (1998). *The scientific practice of professional psychology*. New York: Plenum Press.

Williams, D.I. & Irving, J.A. (1996). Counselling psychology: A conflation of paradigms. *Counselling Psychology Review*, 11(2), 4–6.

Woolfe, R. & Dryden, W. (1996). *Handbook of counselling psychology*. London: Sage.

6 Peer coaching framework: An exploratory technique

Manfusa Shams & Ho Law

Abstract

This paper aims to highlight the technique used to develop a generic peer practice coaching framework, based on our paper, 'Coaching psychology in practice: Developing a generic framework for good practice in coaching community groups', presented in the 3rd European Coaching Psychology Conference, 2011. We hope this technique will generate interests to develop appropriate frameworks underpinned by relevant theories to enhance good peer practice in coaching.

Coaching psychology is developing fast using various appropriate theoretical models, approaches and techniques (Palmer, 2011; Passmore, 2011; Grant, 2011). However, the focus is mainly on developing coaching techniques to serve the coachees appropriately with the use of relevant psychological approaches, principles and theories. Compared to the growth in this part of coaching psychology, less attention is given to draw relevant theories to develop coaching skills and techniques for peer coaching exclusively.

This paper aims to present a generic peer coaching framework to generate interests and debate on the effectiveness of this framework in peer coaching, and to popularise the technique in coaching practices to enhance good practice in peer coaching. A general system theory is used as a methodology to organise the information and to develop the framework.

Original publication details: Shams, M., & Law, H. (2012, June). Peer coaching framework: An exploratory technique. *The Coaching Psychologist, 8*(1), 46–49. Reproduced with permission of The British Psychological Society.

Implementing new ideas in practice is a challenging task (Kitson, 2009), and context plays an important part to formalise ideas with an aim to put new ideas into practice (Dopson & Fitzgerald 2005). It is thus a dilemma for peers to accept views and ideas that are in contradiction to their existing practices and/knowledge repertoire. However, the increasing value of group coaching has been justified by Brown and Grant (2010) in their proposed practical model of GROUP, incorporating the well known GROW model in coaching practice.

The general system modelling approach was developed from systems dynamics by Forrester (1987). It views any organisations (including living organisms) as a system, which, in its basic form consists of input, output, outcome and feedback loop. Systems can be nested to form a complex system. The systems approach has been applied to human systems known as soft systems methodology (Checkland, 1999). Kurt Lewin's (1947) Open Systems Theory in combination with the psycho-dynamic approach has also been used in Executive Coaching (Vaga & Brunning, 2007). We would like to propose a generic peer coaching framework that is grounded in open system theory.

WHAT IS PEER COACHING FRAMEWORK?

A simple definition is that it is a framework to carry out an effective peer coaching session using a set of criteria. The criteria for effective peer coaching are:

- Focused approach using existing resources of the coaches.
- Engagement with the coaching practice using unconditional positive regards.
- Mutually exclusive expectations, values and commitment of the coaches.
- Ability to replace and/or existing skills and knowledge on the pathway to achieving a peer coaching framework.
- Acknowledging the need for personal development, skills enhancement and good understanding of coaching psychology prior to the actual peer coaching sessions.
- Two-directional feedback in a peer coaching session to develop insights in the issues under discussion.
- Use of reflective practice in peer coaching and developing deep insights in problem-based and/or enquiry-based coaching.
- Problematising personal coaching experiences to gain benefits from peer coaching sessions.
- Respecting confidentiality, ethical issues and professional liabilities in all peer coaching sessions.

The proposed framework is offering the following pathway to provide distinctive steps from the start to the end of a peer practice coaching session in the light of diverse skills, approaches and experiences of coaches:

PATHWAY TO EFFECTIVE PEER PRACTICE SESSION

→ Start → find a mutually agreed and best coaching technique/intervention method to apply → start discussion and evaluation through practical examples, cases from each coaches' experience → demonstrate critical thinking on the achieved outcomes from the peer practice coaching sessions → filter out the core elements discussed for further peer practice sessions → continue dialogues to arrive at an agreed and integrated coaching framework → evaluate the effectiveness of the framework in real-world peer coaching practices → modify further and integrate in formal peer coaching practice. The pathway is providing a linear direction.

The general system theory underpinning the generic coaching framework offers the following subsystems: Input=starting a discussion related to coaching, Content=peer coaching practice using a set of criteria, Output=developing an integrated peer coaching framework, and Outcome=application of the framework/ technique to achieve maximum benefits for developing human potentials through peer coaching sessions.

We have developed a framework to facilitate peer coaching (Figure 1).

In the following section, we will describe the technique of developing this framework using the functional elements of all subsystems in open system theory.

SYSTEM CRITERIA TO DEVELOP A PEER COACHING FRAMEWORK

• Input – resources: financial, materials, people/peers, their experience of coaching practice, engagement, commitment.

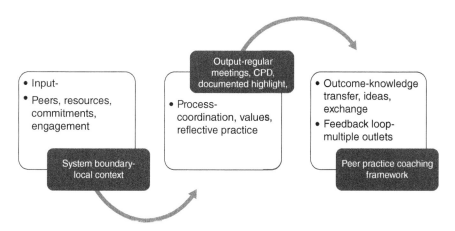

Figure 1 *A generic peer coaching framework using subsystems in Open system model.*

- Systems boundaries – local context, expectations, psychological contract, code of ethics, conduct and practices.
- Process – co-ordination, values (e.g. ethics and unconditional positive regards), reflective practice.
- Output – regular meetings, CPD certificates, reports.
- Outcome – enriched experience, knowledge transfer, new possibilities and opportunities.
- Feedback loop – within the session, outside the session, amongst peers, knowledge sharing, notes / reports dissemination.

The starting point in this framework is 'Input'. This refers to investing both tangible (place, documents) and non-tangible (skills, experiences) resources to initiate peer practice discussion. It also includes experiences of peers, skills and commitments. This part of investing resources is regulated by the local context, psychological contract, code of ethics, conduct and professional liabilities, and termed as 'Systems boundaries'. The 'Process' of peer practice is guided by effective coordination of information, organisations of available resources to inform peers, reflective practice, flexible approach to embrace changes in practice related issues, and acceptance of unconditional positive regards towards others. This is related to the 'Output' part of the framework in which essential functions of an effective group is highlighted, for example, regular meetings, appreciations of peers performance through formal CPD certificates, and regular contributions to selected issues to inform about good practice in coaching in formal settings (conferences, public events, publications). The framework ends with a description of behavioural and / professional 'Outcomes' in terms of enriched experiences, enhanced coaching skills, knowledge transfer, cross-fertilisation of ideas, new possibilities and increasing opportunities to advance peer practice, and coaching psychology in general. The framework can operate like a feedback loop for many other relevant purposes, for example, within the peer practice session, outside the session, amongst peers during knowledge sharing and through formal documentation to inform wider groups of peers and coaching psychologists. We hope this framework will help to develop peer practices in coaching psychology, and meet the challenge of accepting peer coaching practices, based on open system theory.

CONCLUSIONS

We have proposed a technique to develop a generic peer coaching framework with an expectation that our proposed framework for peer coaching will generate interests to apply to peer coaching practices. We also hope that an increasing awareness of the value of peer coaching in coaching psychology will be developed, with an aim to ground all coaching techniques in appropriate theoretical context.

REFERENCES

Brown, W.S. & Grant, M.A. (2010). From GROW to GROUP: Theoretical issues and a practical model for group coaching in organisations. *Coaching: An International Journal of Theory, Research and Practice*, 3(1), 30–45.

Checkland, P. (1999). *Soft Systems Methodology*. Net Library: John Wiley.

Dopson S. & Fitzgerald L. (2005). *Knowledge to action? Evidence-based health care in context*. Oxford: Oxford University Press.

Forrester, J.W. (1987). Lessons from System Dynamics Modelling. *System Dynamics Review*, 3(2), 136–149.

Grant, M.A. (2011). The solution-focused inventory: A tripartite taxonomy for teaching, measuring and conceptualising solution-focused approaches to coaching. *The Coaching Psychologist*, 7(2), 98–106

Kitson, L.A. (2009). The need for systems change: Reflections on knowledge translation and organisational change. *Journal of Advanced Nursing*, 65(1), 217–228.

Lewin, K. (1947) Frontiers of group dynamics. *Human Relations*, 1, 5–41.

Palmer, S. (2011). Revisiting the 'P' in the practice coaching model. *The Coaching Psychologist*, 7(2), 156–158.

Passmore, J. (2011). MI-Balance sheet technique. *The Coaching Psychologist*, 7(2), 151–153.

Shams, M., Law, H. & Stocker-Gibson, C. (2011). *Coaching psychology in practice: Developing a generic framework for good practice in coaching community groups*. Paper presented in the 3rd European Coaching Psychology Conference, London. England.

Vaga, Z. & Brunning, H. (2007). Psychodynamic and systems-psychodynamic coaching. In S. Palmer & A. Whybrow (Eds.), *Handbook of coaching psychology*. London: Routledge.

7 Reflection, note-taking and coaching: If it ain't written, it ain't coaching!

Anthony M. Grant

Abstract

This paper explores issues related to reflection-in-action, an essential tool in the development of coaching expertise, and discusses how note-taking by the coach during the coaching conversation can help develop the coach's skills in this area. Reflection-in-action is in-the-moment reflective use of experience and knowledge so as to better facilitate the coaching process. This requires a high level of self-insight – a clear understanding of one's thoughts, feelings and behavior. Levels of self-insight can be developed by mindfully engaging in exercises designed to raise in-the-moment awareness during the actual coaching process. Structured note-taking is one such approach that has been shown to be effective. The development of these skills allows coaches to be more agile in the coaching process, and helps them work in both structured and unstructured ways with their clients. Case-based examples are presented along with suggestions for the development of these skills.

Keywords

Coaching; self-reflection; note-taking; self-insight

Original publication details: Grant, A. M. (2016, December). Reflection, note-taking and coaching: If it ain't written, it ain't coaching! *The Coaching Psychologist, 12*(2), 49–58. Reproduced with permission of The British Psychological Society.

INTRODUCTION

COACHING is typically thought of as being a conversation that is aimed at fostering some type of purposeful, positive change. It is easy to dismiss such conversations as merely a chat, a fluid exchange of ideas, not dissimilar to the conversations we have everyday in the home or the workplace. On one level this is true, but it is not the whole story. There are a number of things that mark the difference between a purposeful coaching conversation and a goal-focused helpful 'chat' with a friend. Perhaps most important is the coach's *intentional* use of theory and technique in the pursuit of helping the coachee develop new perspectives and making progress towards a desired outcome. This is true regardless of the coaching being formal or informal, or having a skills, performance or developmental focus.

This article explores the complexity of the coaching conversation and highlights some useful techniques for fostering reflection-in-action during the actual coaching conversation. A clear rationale for this approach is presented (see Table 1), and the utility of note-taking during the coaching session is addressed. An effective structured approach to note-taking is then outlined. In addition, this article discusses the importance of written action plans at the end of the coaching session and relates that to the extant literature. The aim of this paper is to disseminate practical methodologies for helping both novice and experienced coaches further develop their coaching skills.

REFLECTION ON ACTION

The term 'intentional' implies purposeful, deliberate action. To be intentional requires the individual to have an awareness of why they are doing that specific action and not some other action. It is this notion that forms the foundation of reflective practice. There is a considerable literature on reflective practice in a wide range of domains starting with Schon (1982) and including reflective practice in education (Schunk & Zimmerman, 1998), nursing and social work (Bulman & Schutz, 2013), and coaching (McGonagill, 2002; Peterson, 2011).

The coaching literature has rightly emphasised the importance of reflective practice, and coaches are typically encouraged to engage in reflective practices either with a supervisor, mentor and peers or by themselves. McGonagill (2002) was one of the first to provide a thorough exposition on reflective practice in coaching, and subsequent works have also tended to emphasise the role of a supervisor in the reflective process (e.g. Hay, 2007; Passmore & McGoldrick, 2009).

Such 'reflection-on-action' involves reflecting on past coaching sessions. This kind of reflective activity goes beyond merely evaluating the coaching session in terms of coaching outcomes. Rather, one assumes an attitude of holistic curiosity, questioning one's own assumptions, values, frames of reference, theoretical understanding and personal emotional responses. This process requires one to step back and observe oneself in a dispassionate, mindful fashion with the aim of creating action steps for both personal and professional development (for details of a range of reflective methodologies see Gibbs, 1988; Johns & Burnie, 2013; Peterson, 2011).

Table 1   *Summarised rationale for this paper*

1.	Reflection-in-action is in-the-moment surfacing and use of experience and knowledge so as to better facilitate the coaching process.
2.	Reflection-in-action is an important tool in the development of coaching expertise.
3.	Refection-in-action requires the use of 'informed intuition' – an informed yet intuitive sense of what is happening in the present moment and various possible courses of action.
4.	The purposeful use of 'informed intuition' requires a high level of self-insight – a clear understanding of one's thoughts, feelings and behaviour.
5.	Self-insight is a central part of the self-regulation and goal-striving process and is strongly related to well-being.
6.	Self-insight can be developed by mindfully engaging in exercises designed to raise in-themoment awareness during the actual coaching process.
7.	Structured note-taking is one such exercise that has been shown to be effective in developing self-insight.
8.	The development of these skills allows coaches to be more agile in the coaching process, and helps them work in both highly structured and unstructured ways with their client

REFLECTION IN ACTION

Reflective practice using 'reflection-on-action' approaches is relatively common place in coaching (Jackson, 2004), and of course 'reflection-on-action' can provide important developmental insights. However, post hoc 'reflection-on-action' approaches are limited in the extent to which they can provide reflective insight during the actual coaching process itself. This kind of in-the-moment reflection is the domain of 'reflection-in-action' reflective practice. To date, the coaching literature has paid less attention to the notion of 'reflection-in-action'.

Where reflection-on-action takes place after an event, reflection-in-action takes places in the 'midst of action' (Schön, 1988). This relies on the ability of a practitioner to 'think on his or her feet' and to use such information to better engage with the task at hand. Schon (1984) describes the process as one in which the individual engages in in-the-moment surfacing, evaluating, restructuring and testing of one's intuitive understanding of the experienced phenomena.

In doing so we access the knowledge, principles and maxims of practice that we have built up over the years, compare this to our present experience and then make changes based on this new appraisal of the situation. The process is sometimes referred to as 'felt-knowing' (Walkerden, 2009). I prefer to think about this as 'informed intuition' (Ericsson, Prietula & Cokely, 2007), and for this we need a good level of personal self-insight. Self-insight can be described as 'the clarity of understanding of one's thoughts, feelings and behaviour' (Grant, Franklin & Langford, 2002, p.821) and is central to any process of purposeful, directed change (Carver & Scheier, 1998). Given that reflection-in-action and the underpinning process of 'informed intuition' are important, both from theoretical and applied perspectives, the question arises as how to enhance them.

THE COMPLEXITY OF REFLECTION-IN-ACTION IN COACHING

To answer this question we fi rst need to consider the complexity of the coaching conversation. Coaching is a highly complex cognitive, emotional and behavioural process and, at any point in the coaching conversation, there are many different cognitive, emotional or behavioural events occurring.

Let's consider an imaginary coaching session and count the number of things we as a coach need to keep track of at any point in time. These include remembering the coachee's name, being aware of the length of the session and when to finish, the various coaching methodologies and techniques we might use during the session, keeping in mind any ideas or suggestions we might want to put forward to the coachee at various points in the session and trying to ignore any extraneous thoughts such as what we might eat for supper or where our car is parked. We may also be thinking about how the coachee presents in the session, their levels of anxiety, concern, concentration and engagement, or their history.

As the session develops we may have questions or observations that we want to bring into the conversation and, being aware that this may not be the right moment to articulate those thoughts, we try to hang on to those questions or observations for use later on. In addition, we will also be paying attention to our own thoughts and feelings. We may notice that a comment from the coachee prompts an unexpected emotional reaction from us and we may think that mentioning that reaction may be useful in raising the coachee's awareness about an issue. Again, we may not want to do that straight away, so we hold on to that idea for use later. At other times we may notice that the conversation seems to becoming somewhat problem-focused and we may make a mental note to ourselves to bring the conversational focus back to the goal for the session. It is clear from this very brief (and incomplete) description of a coaching session that there is a lot going on. The coach needs to keep track of multiple streams of diverse information in order to tap into their 'informed intuition' and engage in reflection-in-action.

Of course, in everyday life such complex cognitive processes take place automatically as we engage in different tasks throughout the day. The difference between our everyday experience and reflection-in-action is that reflection-in-action is engaged in on a conscious, mindful level. Such mindful, constructive reflection is effortful. This is not an easy task. Most people need some kind of prompt or reminder in order to constantly engage in such reflection (Argyris, 2000). Indeed, for many people, the very act of trying to consciously keep track of these varied processes will undermine their ability to place their attention on the coachee. This is because the human brain and our working memory has a limited capacity for storing and manipulating information (Baddeley, 2003).

Discussing reflection-in-action in relation to leaders and managers, Schon (1984) makes the salient point that we all live or work in organisational systems which may either promote or inhibit reflection-in-action. Likewise, coaches work (and practice coaching) in systems that can either promote or inhibit reflection-in-action. The coaching conversation can be thought of as one such system. The question now arises as how we can set up a system within the coaching conversation that promotes and facilitates reflection-inaction and – in doing so – give our working memory a much needed boost.

USING NOTE-TAKING TO FACILITATE REFLECTION-IN-ACTION

One way that the coach can develop their awareness of the many different cognitive, emotional or behavioural events occurring during the coaching session, and use this information to better facilitate the coaching process, is to practice making notes during the coaching session itself. At the Coaching Psychology Unit we have developed a simple, structured method of note-taking that facilitates reflection-in-action during the coaching session. We have taught this method to literally thousands of aspiring and practicing coaches. Indeed, research has found that using this approach in coach training significantly increases the coach's levels of personal self-insight (Grant, 2008).

It is important to note that this type of note-taking is not aimed at recording the exact content of the session and is not done specifically to act as a record of what happened. Rather, this approach aims to function almost like an external 'working memory' support – the coach makes notes using short phrases, keywords, signs or symbols (see Figure 1).

On the left hand side of the paper, the coach keeps track of the main issues being discussed in the coaching session between the coach and the coachee. On the right hand side of the paper the coach keeps track of their own thoughts, feelings, observations, or potential suggestions or questions.

This approach is similar to the Cornell Note Taking System (Pauk & Owens, 2013) used by some university students, where the person taking notes divides the page into several sections by drawing a line across the paper. One section is used to make notes about the content of the lecture – general ideas, arguments, facts and other details. The student does not attempt to write everything down; rather they aim to capture the key points. Another section is used by the student to capture key words or questions that may arise in response to the taught material. For example, in a lecture on Freud a student would write down the main tenants of the lecture in one column (e.g. Freud says there are there are three levels of consciousness; conscious, preconscious and

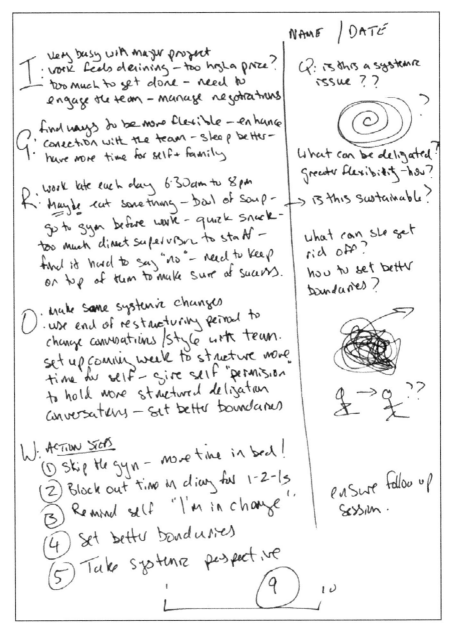

Figure 1   *Example of structured note-taking.*

unconscious) and in the other column the students records personal observations or reflections about the content (e.g., How does this relate to Skinner's approach? How could I test Freud's theory?).

USING I-GROW

In order to provide a useful structure in coaching using this kind of method, I recommend writing the acronym I-GROW down the left hand side of the paper. I-GROW is a simple way of structuring the coaching session into five sections: the presenting Issue, the Goal for the session, exploration of the Reality of the situation, various Options, and finally a Wrap-up stage where specific action steps are delineated and written down (for a detailed discussion of the I-GROW model and its derivatives see Grant, 2011). As the session progresses, the coach makes notes pertaining to each section of the I-GROW model. These do not need to be highly detailed. I often just write down key words or phrases that capture the main content, although sometimes I spend a few minutes to write the goal out in full. On the right hand side the coach makes notes about their internal state and personal reflections on the coaching process. These could include questions that the coach may want to ask the coachee, prompts to use a particular theoretical model, or notes relating to the coach's self-management. You can even use signs or symbols.

ISSUE

On the example in Figure 1, the presenting issue for the coaching session is one of feeling overworked and out of control at work, with a need to engage the team and manage negotiations. This has been noted down on the left hand side. On the right hand side the coach has made the comment 'Is this a systemic issue?' and has drawn a series of concentric circles, which have been used to visually represent a system. The coach may not want to ask a systemic question until later in the session, for example, until after the coachee has unburdened herself of her various frustrations. To ask the question too early may risk alienating the coachee, and to try to keep that question in the coach's mind reduces the coach's attentional capacity. Making a note (or scribbling a symbol) allows the coach to focus in the moment on the conversation as it develops without having to keep remembering to ask that question.

GOAL

As the session progresses the coach makes rough notes about the goals for the session. In this case the goals are about becoming more flexible, enhancing communication with the team, taking more time to connect with family and friends and getting more sleep. In the right hand column the coach has made notes about 'What can be delegated?' and 'How to be more fl exible?' – both important questions that will need to be asked as the conversation develops.

REALITY

In exploring the reality of the situation in this case, a number of issues came to light. The coachee was working long hours, including an early morning gym session several times a week. In addition, the coachee felt she was spending too much time supervising and managing staff rather than trying to coach them into being more self-directed. She also recognised that she found it hard to say 'no' to requests and this contributed to her heavy workload. Notes along these lines were made on the left hand side. The coach made a number of reflective comments on the right hand side, including the observation that this was not a sustainable approach to life, and questioning how she could set better boundaries and what work she could 'get rid of'. The squiggly doodle with an arrow coming out is a symbol that I use when I recognise that the conversation is getting too problem-focused. It represents the sense of confusion that accompanies a problem-saturated conversation and the need to reframe the conversation towards solution construction and the delineation of specific options.

OPTIONS

The next stage is the exploration of options. (Of course, there is a high degree of back and forth iteration in a real coaching conversation. However, for illustrative purposes I am discussing the use of note-taking in coaching as if it were a relatively linear process). In this example, the coachee has identified a number of possible courses of action including making systemic changes, using the end of a restructuring period to change the kinds of conversations being held with the team and setting better boundaries. In the right hand column the coach has draw two stick figures and a question mark. I use this kind of symbol as a prompt for myself to suggest to the coachee to consider holding a specific conversation, if the coachee herself did not come up with that idea.

The skill for the coach here is to be able to make notes about possible courses of action without forcing them on the coachee. We need to let the coachee determine the main thrust of the conversation, whilst offering useful directions for exploration based on our experience and our preferred theoretical approach. It is in the adroit execution of this process that the coach earns their fee.

WRAP-UP

In the last few minutes the session moves into the wrap-up stage. This is the point where specific action steps are delineated. In terms of goal theory, these are specific actionable goals and are equivalent to Gollwitzer's (1999) notion of implementation intentions: specific plans detailing what, where and how actions will be executed.

There is a considerable body of research indicating that the formal setting of implementation intentions leads to better recall of the goal as well as greater goal attainment (cf. Bélanger-Gravel, Godin & Amireault, 2013).

In this example, the action steps are written quite briefly in terms of 'Block out time in diary for 1-2-1s'. However, the simplicity and brevity of these notes belies the amount of time and thought that has gone into their formation. The principle at play here is simplicity: the action steps should be the simplest that will achieve the desired result. The power of the specific action steps springs from the meaning given to them during the coaching conversation. This is then captured and crystallised through the act of the coachee themselves writing the action steps down. The coach sometimes needs to be quite directive at this point in the session. 'Confidence scaling' is a useful technique to use in the final stage in action step planning. The coach simply asks the coachee to rate, on a scale of one to ten, how confident they are that they can do the action steps. Note that we are not asking how confident they are of a successful outcome because that cannot be predicted. Rather we are gauging their self-efficacy at performing the action steps. This is an important point as self-efficacy is a strong predictor of behavioural change and goal attainment (Bandura, 1982). I tend to look for a rating at eight or above. If it is below eight, I suggest simply asking the coachee 'What would it take to move to an eight or nine?' (or one or two points up the scale if lower). In this case the coachee has rated herself at a nine.

IF IT AIN'T WRITTEN, IT AIN'T COACHING!

In many ways, the whole coaching session has been leading up to the delineation of action steps that will help the coachee attain their goal. As coaches we need to pay particular attention to this process if we are to consistently deliver value to our clients. We need to ensure that the coachee is actively engaged in the action planning process. The research strongly suggests that actually writing down actions steps enhances goal attainment (Achtziger, Bayer & Gollwitzer, 2012; Gollwitzer & Brandstätter, 1997). Note, in order to maximise the effectiveness of this coaching strategy, it should be the coachee themselves that writes their action steps down – in a very real sense – *if it ain't written it ain't coaching!* This is not to say that the coach should not keep a note of the action steps. Indeed the coach must do this in order to follow-up in the next session, but the emphasis here is on using note-taking as a means of helping the coachee reach their goals.

A useful structured approach to the writing of action steps is for the coach to ask the coachee what specific actions come to mind, then say to the coachee 'Let's write those down', then ask the coachee to tell you (as the coach) what they've written down, then you (as the coach) write down what they tell you (sometimes giving corrective feedback), and then finally you (as the coach) read out what you've written down to get final agreement from the coachee. Although this may seem somewhat convoluted or even contrived, this is an excellent disciplined practice that can really help the coachee in the goal striving process.

MANAGING THE WRITTEN ACTION-PLANNING PROCESS

Writing notes whilst engaging in a coaching conversation can be challenging both for the coach and the coachee. In my experience, in relation to the coachee, it is very important to explicitly set clear expectations in advance about note-taking. This is particularly important in contexts where note-taking during workplace conversations is not a usual course of events, or where note-taking is typically associated with disciplinary or coercive actions. For example, in some workplaces, if an Human Resources practitioner starts taking notes an employee may react with concern and be less than forthcoming because note-taking may be seen as a preliminary to some kind of disciplinary action. Similarly, in some professions (law, for example), note-taking may be associated with record keeping or legal action. In a heavily unionised workplace where there is deep distrust between employees and management, note-taking may provoke a cautious or defensive response from the coachee, which may result in objections to the note-taking or demands to know how the notes will be used.

All of these difficulties can be quite easily overcome by simply asking the coachee for 'permission' to take notes. Permission asking in this context is as simple as saying; 'Is it OK if I take a few notes while we talk? It helps me concentrate.' Placing a notepad for the coachee on the table and taking the time to set up the coaching environment in advance, by (for example) having notepads and pens on the table before the session, also helps create an atmosphere where note-taking is seen as the norm. Using this approach, I have found that coaches rarely, if ever, encounter resistance to note-taking. If there are objections to note-taking from the coachee after seeking permission, this would signal to me that this is not really a coaching session – rather it is some other kind of conversation.

THE COACH'S RELUCTANCE TO TRY NOTE-TAKING

In my experience there is sometimes more resistance to note-taking from the coach than from the coachee. Some coaches feel that they cannot experiment with such ways of working with coachees, because they (the coach) feel as if the note-taking process makes the coaching 'clunky' or less fluid. Another common fear articulated by coaches is that note-taking may interrupt the rapport process or be seen as disrespectful by the coachee.

These fears are unfounded in my view. The development of any new skill requires conscious practice, which inevitably feels somewhat uncomfortable to start with (Daley, 1999). Many coaches seem to erroneously assume that this will have a negative impact on the coachee. But this is not the case. In the many training sessions I have run over the years, coaches sometimes report that, when taking notes, the coaching conversation felt 'clunky' to them. However, when one asks the coachee about their personal experience, they typically report a perfectly 'smooth' experience. Sometimes we judge ourselves far more harshly than others do!

Similarly, note-taking does not necessarily interrupt the rapport process or be seen as being disrespectful. Indeed, the opposite is often true. The pauses in conversation that sometimes accompany note-taking can be used to add gravitas to the moment; for example, by the coach saying something like 'That sounds like an important point' and then noting it down. Note-taking can also be used to deliberately slow down or speed up a session: having a range of such techniques can only add to the coach's toolkit and extend their repertoire.

USEFUL BY-PRODUCTS OF NOTE-TAKING: COACHING AGILITY AND SELF-INSIGHT

There are a number of benefits that emerge as coaches master the art of note-taking. Firstly, coaches become far more agile in their mindful use of both theory and technique in coaching. I think of this meta-skill as 'coaching agility' – the ability to switch from one approach to another seamlessly and in an efficient and effective manner as the dynamics of the coaching conversation evolve and change, whilst remaining centred and focused. Just as physical agility requires balance, speed and the coordination of various aspects of physical movement, coaching agility requires the coach to have good emotional and cognitive balance, intellectual speed, and the coordination and integration of various theoretical and interpersonal aspects.

Secondly, as coaches engage in this kind of note-taking during the coaching conversation, over time they can develop a greater sense of self-insight (Grant, 2008). Engaging in this kind of structured in-the-moment reflection requires the coach to develop a highly attuned sense of their internal state and personal self narrative. These can be very important self-development aspects, both in relation to the enhancement of one's coaching skills and also in relation to oneself personally. This is because self-insight is a central part of the self-regulation and goal-striving process (Carver & Scheier, 1998) and is strongly related to personal wellbeing (Lyke, 2008).

SUMMARY

It is clear that reflection-in-action is an important tool in the development of coaching expertise. Purposeful reflection-inaction requires a high level of self-insight – a clear understanding of one's thoughts, feelings and behaviour. Engaging in this kind of activity is not easy. We can enhance our ability to engage in reflection-in-action by using note-taking techniques as outlined above. This kind of structured note-taking can be effective in developing coaching agility and self-insight. Self-insight is a central part of the self-regulation and goal-striving process and is strongly related to well-being. In this way, coaches can not only enhance their professional skills but also engage in their own personal development. Given the potential benefits from this kind of structured note-taking, maybe it is true: *If it ain't written – it ain't coaching!*

REFERENCES

Achtziger, A., Bayer, U.C. & Gollwitzer, P.M. (2012). Committing to implementation intentions: Attention and memory effects for selected situational cues. *Motivation and Emotion, 36*(3), 287–300.

Argyris, C. (2000). *Teaching smart people how to learn*. Harvard Business Review, May–June (99–109).

Baddeley, A. (2003). Working memory: Looking back and looking forward. *Nature Reviews Neuroscience, 4*(10), 829–839.

Bandura, A. (1982). Self-efficacy mechanism in human agency. *American Psychologist, 37*(2), 122–147.

Bélanger-Gravel, A., Godin, G. & Amireault, S. (2013). A meta-analytic review of the effect of implementation intentions on physical activity. *Health Psychology Review, 7*(1), 23–54.

Bulman, C. & Schutz, S. (2013). *Reflective practice in nursing*. London: John Wiley & Sons.

Carver, C.S. & Scheier, M.F. (1998). *On the self-regulation of behavior*. Cambridge, UK: Cambridge University Press.

Daley, B.J. (1999). Novice to expert: An exploration of how professionals learn. *Adult Education Quarterly, 49*(4), 133–147.

Ericsson, K.A., Prietula, M.J. & Cokely, E.T. (2007). The making of an expert. *Harvard Business Review, 85*(7/8), 114.

Gibbs, G. (1988). *Learning by doing: A guide to teaching and learning methods*. London: Further Education Unit

Gollwitzer, P.M. (1999). Implementation intentions: Strong effects of simple plans. *American Psychologist, 54*(7), 493–503.

Gollwitzer, P.M. & Brandstätter, V. (1997). Implementation intentions and effective goal pursuit. *Journal of Personality and Social Psychology, 73*(1), 186.

Grant, A.M. (2008). Personal life coaching for coaches-in-training enhances goal attainment, insight and learning. *Coaching: An International Journal of Theory, Research and Practice, 1*(1), 54–70.

Grant, A.M. (2011). Is it time to regrow the grow model? Issues related to teaching coaching session structures. *The Coaching Psychologist, 7*(2), s.

Grant, A.M., Franklin, J. & Langford, P. (2002). The self-reflection and insight scale: A new measure of private self-consciousness. *Social Behavior and Personality*, 30(8), 821–836.

Hay, J. (2007). *Reflective practice and supervision for coaches*. Maidenhead: Open University Press.

Jackson, P. (2004). Understanding the experience of experience: A practical model of reflective practice for coaching. *International Journal of Evidence Based Coaching and Mentoring, Vol. 2, No. 1*.

Johns, C. & Burnie, S. (2013). *Becoming a reflective practitioner* (4th ed.). Chichester, UK: Wiley-Blackwell.

Lyke, J.A. (2008). Insight, but not self-reflection, is related to subjective well-being. *Personality and Individual Differences*, 46(1), 66–70

McGonagill, G. (2002). The coach as reflective practitioner. In C. Fitzgerald & J.G. Berger (Eds.), *Executive Coaching: Practices and Perspectives* (pp.59–88). Palo Alto, CA: Davies-Black.

Passmore, J. & McGoldrick, S. (2009). Super-vision, extra-vision or blind faith? A grounded theory study of the efficacy of coaching supervision. *International Coaching Psychology Review*, 4(2), 145–161.

Pauk, W. & Owens, R.J. (2013). *How to study in college*. Cengage Learning.

Peterson, D.B. (2011). Good to great coaching. In G. Hernez-Broome & L.A. Boyce (Eds.), *Advancing executive coaching: Setting the course of successful leadership coaching* (pp.83–102). San Francisco CA: Jossey-Bass.

Schon, D. (1982). *The Reflective Practitioner*. New York: Basic Books.

Schon, D.A. (1984). Leadership as reflection-inaction. In T.J. Sergiova & J.E. Corbally (Eds.), *Leadership and organizational culture: new perspectives on administrative theory and practice* (pp. 36–63). Illinois: Urbana: University of Press.

Schön, D.A. (1988). *From technical rationality to reflection-in-action*. Cambridge University Press.

Schunk, D.H. & Zimmerman, B.J. (Eds.) (1998). *Self-regulated learning: From teaching to self-reflective practice*. New York, NY: Guilford Press.

Walkerden, G. (2009). Researching and developing practice traditions using reflective practice experiments. *Quality & Quantity*, 43(2), 249–263.

8 Building reflective capability to enhance coaching practice

Louise Kovacs & Sarah Corrie

Abstract

The ability to reflect on our work is increasingly recognised as a vital competence of skilled professional practice. However, reflection is a concept that has proved difficult to define and operationalise which can hamper the ability to devise effective means of enhancing this capability. This article examines the concept of reflection, reviews some of the literature which seeks to inform our understanding of reflective practice, and provides an illustration of its use in coaching research and practice. The article concludes with some recommendations for coaches and coaching psychologists who wish to develop their skills as reflective practitioners.

Keywords

Reflection; reflective practice; reflection-in-action; reflection-on-action; coaching; formulation.

INTRODUCTION

Technical knowledge, while vital to learning and development, is insufficient for preparing individuals for the realities of professional practice. An additional, more experientially-based, form of knowledge is required if professional practice is to prove responsive to individual client need, deliver procedural expertise, and demonstrate more than the mechanical application of tools and techniques. At the heart of this experientially-based form of learning and development lie skills in reflection.

Original publication details: Kovacs, L., & Corrie, S. (2017, June). Building reflective capability to enhance coaching practice. *The Coaching Psychologist, 13*(1), 4–12. Reproduced with permission of The British Psychological Society.

The capacity to reflect on one's work is widely seen as a fundamental component of effective professional practice (see for example, the British Psychological Society's *Standards Framework for Coaching Psychology*, 2008). Nonetheless as a concept, reflection has proved elusive to define and operationalise. A further issue is that the term has been interpreted in diverse ways, as reflection is both a skill and an orientation to one's work (Harper, 2009). This poses challenges for coaching practitioners who wish to find a systematic and effective way of building greater reflective capability into their work. The aims of this article are, therefore, threefold:

1. To enable readers to better understand the nature of reflective practice, and how it can enhance their professional offering to coaching clients;
2. To enable readers to consider how they might use reflection to review and evaluate their practice;
3. To offer some specific methods for enhancing reflective capability that can be applied to current and future learning.

TOWARDS AN UNDERSTANDING OF REFLECTIVE PRACTICE: ORIGINS, THEORIES AND RELEVANCE TO TODAY'S COMPLEX WORLD

Since the publication of his seminal text in 1983, Donald Schön's work on the reflective practitioner (see also Schön, 1987) has gained widespread endorsement and provided the inspiration for broadening understanding of how professional practitioners acquire their knowledge and skill. In consequence, developing skills in reflective practice is now an aim of many disciplines within higher education and Schön's work has been incorporated into a variety of professional training programmes including nursing (Hargreaves, 1997), adult education (Ferry & Ross-Gordon, 1998), counselling and psychotherapy (Stedmon & Dallos, 2009), and sports coaching (Gilbert & Trudel, 2001).

Reflective practice refers to, '…a deliberate pause to assume an open perspective, to allow for higher-level thinking processes' (York-Barr et al., 2001; p.6). The purpose of this pause is to enable practitioners to examine their beliefs, assumptions, goals and methods in order to gain insights that might facilitate improved learning (York-Barr et al., 2001). Drawing on the earlier work of Argyris and Schön (1978), Osterman and Kottkamp (2004) have identified a further function of reflection – namely, helping practitioners become sensitive to, and take steps to resolve, any discrepancies between their espoused theories (that is, their stated beliefs and values about learning, development and practice) and their theories-in-use (what they actually 'do' and the results of their actions).

Perhaps because of these perceived functions, reflection has been particularly emphasised in disciplines that require an integration of academic study and practical application. It is also recognised as a quintessential component of the lifelong learning that an increasingly uncertain and unpredictable employment market necessitates (Lane & Corrie, 2006). Unsurprisingly then, the capacity for reflection has been identified as a critical skill in both coaching and coaching psychology (e.g. Grant, 2016; Hay, 2007; McGonagill, 2002). However, reflective practice can mean different things in different contexts. Wellington and Austin (1996) have identified five distinct orientations which are predicated upon divergent beliefs and values and which influence the extent to which reflective practice is used as well as its outcomes:

1. The immediate: an orientation focused exclusively on achieving the task at hand. Practitioners with this orientation rarely use reflective practice;
2. The technical: reflection is seen as a tool for directing practice often within predetermined standards or guidelines;
3. The deliberative: emphasising the discovery of personal meaning, and the attitudes and values of learners;
4. The dialectic: an orientation which rejects authorised discourses around knowledge and its parameters in favour of political and social awareness and activism;
5. The transpersonal: an orientation which seeks to develop the inner self and the relationship between the internal and external world for the purposes of personal liberation.

These orientations are offered not as competing perspectives but rather as different ways in which reflective practice can be approached, with an invitation to practitioners to recognise their own favoured orientations as well as appreciate those of others.

Regardless of the orientation adopted, there is some consensus that reflective practice refers to how insights and understandings can be gained from learning through experience (Boud et al., 1985; Mezirow, 1981). This in turn relies upon the practitioner being both self-aware and able to critically evaluate their decisions and reactions in practice-based contexts. This process of learning from experience can be better understood through considering Schön's (1983) original distinction between *reflection-in-action*, and *reflection-on-action*. Reflection-in-action refers to an internalised, often intuitive form of knowledge that is acquired over time. It is equated with the notion of 'thinking on our feet' and for Schön, is often triggered in the context of being surprised (e.g. where a client responds to an intervention in a way that the coach did not predict). A consistent feature of effective practice, this enables the practitioner to go beyond the rote application of models or techniques in order to practise with greater artistry and to devise novel, bespoke solutions for the needs of individual clients.

Nonetheless, if the learning acquired through reflection-in-action is to be made available for future practice, it must be subjected to a more deliberate and conscious process of review and consolidation. This is the essence of 'reflection-on-action'. As

Grant (2016) suggests, this type of reflective activity transcends an examination of outcomes and assumes, '…an attitude of holistic curiosity, questioning one's own assumptions, values, frames of reference, theoretical understanding and personal emotional responses' (p.50). This process of reviewing practice after it has occurred is understood by many scholars as primarily an analytical process (see Merriam et al., 2007) that facilitates new perspectives which can inform behavioural change. The ongoing commitment to consciously revisiting our experiences, examining them, choosing what to do differently and then acting accordingly allows for a process of continuous learning and growth. This cyclical process has been captured most famously by Kolb (1984) as well as those who have adapted it (e.g. Gibbs, 1988; and Boud et al., 1985, who have emphasised the need to include our affective responses within the reflective process). These experiential learning models are one approach through which reflective capability can be taught and developed (see for example, Gibbs' Reflective Cycle (1988) which has been applied in healthcare education and offers an approach to structuring reflective learning).

In their work on developing an understanding of reflection in the context of cognitive behaviour therapy (CBT), Haarhoff and Thwaites (2016) have identified and differentiated four uses of the term:

1. Reflective *practice*: that is, the act of reflecting on practice-based experience including the personal reactions of the practitioner. This may occur in the context of supervision, self-supervision and through use of reflective diaries;
2. Reflective *skill*: that is, the ability to reconstruct events in one's mind, including exploration of one's own reactions and behaviours;
3. Reflection as a *process*: comprising the three elements of focused attention on a specific issue, reconstructing the event, and conceptualising and synthesising the dilemma through self-analysis and problem-solving;
4. The reflective *system*: that is, the 'engine' which lies at the heart of the practitioner's knowledge and skill and which enables the therapist to adapt their expertise to the needs of the individual client.

The reflective system features centrally in the Declarative Procedural Reflective model originally devised by Bennett-Levy (2006) to better understand and support the development of a wide range of skills in CBT therapists. In brief, he distinguishes *declarative knowledge* (that which is obtained through traditional methods of learning such as reading and attending lectures); *procedural knowledge* (the ability to draw upon an increasingly sophisticated network of tacit 'rules' that guide a practitioner's moment-to-moment decision-making) and the *reflective system* (which contains no discipline-specific knowledge of its own but which drives the process of learning through integrating understanding derived from the other systems). Haarhoff and Thwaites (2016) emphasise that the relationship between the reflective system and the declarative and procedural systems is a two-way process and highlight how the process of reflection may differ as a function of experience. For example, novice practitioners will have relatively limited declarative and procedural knowledge and so the reflective system will be primarily needed to support the development of discipline-specific knowledge and skill. In contrast, for more experienced practitioners, prior knowledge and skills will both shape, and be shaped by, the reflective system in the refinement of expertise (Bennett-Levy, 2006).

Being able to reflect in, and on, action is necessary because, beyond the safety of the structured learning environment, practitioners are inevitably confronted with varying degrees of complexity, uncertainty and ambiguity which they must be able to navigate. This more 'messy' reality is a defining feature of professional practice in which the problems encountered typically defy the clear, neat application of theory and evidence. As Schön observed:

> In the varied topography of professional practice there is a high ground where practitioners can make effective use of research-based theory and technique, and there is a swampy lowland where situations are confusing 'messes' incapable of technical solution. The difficulty is that the problems of the high ground, however great their technical interest, are often relatively unimportant to clients or to the larger society, while in the swamp are the problems of greatest interest (1983, p.42).

If reflective practice supports the ability to navigate the messiness that characterises problems in the 'real world', then there has never been a time when reflection is more essential for coaching practitioners to include amongst their armoury of skills. Arguably, professional practice today requires a greater ability to manage complexity than ever before. Coaches and their clients are living and working in a volatile, uncertain, complex and ambiguous world (Barber, 1992). Many coaching assignments now take place in contexts where single models have limited benefit and linear ways of thinking about cause and effect do not apply. In such contexts, coaching practitioners are having to develop new ways of conceptualising the issues with which their clients present, and acquire new means of defining, delivering and enabling the process of change. Consequently, developing approaches for working with complexity has been an increasing focus of the coaching literature (see Cavanagh & Lane, 2012; Kovacs, 2016).

BEING REFLECTIVE ABOUT THE REFLECTIVE PRACTICE: THE LIMITS OF THE EVIDENCE-BASE

Despite wide endorsement, the notion of reflective practice is not without its critics (see Usher et al., 1987), or its challenges.

Although widely endorsed as an essential component of effective professional practice, there is little rigorous research that has directly linked the benefits of reflective practice to improved outcomes for clients. There is some evidence which supports the benefits to professionals such as gaining insights into practice, growing self-awareness and changing perspectives on issues (Morrison 1996), but as Loughran (2000; cited in Finlay, 2008) has observed, the appeal of reflection may lie in its intuitive 'fit' with our collective assumptions about what underpins skilled professional practice, rather than what has been empirically substantiated.

An alternative explanation for the apparent lack of evidence for reflective practice, and as noted at the beginning of this article, is that the phenomenon itself does, to an extent, defy definition. It does not, therefore, lend itself well to operationalisation and measurement. Reflection is perhaps best understood as a 'meta-competence' and as such, its impact on practice may occur through a series of indirect meta-effects rather than through any simple causal chain that can be readily identified and replicated. Where this is overlooked, unintended consequences may arise. For example, Finlay (2008) has highlighted how reflective practice has sometimes been adopted in an attempt to rationalise existing practice – an example of reflective practice being used in a distinctly unreflective way. Equally, experiential learning models, whilst having benefits for the teaching and development of reflective practice may, if applied too rigidly, result in a mechanistic application that leaves little scope for practitioners to develop their own context-dependent approaches (Quinn, 2000).

There are also challenges at the level of engagement. For some, reflective practice can be difficult and unsettling. In teacher training, for example, many student teachers found the process painful as they gained awareness of their lack of expertise and of the complexity of the issues they were exploring (Morrison, 1996). In the field of nursing, practitioners may feel they have 'lost their way' as their existing assumptions and knowledge are challenged (Brookfield, 1993). These examples highlight that reflective practice needs to be dovetailed to the needs, experience and readiness of the individual. For coaching practitioners who are at an early stage of their career and professional development journey, it may be most appropriate to develop their reflective capacity in the supportive environment of learning groups or supervision rather than through individual reflection activities.

A further challenge to embedding reflection in practice is both a physiological and psychological one. Reflection entails an active and conscious processing of thoughts and reactions, which requires self-control, energy and the right conditions (Arnsten, 2009). Some of the difficulty in creating space to think in today's world of information-overload is driven by our neurochemistry. A highly task-focused orientation, switching between tasks and multi-tasking, produce dopamine which can engender a feeling of personal productivity whilst actually depleting effectiveness (Crabbe, 2014). For example, multi-tasking has been noted to increase by 40 per cent the amount of time needed to complete tasks (Meyer & Kieras, 1997). In contrast, although the time spent in reflective activities may well lead to more significant outcomes it is less likely to be accompanied by a release of dopamine and may, therefore, feel less satisfying.

How, then, should we as coaching practitioners respond to the call to be reflective, whilst at the same time acknowledging the limitations of the current evidence-base? In the next section, we present a case study which provides an illustration of how reflective practice was used as a 'backbone' to a substantial piece of coaching research. This provides a basis for the final section in which we offer some specific recommendations for coaching practitioners who seek to develop their own reflective capability.

BUILDING REFLECTIVE CAPABILITY: A CASE STUDY

For one of us (LK), the development of reflective capability became an essential component of her doctoral research as well as her coaching practice. The research project involved developing, implementing and evaluating a framework that applied case formulation to executive coaching. Reflective capability was required for the researcher (who also delivered the coaching to all the research participants) to investigate and evaluate the complexities entailed in the application of the framework to coaching practice. A secondary aim of the research was to understand the coach's developmental experience, identify the mechanisms for any development and use these data to make recommendations to other coaching psychologists for their professional development.

Several methods of reflection were employed during the study, which were based on Kolb's (1984) experiential learning framework and used reflective questions adapted from Fook and Gardener (2006; see Table 1). The researcher's reflections on coaching sessions were used as a distinct method of data collection and entailed recording each session, reviewing the recordings, and writing reflections on the session. A written learning journal was also maintained throughout the project. This was used for capturing and synthesising information, ideas and knowledge, and reflecting on their application to coaching practice. Reflections in the journal also identified themes and patterns emerging from both the session reflections and the learning journal itself. In addition, formulation is an inherently reflective practice. Developing formulations for each of the coaching clients both required and assisted in developing reflective capability, synthesising information, developing hypotheses, making links between data, and reflecting on the progress of the coaching.

One pattern that emerged from the data analysis of the learning journal was a change in the nature of the reflections over the period of the research. Early in the research many of the entries took the form of reflections on practice, such as reviewing the coaching techniques used, what went well and what might be more effective. As the research progressed, the reflections became increasingly focused on the researcher's professional and personal selves. For example, after one session the researcher reflected on the anger she felt on behalf of her client. The journal entry for this incident considered what had triggered this response in the researcher, and these reflections helped her identify how a perceived transgression of values, a challenge to assumptions and beliefs about how people in the workplace should behave, and a difference in cultural norms led to her reaction.

In reviewing the data from this case study, reflective practices were identified as one of the primary mechanisms of coach development. The discipline of maintaining a commitment to reflective practices for the duration of the doctorate led to several key outcomes. First, the regular practice of reflection-on-action increased the researcher's ability to reflect-in-action. The learning journal entries captured the increasing awareness of emotions and reactions and how these were managed or used in sessions. Second, the development and ongoing use of the PAIR (purpose-account-intervenereflect) framework (Kovacs, 2016) enabled reflective practice through applying formulation and a process of post-session reflection. Experiencing the benefits to personal and professional development of a sustained commitment to reflection created a habit that is now embedded in the researcher's professional practice.

HOW TO PROMOTE REFLECTIVE PRACTICE: SOME RECOMMENDATIONS

As noted previously, understanding of 'reflective practice' can vary considerably as a function of both intellectual orientation and discipline-specific considerations (Finlay, 2008). Arguably, the field of coaching is yet to determine its own definition of this complex phenomenon or to determine its position on how reflection might enable best practice for our clients. In the absence of clear guidance, we offer some recommendations emerging from practice-based evidence that might represent an aid to decision-making for the individual practitioner. As illustrated by the case study, bringing reflective practice into the heart of coaching requires sustained effort. Therefore, before embarking on this endeavour it is important to be clear about what you want reflection to contribute to your work. Is your primary concern developing greater understanding of your work with a specific client, or are you seeking to embed a learning process that will support your work over time? Are you seeking a cross-sectional perspective that will increase your insight into what happened in a specific session, or wanting to develop a reflective 'habit' that will help sustain you through a period of study? Are you primarily concerned with self-reflection, general reflective skills, reflection-on-action or reflection-in-action? These outcomes cannot all be achieved at the same time although, as with the case study above, a focus on one area may build reflective capacity more broadly.

With clarity of purpose established, consideration can be given to identifying the most appropriate tools, approaches and forms of support to achieve this purpose and that are best suited to your preferences. Reflection does not have to be a written or introspective process but can take the form of reflection with others, such as in supervision or peer practice groups. Reflections can be captured using audio or video recordings, drawing mind-maps or through creating illustrations.

Regardless of the method used, one of the core elements of reflective practice is the use of incisive questions, which may be used in conjunction with a model of reflection such as Gibbs (1988) or Kolb (1984). Table 1 provides some examples of questions (adapted from Fook & Gardner, 2006) that may be useful starting points in different situations and which we offer to the reader in the hope that they might facilitate a personalised approach.

Table 1   *Questions to support the development of reflective practice.*

- Reflection-on-practice:
  - What worked well? What does working well mean in this context?
  - What was not as effective? What does not effective mean in this context?
  - What do my responses to the questions above reveal about the hypotheses I hold about the client and their situation?
  - What would I do differently next time?
- In building capability for reflection-in-action, it can be helpful to listen to recordings of sessions. This provides an opportunity to re-live the session and consider:
  - What did I miss, or was not considering, in the moment?
  - What was going through my mind and what did that lead to?
  - What was my line of enquiry?
  - What hypotheses was I holding in mind and how did I go about testing these?
  - What could I have done differently and in what way might that have changed the conversation?
- In building capability for reflection-on-action, some questions to hold in mind include:
  - What is the pattern here? What might this pattern mean?
  - How does this interaction make me feel and what might that mean?
  - How are my emotions, beliefs or assumptions influencing my ability to work with the client at this point?
  - What hypotheses am I forming and how can I test these?
- For developing the ability for greater self-reflection:
  - What does this situation or case tell me about my values and assumptions?
  - What different assumptions or beliefs would help me act differently next time? What would be the potential impact on the client?
  - Am I applying the theories in which I am trained or just going with the flow and my gut feel? What are the implications of this?
  - How did my beliefs and assumptions interact with the social context in this situation? What impact did this have on the coaching and the client?

While incisive questions are a useful tool, additional approaches can be applied that can help embed and sustain reflective practice. These include:

- Introducing a discipline of reflecting on each session. Both successes and disappointments in coaching interactions and outcomes can be useful sources of reflective material revealing patterns that lead to insights for clients, and the coach's professional and personal development (Kovacs 2016).
- Recording sessions over a period of time, or intermittently with different clients. These recordings can be used for personal review alone, or shared in supervision (Carson 2008).
- Keeping a reflective diary (written, spoken or video) that you review periodically to identify and capture themes across your work (Thorpe 2004, Hay, 2007).

- Use of peer supervision or a critical friend (Gilbert & Trudel 2001, and see McNicoll & Baker, 2012, for examples of tools that can be used for supervision and mentoring groups).
- Note-taking in sessions (see Grant, 2016). This can support reflection-in-action given that not only is key information noted but the coach's thoughts and reflections on the client and the session content are also captured.
- Developing formulations, which assist in synthesising data, developing hypotheses, seeing links, and bringing new perspectives to a client's situation (Kovacs, 2016).

It may take some experimentation and practice before you strike the right approach for your purpose and preferences. Moreover, as illustrated by the case study above, it is useful to periodically review and evaluate your reflective practices, which aids in embedding reflection in your work at multiple levels, including on the effectiveness of your current reflective practices.

CONCLUSION

It is beyond the scope of this article to critically review the literature on reflective practice in its entirety. Nonetheless, by identifying some of the main contributions to this literature, the aim has been to sharpen understanding of reflective practice and to consider how its more conscious application might support our work as coaching practitioners. Ultimately, reflection is only one of myriad reasoning skills needed for professional practice. However, as Ghaye (2000) observes, 'Maybe reflective practices offer us a way of trying to make sense of the uncertainty in our workplaces and the courage to work competently and ethically at the edge of order and chaos...' (p.7). Reflective practice, it would seem, has much to teach us, if we are willing to invest the time and energy in reaping the benefits it has to offer.

REFERENCES

Argyris, C. & Schön, D.A. (1978). *Organisational learning: A theory of action perspective*. San Francisco, CA: Jossey-Bass.

Arnsten, A.F.T. (2009). The emerging neurobiology of attention deficit hyperactivity disorder: The key role of prefrontal association cortex. *Journal of Pediatrics*, 154, 1–43.

Barber, H.F. (1992). Developing strategic leadership: The US army war college experience. *Journal of Management Development*, 11, 4–12.

Bennett-Levy, J. (2006). Therapist skills: A cognitive model of their acquisition and refinement. *Behavioural and Cognitive Psychotherapy*, 34, 57–78.

British Psychological Society, Special Group in Coaching Psychology (2008). *Standards Framework for Coaching Psychology, 2008*. Leicester: BPS.

Brookfield, S.D. (1993). On impostership, cultural suicide, and other dangers: How nurses learn critical thinking. *Journal of Continuing Education in Nursing*, 24, 197–205.

Boud, D., Keogh, R. & Walker, D. (1985). *Reflection: Turning experience into learning*. New York: Kogan Page.

Carson, F. (2008). Utilizing video to facilitate reflective practice: Developing sports coaches. *International Journal of Sports Science and Coaching*, 3, 381–390.

Cavanagh, M.J. & Lane, D. (2012). Coaching psychology coming of age: The challenges we face in the messy world of complexity? *International Coaching Psychology Review*, 7, 75–90.

Crabbe, T. (2014). *Busy: How to thrive in a world of too much*. London: Piatkus.

Ferry, N. & Ross-Gordon, J. (1998). An inquiry into Schön's epistemology of practice: Exploring links between experience and reflective practice. *Adult Education Quarterly*, 48(2), 98–112.

Finlay, L. (2008). Reflecting on reflective practice. A discussion paper prepared for PBPL CETL (www.open.ac.uk/pbpl. Available at: http://www.open.ac.uk/opencetl/sites/www.open.ac.uk.opencetl/files/files/ecms/web-content/Finlay(2008)-Reflecting-on-reflective-practice-PBPLpaper-52.pdf. Accessed on 11 March 2017.

Fook, J. & Gardner, F. (2006). *Practising critical reflection: A resource handbook*. Maidenhead, Berkshire: Open University Press.

Ghaye, T. (2000) Into the reflective mode: bridging the stagnant moat. *Reflective Practice*, 1(1) 5–9.

Gibbs, G. (1988) *Learning by doing: A guide to teaching and learning methods*. Oxford: Further Education Unit, Oxford Polytechnic.

Gilbert, W. & Trudel, P. (2001). Learning to coach through experience: Reflection in model youth sport coaches. *Journal of Teaching in Physical Education*, 21, 16–24.

Grant, A.M. (2016). Reflection, note-taking and coaching: If it ain't written, it ain't coaching! *The Coaching Psychologist*, 12(2), 49–57.

Haarhoff, B. & Thwaites, R. (2016). *Reflection in CBT*. London: Sage.

Hargreaves, J. (1997). Using patients: Exploring the ethical dimension of reflective practice in nurse education. *Journal of Advanced Nursing*, 25, 223–229.

Harper, D. (2009). Preface: Learning from our work. In J. Stedmon & R. Dallos (Eds.) *Reflective practice in psychotherapy and counselling*. Maidenhead, Berkshire: Open University Press.

Hay, J. (2007). *Reflective practice and supervision for coaches*. Maidenhead, Berkshire: McGraw-Hill.

Kolb, D.A. (1984). *Experiential learning: Experience as the source of learning and development*. Englwood Cliffs, NJ: Prentice Hall.

Kovacs, L.C. (2016). *Enabling leaders to navigate complexity: An executive coaching framework*. Unpublished doctoral thesis, Middlesex University.

Lane, D.A. & Corrie, S. (2006). *The modern scientist-practitioner. A guide to practice in psychology*. Hove, East Sussex: Routledge.

Loughran, J.J. (2000) Effective Reflective practice, A paper presented at *Making a difference through reflective practices: Values and actions* conference. University College of Worcester, July 2000.

McGonagill, G. (2002). The coach as reflective practitioner. In C. Fitzgerald & J.G. Berger (Eds.) *Executive coaching: Practices and perspectives* (pp.59–88). Palo Alto, CA: Davies-Black.

McNicoll, A. & Baker, W. (2012). *The power of peer supervision. Tools for supervision & mentoring groups*. Auckland, New Zealand: New Zealand Coaching & Mentoring Centre.

Merriam, S.B., Caffarella, R.S. & Baumgartner, L.M. (2007). *Learning in adulthood: A comprehensive guide (3rd edn)*. San Francisco, CA: Wiley.

Meyer, D.E. & Kieras, D.E. 1997. A computational theory of executive cognitive process and multiple-task performance: Part 1. Basic mechanisms. *Psychological Review*, 104, 749–791.

Mezirow, J. (1981) A critical theory of adult learning and eduaciton. *Adult Education*, 32(1), 3–24.

Morrison, K. (1996). Developing reflective practice in higher degree students through a learning journal. *Studies in higher education*, 21, 317–332.

Osterman, K.F. & Kottkamp, R.B. (2004). *Reflective practice for educators: Professional development to improve student learning* (2nd edn). Thousand Oaks, CA: Corwin Press.

Quinn, F.M. (2000) Reflection and reflective practice. In C. Davies, L. Finlay & A. Bullman (Eds.) *Changing practice in health and social care* (pp.81– 90). London: Sage (Original work published in 1988 and reproduced in 2000)

Schön, D.A. (1983). *The reflective practitioner: How professionals think in action*. New York: Basic Books.

Schön, D.A. (1987). *Educating the reflective practitioner*. New York: Basic Books.

Stedmon, J. & Dallos, R. (2009). *Reflective practice in psychotherapy and counselling*. Maidenhead, Berkshire: Open University Press.

Thorpe, K. (2004). Reflective learning journals: From concept to practice. *Reflective Practice, 5*, 327–343.

Usher, R., Bryant, I. & Johnston, R. (1987). *Adult education and the post-modern challenge: Learning beyond the limits*. New York: Routledge.

Wellington, B. & Austin, P. (1996). Orientations of reflective practice. *Educational Researcher*, 38(3), 307–316.

York-Barr, J., Sommers, W.A., Ghere, G.S. & Montie, J. (2001). *Reflective practice to improve schools: An action guide for educators*. Thousand Oaks, CA: Corwin Press.

Section 4
Wellbeing Coaching
Introduction

David Tee & Jonathan Passmore

Coaching started its growth in the 1980s and 1990s with a strong focus on supporting people in making life choices or improving the quality of their lives. 'Life coaching' as it was labelled remains popular in North America, although the use of the term in Europe and Asia Pacific has virtually disappeared, reflecting the poor reputation which life coaching acquired from untrained or under-trained practitioners who were often attempting to work with complex psychological issues.

In many parts of the world, the term 'life coaching' has been replaced by the term 'wellbeing coaching'. The focus remains similar, but often wellbeing coaches are trained psychologists or have been trained in psychologically informed models, thus equipping them with the skills to work with more complex cases.

It may be helpful at this point to differentiate between 'life' or personal coaching and 'health' coaching, which form two strands of wellbeing coaching.

The use of coaching in health has grown significantly over the past decade in the UK and globally (Evidence Centre, 2014; Salathiel & Passmore, 2021). Over 300 papers have been published, with the approach now widely used by nurses, doctors and allied health professionals such as physiotherapists and health advisors (Salathiel & Passmore, 2021).

As with all areas of coaching, different authors have emphasised different aspects of the practice in their various definitions:

'a patient-centred process that is based upon behaviour change theory and is delivered by health professionals with diverse backgrounds. The actual health coaching process entails goal setting determined by the patient, encourages self-discovery in addition to content education, and incorporates mechanisms for developing accountability in health behaviours' (Evidence Centre, 2014, p. 3).

Coaching Practiced, First Edition. Edited by David Tee and Jonathan Passmore.
© 2022 John Wiley & Sons Ltd. Published 2022 by John Wiley & Sons Ltd.
DOI: 10.1002/9781119835714.s04

'the practice of health education and health promotion within a coaching context, to enhance the wellbeing of individuals and to facilitate the achievement of their health-related goals' (Palmer et al., 2005, p. 91).

"health coaching is a client-centred process that draws on psychological, evidence-based models of behavioural change to help clients make effective and sustained changes in their thoughts, feelings and behaviours, and thus contributes to enhanced wellbeing and quality of life" (Salathiel & Passmore, 2021, p. 4).

What is less clear from these definitions is where health coaching starts and finishes. If coaching is employed to help individuals with chronic conditions and to improve health outcomes, does this include approaches such as motivational interviewing, which are widely used for drug and alcohol treatment, or brief solution-focused therapy and cognitive-behavioural therapy, which might be considered to be included within some of these definitions above, but which the practitioner delivering it might consider to be counselling or therapy? This lack of a more clearly defined boundary has made it difficult to study and compare coaching interventions within the health arena (Boehmer et al., 2016).

One useful, although controversial, distinction we have offered is to use the time focus of the conversation, with coaching focused on future behavioural change for health improvement, while counselling or therapy are focused on coping with, managing or making sense of the past.

"Health coaching is a client-centred future-focused process that draws on psychological, evidence-based models of behavioural change to help patients and service users make effective and sustained changes in their thoughts, feelings and behaviours in the present, and contributes to future enhanced wellbeing and quality of life" (Salathiel & Passmore, 2021, p. 4).

Like health coaching, wellbeing (or life) coaching has become a popular means of helping non-clinical populations in enhancing their wellbeing through reflective and goal-setting practices within a one-to-one Socratic relationship (Green et al., 2006). Wellbeing coaching can be broadly defined as a collaborative solution-focused, result-orientated and systematic process in which the coach facilitates the enhancement of life experience and goal attainment in the personal life of normal, non-clinical clients. In other words, life coaching has often been considered to be coaching outside of the work arena.

One possible distinction between life coaching and health coaching is that health coaching is often defined in terms of the qualification of those providing it. Health coaching is coaching delivered by health professionals, while wellbeing coaching is delivered by those outside of the health sector. This is a less-than-perfect distinction but may be worth holding in mind as we explore the four papers in this section.

In the first paper, Kasia Szymanska (2006) explores the issue of depression, how coaches can identify the signs in clients and what steps they need to take to support and appropriately refer clients to other helping professionals or clinical services. She identifies nine possible symptoms to look out for:

1. Low mood.
2. A lack of interest or pleasure in everyday activities.

3. Weight loss or weight gain.
4. Sleep disturbance.
5. A sense of being slowed down.
6. A lack of energy or fatigue.
7. Feeling worthless, feeling guilty or low self-esteem.
8. Poor concentration.
9. Thoughts of suicide.

In the second paper, Szymanska (2007) explores anxiety, including panic disorders and social phobias, again identifying signs and possible actions which the coach can take to support their client. She notes that the signs for general anxiety disorder (GAD) may include:

- Irritability
- Worrying
- Poor concentration
- Difficulties in sleep
- Muscle tension
- Restlessness

Szymanska also notes interventions may include step-by-step engagement with fears (immersion), breath retraining, cognitive restructuring of automatic thoughts and psycho-social educational interventions.

In the third paper, Szymanska (2009) continues this exploration into anxiety, including post-traumatic stress disorder (PTSD), obsessive compulsive disorder (OCD) and acute stress disorder (ASD).

In the final paper in this series, Peter Duffell and Carmelina Lawton-Smith (2015) explore the role of emotions in coaching. They highlight the difficulty of defining emotions and, without training in psychology or understanding of human emotions, coaches may find it hard to work with emotions effectively. They share how the role of language can be a useful tool for identifying, recalling and exploring the meaning of emotions and the events which surround them, providing new insights for clients through the coaching conversation.

REFERENCES

Boehmer, K. R., Barakat, S., Ahn, S., Prokop, L. J., Erwin, P. J., & Murad, M. H. (2016). Health coaching interventions for persons with chronic conditions: A systematic review and meta-analysis protocol. *Systematic Reviews*, *5*(1), 146.

Duffell, D., & Lawton-Smith, C. (2015) The challenges of working with emotion in coaching. *The Coaching Psychologist*, *11*(1), 32–42.

Green, L. S., Oades, L. G., & Grant, A. M. (2006). Cognitive-behavioural, solution-focused life coaching: Enhancing goal striving, well-being, and hope. *The Journal of Positive Psychology*, *1*(3), 142–149.

Palmer, S., Stubbs, I., & Whybrow, A. (2005). Health coaching to facilitate the promotion of healthy behaviour and achievement of health-related goals. *International Journal of Health Promotion*, 14(3), 91–93.

Salathiel, E., & Passmore, J. (2021). *Does health coaching work: A critical review of the evidence of coaching in health care systems*. Henley on Thames: Henley Business School. ISBN 978-1-912473-30-4.

Szymanska, K. (2006). The impact of depression on the coaching process: How to recognise the signs and what to do next? *The Coaching Psychologist*, 2(3), 29–32.

Szymanska, K. (2007). Anxiety and the coaching relationship: How to recognise the signs and what to do next? *The Coaching Psychologist*, 3(2), 85–89.

Szymanska, K. (2009) Anxiety and the coaching relationship: How to recognise the signs and what to do next (Part 2). *The Coaching Psychologist*, 5(1), 39–42.

The Evidence Centre (2014) *Does Health Coaching Work? A Rapid Review of Empirical Evidence*. Health Education East of England: NHS.

9 The impact of depression on the coaching process: How to recognise the signs and what to do next

Kasia Szymanska

Abstract

This paper addresses how to manage clients with depression in the coaching relationship. The symptoms of depression are discussed, as are the strategies used to work with clients and if required the subsequent referral process for psychotherapy.

Keywords

Depression; symptoms; self-help; guidelines; cognitive behaviour therapy.

Depression is a growing problem in the UK. Given this information, it is likely that the majority of coaching psychologists reading this article will have worked or will go on to work with clients who have been depressed or are currently suffering from depression. Indeed some may have experienced it themselves.

Depression can be viewed on a continuum, with low mood at one end of the continuum and major clinical depression at the other. While clients with major

Original publication details: Szymanska, K. (2006, December). The impact of depression on the coaching process: How to recognise the signs and what to do next. *The Coaching Psychologist, 2*(3), 29–31. Reproduced with permission of The British Psychological Society.

Coaching Practiced, First Edition. Edited by David Tee and Jonathan Passmore.
© 2022 John Wiley & Sons Ltd. Published 2022 by John Wiley & Sons Ltd.
DOI: 10.1002/9781119835714.ch09

depression may not necessarily seek coaching, it is possible that a client may develop symptoms of depression whilst receiving coaching or that clients' currently being coached are already mildly to moderately depressed but adept at hiding their symptoms. Therefore, from a professional perspective, coaching psychologists would benefit from:

a. recognising the symptoms of depression;
b. if appropriate, having the skills to work with clients experiencing depression;
c. knowing where to refer clients on if they require therapy as opposed to coaching.

This article aims to address all three points, with an overall aim of providing coaching psychologists with a brief and jargon-free guide to depression.

According to Aaron Beck (1979), 'a typical depression usually starts off mild, reaches a peak of severity, and then generally declines in intensity.' In addition he states that 'depression tends to be episodic with periods of symptom-free intervals' (p.23). The reasons for the onset of depression are varied and can be the result of an interaction between life events, genetic, psychological and environmental factors.

One of the most common depressions is 'major depression'. According to the DSM-IV-TR a formal diagnosis is made if a client experiences *at least five* of the following symptoms over a *two-week period*.

1. Low mood.
2. A lack of interest or pleasure in everyday activities.
3. Weight loss or weight gain.
4. Sleep disturbance (commonly clients report waking up early and being unable to go back to sleep).
5. Feeling agitated and a sense of being slowed down.
6. A lack of energy or fatigue.
7. Feeling worthless, feeling guilty or reporting a low self-esteem.
8. Poor concentration.
9. Thoughts of suicide.

In the clinical context, practitioners can readily use these guidelines to assess levels of depression and risk. However, as the philosophy and practice of coaching differs significantly from clinical work, it is important for coaching psychologists to differentiate between ordinary low mood and clinical depression. Integral to this process is a strong coach-client alliance, coupled with this, the following points which are by no means exhaustive, may aid the coaching psychologist in determining whether their client is depressed.

a. If your client refers to feeling depressed or expresses a general sense of hopelessness about the future, explore with them what they mean by this. It is important not to ignore it, even if you believe that you know your client well. Hopelessness in particular can be a sign of suicidal ideation or intent.

b. If your client complains of feeling low and shows little interest in work, family or social activities, ask them how long they have being feeling this way and what activities they no longer engage in. As depression worsens clients frequently give up doing things they enjoy such as exercise and seeing friends, leading to a decrease in mood.

c. Their thinking may be consistently negative. Specifically, they may be hard on themselves and be self-critical, e.g. 'I must perform well' or 'I'm always getting it wrong'; negative about the world, e.g. 'Life is just a hard slog' and negative about the future, e.g. 'Why bother doing this job, it's never going to get me anywhere anyway'.

d. The client may present with pervasive low confidence which in turn may be due to poor self-esteem.

e. A prior history of depression can be predictive of a relapse.

f. If your client has experienced stressful life events recently they may be at greater risk of developing depression (Kendler *et al.*, 1999; Maciejewski *et al.*, 2000).

Whether to work with a client experiencing depression can be difficult to judge as it can depend on a number of factors such as, the severity of the client's illness, your client's insight into their illness, the impact of the depression on the coaching process, the coaching psychologist's own style of working, own experiences and confidence in the process. Before the coaching psychologist makes a decision, any concerns are best discussed initially with the coaching psychologist's own supervisor before being addressed with the client.

If the client continues in coaching as their depression seems to be mild to moderate, there are a number of options available to them. They could have counselling or therapy as well as coaching. The recent NICE guidelines suggest that problem solving, cognitive behaviour therapy or counselling (2004b), are the most suitable treatments for moderate depression. In addition clients may also benefit from some suggestions from the coaching psychologist or respond to the application of self-help materials to manage depression. Below is a short list of therapeutic/self-help strategies which can be adopted in the coaching context:

- A discussion about supervised exercise together with a regular review of the client's progress;
- Teaching your client to identify their negative thinking patterns, challenge these patterns and replace them with more realistic ways of thinking (to learn more about this process see, e.g. Feeling Good: The New Mood Therapy by Burns (1999);
- Asking your client to access self-help texts and/or self-help CD ROMS (Williams, 2001; Whitfield & Williams, 2006). For example, *Overcoming depression* by Gilbert (2000) is a step-by-step self-help manual designed to be used alone or in conjunction with therapeutic input While both 'Beating the blues' available at www.ultrasis.com and 'Overcoming depression' at www.calipso.co.uk are effective CBT-based computerised self-help programmes designed to train clients in the acquisition of skills to manage symptoms of depression (Whitfield & Williams, 2006).

If your client slides into major depression, NICE recommends therapy, in particular cognitive behaviour therapy and/or medication. At this stage it is usually preferable that coaching is put on hold while the client seeks alternative support. If your client asks for information about therapy, there are three key organisations (in addition to the Society's website) to recommend that have accredited or recognised practitioners:

- The British Association for Cognitive and Behavioural Psychotherapy (BABCP). Website: www.babcp.org.uk
- The British Association for Counselling and Psychotherapy (BACP). Website: www.bacp.co.uk.
- The United Kingdom Council for Psychotherapy (UKCP). Website: www.ukcp.org.uk

What is important at this juncture, is that the coaching psychologist, does not attempt to offer psychotherapy in addition to or instead of providing coaching to the client, otherwise boundaries can easily become blurred and this may be to the client's detriment. Clients may benefit from receiving therapy in parallel with the coaching, but not necessarily both from the same person. A good example would be a senior employee receiving executive coaching to help him or her deal with presentations whilst also being in cognitive therapy for moderate depression which was not sufficiently debilitating for the employee to take sickness leave.In conclusion, an understanding of mental health issues can be an asset to coaching psychologists, who armed with knowledge about the signs of depression can make an informed decision about how to support their clients who are experiencing depression either within the coaching relationship or outside of it.

REFERENCES

American Psychiatric Association (Eds.) (1994). *Diagnostic and Statistical Manual of Mental Disorders –4th edition (DSM-IV-TR)*. Washington, DC: American Psychiatric Association.

Beck, A.T., Rush, A.J., Shaw, B.F. & Emery, G. (1979). *Cognitive therapy for depression*. New York: Guilford Press.

Burns, D.D. (1999). *Feeling good: The new mood therapy*. New York: HarperCollins.

Gilbert, P. (2000). *Overcoming depression: A self-help guide using cognitive behavioural techniques*. London: Robinson.

Kendler, K., Karkowski, L. & Prescott, C. (1999). Causal relationship between life events and the onset of major depression. *American Journal of Psychiatry*, 156, 837–841.

Maciejewski, P., Prigerson, H. & Mazure, C. (2000). Self-efficacy as a mediator between life events and depressive symptoms. *The British Journal of Psychiatry*, 176, 373–378.

National Institute for Clinical Excellence (2004b). *Depression: Management of depression in primary and secondary care. Clinical Guidelines 23*. London: National Institute for Clinical Excellence.

Whitfield, G. & Williams, C. (2006). The impact of a novel computerized CBT CD Rom (Overcoming depression) offered to patients referred to clinical psychology. *Behavioural and Cognitive Psychotherapy*, 34, 1–11.

Williams, C. (2001). Use of written cognitive behavioural therapy self-help materials to treat. depression. *Advances in Psychiatric Treatment*, 7, 233–240.

10 Anxiety and the coaching relationship: How to recognise the signs and what to do next

Kasia Szymanska

Abstract

This paper addresses how to recognise and manage symptoms of anxiety in the coaching relationship.

Keywords

anxiety, symptoms, strategies, panic, specific phobia, social phobia and Generalised Anxiety Disorder.

The second in the series on coaching psychology and mental health issues, this paper focuses on anxiety. From a clinical perspective, anxiety is a generic term which encompasses a number of related disorders as formalised in the DSM-IV-TR. These include panic disorder, specific phobia, social phobia, Generalised Anxiety Disorder (GAD), Post-traumatic stress disorder (PTSD), Acute Stress Disorder (AST) and Obsessive Compulsive Disorder (OCD) and health anxiety.

This paper will address the symptoms of the first four disorders, panic, specific phobia, social phobia and GAD and focuses on a selection of strategies coaching psychologists can adopt to support clients in managing their symptoms.

Original publication details: Szymanska, K. (2007, August). Anxiety and the coaching relationship: How to recognise the signs and what to do next. *The Coaching Psychologist, 3*(2), 85–89. Reproduced with permission of The British Psychological Society.

Anxiety is a familiar component of the coaching relationship. Clients can present with milder forms of anxiety contextualised within their presenting issues such as increased levels of worrying, concern or physiological symptoms e.g. tension, or anxiety can be so debilitating, such as social phobia that it impacts not only on the individual but also their ability to function in the work environment, in social settings and on their general quality of life. Figures derived from The Office for National Statistics Psychiatric Morbidity Report (2000) suggest that anxiety and depression are some of the common disorders in UK and that some nine per cent of adults experienced symptoms of anxiety in 2000, while 20 per cent reported increased levels of worrying.

PANIC DISORDER

A&E is frequently the first port of call for individuals with symptoms of panic, (Katerndahl, 2002). Often, the 'diagnosis' of panic can engender a sense of relief and together with the use of medication, e.g. propranolol and/or the use of avoidance as a 'coping' strategy serves to reduce the frequency of symptoms.

In the coaching arena clients often present with symptoms embedded within specific scenarios associated with the workplace such as giving presentations, participating in meetings and transportation, e.g. planes and car journeys.

Some of the more common symptoms of panic include:

1. Physiological symptoms such as an increased heart rate, tightness in the chest, dizziness, sweating, shaking and fainting. Often clients are more likely to have fear of having the latter two symptoms rather then experiencing them.
2. Variations of the following negative cognitions, such as 'I'm going to have a heart attack', 'This is terrible', 'Everyone is looking at me', 'I'm so weak', 'I'm so stupid' and I'm going to make a fool of myself.'

For some clients panic attacks occur in conjunction with agoraphobia.

SPECIFIC PHOBIAS

The DSM-IV-TR defines a phobia as 'marked and persistent fear that is excessive or unreasonable.' It can effect up to 1.9 per cent of the population (The Office for National Statistics, 2000) and can be applied to objects, situations or specific issues such as planes, animals, lifts, blood, heights, airplanes, thunder storms and fear of choking or vomiting.

It is characterised by complete or partial avoidance and often pre-empted by anticipatory anxiety which can include physiological symptoms and negative cognitions, e.g. 'I know I'll panic if the lift stops.'

SOCIAL PHOBIA

Social phobia which often begins in adolescence is characterised by a fear of behaving in embarrassing or humiliating way and the fear of being scrutinised by others. It is often accompanied by shyness and can lead to symptoms of panic either in situ or as part of the anticipatory fear.

A central theme which dominates social phobia is an increase in self-consciousness leading to unhelpful spiral of sensation awareness and negative interpretation of symptoms and emotions. For example, a client walking into a networking meeting on their own may think about the fact they are walking into a room full of people they don't know. This may lead to 'butterflies' or a feeling of anxiety, which in turn can be interpreted as weak by the person leading to a series of further physiological and cognitive symptoms such as blushing and heart racing.

GAD

The DSM-IV-TR defines GAD as, 'Excessive anxiety and worry (apprehension expectation) occurring more days then not for at least six months, about a number of events or activities (such as work or school performance).'

Some of the components of GAD include:

- High levels of worrying;
- Poor concentration;
- Difficulties in sleeping;
- Muscle tension and restlessness;
- Irritability.

The key feature of GAD is increased worrying about most things, which Leahy (2006) describes as the 'what if disease'. Clients can often worry about worrying which can in turn lead to heightened anxiety and episodes of depression.

As with depression (Szymanska, 2006), the decision to work with clients who experience any of the above disorders depends on a number of factors, the severity of the client's problems, the impact of anxiety on the coaching process, the coaching psychologist's skills and confidence in using the strategies and your client's motivation to work on these issues.

Counselling/clinical psychologists work *with* the disorders while coaching psychologists may work with *aspects* of the disorders, presented as part of the ongoing case formulation.

Clients with longstanding patterns of thinking/behaviour underpinned by anxiety or severe symptoms of anxiety which can impact on the coaching process may benefit from seeing a counselling/clinical psychologist before they start coaching. For example, I once saw a client for coaching who presented with low levels of motivation. He had being offered a senior role within the company which he was reticent about accepting. The position involved a substantial amount of travel and taking clients out for dinner. After careful questioning it transpired that while the client was under a considerable amount of stress and was concerned about achieving the 'perfect' life/work balance, which could be addressed in coaching, one of the main causes of his stress was a fear of choking when eating with others. The client had choked four times in the last two years when eating with colleagues and now was anticipating choking and making 'a fool' of himself. In addition it seemed that the fear of choking could be traced back to his mother who before her death was unable to eat or drink without choking. Wearing my coaching psychologist's hat at the time, I referred the client for cognitive therapy to manage his fears and then saw him to focus on strategies to manage pressure.

Therapeutic strategies which can be adapted to support clients with panic, specific phobias and social phobias.

Psycho-education/self-help materials: primarily psycho-education has a powerful impact as a normalising tool. For many clients it is a relief to see 'their' symptoms in black and white and for clients who believe that the manifestation of symptoms is the first step towards madness, knowing that others experience similar symptoms can serve to reduce their conviction in the idea of 'I'm going mad.'

Breathing re-training: The onset of physiological symptoms, such as tightness in the chest and a rapid heart beat, can induce catastrophic misinterpretation, e.g. 'I'm having a stroke'.

Clients with physiological symptoms should be seen by a doctor to rule out organic reasons for their symptoms, if there are none, clients may benefit from breathing re-training as a strategy to manage their symptoms. Hyperventilation or over breathing can lead to an imbalance of oxygen and carbon dioxide in the blood leading to symptoms such as chest pains or tingling. Consistent application of breathing strategies can help clients reduce sensations and recognise that they are harmless (Taylor, 2000).

Confronting fears on a step-by-step basis: applicable in the main to symptoms of panic, specific phobias and social phobia, confronting fears using small steps has the impact of increasing self-efficacy and a sense of self-control. Clients have a choice, to continue to feel fear/anxiety which tends to involve avoiding situations or take control and address the issue, short term pain for long term gain! A written assignment focusing on the costs and benefits of avoiding dealing with their current situation versus the costs and benefits of step-by-step confrontation can be beneficial as an initial step towards change. The second step is to draw up a list of situations the client avoids, starting with the easiest first before encouraging your client to face the next scenario and so on, whilst closely monitoring outcomes. To facilitate positive results clients should be encouraged to stay in each situation until their fear has reduced, leading to habituation.

Positive self-talk/cognitive restructuring: negative self-talk is a dominant component of psychological problems. For example, a fear of panicking/fainting on the tube (anticipatory anxiety) can lead to an increase in physiological symptoms, expectations of failure, and avoidance of the issue (both cognitive and behavioural). To increase the chances of success client negative self-talk needs to be identified and restructured, initially during sessions and then practised by the client whilst undertaking tasks.

To restructure negative self-talk the following Socratic questions can be implemented:

Where is the evidence that …?

What would you say to a friend/colleague in the same situation?

How likely is it that the worst will happen? What are the costs/benefits of thinking this way?

What is a better way of thinking about this situation?

If my thoughts were presented as evidence in court would they stand up for scrutiny by the judge?

Reduction in safety behaviours: safety behaviours are employed to manage difficult situations, e.g. sitting by the door in a meeting to be near an escape route, avoiding eye contact with colleagues to reduce the chances of being asked questions and sitting down to avoid dizziness and fainting. Clients often describe these strategies as essential coping mechanisms; however, they only serve to reinforce anxiety and fear.

Self-monitoring and discussion during sessions can heighten awareness of safety behaviours. While focusing on the negative consequences of specific behaviours is a precursor for relinquishing their gradual application. So when discussing avoiding eye contact with colleagues in meetings with a client who tended to avoid large groups of colleagues for fear of saying the 'wrong thing', we focused on the negative consequences of her behaviour, such as, that means that people are less likely to speak to you, they may even find you unapproachable, or think you are uninterested in working for the company and it only intensifies your lack of confidence. We then went onto practise communication skills and cognitive restructuring in the session before she went on to use the strategies in the workplace.

Worry management: in addition to being a predominant feature of GAD, worrying is a common human trait. It tends to become problematic when it is unremitting, seen as beneficial (e.g. as a problem solving strategy) and when clients start to worry about worry! In his book on handling worrying Leahy (2006) describes the worst strategies clients can use to manage worries, such as trying to use thought stopping, being more positive, checking and ruminating.

A number of strategies can be used to help clients manage worries: identifying worries in writing can loosen a client's belief in their validity; focusing on the costs and benefits of worrying or specific worries can have the same impact; setting aside a short time each day to focus on worries and their solutions (Borkovec et al., 1983b); and writing down a list of reasons as to why worrying is *not* helpful.

CONCLUSION

Being such a ubiquitous condition, the body of evidence based strategies developed to manage anxiety is firmly in place, so for clients who do not want to seek psychotherapy or have low grade symptoms embedded within coaching specific contexts, adapting strategies used in the therapeutic arena can break the cycle of anxiety, increase self-efficacy and motivation. To reduce the chances of relapse, clients need to be encouraged to use these strategies regularly and with vigour.

REFERENCES

American Psychiatric Association (Eds.) (1994). *Diagnostic and Statistical Manual of Mental Disorders* (4th ed., DSM-IV-TR). Washington, DC: American Psychiatric Association.

Borkovec, T.D., Wilkinson, L., Folensbee, R. & Lerman, C. (1983b). Stimulus control applications to the treatment of worry. *Behaviour Research and Therapy, 21,* 247–251.

Katerndahl, D.A. (2002). Factors influencing care-seeking for a self-defined worst panic attack. *Psychiatric Services, 53,* 464–470.

Leahy, R. (2006). *The worry cure: Stop worrying and start living*. London: Piatkus.

Szymanska, K. (2006). The impact of depression on the coaching process: How to recognise the signs and what to do next. *The Coaching Psychologist, 2(3)*, 29–31.

Taylor, S. (2000). *Understanding and treating panic disorder: Cognitive-behavioural approaches*. Chichester: John Wiley.

The Office for National Statistics (2000). *Psychiatric morbidity among adults living in private households in Great Britain*.

11 Anxiety and the coaching relationship: How to recognise the signs and what to do next (Part 2)

Kasia Szymanska

Abstract

This article addresses the symptoms of Post-Traumatic Stress Disorder, (PTSD), Acute Stress Disorder (AST) and Obsessive Compulsive Disorder (OCD) and health anxiety, with the aim of familiarising coaching psychologists with the symptoms of the above disorders and the strategies which can be implemented within the coaching arena to provide coachee support.

Keywords

Post-Traumatic Stress Disorder (PTSD), Acute Stress Disorder (AST), Obsessive Compulsive Disorder (OCD), health anxiety, self-help and strategies.

Original publication details: Szymanska, K. (2009, June). Anxiety and the coaching relationship: How to recognise the signs and what to do next (Part 2). *The Coaching Psychologist, 5*(1), 39–41. Reproduced with permission of The British Psychological Society.

PTSD AND ASD

Previously referred to as railway spine, irritable heart and shell shock, PTSD was only recognised as a medical condition and included in the *DSM-III* in 1980, post the Vietnam War.

The key features of PTSD following the experience of a traumatic event or witnessing an event, include, re-experiencing the event often in the form of flash backs or nightmares: avoidance of the trauma in the form of distraction, i.e. not thinking or talking about the trauma and avoiding locations and individual associated with the trauma; increased arousal such as hyper-vigilance and sleep problems.

In addition to the above, common symptoms presented include: poor concentration, panic, tension, sadness, guilt, blame, shame, frustration, anger, decrease/increase in ability to work, tendency to function on automatic pilot and increase in alcohol consumption.

A diagnosis of PTSD can only be made once the individual has had the symptoms for one month or more. Further categorisations of PTSD include, chronic and delayed onset PTSD, the latter being PTSD which develops six months or more after the traumatic experience.

In the time frame prior to the diagnosis of PTSD, individuals can be diagnosed with Acute Stress Disorder or ASD. Three or more of the following symptoms constitute a diagnosis: feeling numb, a lack of awareness of their surroundings, depersonalisation or derealisation and dissociate amnesia. Depersonalisation is characterised as feeling detached from your body, or being in a dream state while during derealisation the world around the person seems unreal.

Although not included in the *DSM-IV-TR* and in the NICE Guidelines, there is a growing body of evidence (Scott & Stradling, 1992; Randall, 1997) to suggest that bullying in the workplace can in effect contribute to the development of symptoms of PTSD. Tehrani (2004) found that following a formal assessment of 165 care professionals, of the 67 that had experienced being bullied, 44 per cent exhibited signs of PTSD, such as: feeling numb; tense: irritable; avoiding situations or others; feeling guilty or experiencing self blame and thinking about the bullying when involved in different activities.

STRATEGIES ADAPTED TO WORKING WITH COACHEES WHO HAVE EXPERIENCED TRAUMATIC EVENTS

Working directly on the symptoms of trauma with coachees is not recommended, coaching psychologists who on the basis of assessment suspect coachees have symptoms of PTSD should refer them for a formal assessment to a clinical practitioner. If this leads to diagnosis and therapy for treatment, it is possible that once the therapy has being concluded coaching psychologists can then work with the coachee on issues such as stress management and assertion training, if applicable. If, however, the coachee is receiving coaching for an unrelated issue and during the coaching relationship it becomes evident that the coachee has experienced a recent trauma, normalisation of trauma responses within a boundaried discussion can be helpful, its only if the person's distress continues to impact on their personal and professional functioning weeks after the trauma that clinical professional support is recommended.

OBSESSIVE COMPULSIVE DISORDER (OCD)

OCD is characterised by the persistent reoccurrence of thoughts or ideas and/or compulsions or acts performed in reputed manner leading to high levels of anxiety. For a diagnosis to be made, the obsession and compulsions need to take more then one hour a day and individuals need to recognise that that their obsessions and compulsions are excessive and that they cause distress which impacts on the person's daily routine and functioning. Some of the more common forms of OCD include: contamination fears, e.g. HIV, religious thoughts, sexual images, thoughts of violence, and concerns about order, symmetry and exactness, e.g. repeating acts, repeated checking that e-mails have been sent to the right person and checking that the oven is switched off, arranging acts hoarding and counting (Veale & Wilson, 2005). According to the NICE Guidelines (2005) some one to two per cent of the population suffer from OCD.

STRATEGIES ADAPTED TO WORKING WITH COACHES WITH ASPECTS OF OCD

As with ACT and PTSD working directly with coahees who have OCD is inappropriate, a clinical diagnosis and referral for cognitive behaviour therapy is preferable. For coachees who do not want therapy, self-help can be effective; there are a number of books on the market which provide valuable information and resources on how to ease obsessions and compulsions. For coachees who present with mild forms of OCD it can also be helpful to normalise aspects of obsessional thinking and compulsive behaviour, almost everyone has at one time experienced unwanted thoughts or gone back to check that the front door is closed or checked more then once that the iron is unplugged.

HEALTH ANXIETY

Health anxiety involves a preoccupation with thought that one is or will be physically ill. Also known as hypochondriasis, it can relate to a fear of developing physical illnesses such cancer, multiple sclerosis, HIV and heart attacks. For example, an individual may believe that hearing their heart beating must be a sign of a heart problem, while another may think that forgetting words is a sign of dementia.

Health anxiety is perpetuated by checking for signs of illness and often by repeated visits to doctors and consultants in order to get a firm diagnosis or to have certainty. Diagnoses which do not fit in with the individual's viewpoint are often rejected or the reassurance from the doctor that they are not ill is often initially accepted then discounted quickly leading to individuals visiting doctor after doctor looking for verification of symptoms which in parallel leads to an increase in symptoms of anxiety. In therapy, individuals can also use the session to try and persuade their therapist that their symptoms have a medical cause or refer to their symptoms as 'medically unexplained'.

The cause of health anxiety can vary; it can be triggered by a stressful event or a death of a family member of friend or a serious illness.

STRATEGIES ADAPTED TO WORKING WITH COACHES WITH ASPECTS OF HEALTH ANXIETY

While it is not appropriate to focus on managing health anxiety in the coaching, health anxiety responds well to psychotherapeutic intervention. As with PTSD, ASD and OCD coachee's who experience mild levels of health anxiety may benefit from reading literature related specifically to health anxiety. It is preferable not to direct the coachee to do their own search on the internet for information as this only serves to perpetuate the anxiety cycle as the individual looks for information to substantiate their anxiety related thoughts.

For information about how to find suitable therapy for this condition see Szymanska (2006). While an informative series of self-help books which includes a book on health anxiety is published by Constable and Robinson.

CONCLUSION

In the first and second parts of this series on clinical disorders the focus was on the depression, specific and social phobias and the generalised anxiety disorders. It is much more likely that coaching psychologists will work with clients experiencing aspects of any of the above then with the disorders covered in this paper. Coachees whose symptoms of the disorders outlined impact on the coaching relationship to the extent that the focus on the original goals of coaching is impossible, would benefit from therapy rather than coaching.

REFERENCES

American Psychiatric Association (Eds) (1980). *Diagnostic and Statistical Manual of Mental Disorders – 3rd ed. (DSM-III)*. Washington, DC: Author.

American Psychiatric Association (Eds) (1994). *Diagnostic and Statistical Manual of Mental Disorders – 4th ed. (DSM-IV-TR)*. Washington, DC: Author.

National Institute for Clinical Excellence (2005). *Obsessive Compulsive Disorder: Core interventions in the treatment of obsessive-compulsive disorder and body dysmorphic disorder*. London: Author.

Randall, P. (1997). *Adult bullying; perpetrators and victims*. London: Routledge.

Scott, M.J. & Stradling, S.G (1992). *Counselling for Post-Traumatic Stress Disorder*. London: Sage.

Szymanska, K. (2006). The impact of depression on the coaching process: How to recognise the signs and what to do next. *The Coaching Psychologist*, 2(3), 29–31.

Szymanska, K. (2007). Anxiety and the coaching relationship: How to recognise the signs and what to do next (Part 1). *The Coaching Psychologist*, 3(2), 85–89.

Tehrani, N. (2004). Bullying: A source of stress of chronic post-traumatic stress? *British Journal of Guidance & Counselling*, 32(3), 357–366.

Veale, D. & Wilson, R. (2005). *Overcoming Obsessive Compulsive Disorder: A self-help guide using cognitive and behavioural techniques*. London: Constable and Robinson.

12 The challenges of working with emotion in coaching

Peter Duffell & Carmelina Lawton-Smith

Abstract

The role of emotion in coaching has attracted significant recent debate and this article summarises three potential perspectives that coaches may be using in respect of emotion. It then goes on to highlight a number of potential issues that need further exploration. Firstly, defining emotion remains a complex area of debate and without a shared understanding with clients of what is meant by 'emotion', coaches may find it hard to work with effectively. Secondly, dealing with emotion in the coaching interaction often relies on the recounting and recalling of a previous event and is therefore subject to memory. The coach is working with the account of the event from memory, rather than the event itself. This has implications for the role of the coach in dealing with the subsequent client meaning making of emotional events. Lastly, the limitations of language may influence the coaching interaction when discussing emotions, leading to unhelpful consequences. Some suggestions are made to help inform coaching practice when working with emotion.

Keywords

emotion, coaching, memory, language.

The role of emotion in organisational coaching has attracted significant interest in recent years (Bachkirova & Cox, 2007; Cox & Bachkirova, 2007; Cox & Patrick, 2012). In this article we will summarise three prevailing perspectives in relation to emotions in coaching and go on to highlight remaining challenges for coaches when working with emotions.

Original publication details: Duffell, P., & Lawton-Smith, C. (2015, June). The challenges of working with emotion in coaching. *The Coaching Psychologist, 11*(1), 32–41. Reproduced with permission of The British Psychological Society.

INTRODUCTION

Approaches to emotion in coaching could be categorised into three potential perspectives.

The first perspective potentially held by coaches is that emotion is a topic to be *ignored* because emotion has no place in the organisational context, and the main aim of the coach is to enable rationality to prevail (Cox & Bachkirova, 2007), or to refer the client to alternative support. Such views may be pertinent for internal coaches or when coaching is provided for a defined area of performance. The second approach accepts the significance of emotions but takes the perspective that they are *inconvenient* and need to be managed and controlled. This view is characterised by the growth in Emotional Intelligence resources (Goleman, 2013), and by coaches who aim to help clients recognise and manage their emotional reactions. The third perspective, emerging as a stronger force in recent years, regards emotions as *information* that can be valuable in the coaching process, (Cremona, 2010). This review will expand on each of these perspectives and highlight some remaining issues for coaches when working with emotion.

EMOTIONS ARE TO BE IGNORED AND ARE IRRELEVANT OR UNHELPFUL

Historically, emotion was treated with caution in the coaching field, with some arguing that the emergence of difficult emotions often signalled a transition across the counselling boundary. Cox and Bachkirova (2007) highlight an early view from the International Coaching Federation (ICF) that 'Coaching assumes the presence of emotional reactions to life events that clients are capable of expressing and handling their emotions. Coaching is not psychotherapy' (p.183). This infers that coaches would potentially have considered referral in situations that generated strong emotions. Askew and Carnell (2011) suggest coaches might be wary of 'trespass', so tend to distance themselves from emotion. However, the ICF has since changed its perspective on this point and now advises that coaches should be able to work with strong emotions (ICF, 2013). It has also been suggested that lack of emotional investigation may negatively impact the coaching relationship (Patrick, 2004) resulting in a less effective engagement, hence 'Emotion work' (Cox & Patrick, 2012), is now seen as important within the coaching field. Cox (2013) advocates that an aversion to dealing with emotion in coaching 'should be seen as misplaced since feelings are the initial mechanisms through which understanding is ultimately achieved' (p17).

It may, in fact, be almost impossible to operate as a coach without dealing with client emotion leading to suggestions by Cox and Bachkirova (2007), that emotion be considered in coach training. In their study, none of the coaches involved appeared able to avoid working with emotion in their practice. However, a number of those coaches still reported that emotions were considered 'unhelpful' to the coaching process and some would still refer any client expressing painful emotions. Yet even when coaching is clearly performance based, such as sales or presentation coaching, emotional reaction can often block improved performance, so attempts to ignore client emotion may limit the effectiveness of coaching.

EMOTIONS ARE INCONVENIENT AND NEED TO BE REGULATED

The second coaching perspective to difficult emotions regards regulation as the required approach. This is characterised by Emotional Intelligence psychometrics (Bar-On, 2000) often used by coaches to draw attention to emotions that the organisation, or the individual, might prefer to be managed or suppressed.

Richards and Gross suggest that there are two forms of emotion regulation; 'response focused regulation mops up one's emotions; antecedent-focused regulation keeps them from spilling in the first place' (2000, p.1308). These strategies are also referred to as reappraisal (response-focused) and suppression (antecedent-focused). Since suppression is a preventative emotional regulation strategy it requires continual self-monitoring and self-corrective action throughout a potentially emotional event (Gross, 2002). It is suggested that such monitoring requires a continual outlay of cognitive resources, reducing the capacity to process events, which can affect future recall. Reappraisal, by contrast, is reactive, therefore does not require continual self-regulatory effort during the emotional event. The type of regulatory strategy employed might therefore have an impact on the memory of the emotional event, with suppressed events being harder to recall in detail. This has clear implications for how the event may be relayed to a coach some time later. A client who is struggling to remember the detail of an emotional event may have genuine difficulty in recalling the detail which can make it hard for the coach and client to explore the event meaningfully. Alternatively the coach may mistake this as a signal that the event was not significant and fail to investigate and challenge, thus denying the client the opportunity to work with the coach to make sense of strong emotional signposts that could support development.

Encouraging suppression strategies therefore will increase the cognitive load, thus reducing the resources clients have available to remember and subsequently make sense of their emotional experiences as a source of learning. Consequently, if emotions are treated only as something to be monitored and regulated the client learning may be limited.

EMOTIONS ARE INFORMATION TO BE TO BE ACCEPTED OR ANALYSED

Employing suppression means that emotions are never accepted or analysed, despite the potential for these emotion to provide valuable insight. Emotions arise when something happens of importance to an individual (Gross, 2002). By uncovering the object of that emotion the coach and client can gain awareness of deeply held principles and existing behavioural strategies to deal with that emotion (Bachkirova & Cox, 2007). There are indications that knowledge of client emotions may be helpful in coaching (Cremona, 2010; Grant, 2012; Gyllensten et al., 2010). Some suggest that approaches such as Rational Emotive Behavioural Coaching can help clients 'understand both their values and their emotions' (Fusco, Palmer & O'Riordan, 2011). Gestalt coaching based on the 'paradoxical theory of change' (Beisser, 1970) would also suggest that awareness and acceptance of powerful emotion can be the trigger for change. Emotions can, therefore, provide a 'signpost' to core principles or values that the client has not acknowledged or is unaware of. High emotion often results when a deeply help principle is violated, so, for example, a client who describes anger at a change of reporting line may benefit from understanding the main reason behind that anger. For some it may be that the decision was taken without consultation, for another the anger may result from a perceived loss of power. Understanding the focus, or the object of the emotion can, therefore, aid self-knowledge.

Since emotions have an object they are described as intentional (Chamberlain & Broderick, 2007), this is in contrast to a 'mood' that is often free flowing with no clear object as the focus of that mood. Emotions frequently arise when comparing expected progress, against actual progress towards a goal (Carver, 2006) and are particularly relevant when the goal is of significant importance for the individual (Koole, 2009). This may reflect a disparity in what an individual feels 'should happen' vs. what they perceived 'did happen' such as the duty of consultation, where none was used. However, the resulting emotion can impede or promote progress towards the goal. For example, an individual seeking promotion who experiences failure and disappointment may feel negative emotion which diverts energy and may impact the motivation to work towards the desired goal. The fact that an emotion exists and creates the desire for regulation (Thompson, 2011) can provide valuable information in the coaching context and raise client awareness. In a situation where a client claims that a promotion was not important but reports anger at how the interview was handled, could benefit from working through this incongruence in a coaching context. Exploring such incongruence can help the client identify a more fundamental problem that may underlie the reaction, possibly revealing competing commitments (Kegan & Lahey, 2009) of which they were unaware.

Incongruence between inner feelings and outer behaviour may also be the result of using suppression, which if engaged long term, can make people feel inauthentic and negative about themselves (John & Gross, 2004). Coaches are well placed to explore such feelings of incongruence and inauthenticity in the confidential client space. Therefore emotions can be a valuable source of information to both the coach and the client, often indicating the presence of significant issues that need to be surfaced to enable awareness and sense-making. However, using emotions in coaching as information to be accepted and analysed, while valuable, presents a number of issues for practicing coaches. Below we detail three key problems that coaches need to be aware of in coaching practice when working with emotions.

THE DEFINITION PROBLEM

Despite the interest and long research history, there is as yet no agreed definition of emotions. This is problematic in coaching, because when we talk about emotion it would be valuable for both the client and the coach to share a mutual understanding. In fact, the definition of emotion is described as one of the 'perennial problems in the field of emotion' (Frijda, 2008, p.68). The question of what is an emotion is not an abstract one, as in marketing the emotional impact of advertising on consumer behaviour has significant consequences backed by extensive research (Chamberlain & Broderick, 2007). There appear to be two main issues. Firstly, emotions are deeply personal with multiple-emotions often experienced at the same time (Plutchik, 2001). Whilst everyone is familiar with emotion, each individual may have their own experience of it (Ekman, 1992). Secondly, Le Doux (1998) comments that 'emotion is only a label as it does not refer to something the brain has or does' (p.16). This infers that emotion is merely a construct for talking about brain and mind. In addition, since emotion is hard to gauge or measure, especially in other people, it is described as 'the most vexing problem in affective science' (Mauss & Robinson, 2011, p.209).

Kleinginna and Kleinginna addressed this 'vexing problem' and concluded that 'emotion is complex and can give rise to affective experiences, cognitive processes, physiological adjustments or behaviours' (1981, p.355). This broad scope means that theorists focus on different elements, resulting in numerous, divergent definitions (Frijda, 2008). Mauss and Robinson, note that there is no 'thing' (2011, p.14) that defines emotion because of the multiple variables. However, despite numerous approaches, there is some common ground in the literature, with six areas emerging as consistent in theoretical thinking about emotion:

1. *Conscious and unconscious appraisal*: Fredrickson (2001) outlined a broadly affective definition proposing that emotion begins with an individual's assessment of the personal meaning of an event. She expanded this, suggesting *The challenges of working with emotion in coaching* conscious and unconscious appraisal processes might trigger cascades of response tendencies resulting in things such as cognitive processing. Other authors support this view, referencing affective phenomena,

multi-component response systems and conscious or unconscious appraisal (Chamberlain & Broderick, 2007; Garland et al., 2010).

2. *Physiological responses and behaviour*: Emphasises physiological definitions that emotions are short-lived experiences producing co-ordinated changes in thoughts, actions and physiological responses (Fredrickson & Branigan, 2005). Emotions are also suggested as exerting sweeping influence on behaviour (Koole, 2009).

3. *Positive and negative emotion*: Fredrickson (2003) highlights the lack of differentiation between positive and negative emotion. This idea is developed further by other authors who suggest that there is positive and negative affect in emotion (Gross & Thompson, 2007), and that they can co-exist (Zembylas, 2008).

4. *Evolution*: Fredrickson (2003), for example, refers to evolutionary reasons for negative emotion (fight or flight) and that it is possible that the body is predisposed to particular emotions in certain circumstances.

5. *Cognition and motivation*: More recent research suggests that some emotions, such as fear, are easier to trigger, whilst others require more cognition (Brown & Brown, 2013), with several authors suggesting that emotion and cognition are inseparable (Baker, 2007; Le Doux, 1991).

6. *Fast and slow thinking*: That there are two different mental processes involved that work at different speeds (Kahneman, 2011). This accords with earlier thinking that emotions allow us to begin to deal with fundamental life-tasks, without elaborate planning (Ekman, 1992).

These areas are not mutually exclusive, for example, Howard (2006) suggests that emotions help us to quickly assess what is going on in our social and physical environment, informing reactions that promote survival and well-being. This neatly combines thinking on evolution and fast and slow thinking. Consequently, what we tend to see in the literature are more practically rooted definitions that combine elements from each of these areas. For example, Fredrickson and Cohn (2008), who refer to emotions as being about some personally meaningful circumstance, which are typically short lived, and occupy the foreground of consciousness. These more limited definitions may be valuable to coaching by providing aspects of focus for the coach. Hence they direct the coach towards the conscious emotions, physiological changes or cognitive impacts that their clients have experienced. These can be areas that may provide valuable insight for the client. Bringing painful emotions into conscious awareness is proposed to be an important aspect of the coaching process (Cox, 2013). Despite the lack of definition coaches can focus on each of the six areas described above to help clients' sense making. They can discuss the degree to which the client reaction is conscious or unconscious and the physical reactions and behaviour cycle that may often be the result of a valuing process that labels the event as positive or negative.

Insight can also be gained from evaluating the degree to which emotions are the result of fast (automatic) or slow thinking and relating this to evolutionary processes to help gain understanding.

THE MEMORY PROBLEM

It has been suggested that using a *'suppression'* regulatory strategy creates a higher cognitive load which may result in poorer recall of an emotional event. Research by Richards and Gross (2000) supported this, finding that events subject to strong emotional regulation are more poorly recalled some weeks later. This means that a client wanting to discuss a past emotional event with a coach may struggle to fully recall the situation, so the coach may gain an incomplete account of what was happening for the client at the time. This brings the paradoxical situation that the strongest emotional events that a client may want to unravel and discuss, may be subject to the poorest recall containing reduced descriptive details that necessarily limits the deconstruction and analysis that is possible in the subsequent coaching interaction. Both coach and client are effectively working with partial information.

Furthermore, it is suggested that what people remember is related to their personal commitment to a remembered event, and that they rationalise what they remember by modifying it into something with which they feel comfortable (Foster, 2009). Foster contends that when we remember past episodes, some elements are easily recalled whereas others may be re-constructed rather than reproduced. Hassabis and Maguire assert that 'well-known memory errors and inconsistencies, such as misattribution provide further tacit evidence for constructivist views of episodic memory' (2007, p.300).

So there is a danger that personal constructivism completes imperfect memories in order to make sense of the fragments that are contained in memory. This reconstruction may rely on autobiographical self-knowledge which leads to plausible but inaccurate recollection of past experiences (Koriat et al., 2000). The client who gives a very different account of an altercation with a colleague, to the briefing the coach received from HR, may be demonstrating a genuine recall issue, rather than lack of awareness or concealment.

Of further concern is that when our memories are put to the test, individuals do not discriminate well between true events and reconstructions used to make sense of the event (Henriksen & Kaplan, 2003; Loftus & Ketcham, 1996). It is also suggested that people may bring fragments of memory together and actually construct rather than re-construct a memory (George, 2013; Gross, 2002). There are further suggestions that memories are normalised and that questions associated with memory are answered with a level of generality (Koriat et al., 2000) which may reduce their intensity and quality.

These findings, plus the potential impact of suppression strategies suggest the most stressful and cognitively demanding events may be those remembered with least saliency so may with time become very 'forgettable' and as a result what might be considered critical incidents, may not be brought to the coaching space at all. Barrett (2004) proposes that if we want to know something about how a person is feeling, we should ask. Yet the memory problem suggests asking may be a very poor reflection of the true emotion at the time. Cox (2013) draws attention to how coaches employ this 'episodic memory recall' with such tools as visioning and suggests this construction of events should not present an issue as it can be a 'powerful way of embodying past experience and bringing it into the session, thus enabling any obvious bias or internal inconsistency to be articulated and challenged' (p.21). In addition, when we ask clients to recall and discuss an event 'the event does not come back to the client as it was experienced, it comes to the client afresh, with new insights' (Cox, 2013, p.21). This could be negative or positive for the coaching interaction. While the memory may have elements that have been reconstructed and, therefore, are not reflective of the event at the time, it may also include reflection that brings new insights. In either case, the coaching is working not with a contemporary record, but with a post-reality construction.

Coaches, therefore, need to be mindful of the limitations of memory in three ways. Firstly during strongly emotional events, recall and recollection may be impaired resulting in more limited detail of the event when subsequently recounted to a coach. Secondly, the events that are brought to coaching may not be those that were most salient at the time as the high emotion during the event may have reduced the scale of the event in memory. Thirdly, the emotion itself may be re-constructed with new meaning making following the event that was not evident at the time (Loftus, 1997). The coach should, therefore, be circumspect about dwelling on single emotionally charged events and consider multiple events over a period of time to better inform client sense making. A client who is asked to continually analyse and discuss a single emotional event may become more entrenched in their view that the memory is complete and, therefore, less open to challenge and re-evaluation. Continued focus in the coaching interaction may, therefore, re-enforce an erroneous view the client may have of an emotionally charged event.

THE LANGUAGE PROBLEM

When conveying information about an emotional event the client construction will be affected by memory, but it will also be bound by the client cognitive frame. The meaning of words such as 'suffering' or 'sadness' may take on a very different conception depending on the personal 'frame' of the speaker. Frames are the mental structures and personal constructs that encode a feeling into language (Lakoff, 2004; Wine, 2008). The coach will similarly evoke their own frames in the questions that they ask and in decoding the words used by their client, creating the potential for significant misunderstanding. This may not manifest in terms of overt discussion but might inform how the conversation progresses. Coaches, therefore, need to be wary of how the use of language colours their work with a client. Clean Language (Tompkins & Lawley, 1997) tries to address this issue but may not be favoured by all coaches or clients. Coaches, therefore, need to be mindful of how emotions are conveyed in language. For example, the tendency to categorise emotions as either positive or negative can be an unjustified automatic response. Lazarus (2003) highlights that emotions often seen as positive, such as Hope, might also have a negative side, which equates to anxiety. Emotions are, therefore, experi-enced as complex phenomena that may not be adequately reflected through the use of existing words in a linear structure and some tools are now available to help clients articulate their felt experiences (Duffell & Lawton Smith, 2014).

In addition, the language used by the coach has the potential to influence the client and the subsequent interaction. Steel and Aronson (1995) demonstrated how a 'stereo-type threat' can affect performance on a task for ethnic minorities. The language used to introduce an ability assessment task was found to affect the ultimate results in line with general stereotypes. Participants effectively fulfilled the stereotypical label that they applied to themselves.

We can also refer to the Principle of Consistency (Yeung, 2011), when people hear themselves being described in a certain way, they may unconsciously seek ways to behave consistently with the description. Therefore, if a coach were to paraphrase an emotion as 'anxiety' it may cause the client to in some way adapt and behave in a way consistent with the description that has been introduced by the coach. So paraphrasing, or clarifying understanding with new words, may not be a helpful intervention and could impede development. Therefore, the coach needs to be aware of the implica-tions of language and be alert to maintain the role of investigation and challenge, of both themselves and the client.

Coaches, therefore, need to beware of the way they use language with the client descriptions of emotion. For example, a coach may conclude that a client is describing a situation that was 'frustrating' for the client, based upon the coaches' personal cate-gorisation of this emotion. This may not align with either the clients' categorisation or emotional description of how they felt. Self-confident clients may be quite happy to correct the coaches understanding, but there is a risk that the client adopts the coaches' 'label'. In either case, the subsequent coaching conversation will not be authentic to the clients' original emotional experience.

CONCLUSION

Emotions in the coaching context are often viewed in one of three ways by coaches. They might be seen as irrelevant to the organisational context or as an inconvenient attribute to be regulated and controlled. Both these seem limited strategies for the coaching relationship because emotions can be the source of a wealth of information that can inform both the client and the coach. It is clear that emotions arise when something of significance happens to the individual (Gross, 2002). We therefore con-tend that emotions are an important and valuable aspect that can provide information and be the focus for analysis that can inform and support effective coaching.

However, working with emotions in coaching remains problematic due to three key issues:

Firstly, while emotion as a subject is well studied, it suffers from practical and theoretical definitional issues. To address this potential problem we suggest working with six key areas that appear to be common to most definitions of emotion in order to avoid distraction by semantic concerns and build a shared understanding.

A second issue for coaches is that the emotion a person feels, at the time of an event, is very difficult to measure and may not be accurately recalled later because of the impact of an emotion regulation strategy or because of inaccuracies in memory. Memory of events may be limited by the cognitive overload at the time or be constructed to re-interpret experiences, after the event. This means that a coach may find the recall of the most significant events is limited or subsequently dismissed as less important than it was at the time. Coaches also need to be aware that they may be working with a re-construction of the event that is subject to both new information and to perceptual bias influenced by a number of processes. Coaches might, therefore, need to treat with caution the client narrative of emotional events. This may require an attitude of interested curiosity, rather than adopting the recollection as a matter of true record. Coaches can also try to avoid excessive focus on a single event that may otherwise cause further strengthening of the construction.

Lastly, emotions remain a very individual experience that is bound by the personal constructs and language of the individual. How far the coach can really appreciate the personal meaning making and semantic frame used by the client may have implications for how they work together. Coaches need to maintain awareness of how their own language and interpretations might influence emotions. The Clean Language approach deals with this explicitly but there may be ways for coaches to adopt some of the ideas without becoming 'Clean Coaches'. Awareness of their own language and a curiosity about what clients infer in their choice of words can go some way to avoiding assumptions of meaning. Coaches might therefore reflect on four key questions about their practice:

- How can I help the client see emotions as valuable and informative?
- How can I build a common understanding of the emotional experience with my client?
- What investigative strategies will help gain the maximum insight to minimise the memory problem?
- How might my own language be influencing our interactions?

Emotion and its associated processes can be very informative for both coaches and clients, however, further research is needed to support coaches who wish to work with emotions in coaching. Many potential impacts remain unexplored and while awareness and curiosity are valuable assets, coaches would benefit from further empirically based advice of how to address emotional aspects of coaching.

REFERENCES

Askew, S. & Carnell, E. (2011). *Transformative coaching: A learning theory for practice.* London: Institute of Education, University of London.

Bachkirova, T. & Cox, E. (2007). Coaching with emotion in organisations: Investigation of personal theories. *Leadership & Organization Development Journal*, 600–612.

Baker, R. (2007). *Emotional processing: Healing through feeling.* Oxford: Lion Hudson.

Bar-On, R. (2000). Emotional and social intelligence: Insights from the Emotional Quotient Inventory (EQ-i). In R. Bar-On & J.D.A. Parker (Eds.), *Handbook of emotional intelligence* (pp.363–388). San Francisco, CA: Jossey-Bass.

Barrett, L.F. (2004). Feelings or words? Understanding the content in self-report ratings of experienced emotion. *Journal of Personal Social Psychology*, 87(2), 266–281.

Beisser, A. (1970). The paradoxical theory of change. In J. Fagan & I.L. Shepard (Eds.), *Gestalt therapy now* (pp.70–80). California: Science and Behavior Books.

Carver, C.S. (2006). Approach, avoidance and the self-regulation of affect and action. *Motivation & Emotion*, 30, 105–110.

Chamberlain, L. & Broderick, A.J. (2007). The application of physiological observation methods to emotion research. *Qualitative Market Research: An International Journal*, 10(2), 199–216.

Cox, E. (2013). *Coaching understood.* London: Sage.

Cox, E. & Bachkirova, T. (2007). Coaching with emotion: How coaches deal with difficult emotional situations. *International Coaching Psychology Review*, 2(2), 178–189.

Cox, E. & Patrick, C (2012). Managing emotions at work: How coaching affects retail support workers' performance and motivation. *International Journal of Evidence Based Coaching & Mentoring, 10(2).*

Cremona, K. (2010). Coaching and emotions: An exploration of how coaches engage and think about emotion. *Coaching: An International Journal of Theory, Research and Practice*, 3(1), 46–59.

Duffell, P. & Lawton Smith, C. (2014). More than a feeling. *Coaching at Work*, 9(3), 33–36.

Ekman, P. (1992). An argument for basic emotions. *Cognition and Emotion*, 6(3), 169–200.

Foster, J.K. (2009). *Memory, a very short introduction.* Oxford: Oxford University Press.

Fredrickson, B.L. (2001). The role of positive emotions in positive psychology: The broaden and build theory of positive emotions. *American Psychology*, 56(3), 218–226.

Fredrickson, B.L. (2003). The value of positive emotions. *American Scientist*, 91(394), 330–335, July–August.

Fredrickson, B.L. & Branigan, C. (2005). Positive emotions broaden the scope of attention and thought-action repertoires. *Cognitive Emotion*, 19(3), 313–332.

Fredrickson, B.L. & Cohn, M.A. (2008). Positive emotions. In M. Lewis, J.M. Haviland-Jones & L.F. Barrett (Eds.), *Handbook of emotions* (pp.777–796). London: Guilford.

Frijda, N.H. (2008). The psychologists' point of view. In M. Lewis, J.M. Haviland-Jones & L.F. Barrett (Eds.), *Handbook of emotions* (2nd ed., pp.68–77). New York: Guilford.

Fusco, T., Palmer, S. & O'Riordan, S. (2011). Can coaching psychology help develop authentic leaders? Part two. *The Coaching Psychologist*,7(2), 127–131.

Garland, E.L., Fredrickson, B.L., King, A.M., Johnson, D.P., Meyer, P.S. & Penn, D.L. (2010). Upward spirals of positive emotions counter downward spirals of negativity: Insights from the broaden-and-build theory and affective neuroscience on the treatment of emotion dysfunctions and deficits in psychopathology. *Clinical Psychology Review*, 30, 849–864.

George, A. (2013). I could have sworn… Interview with psychologist Elizabeth Loftus. *New Scientist*, 219(2931), 28–29.

Goleman, D. (2013). *Focus: The hidden driver of excellence*. London: Bloomsbury Publishing.

Grant, A.M. (2012). An integrated model of goal-focused coaching: An evidence-based framework for teaching and practice. *International Coaching Psychology Review*, 7(2), 146–165.

Gross, J.J. (2002). Emotion regulation: Affective, cognitive, and social consequences. *Psychophysiology*, 39, 281–291.

Gyllensten, K., Palmer, S., Nilsson, E-K., Regner, A. M. & Frodi, A. (2010). Experiences of cognitive coaching: A qualitative study. *International Coaching Psychology Review*, 5(2), 98–108.

Hassabis, D. & Maguire, E. (2007). Deconstructing episodic memory with construction. *Trends in Cognitive Science*, 11(7), 299–306.

Henriksen, K. & Kaplan, H. (2003). Hindsight bias, outcome knowledge and adaptive learning. *BMJ Quality & Safety Health Care*, 12 (Supplement II), ii46–ii50.

Howard, A. (2006). Positive and negative emotional attractors and intentional change. *Journal of Management Development*, 25(7), 657–670.

International Coach Federation (ICF) (2002). *ICF Core Competencies*.

International Coach Federation (ICF) (2013). ICF Core Competencies. Accessed 16 April 2013, from: http://www.coachfederation.org/icfcredentials/core-competencies/

John, O.P. & Gross, J.J. (2004). Healthy and unhealthy emotion regulation: Personality processes, individual differences and life span development. *Journal of Personality*, 6(6), 1301–1334.

Kahneman, D. (2011). *Thinking, fast and slow*. London: Penguin.

Kegan, R. & Lahey, L. (2009). *Immunity to change*. Boston: Harvard Business Press.

Kleinginna, P.R. & Kleinginna, A.M. (1981). A categorised list of emotion definitions, with suggestions for a consensual definition. *Motivation and Emotion*, 5(4), 345–379.

Koole, S.L. (2009). The psychology of emotion regulation: An integrative review. *Cognition & Emotion*, 23(1), 4–41.

Koriat, A., Goldsmith, M. & Pansky, A. (2000). Toward a psychology of memory accuracy. *Annual Review of Psychology*, 51, 481–537.

Lakoff, G. (2004). *Don't think of an elephant*. White River Junction, VT: Chelsea Green.

Lazarus, R. (2003). Does the positive psychology movement have legs? *Psychological Inquiry*, 14(2), 93–109.

Le Doux, J.E. (1991). Emotion and the Limbic system concept. *Concepts in Neuroscience*, 2, 169–199.

Le Doux, J.E. (1998). *The emotional brain*. London: Phoenix, Orion Publishing Group.

Loftus, E.F. (1997). Creating false memories. *Scientific American*, 277(3), 70–75.

Loftus, E. & Ketcham, K (1996). *The myth of repressed memory, false memories and allegations of sexual abuse*. New York: St. Martin's Griffin.

Mauss, I.B. & Robinson, M.D. (2011). Measures of emotion: A review. *Cognitive Emotion*, 23(2), 209–237.

Patrick, C. (2004). *Coaching: Should we enquire into emotional aspects of the client's experience?* Oxford Brookes University: MA Thesis.

Plutchik, R. (2001). The nature of emotions. *American Scientist*, 89, 344–350.

Richards, J.M. & Gross, J.J. (2000). Emotion regulation and memory: The cognitive cost of keeping one's cool. *Journal of Personality and Social Psychology*, 79(3), 410–424.

Steele, C.M. & Aronson, J (1995). Stereotype threat and the intellectual test performance of African Americans. *Journal of Personality and Social Psychology*, 69(5), 787–789.

Thompson, R.A. (2011). Methods and measures in developmental emotions research: Some assembly required. *Journal of Experimental Child Psychology*, 110, 275–285.

Tompkins, P. & Lawley, J. (1997). Less is more… the art of clean language. *Rapport: The Magazine for NLP Professionals*, 35, 36–40.

Wine, L. (2008). Towards a deeper understanding of framing, footing and alignment. *The Forum*, 8(2).

Yeung, R. (2011). *I is for Influence: The new science of persuasion*. London: Macmillan.

Zembylas, M. (2008). Adult learners' emotions in online learning. *Distance Education*, 29(1), 71–87.

Section 5
Workplace Coaching

Introduction

David Tee & Jonathan Passmore

Coaching psychology, as with psychology in general, lacks a grand unifying theory. Similarly, there is no consistently used or defined set of terms and, occasionally, it seems there is an assumed understanding as to the meaning of particular phrases or labels. 'Workplace coaching' may be such an example. In our introduction to Section 4, we were able to share various definitions of 'health coaching'. It may be that coaching within an organisational context dominates the research and practice fields to such an extent that writers do not feel a need to define workplace coaching in the same way they do health coaching, educational coaching or other context-specified fields.

An opportunistic glance in the index of coaching and coaching psychology text-books either finds the term 'workplace' absent or followed by the phrase 'See also', with pointers to executive coaching, leadership coaching and other terms that include anything related to organisational life. It is this extant, broader conceptualising of the term that we used in determining papers to include in this section. This is not to suggest that we do not recognise the diversity of organisational settings in which a coach may work. To offer one example, are the considerations of coaches working with C-level executives in multinational organisations (Wasylyshyn, 2020) the same as those working with the bosses of small family owned businesses (Shams & Lane, 2020)?

There are instances where workplace coaching has been more narrowly defined. Bozer and Jones (2018, p. 342) offer the following definition:

"...coaching provided to all levels of employees by external or internal coaching practitioners who do not have formal supervisory authority over the coachee."

This definition has utility in differentiating one approach to coaching in organisational settings, where the coach holds no position of formal authority over the client, against coaching where it is a line manager using a coaching approach when working

Coaching Practiced, First Edition. Edited by David Tee and Jonathan Passmore.
© 2022 John Wiley & Sons Ltd. Published 2022 by John Wiley & Sons Ltd.
DOI: 10.1002/9781119835714.s05

with an employee (see Alford & Cantrell, 2018; Onyemah, 2009). This second approach has been labelled by Joo et al. (2012) as manager-as-coach (or MAC). Workplace coaching, with a coach detached from the client's chain of command and therefore more overtly neutral, might more readily allow the development of coach-client trust and the creation of a 'safe' coaching space (Jones et al., 2018).

However, the term 'workplace coaching' may be problematic in assuming a narrow use of the term 'work' – that is, activity carried out as part of paid employment. Kinder et al. (2013) point to examples of work, including unpaid or voluntary roles, adult students on university courses and the effort exerted by an unemployed person in seeking a job. This broader recognition may even be extended to include housework or care for vulnerable family members. Warr (2013) therefore provides the following definition of work:

> "…an activity with a purpose beyond enjoyment of the activity itself. It can be arduous and / or tedious, involving effort and persistence beyond the point at which it is pleasurable. The term connotes difficulty and a need to labour or exert oneself against the environment; the objective is to achieve something that is physically and / or psychologically difficult."
>
> (p. 3)

Adopting Warr's description of work, we propose to build upon Bozer and Jones's (2018) definition, identifying workplace coaching as 'coaching where the coach holds no formal position of authority over the client and with a primary focus on client roles and activities which hold a purpose beyond enjoyment of the activity itself'. This definition accommodates coaching focused upon paid employment, university study, unpaid internships and job-seeking efforts by unemployed coaching clients.

We hope this redefining of the term may lend itself to situating individual studies within a clearer conceptualisation, leading to a building of a shared research vocabulary, cross-researcher harmonisation on the boundaries of current evidence and understanding and, from that, a more consistent focus on key variables and constructs of interest in advancing the practice of and benefits from workplace coaching.

For the opening paper in this section, Mary Watts and Sarah Corrie detail the LLG (Lead, Learn and Grow) model, intended for leadership coaching and with its theoretical roots in transformational leadership, leader-member exchange theory and the work of Grayson and Speckhart (2006) on leader-follower relationships. The model was 'road tested' at a coaching psychology conference, with the thoughts as to how it could be applied in practice detailed within the paper.

Vicky Ellam-Dyson and Stephen Palmer's 'Leadership Coaching? No thanks, I'm not worthy' paper is interesting not least because it was borne out of a research project, but one for which half the targeted participants declined the opportunity to receive funded executive coaching. The purpose of the paper evolved into exploring how we may encourage individuals with conditional self-acceptance to engage in coaching. Suggestions for practice concerning the types of goals most likely to be effective and how to work with clients that may have deep seated psychological issues are provided.

A team coaching model, derived from principles of CBC, is detailed in the third paper for this section. Ulrika Hultgren and colleagues propose a technique for adapting an individual coaching CBC model (PRACTICE) to use for team work specifically intended to increase wellbeing. The authors present a three-session approach, detailing the key elements to be covered within each session so that a structured approach to problem-solving can be provided.

Finally, how might we as coaching psychologists work with a client that has experienced a loss of sense of self? In Tessa Dodwell's paper, the notion of what is understood by the term self is variously considered, before key considerations for engaging in this client work are detailed: the trigger for this lost sense of self, the client's ego development, the client's understanding of self-construction and the coach approach. A case study concerning a partner in a law firm is helpfully provided to illustrate how these considerations may be applied to client work.

REFERENCES

Alford, C., & Cantrell, K. (2018). Using coaching skills to lead. *Journal of Practical Consulting, 6*(1), 102–107.

Bozer, G., & Jones, R. J. (2018). Understanding the factors that determine workplace coaching effectiveness: A systematic literature review. *European Journal of Work and Organizational Psychology, 27*(3), 342–361. https://doi.org/doi.org/10.1080/1359432X.2018.1446946

Grayson, D. & Speckhart, R. (2006). The Leader-Follower Relationship. Leadership Advance Online, *VI*, 1–6. Retrieved from: https://www.regent.edu/acad/global/publications/lao/issue_6/pdf/grayson_speckhart.pdf

Jones, R. J., Woods, S. A., & Zhou, Y. (2018). Boundary conditions of workplace coaching outcomes. *Journal of Managerial Psychology, 33*(7/8), 475–496. https://doi.org/doi.org/10.1108/JMP-11-2017-0390

Joo, B., Sushko, J., & McLean, G. (2012). Multiple faces of coaching. *Organization Development Journal, 30*(1). 19–38

Kinder, A., Nind, K., Aitchison, D., & Farrell, E. (2013). Counselling and Personal Development. In: R. Lewis, & L. Zibarras (Eds.), *Work and Occupational Psychology: Integrating Theory and Practice*. SAGE Publications Ltd.

Onyemah, V. (2009). The effects of coaching on sales peoples' attitudes and behaviors – A contingency approach. *European Journal of Marketing, 43*(7/8), 938–960. https://doi.org/doi.org/10.1108/03090560910961461

Shams, M., & Lane, D. (2020). Team coaching and family business. *The Coaching Psychologist, 16*(1), 25–33.

Warr, P. (2013). *Work, Happiness and Unhappiness*. Lawrence Erlbaum Associates, Inc.

Wasylyshyn, K. (2020). A road resisted: 'Fakers' in executive coaching and how to avoid wasting company resources on them. *The Coaching Psychologist, 16*(1), 34–40.

13 Growing the 'I' and the 'We' in Transformational Leadership: The LEAD, LEARN & GROW Model

Mary Watts & Sarah Corrie

Abstract

This paper presents the LEAD, LEARN & GROW Model of leadership development – an approach emerging from practice-based insights – and describes how the Model was received by coaching psychologists in the context of a workshop facilitated by the first author at the Annual Conference of the Special Group in Coaching Psychology (SGCP) in December 2012. Participants' reactions to the Model suggested that it had face validity and was a potentially useful framework for leadership coaching; thus, the idea for this article was born. In this article the authors describe both the model and the workshop in which it was explored and developed. Ideas and discussion emerging from the workshop participants have been incorporated into the article, which concludes with a series of questions offered as aids for further reflection and guidance in the application of the LEAD, LEARN & GROW Model.

Keywords

Leadership; transformational leadership; lead; learn;grow;

Original publication details: Watts, M., & Corrie, S. (2013, December). Growing the 'I' and the 'We' in transformational leadership: The LEAD, LEARN & GROW model. *The Coaching Psychologist, 9*(2), 86–99. Reproduced with permission of The British Psychological Society.

Leadership development is a popular area of coaching and arguably, few areas have received as much attention in the coaching and coaching psychology literatures. It has been observed that the 'case' for leadership coaching is compelling (Bond & Naughton, 2011); leadership skills are likely to prove critical for organisations' survival in a climate that is increasingly complex, unpredictable and competitive. As such, organisations increasingly require effective leaders at all levels (Clutterbuck, 2007; Jarvis, Lane & Fillery-Travis, 2006).

Leadership has been investigated from numerous perspectives. The academic and professional literatures comprise multiple theories, models and research studies that span leadership behaviour patterns (see Wasylshyn's, 2008, identification of remarkable, perilous and toxic behaviour patterns in business leaders); the reasons for which leaders seek coaching (Stern, 2004) and the effectiveness of leadership coaching (e.g. Dagley, 2006; de Haan & Duckworth, 2013) amongst others. There is also a growing literature on self-leadership which emphasises that the qualities of effective leadership can be usefully self-directed to facilitate the accomplishment of personal life and career goals (see, for example, Bryant & Kazan, 2013).

The LEAD, LEARN & GROW Model (LLG Model) is a recent contribution, inspired by existing leadership models, that offers a framework through which the activities of leadership can be better understood, and through which leaders — of all varieties and in all settings — can be assisted to develop their own and others' potential. The LLG Model was developed by the first author (Watts, 2012a), herself a coaching psychologist and senior leader, and depicts three areas of activity that her experience has shown to be significant to the culture and impact of leadership. As such, the LLG Model can be considered an example of 'practice-based evidence' (Barkham & Mellor-Clark, 2000) that was tested further through participants' reactions in the context of a workshop on leadership.

In this article, we provide a brief description of the LLG Model. We then give a brief outline of the process by which the LLG Model was communicated to delegates at the Annual Conference of the SGCP, in December 2012. We incorporate the ideas emerging from the group as an illustration of how the participants engaged with the LLG Model and how they used the workshop to assist their own leading, learning and growing. Finally, we provide some questions which can assist the personalising of the LLG Model to different professional contexts.

THE SCHOLASTIC FOUNDATION OF THE LEAD, LEARN & GROW MODEL

The LLG Model is informed by Transformational Leadership (e.g. Bass, 1985; Bass & Avolio, 1994) and Leader-Member Exchange (Graen & Uhl-Bien, 1995) theories. Although a comprehensive review of these theories is beyond the scope of this article, a brief review of their key principles provides a helpful orientation to the description of the LLG Model that follows.

Succinctly, in transformational leadership theory, transformational leaders are described as those who inspire their followers to shape their motives, aspirations, values and goals so that personal aspirations become aligned with the identity and vision of the organisation. This is in contrast to transactional leadership whereby leaders tend to shape the behaviour and motivation of their followers through systems of reward and punishment (Bass, 1985; Bass & Avolio, 1994). The relationship between transformational leadership and followers' attitudes, behaviours and performance has been well-documented (see, for example, Judge & Piccolo, 2004) and a variety of sources of influence have been implicated. These include relational identification, perceptions of trust and fairness, psychological empowerment and leader-member exchange (see Walumbwa & Hartnell, 2010; Yukl, 1998).

According to Leader-Member Exchange Theory (LMX; Graen & Uhl-Bien, 1995) those in leadership roles form unique relationships with each of their subordinates, and the quality of these leader-member exchanges influences subordinates' access to information and resources, level of responsibility and performance. LMX is concerned with how organisational effectiveness can be enhanced through creating positive interpersonal relationships between leader and follower, with high leader-member exchange relationships distinguishable by their strong reciprocal support and loyalty (Sparrowe & Liden, 1997). LMX has been associated with range of criteria concerning organisational effectiveness including employee performance, employee satisfaction and staff retention (Gerstner & Day, 1997).

A third perspective that has informed the development of the LLG Model is that of Grayson and Speckhart who have challenged the exalted role that leadership enjoys within contemporary society. Specifically, they argue that, '…the glory of being number one and the shame of being number two' (2006, p.1) which pervades both organisations and society more broadly has prevented adequate investigation of how to develop robust and capable *followers*. This, they propose, has had the unintended consequences of undermining organisational performance and encouraging individuals who are not best suited to leadership positions to strive for such roles. Moreover, the rapidly changing professional and economic climate in which organisations operate is forcing a re-examination of traditional beliefs about leadership (Grayson & Speck-hart, 2006). With developments in technology as well as changes in the structure of organisations, traditional notions of the designated leader as the source of knowledge, information and expertise are being challenged. The distinction between leaders and followers is being re-examined, with leadership and followership increasingly understood as intertwined, rather than dichotomous, roles (see Amar, 2001; Raelin, 2003).

Perspectives such as these invite fresh ideas on how to coach individuals in order to enhance their leadership potential and are consistent with the values underpinning the LLG Model. For example, at the heart of the LLG Model lies the intention to facilitate others in looking at, and questioning, their own values and beliefs about leadership roles, as well as their own leadership prac- tices. More specifically, the LLG Model is underpinned by the following beliefs:

1. Leadership and leadership coaching are for all, not just a select few. Learning how to nurture leadership potential in ourselves and in others can be both productive and enjoyable. (This is consistent with the notion that leadership and followership are intertwined concepts, that those in 'follower roles' exercise considerable influence on organisational effectiveness and that in the context of a specific project or task, there can be shifts in leadership as a function of who holds expertise in specific domains.)
2. Inspirational and transformational leadership can be used to bring hearts, minds and skills together in creative, humane and fun ways, in order to change and improve both large and small aspects of our world. (This is consistent with the principles and values underpinning Transformational Leadership and Leader-Member Exchange Theory.)
3. We need to broaden our collective understanding of leadership. After John Quincy Adams (quoted in *The Positivity Blog*, 2012), if your actions inspire others to dream more, learn more, do more and become more, then you are a leader. (This perhaps implies that traditional conceptualisations of leadership may need redefining if they are to prove fit for purpose in a rapidly changing world.)

DEVELOPING ENHANCING LEADERSHIP POTENTIAL: AN INTRODUCTION TO THE LEAD, LEARN & GROW MODEL

Drawing on the scholastic foundations described above, the LLG Model is now described and presented diagrammatically in Figure 1.

At the heart of the model lie two critical constituents of leadership – the 'I' and the 'We'. The 'I' refers to the designated leader and the 'We' the individuals, team or teams whom it is intended that the leader leads. The 'I' and 'We' are in a symbiotic relationship and impact in positive or less positive ways on the culture and outcomes within an organisation. The Model also depicts the important ideal that 'I' and 'We', separately and together, are involved in leading, learning and growing. The inter-relationship of these three elements impacts significantly on the style and culture of leadership.

Encasing the 'I' and 'We' and the LEAD LEARN & GROW, are the Tracking, Hindsight and Evaluation circle. As leaders we must take responsibility for keeping track of the impact of our actions, engaging in formal evaluation at appropriate times and also engaging in a more personal form of hindsight which often comes about after action. Reflection may occur in, and on, action. Hindsight is similar but will take account of our reflections, the tracking and the evaluation so that we can draw the various learnings together and take them forward in a planned and constructive way into new ventures. Regular and effective engagement in each of these is critical to effective and ethical leadership practice.

Figure 1 is unpacked further in Figures 2 and 3. These depict the 'I' and 'We' as each sitting on a stool. These stools, if strong and well-balanced, can effectively support both the 'I' and the 'We' as they engage in the leadership endeavour.

Figure 2 shows 'I', as a leader, sitting on a stool with three strong legs. There is a LEAD leg, a LEARN leg and a GROW leg as depicted by the middle circle in the LLG Model (Figure 1). Holding the legs firmly in place so that they don't collapse under the weight of the 'I' are the three strong bars of Tracking, Hindsight and Evaluation, the outer circle of Figure 1. As the weight of leadership activity increases these three bars become increasingly important.

Starting with the 'I' LEAD leg, attention is drawn to the place of inspiration in leadership. This may come directly from the leader, or the leader may facilitate others in being inspirational – ideally both will occur in the context of transformational leadership (see Bass & Avolio, 1994). However, generating a trusting environment in which people are willing and feel safe to contribute their ideas and actions requires more than just inspiration. It is suggested that what is required is a leader who can listen to others and to themselves; who can empathise with, appreciate and empower others, and who can also work to develop strengths in themselves and others.

Figure 1   *The LEAD, LEARN & GROW Model.*

The 'I' LEARN leg draws attention to the fact that even as a leader there is much to be learnt on an on-going basis, that learning is never complete and there must be a genuine interest and belief in the value of that learning in order for it to be personalised and effectively applied to the practice of leadership.

'I' LEAD and 'I' LEARN together contribute to the development of the third leg of leadership which is 'I' GROW. This can be taken literally in the sense that if I lead and I learn, I also have the opportunity to grow as a person and to facilitate the growth of those I lead. However, the 'I' GROW 'leg' goes beyond this and draws upon the GROW model used in coaching (Whitmore, 2002). Leadership, in whatever context and at whatever level, gives rise to many issues. Many of these issues can be made transparent and openly debated if the multiplicity of goals, shared and personal realities and possible ways forward are identified and creatively debated.

Figure 3 is very similar to Figure 2 but depicts the 'We' as supported by a three-legged stool again with the supportive struts

of Tracking, Hindsight and Evaluation. The 'We' LEAD leg demonstrates that leadership is not just down to the designated leader – the Listening, Empathising, Appreciating and Developing that are so important for the leader are also important to the wider team or organisation. Likewise, with the 'We' LEARN and the 'We' GROW legs, those elements that apply to the leader apply also to the wider team and transformational change is likely to come about when the **'I'** and 'We' evolve mutually and collaboratively.

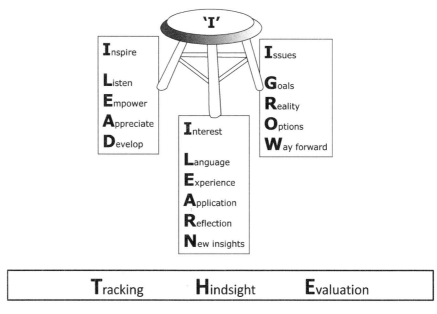

Figure 2   *The 'I Stool in the LEAD, LEARN & GROW Model.*

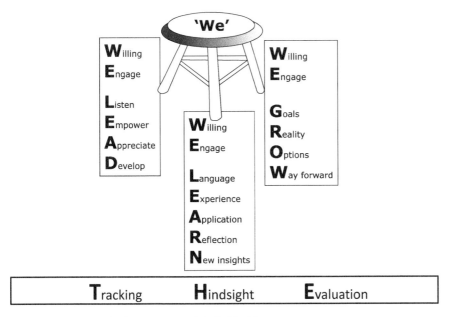

Willing
Engage
Listen
Empower
Appreciate
Develop

Willing
Engage
Language
Experience
Application
Reflection
New insights

Willing
Engage
Goals
Reality
Options
Way forward

Tracking   **H**indsight   **E**valuation

Figure 3   *The We Stool in the LEAD, LEARN & GROW Model.*

INTRODUCING THE LEAD, LEARN & GROW MODEL IN A WORKSHOP CONTEXT

The context for the workshop was a master class on leadership for the annual conference of the SGCP in 2012. This was delivered by the first author. The second author was a participant and her personal reflections and applications of the model, as well as subsequent collaboration, have contributed much to this paper. The workshop represented an opportunity to test whether the model had face validity with a wider audience of practitioners delivering coaching interventions and also to provide partic-ipants with an opportunity to reflect upon their own Leading, Learning and Growing. The conference abstract described the workshop as follows:

'Leadership is for all, not just a select few. Learning how to 'grow' leadership both in our-selves and in others can be fun and productive. This workshop focuses on how we can do this. The first part builds the foundation for this using the LLG Model, drawing particular attention to the 'I' – 'We' dynamics. The second part builds on this by integrating personal insights, psychological theory and research with the model and the wider application of this in multiple contexts. The workshop is highly interactive and contains a number of recurring themes but one of the key messages is that although there is considerable work to be done in the leadership area, coaching psychologists are in an ideal position to use their knowledge and skills, in a collaborative manner, to bring about change'

(Watts 2012b).

Prospective participants were advised that all that was necessary to bring to the workshop was an open, flexible and curious mind, a willingness to share ideas and to listen to the ideas of others, and a desire to learn. This workshop description attracted 20 participants, equally divided between men and women. The majority of the participants were coaching psychologists but at least one was a non-psychologist member of the SGCP who brought with her considerable leadership coaching experience. The diverse experiences of the participant group added richness to the discussions and shared learning experience. The workshop was designed to be collaborative with participants working together to generate visionary approaches to leadership and leadership development relevant to their own personal and professional contexts.

The workshop was delivered in two distinct but inter-related parts, as follows:

In Part 1, the LLG Model was presented and discussed in detail. The underlying vision of leadership as a capability that we all need to acquire was emphasised. It was also proposed that before we can lead others we must know what it means to lead ourselves, to take responsibility for our learning and have the skills and confidence to do this. Leadership and learning, it was suggested, go hand in hand and leadership without development produces stasis.

Part 2 was a natural progression from Part 1, emphasising implementation of the model and translating the underlying vision into a workable reality. Specifically, participants were encouraged to draw upon their own experience and knowledge to think creatively about the potential application of the model to enhancing leadership in different domains such as leadership coaching; current theory and research; and ideas for new research to enhance practice. Participants worked in small groups to generate ideas and recorded key points for presentation to the whole group for the purposes of generating discussion and ideas that could be usefully taken away from the workshop to assist further reflection.

DEVELOPING APPROACHES TO LEADERSHIP USING THE LEAD, LEARN & GROW MODEL: IDEAS GENERATED IN A WORKSHOP SETTING

The purpose of the workshop was to present the model as a particular approach that participants could usefully reflect upon, critique and incorporate into their own professional practice. Critiquing the model was particularly encouraged as a means of enabling deep thought and reflective practice. Participants were encouraged to link their critiques as closely as possible with personal experiences, reading and research evidence. A second aim was to share an aspiration for coaching psychology as taking a visionary outlook in respect of leadership coaching.

Participants engaged actively with these aims, and numerous points for discussion arose as they considered their own experiences and practice through the lens of the LLG Model. For example, the alignment of different perspectives and perceptions was identified as one of the major challenges of leadership. Examining such differences through the 'I' LEARN and 'We' LEARN 'legs' of the stools generated discussion about how diverse perspectives might be capitalised upon, as well as the critical importance of ascertaining understanding, perception and interpretation.

Whilst the 'We' stool depicts willing engagement, participants also considered how there can sometimes be a disjuncture between the 'I' and the 'We' (that is, between the leader and those whom it is intended that he or she leads). This may lead to a complete leadership breakdown. At the same time, using Figures 4, 5 and 6, participants discussed how the notion of willing engagement does not require total alignment in thinking. The 'I' and 'We' may have totally disconnected, partially aligned or totally aligned thinking; it is not possible to make a blanket statement about which is best. There will be occasions when discon-

nected thinking is inevitable and when careful listening, empathising, sharing of insights and experience will be critical to enabling new goals and options to emerge. Sometimes thinking will be partially aligned and an element of shared understanding may make it easier and safer to tackle those areas of difference that are slowing progress and mutual aspirations and actions. Totally aligned thinking as shown in Figure 5 may at first appear a good thing (as, for example, might be the case in a surgical team where agreement about the procedures to be followed during an operation is critical to success). However, there are times when total alignment can stultify thinking and action and when the team would benefit from the views of an 'outsider'.

Figure 4 *Disconnected Thinking.*

Figure 5 *Partially Aligned Thinking.*

Figure 6 *Totally Aligned Thinking.*

Discussion about the contexts in which leadership coaching can play a significant role led to a consideration of the ideas represented in Figures 7, 8 and 9.

Figure 7 was used to depict a situation where a leader and his or her team are starting out in a new relationship. They are starting from a neutral position that entails good enough functioning that has the potential to be much better or worse. The arrows showed how the leader has the capacity to impact the wider team and vice versa but that nothing is changing. The leadership is neither leading to an improved situation nor deterioration. There is stasis.

Using Figure 8, the participants discussed a negative model of interdependence. The impact of the leader is to cause the 'We' (team), to deteriorate in their functioning. A negative trend has started which impacts the leader who also deteriorates in his or her functioning. If not arrested this is likely to be the start of a negative spiral. The critical question is how can this be arrested and reversed – or better still avoided in the first place. One suggestion was the active application of the LLG Model, supported by a coaching psychologist or coach. Figure 9 shows the application of the LLG Model as starting with the leader but being applied to the wider team. This triggers a positive trend, improving the functioning of the leader and the team.

Participants examined how thoughtful and skilled coaching could be used to reverse negative trends and to promote positive relations and actions, and the LLG Model was identified as providing a useful conceptual framework for achieving this. For example, very simple measures such as teaching core listening skills and the capacity to appreciate others were recognised as an initial point of entry into creating change. Learning to reflect and entertain new ideas and insights can follow, as can learning to engage with others in developing goals and identifying possible ways of achieving these. It is often hard to accept that our own reality is just that – our own and not that of others. As Kelly (1955) observed, we all construct a complex web of world views which may be difficult to understand and even more difficult to change. It is the multiplicity of differing views that can be both the greatest of assets and the greatest of hindrances in transformational leadership.

The 'I' LEARN leg speaks to the need in leaders to have a genuine interest in learning, and an appreciation of the importance of language, experience, the application of that experience, reflection and insights. We tend to assume that if we speak the same language, we understand the other and what is meant by his or her words. We overlook the subtlety of language, the cultural differences in its use, the nonverbal language that we all use and the vast complexity of communicating effectively with others. We often misunderstand others and they us, leading at best to unplanned or ineffective actions and very often to ill-feeling. Equally problematic is when we misunderstand ourselves – our internal dialogue of thoughts, feelings and behaviours. Language, in its various shapes and forms, is never, therefore, to be taken for granted. Equally, we may have vast amounts of experience but if we never learn from it and find

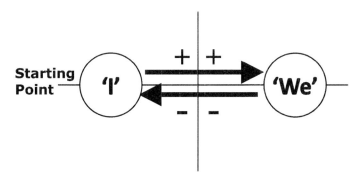

Figure 7   *Static - Model of interdependence between the I and 'We' in leadership.*

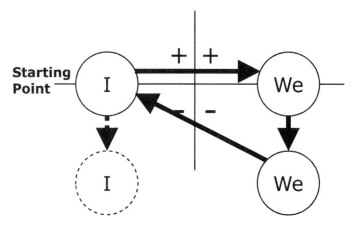

Figure 8 *Negative – Model of interdependence between the 'I' and 'We' in leadership.*

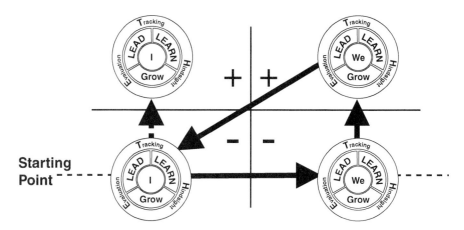

Figure 9 *Positive – Model of interdependence between the 'I' and 'We' in leadership: Applying the LEAD, LEARN & GROW Model.*

ourselves locked in a cycle of repetitive application, it is as though we have only one, perhaps unproductive experience. Personal reflections and insights are critical to transforming our experience and the application of this in creative and transformative ways (Kelly, 1970; Jarvis, 2006, 2012a; 2012b; 2012c; Watts 2012c). Equally, the 'I' LEAD and 'I' LEARN work together – listening to and appreciating others elaborates a leader's experience and reflections facilitating 'I' GROW.

Each leg of the stool has an important part to play in supporting the development and actions of the transformational leader. Over-emphasis of one at the expense of the others will lead to a stool with unbalanced legs. Attention has already been drawn to the three struts that hold the legs together – the Tracking, Hindsight and Evaluation struts. It was noted by the participants that a leader may choose not to strengthen all three legs of the LLG Model at the same time; it may be preferable to focus on developing the team (the We) or one or other of the legs specifically. Equally in a coaching contract, discerning decisions will need to be made about which leg or legs to prioritise, for how long and for what reasons.

HOW THE LLG MODEL CAN BE USED IN COACHING PRACTICE

The LLG Model generated considerable interest and enthusiasm. Feedback from the participants indicated that it was deemed relevant to their needs as coaching psychologists, could be creatively and flexibly applied to enhance leadership potential (in self and in coachees), and could be personalised through an integration with participants' own knowledge and experience.

The LLG Model is not necessarily applicable to all leadership contexts. Rather, it is offered as a framework that can enable individuals, teams, and organisations (as well as those who coach them) to consider the essentially relational nature of leadership, and the kinds of learning, leading and growing that may be required to flourish and enable others to flourish in any given setting. Within a coaching contract, the LLG Model can be used as vehicle through which some of the core concepts of transformational leadership can be explored, specific manifestations of the leader-member exchange identified, and particular areas of strength and need explored. For example, it may be that a coachee is skilled in creating a context in which members of the team deem it safe to contribute innovative ideas (the LEAD leg) and remaining open to diverse perspectives (the LEARN leg), but experiences discomfort at the idea of growing in understanding through drawing on the expertise of members of the team (the GROW leg). Identifying the 'I' GROW leg as a source of development can then enable coach and coachee to consider interventions that serve to strengthen this aspect of leadership behaviour. This might include examining potentially unhelpful cognitions about the leader needing to be the primary, or even sole, source of information and expertise.

In contrast to management which essentially entails working within defined, existing parameters, Stokes and Jolly (2010) propose that leadership focuses primarily on what is 'not known' – that is, the capacity to anticipate what will be necessary to function effectively in the future. They make the case that leadership is more concerned with people and relationships than with tasks and procedure, and that effective leadership requires a shift of mindset from one of controlling events to one of enabling others. It is precisely this change of perspective for which they propose that executive coaching is often sought. Equally, the capacity of leaders to inspire and empower – and to see this capacity as a focus of coaching interventions - was identified as vital in our current professional, social and economic climate, and standing in stark contrast to leaders engaging in defensive practices (such as a failure to develop their staff) due to a fear of being undermined and surpassed.

The discussions over the course of the master class generated much creative thinking and many useful questions which enabled participants (and indeed the authors themselves) to refine their understanding of how the LLG Model might be usefully applied in a variety of leadership contexts. Three messages appeared to have been particularly impactful; namely that: (1) leadership is for everyone; (2) individuals are not necessarily born knowing how to lead, it is a skill that can be acquired; and (3) before we can lead others we need to learn what it means to lead ourselves. From these three overarching themes a series of additional questions emerged which are included here in the hope that they might enable reflection and experimentation in a variety of leadership contexts:

1. What are the leadership contexts in which it is preferable to have alignment of the 'I' and the 'We' and in which is it preferable to embrace divergence?
2. What drives particular patterns and styles of leadership behaviour in a particular organisation, at a given point in time? How can identifying these drivers enable a more effective intervention strategy in the context of leadership coaching?
3. Who and what makes a good leader?
4. What kinds of leading, learning and growing are most associated with ineffective, moderately effectively and highly effective leaders?
5. Who represents the 'We' in the context of any leadership coaching contract? How many others are impacting the I'—'We' relationship?
6. How does the LLG Model apply to models of collective leadership, and how does it apply in challenging situations where very often the 'We' is wanting an individual to 'step out front' and take charge?

At the heart of the LLG Model lies the intention to create a forum, with some visual and conceptual prompts, that can facilitate others in looking at, and questioning, their own coaching and leadership practices. It is hoped that this might encourage and enable individuals, teams, and wider systems to think about the organisations in which they live and work through fresh eyes. This hope appeared to have been realised through the way in which the participants engaged with the workshop.

ACKNOWLEDGEMENTS

Ideas and discussion emerging from the workshop participants have been incorporated within the article and thanks go to them, both for their attendance and for their lively and creative participation. Particular thanks go to Peter Savage, who has corresponded with the authors after the workshop and provided suggestions that have helped shape the article. Special thanks go also to Gary Herd for producing such clear visual depictions of the LLG Model based on the first author's drawings.

REFERENCES

Adams, J.Q. (2012). Quoted in *The Positivity Blog: 25 great quotes on leadership*. Accessed 24 July 2013, from: www.positivityblog.com (produced by Henrik Edberg).

Amar, A.D. (2001). *Managing knowledge workers: Unleashing innovation and productivity*. Westport, CT: Quorum Books.

Barkham, M. & Mellor-Clark, J. (2000). Rigour and relevance: The role of practice-based evidence in the psychological therapies. In N. Rowland & S. Goss (Eds.), *Evidence-based counselling and psychological therapies: Research and applications* (pp.127-142). London: Routledge.

Bass, B.M. (1985). *Leadership and performance beyond expectations*. New York: Academic Press.

Bass, B.M. & Avolio, BJ. (1994). *Transformational leadership: Improving organizational effectiveness*. Thousand Oaks, CA: Sage.

Bryant, A. & Kazan, A. (2013). *Self leadership: How to become a more successful, efficient, and effective leader from the inside out*. New York: McGraw-Hill.

Bond, A.S. & Naughton, N. (2011). The role of coaching in managing leadership transitions. *International Coaching Psychology Review, 6*(2),165-179.

Clutterbuck, D. (2007). *Coaching the team at work*. London: Nicholas Brealey.

Dagley, G. (2006). Human resource professionals' perceptions of executive coaching: Efficacy, benefits, and return on investment. *International Coaching Psychology Review, 1*, 34-45.

De Haan, E. & Duckworth, A. (2013). Signalling a new trend in executive coaching outcome research. *International Coaching Psychology Review, 8*(1),6-19.

Gerstner, C.R. & Day, D.V. (1997). Meta-analytic review of leader-member exchange theory: Correlates and construct issues. *Journal of Applied Psychology, 82*, 827-844.

Graen, G.B. & Uhl-Bien, M. (1995). Relationship-based approach to leadership: Development of leader-member exchange (LMX) theory of leadership over 25 years: Applying a multi-level multi-domain perspective. *Leadership Quarterly, 6*, 219-247.

Grayson, D. & Speckhart, R. (2006). The leader-follower relationship: Practitioner observations. *Leadership Advance Online, VI*, 1-4.

Jarvis, J., Lane, D.A. & Fillery-Travis, A. (2006). *The case for coaching: Making evidence-based decisions on coaching*. London: Chartered Institute of Personnel and Development.

Jarvis, P. (2006). *Towards a comprehensive theory of human learning*. Abingdon, Oxon: Routledge.

Jarvis, P. (2012a). Introduction: Human learning. In P. Jarvis & M.H. Watts (Eds.), *The Routledge international handbook of learning* (pp.1-4). Abingdon, Oxon: Routledge.

Jarvis, P. (2012b). Non-learning. In P. Jarvis & M.H. Watts (Eds.), *The Routledge international handbook of learning* (pp.94-99). Abingdon, Oxon: Rout-ledge.

Jarvis, P. (2012c). Adult learning: Andragogy versus pedagogy or from pedagogy to andragogy. In P. Jarvis & M.H. Watts (Eds.), *The Routledge international handbook of learning* (pp.134-143). Abingdon, Oxon: Routledge.

Judge, TA. & Piccolo, R.F. (2004). Transformational and transactional leadership: A meta-analytic test of their relative validity. *Journal of Applied Psychology, 89*, 755-768.

Kelly, GA. (1955). *The psychology of personal constructs, Vols 1 and 2*. New York: W.W. Norton.

Kelly, GA. (1970). A brief introduction to personal construct psychology. In D. Bannister (Ed.), *Perspectives in personal construct theory* (pp.1-30). London: Academic Press.

Raelin, J. (2003). *Creating leaderful organisations: How to bring out leadership in everyone*. San Francisco: Berrett-Koehler Publishers, Inc.

Sparrowe, R.T. & Liden, R.C. (1997). Process and structure in leader-member exchange. *Academy of Management Review, 22*, 522-552.

Stern, L.R. (2004). Executive coaching: A working definition. *Consulting Psychology Journal: Practice and Research, 56,* 154-162.

Stokes, J. & Jolly, R. (2010). Executive and leadership coaching. In E. Cox, T. Bachkirova & D. Clutterbuck (Eds.), *The complete handbook of coaching* (pp.245-256). London: Sage.

Walumbwa, F.O. & Hartnell, C.A. (2011). Understanding transformational leadership-employee performance links: The role of relational identification and self-efficacy. *Journal of Occupational and Organizational Psychology, 84,* 153-172.

Wasylshyn, K.M. (2008). Behind the door: Keeping business leaders focused on how they lead. *Consulting Psychology Journal: Practice and Research, 60,* 314-330.

Watts, M.H. (2012a). *Leadership seminar presented to counselling psychology doctoral students on 21 February 2012.* London: City University.

Watts, M.H. (2012b). *Growing the 'I' and the 'We' in Transformational Leadership: A vision for coaching psychology.* Birmingham: Masterclass presented at the British Psychological Society Special Group in Coaching Psychology Annual Conference, 6 December 2012.

The Coaching Psychologist, Vol. 9, No. 2, December 201399The Coaching Psychologist, Vol. 9, No. 2, December 201399 Watts, M.H. (2012c). Autism spectrum conditions & learning. In P. Jarvis & M.H. Watts (Eds.), *The Routledge international handbook of learning* (pp.298-308). Abingdon, Oxon: Routledge. *The Coaching Psychologist, Vol. 9, No. 2, December 201399The Coaching Psychologist, Vol. 9, No. 2, December 201399*

Whitmore, J. (2002). *Coaching for performance.* Boston, MA: Nicholas Brealey.

Yukl, G. (1998). *Leadership in organisations* (4th ed.). Englewood Cliff, NJ: Prentice Hall.

14 Leadership Coaching? No thanks, I'm not worthy

Vicky Ellam-Dyson & Stephen Palmer

Abstract

The question of what encourages or discourages individuals to be coached, or not, is an interesting one. Particularly when the coaching is being funded and it has been positioned as a useful tool to aid the transition to a more senior position. In a study intended to follow 41 executives through the coaching process almost half of the participants declined the opportunity to receive coaching. It is possible that this is related to avoidance behaviour. In previous research avoidance behaviours have been linked to maladaptive beliefs and demands, such as low self-worth/acceptance, perfectionism and low frustration tolerance. Beliefs data for the coaching and no-coaching group were compared and it was found that those who chose not to be coached had significantly lower unconditional self-acceptance than those that were coached. Implications of the findings in terms of how they relate to potential leadership effectiveness are discussed, along with suggestions for organisations and coaches regarding how to overcome these issues. This paper also describes the pitfalls at various stages in the research which resulted in an unavoidable change of focus and alternative research questions, but also led to unexpected important findings.

Keywords

coaching, leadership transition, unconditional self-acceptance, contingencies of self-worth, frustration tolerance, perfectionism.

Original publication details: Ellam-Dyson, V., & Palmer, S. (2011, December). Leadership coaching? No thanks, I'm not worthy. *The Coaching Psychologist*, 7(2), 108–117. Reproduced with permission of The British Psychological Society.

Coaching often forms part of leadership development programmes, with organisations investing in methods to aid successful transition up the leadership ladder. It can assist leaders in developing the skills, behaviours and attitudes required to equip them to cope with the transition and the demands of the new role (Kombarakaran et al., 2008). De Haan (2005) reports that coaching is continually growing in popularity and status, and that the stigma of being coached is reducing as leaders recognise the value in working with other professionals to help them to grow and develop. However, some leaders do still consider there to be a stigma attached to seeing a coach. They believe it signifies the presence of remedial problems that need fixing, and they are concerned about what others will think if they know that they are being coached (O'Shaughnessy, 2001; Underhill, McAnally & Koriath, 2007). In consideration of this, organisations are realising that to engage employees in coaching it is important to position it as a positive endeavour, as a tool to aid successful transition, one which will help leaders to thrive in their new role. Creating a coaching culture is important for changing attitudes to coaching; organisations need to develop an environment where continual growth, change and development are valued by all across the organisation (Clutterbuck & Megginson, 2005). It is recognised also that forcing or coercing individuals into going to coaching can be problematic and can result in resistance to coaching (Hardingham et al., 2006). Hardingham and colleagues (2006) describe the choice spectrum which moves from total choice to total coercion, proposing that the further along the spectrum towards total coercion the coachee perceives they are the more difficult it will be to engage them in the coaching process. It would seem then that engagement in coaching is more likely if it is viewed as a positive tool for change, and that individuals have subscribed to the concept of change and development and see it as a choice.

However, consider this real life example: coaching has been positioned as a positive development tool to a group of fast track leaders, those who have been selected for showing high potential. Almost half of them declined the opportunity to receive coaching, despite it being part of a talent management programme specifically designed for them, on which they had willingly embarked. Each participant had an opportunity to meet with a coach during a development centre day to discuss what their coaching objectives could be. What might have influenced their decision not to be coached?

It is considered here that avoidance behaviours may explain the choice not to be coached. Avoidance behaviours are explained in the rational emotive behaviour (REB) approach as being a consequence of rigid irrational beliefs and demands, with particular focus on beliefs pertaining to perfectionism, low frustration tolerance and low self-acceptance (Ellis, 1995). Perfectionist beliefs such as 'I must <u>never</u> make mistakes, and if I do I am a <u>failure</u>' can result in an extreme fear of failure, worrying about making mistakes and anxiety about what others think. Low frustration tolerance beliefs such as 'life <u>must</u> <u>always</u> be easy otherwise it is <u>intolerable</u>' influence how individuals cope when faced with challenging situations. Such rigid beliefs and demands can lead to procrastination and avoidance as individuals strive to preserve or protect their self-worth and self-esteem (Ellis, 1995). Low self-acceptance beliefs are also reported to influence avoidance behaviours (Crocker & Knight, 2005; Ellis, 1995). Crocker and Knight (2005) suggest that self-acceptance is based on contingencies of self-worth. Contingencies of self-worth are a set of outcomes on which individuals base their self-esteem and sense of worth (Cooper-smith, 1967). Contingencies of self-worth differ across individuals; some may base their self-worth on competencies whilst others may base their worth on approval or disapproval from others. We all want to believe that we are valuable and worthy and as such we typically seek out the emotional highs associated with our contingencies of self-worth; engaging in activities in which we can prove our worth and avoiding those that may result in failure and feelings of low self-worth (Crocker & Knight, 2005).

One aim of the research described in this paper was to explore whether rigid evaluative core beliefs were present in the executives taking part and whether they were correlated with potential derailment behaviours. Another aim of the research was to observe the extent to which coaching can help rigid beliefs to become more flexible and, therefore, help with developing more positive behaviours. As a consequence of the dropout of almost half of the participants it became possible to explore differences in beliefs for those being coached and those choosing to decline coaching, as discussed below.

RESEARCH OUTLINE

A public sector department selected 41 managers as potential future senior civil servants from a group of 100 managers that had taken part in an assessment centre initiative. The 41 managers were then engaged in a talent management programme to help them transition to more senior positions. The programme involved development centre days, action learning days, and six hours of coaching for each manager. The public sector department teamed up with a researcher from City University London (VED) to conduct a study looking at the influence of the coaching for meeting the objectives set for their transition plan. The organisation was interested in understanding their employee's attitudes to coaching and whether the coaching had made a difference. They specifically wanted to look at general perceptions of coaching, levels of motivation and enthusiasm to be coached, expected success of coaching, expected levels of line manager support, and what quality the coachees felt was most important in a coach. Post-coaching they wanted to understand the levels of satisfaction with the coaching, the extent to which objectives had been met, the extent to which coachees now believed they were equipped to cope with the demands of a more senior position, the criteria they used to select their coach, the line managers actual support, and what they believed could have been done differently.

The researcher was particularly interested in observing pre- and post-coaching measures of the participant's beliefs and behaviours to determine whether these changed as a consequence of coaching. The beliefs of interest were those pertaining to perfectionism, frustration tolerance, and unconditional self-acceptance. The behaviours were outlined in the organisations 360° feedback tool, results of which would be collected by the organisation and provided to the researcher. As the approaches used in coaching were likely to be different across participants, due to the coaching being carried out by a number of coaches with different styles, controls were put in place to measure the extent to which different types of coaching were used with each individual; for example, cognitive behavioural coaching, as some methods of coaching target beliefs and behaviours more directly than others.

Due to a change in the 360° feedback tool used by the organisation during the research period it became untenable to compare pre- and post-coaching behaviours as the data could not be matched. However, as the beliefs data was being collected via standardised questionnaires selected by the researcher there was still potential to observe any changes in individuals' beliefs as a consequence of coaching and the data collection went ahead as planned with all 41 managers completing a set of questionnaires. It was hypothesised that there would be lower scores for perfectionism, lower scores for frustration discomfort, and higher scores for unconditional self-acceptance after the coaching. Ethical approval for this study was granted by the research committee at City University London.

RESEARCH DESIGN

Information was collected via paper-based and online surveys to provide quantitative and qualitative data for analysis. Initially this was to be collected pre- and post-coaching from one participant group; the coaching group (N=41). It was recognised that a control group was required ideally to compare outcomes for the coaching group to a no-coaching group. The ideal design for research is the use of randomised control trials, but these can be difficult in applied settings due to issues of fairness and ethics (Clark-Carter & Marks, 2004). A waiting list group design was considered but this would have put the first group of coachees at an advantage if opportunities for promotion came up during the waiting period. Data collection for the coaching group proceeded whilst a control group was sought. (See Ellam-Dyson & Palmer [2008] for more details regarding the challenges of researching executive coaching in applied settings.)

MATERIALS

A set of pre-coaching and post-coaching questionnaires were used. The beliefs to be observed were those pertaining to perfectionism, frustration tolerance, and unconditional self-acceptance. These were measured using standardised questionnaires. The Perfectionism Inventory (PI; Hill et al., 2004) consists of 59 items measuring two main constructs of perfectionism; self-evaluative perfectionism and conscientious perfectionism. The items are rated on a five-point Likert scale ranging from 1=strongly disagree to 5=strongly agree. The Frustration Discomfort Scale (FDS; Harrington, 2005) consists of 28 items measuring four constructs of frustration discomfort; achievement, emotional intolerance, entitlement, and discomfort intolerance, as well as total frustration tolerance. Participants were required to rate their agreement to the 28 statements, also on a five-point Likert scale. The Unconditional Self-Acceptance Questionnaire (USAQ; Chamberlain & Haaga, 2001) contains 20 items presented as statements to which participants were required to rate their level of agreement using a seven-point Likert scale; 1=almost always untrue, 2=usually untrue, 3=more often untrue than true, 4=equally as often untrue and true, 5=more often true than untrue, 6=usually true, 7=always true. Some items were reverse scored as some statements were negatively worded whilst others were positively worded.

Participants also completed a pre-coaching questionnaire about their attitudes to coaching; whether they had been coached before or knew somebody else that was coached, their perceptions of the usefulness of coaching to achieve their objectives, their levels of motivation and enthusiasm to be coached, their line managers' perception of coaching, and the level of support they expected from their line manager in assisting them to attend coaching. This was a 14-item questionnaire with a mix of scales, where some questions were to be scored on a five-point Likert scale, others required a yes or no answer, and the final question was qualitative and required a written response. A post-coaching questionnaire was also developed to capture satisfaction with the coaching, level of success in reaching objectives, the usefulness of the coaching for aiding the transition, line managers' actual support, and how they had selected their coach. This was an 18-item questionnaire requiring responses based on a mix of quantitative scales and qualitative written responses. A further questionnaire was developed part way through the research to capture data from a no-coaching group at Time 2. This was a five-item questionnaire asking participants to rate the extent to which different factors had affected their decision not to be coached, with the opportunity to provide qualitative data.

PROCEDURE

Time 1 measures were collected from all participants ($N=41$) at four development centre events, held on four separate days with approximately 10 attendees at each event. These events were organised as part of the talent management programme for the selected managers to meet other participants, take part in group exercises, and meet with coaches to determine which leadership skills they needed to develop and set their objectives for coaching. Participants completed paper-based versions of the beliefs questionnaires and the attitudes to coaching questionnaire. Following the development centre days the participants were expected to take part in their six hours of coaching over the following 12-month period. As each person concluded their coaching they were contacted to complete online post-coaching surveys to capture the beliefs data and the outcomes data.

Table 1 *Time intervals for data collection for coaching and no-coaching groups.*

Group	Time 1	Time 2
Coaching	Complete beliefs and pre-coaching questionnaires. Start coaching.	Complete questionnaires for beliefs and outcomes.
No coaching	Complete beliefs and pre-coaching questionnaires. No Coaching.	Complete questionnaires for beliefs and reasons for not being coached.

Twelve months on, unexpectedly, almost half of the individuals had chosen not to be coached ($N=20$). This was unfortunate in terms of reducing the sample but it did overcome the issue of not having a control group in place. Given that there were now two groups to observe it was possible to test the full hypothesis by comparing beliefs data collected at Time 2 for the coaching and no-coaching groups. Table 1 shows the revised time intervals for the data collection.

It was considered important to capture data about why the no-coaching group had chosen not to be coached and an additional Time 2 questionnaire was developed. It included questions about practical and personal elements such as the process for selecting coaches, the choice of coach's available, time implications, knowledge of coaching benefits, feeling at ease to discuss issues, confidentiality, and line manager's support. Having the two comparison groups also offered an interesting opportunity to tap into any differences in the beliefs of those choosing to be coached and those declining coaching. This data was expected to offer some great insights into what discourages individuals from being coached.

Hence four new questions were posed:

1. Were there any significant differences in the extent to which beliefs changed between the coaching group and the no-coaching group at Time 2?
2. What were the reasons for the no-coaching group choosing not to be coached?
3. Were there any significant differences in the levels of beliefs for the coaching group and the no-coaching group at Time 1?
4. Were there any differences in the attitudes to coaching for the coaching group and no-coaching group?

RESULTS

The main aim of the research had been to compare the beliefs at Time 1 and Time 2 to observe any differences as a consequence of coaching (coaching group) or the passing of time (no-coaching group). Unfortunately, after persisting for several months, none of the no-coaching group (N=20) completed the Time 2 questionnaires. Moreover, of the coaching group (N=21) only nine completed the Time 2 question-naires. Thus, there was not enough Time 2 data to draw any useful comparisons between Time 1 and Time 2. Nor were there any data to indicate why some participants had chosen not to be coached. Thus, the original hypothesis could not be tested, nor could questions 1 and 2 be answered. It is acknowledged that as we reached this point in the research it was a particularly demanding time for this Government department; the research was therefore not considered a priority and the required resources were now unavailable to assist with data collection. Such are the frustrations of carrying out applied research.

Nonetheless, there was still a pool of pre-coaching attitudes to coaching and beliefs data available for analysis from all 41 public sector managers and questions 3 and 4 could still be addressed. It was considered particularly interesting to compare the beliefs of the coaching group and no-coaching group to observe whether there were any differences in perfectionism, frustration tolerance, and unconditional self-acceptance at Time 1, pre-coaching.

The beliefs data for the two groups were compared and analysed. When calculating the frustration tolerance scores higher scores on the FDS are indicative of higher levels of frustration, hence lower scores are more preferable than high scores. Items in the scale include 'I can't stand doing tasks when I am not in the mood'. Higher scores on the PI indicate higher levels of perfectionism. Examples of conscientious perfectionism items include 'I drive myself rigorously to achieve high standards'. Examples of self-evaluative perfectionism items include 'If I make mistakes people might think less of me'. Lower scores for perfectionism are more preferable than higher scores. Higher scores on the USAQ indicate higher levels of unconditional self-acceptance. Some items were reverse scored. As such, a high level of agreement for the statement 'I feel worthwhile even if I am not successful in meeting certain goals that are important to me' indicates high levels of unconditional self-acceptance. Conversely, a high level of agreement for the statement 'My sense of self-worth depends a lot on how I compare with other people' is indicative of conditional self-acceptance. A higher overall score for the USAQ is preferable.

The data were analysed using an independent samples t-test. There were no significant differences between the attitudes to coaching for the two groups. There was no significant difference in the conscientious perfectionism scores for the coaching group (M=86.38, SD=16.70) and the no coaching group (M=84.85, SD=14.06); $t(39)$=.317, p=.753. There was also no significant difference in the self-evaluative perfectionism scores for the coaching group (M=79.24, SD=17.04) and the no-coaching group (M=87.65, SD=18.01); $t(39)$=-1.537, p=.132. The difference in the total frustration tolerance scores (FDS total) for the two groups was also non-significant; coaching group (M=78.24, SD=9.21) and no-coaching (M=76.95, SD=9.18); $t(39)$=.448, p=.656, as shown in Table 2 along with the mean values for the four sub-categories of frustration tolerance. However, interestingly, the no-coaching group had significantly lower scores for unconditional self-acceptance (M=84.20, SD=14.02) than the coaching group (M=92.81, SD=10.28); $t(39)$=2.250, p=.030), also shown in Table 2.

Table 2   *Time 1 beliefs scores for the coaching and no-coaching groups*

	Coaching (N=21) Mean	No-Coaching (N=20) Mean
Frustration Tolerance		
Achievement	22.81	21.15[1]
Entitlement	20.95	20.30[1]
Emotional Intolerance	18.90	19.95[1]
Discomfort Intolerance	15.57	15.55[1]
FDS Total	78.24	76.85[1]
Perfectionism		
Self Evaluative	79.24	87.65[1]
Conscientious	86.48	84.85[1]
Unconditional Self-Acceptance	92.81	84.20[2]*

[1]=higher scores preferable; [2]= lower scores preferable; * = significant at $p<.05$.

DISCUSSION

The influence of findings on the research questions

The original aim of the research was to explore changes in beliefs and behaviours pre- and post-coaching, with a hypothesis that perfectionism scores would be lower, frustration discomfort scores would be lower, and unconditional self-acceptance scores would be higher in the coaching group after coaching. Unfortunately, this could not be tested due to the lack of post-coaching (Time 2) data for comparison. In light of a control group forming as a number of participants ($N=20$) chose not to be coached, four subsequent questions were posed based on the apparent opportunity to do some Time 2 and between group comparisons. However, the unfortunate lack of Time 2 data then meant that questions 1 and 2 could not be answered. Nonetheless, questions 3 and 4 could still be addressed with the Time 1 data and it was considered that the data might bring useful insights into what contributed to the no-coaching group choosing not to be coached.

There were no significant differences in the attitudes to coaching or the frustration tolerance scores for the two groups. The difference between the perfectionism scores was also non-significant, though it was observed that the no-coaching group did score more highly for self-evaluative perfectionism. The statistically significant difference in the two groups for unconditional self-acceptance was a really interesting finding, particularly when low/conditional self-acceptance is a factor that is likely to influence the confidence to lead. In other words, the people that were likely to need the coaching to help them build the confidence to cope with their transition and the demands of a new role were those avoiding it.

The influence of self-acceptance on avoidance behaviours

As discussed earlier, self-acceptance is based on contingencies of self-worth (Crocker & Knight, 2005). For individuals who experience conditional self-acceptance their contingencies of self-worth must be met for them to feel worthy and to maintain their self-esteem. Where individuals want to prove their success and experience high self-esteem in relation to their contingencies of self-worth they are likely to set and pursue self-validation goals in those domains (Crocker & Park, 2004). If, however, they perceive that failure could be a possibility they may disengage from the tasks required to reach the goal, perhaps deciding it does not matter after all, which is preferable to risking the loss of self-esteem and

Meanfeelings of low self-worth if failure does occur (Crocker & Knight, 2005). It is considered that participants in this study that did not engage in coaching may have been driven by preservation of self-worth and self-esteem. However, the data is not available to substantiate this.

Crocker and Knight (2005) outline some of the consequences of pursuing self-esteem by proving one's worth to oneself and others. It is interesting to consider how these may influence leadership. They suggest that focusing on proving one's worth can interfere with building and maintaining relationships, as people tend to be focused on themselves at the cost of others feelings and needs (Crocker & Park, 2004). From a leadership perspective, a lack of interpersonal sensitivity and poor relationship building are suggested contributors to leadership derailment (Bentz, 1985; McCall & Lombardo, 1983). Pursuit of self-esteem through proving self-worth also has implications for learning, particularly for those who set self-validation goals, as they see mistakes, criticism and negative feedback as threats rather than opportunities to learn, grow, and develop (Crocker & Knight, 2005). Furthermore, it can negatively influence goal attainment. As discussed above, where goal attainment may start to look uncertain individuals may disengage to avoid possible failure. It is interesting to consider whether this could be a contributor to a laissez-faire style of leadership, where leaders avoid getting involved in important issues, avoid decision making, and offer little in terms of direction or support to their followers (Bass, 1985). This self-validation approach can also have consequences for mental health, such as stress and depression (Crocker & Knight, 2005).

LIMITATIONS OF THE RESEARCH

Of course, without the feedback from those who chose not to be coached it is not possible to say exactly what led to their decision. Perhaps the low levels of unconditional self-acceptance led them to decide that a more senior role was in fact too daunting, and perhaps having not been coached provided an excuse not to apply for any upcoming openings for more senior positions. This kind of strategy has been referred to as self-handicapping, where individuals create obstacles to their own success in order to have an excuse ready if failure occurs (Jones & Berglas, 1978; Kearns, Forbes & Gardiner, 2007). Without the data to establish who in fact went ahead and moved into more senior positions this inference can obviously not be substantiated. With gaps in the data it cannot be asserted unequivocally that low unconditional self-acceptance was a main factor in this decision and it is recognised that there are other factors that may well have fed into this decision. However, the findings reported here do show significant differences between the two groups in their levels of unconditional self-acceptance and this data should not be ignored.

SUGGESTIONS FOR LEADERSHIP COACHING

Given the outcomes of the study described in this paper, a pressing question is 'How do we encourage individuals with conditional self-acceptance (i.e. low unconditional self-acceptance) to engage in coaching?' The answer potentially lies in the suggestion of building a coaching culture, where learning and development are accepted, indeed expected throughout the organisation (Clutterbuck & Megginson, 2005). Farson and Keyes (2002) suggest that an environment that encourages risk taking and recognises failures as opportunities to learn is important in encouraging individuals to embrace challenges and reduce the fear of failure.

What can be done to avoid the pitfalls of conditional self-acceptance for those who do engage in coaching and are working on leadership development? Crocker and Knight (2005) suggest that it is important to avoid setting goals that are primarily focused on boosting one's self-esteem, but instead to focus on goals that contribute to others' successes. They also suggest setting learning goals instead of self-validation goals. Anderson (2002) explains that he has worked with a surprising amount of executives who have a lack of self-worth and low self-acceptance. He uses techniques drawn from the rational emotive behaviour approach to uncover the beliefs linked to the behaviours and to help the coachees move forward. One example from his work includes the vice president of a dynamic organisation who had problems with relationships, fear of confrontation, problems with delegation and insecurity dealing with her boss. It became apparent that her behaviours were caused by a lack of self-worth. In another client example, Anderson (2002) found that a brilliant and very quick-minded IT manager had little tolerance for those not performing to his level, deemed himself the judge of their competence, and consequently had difficulties with relationships with his colleagues. He was very intense and prone to holding demanding 'must' beliefs. It was uncovered that as well as frustration tolerance issues he also had low unconditional self-acceptance and felt neglected, ignored and without worth. Palmer and Gyllensten (2008) report a case study of a client who presented with depression and had problems with procrastination. As part of the case conceptualisation, it was hypothesised that her procrastination was related to a belief that, 'If I do not do a perfect job then I am inadequate' (Palmer & Gyllensten, 2008, p.44). Anderson (2002) clarifies that working with these issues can take time, but that clients report it to be a very worthwhile process. Palmer (2009) describes how the rational emotive behaviour approach can be used in coaching with clients to assist them in adapting beliefs and developing more positive behaviours.

Berglas (2002) emphasises how important it is that coaches have the ability to be able to recognise when clients may have deep seated psychological difficulties. He gives an example of an executive who is assigned a coach who focuses purely on raising the executive's assertiveness through role playing, completely missing the fact that the coachee had a morbid fear of failure. The executive became afraid of being exposed as a fake when putting into practice his new 'assertive self', as it didn't mirror how he really felt inside. As a consequence the coachee became severely depressed. Berglas (2002) suggests that the requirement for quick fixes as well as a lack of psychological awareness can also result in coaches turning to behavioural solutions. He emphasises not just the importance of recognising that there may be psychological issues to work with, but that they take time to work with and resolve, as suggested by Anderson (2002). It should not be about quick fixes. He believes that executive coaches who have not had rigorous psychological training can in actual fact do more harm than good when they fail to recognise or simply ignore problems they don't understand.

In summary, in a study involving public sector fast track leaders it was found that those who chose not to be coached had significantly lower unconditional self-acceptance than those who were coached. Whilst there may be numerous reasons for the choice not to be coached, the findings regarding self-acceptance should not be ignored. Low unconditional self-acceptance and low self-worth can influence leadership behaviours, which can be addressed in coaching, but it does require awareness of the coach/coaching psychologist that psychological difficulties exist. If behaviours are influenced by psychological issues the coach/coaching psychologist should avoid using purely behavioural techniques to influence change as this may only serve to mask the real issue and can result in more severe problems (Berglas, 2002). With regards how to engage individuals in coaching in the first place, with focus here on those that have low unconditional self-acceptance, it is suggested that organisations develop an environment that encourages learning, development and risk taking and promotes coaching as a positive tool to aid this process. It is recognised that other factors can influence the decision not to be coached. This paper addresses one possible factor.

REFERENCES

Anderson, J.P. (2002). Executive Coaching and REBT: Some comments from the field. *Journal of Rational Emotive and Cognitive Behaviour Therapy*, 20(3–4), 223–233.

Bass, B.M. (1985). *Leadership and performance beyond expectation*. New York: Free Press.

Bentz, J.V. (1985). A view from the top: A 30-year perspective of research devoted to the discovery description and prediction of executive behaviour. Paper presented at the 92nd Annual Convention of the American Psychological Association, Los Angeles, August.

Berglas, S. (2002). The very real dangers of executive coaching. *Harvard Business Review*, 80(6), 86–92.

Clark-Carter, D. & Marks, D.F. (2004). Intervention studies: Design and analysis. In D.F. Marks & L. Yardley (Eds.), *Research methods for clinical and health psychology* (pp.145–165). London: Sage.

Clutterbuck, D. & Megginson, D. (2005). *Making coaching work: Creating a coaching culture*. London: Chartered Institute of Personnel and Development.

Coopersmith, S. (1967). *The antecedents of self-esteem*. San Francisco: W.H. Freeman.

Crocker, J. & Knight, K.M. (2005). Contingencies of self-worth. *Current Directions in Psychological Science*, 14, 200–203.

Crocker, J. & Park, L.E. (2004). The costly pursuit of self-esteem. *Psychological Bulletin*, 130, 392–414.

de Haan, E. (2005). From stigma to status: Coaching comes of age, Communique, Summer, 4.

Ellam-Dyson, V. & Palmer, S. (2008). The challenges of researching executive coaching. *The Coaching Psychologist*, 4(2), 79–84.

Ellis, A. (1995). *Better, deeper and more enduring brief therapy: The Rational Emotive Behaviour Approach*. New York: Brunner/Mazel.

Farson, R. & Keyes, R. (2002). The failure-tolerant leader. *Harvard Business Review*, 80(8), 64–71.

Hardingham, A., Brearley, M., Moorhouse, A. & Venter, B. (Eds.) (2004). *The coach's coach: Personal development for personal developers*. London: CIPD.

Harrington, N. (2005). The Frustration Discomfort Scale: Development and psychometric properties. *Clinical Psychology and Psychotherapy*, 12, 374–387.

Hill, R.W., Huelsman, T., Furr, M., Kibler, J., Vicente, B. & Kennedy, C. (2004). A new measure for perfectionism: The Perfectionism Inventory (PI). *Journal of Personality Assessment*, 82(1), 80–91.

Jones, E.E. & Berglas, S. (1978). Control of attributions about the self through self-handicapping strategies: The appeal of alcohol and the role of underachievement. *Personality and Social Psychology Bulletin*, 4, 200–206.

Kearns, H., Forbes, A. & Gardiner, M. (2007). A cognitive behavioural coaching intervention for the treatment of perfectionism and self-handicapping in a non-clinical population. *Behaviour Change*, 24(3), 157–172.

Kombarakaran, F.A., Yang, J.A., Baker, M.N. & Fernandes, P.B. (2008). Executive coaching: It works. *Consulting Psychology Journal: Practice and Research*, 60(1), 78–90.

McCall, M. & Lombardo, M. (1983). *Off the track: Why and how successful executives get derailed. Technical Report No. 21*. Center for Creative Leadership, Greensboro, NC.

O'Shaughnessy, S. (2001). Executive coaching: The route to business stardom. *Industrial and Commercial Training*, 33(6), 194–197.

Palmer, S. (2009). Rational coaching: A cognitive behavioural approach. *The Coaching Psychologist*, 5(1), 12–18.

Palmer, S. & Gyllensten, K. (2008). How cognitive behavioural, rational emotive behavioural or multimodal coaching could prevent mental health problems, enhance performance and reduce work-related stress. *Journal of Rational Emotive and Cognitive Behavioural Therapy*, 26(1), 38–52.

Underhill, B.O., McAnally, K. & Koriath, J.J. (2007). *Executive coaching for results: The definitive guide to developing organisational leaders*. San Francisco: Berrett-Koehler.

15 Can cognitive behavioural team coaching increase well-being?

Ulrika Hultgren, Stephen Palmer &
Siobhain O'Riordan

Abstract

This paper aims to describe a model for cognitive behavioural team coaching (CBTC), derived from existing cognitive behavioural theories and individual coaching models. In an organisational context coaching a team to increase well-being, instead of separate individuals, would appear on face value to be more effective. However, it is appropriate to explore what the existing literature can tell us about team coaching, well-being and stress as well as the possible relationships between these areas. There also seems to be a need for clarification of the term 'team coaching', so it can be differentiated from other team activities and this is a theme that will be explored in this paper.

A proposed pilot study is also described, aiming to investigate if CBTC can increase well-being and lessen strain among team members in an organisational setting by using an individual CBC model adapted to team conditions.

Keywords

Well-being, team coaching, cognitive behavioural team coaching, stress; coaching psychology.

Original publication details: Hultgren, U., Palmer, S., & O'Riordan, S. (2013, December). Can cognitive behavioural team coaching increase well-being? *The Coaching Psychologist*, 9(2), 100–110. Reproduced with permission of The British Psychological Society.

WELL-BEING, STRESS AND INNOVATION

There are a vast number of research studies regarding what constitutes high performance and innovative teams. Published research regarding connections between teams, coaching, well-being and stress, are fewer.

Teams consist of individual team members and research regarding individuals is more accessible when it comes to wellbeing and stress. The World Health Organisation (WHO) states in the *Mental Health Declaration for Europe* that 'mental health and mental well-being are fundamental to the quality of life and productivity of individuals, families, communities and nations, enabling people to experience life as meaningful and to be creative and active citizens' (WHO, 2005). Well-being is a focus both in research and by governments, for example, countries in the EU measure their inhabitants' wellbeing regularly. Well-being as a term inhabits different aspects of an individual's perception of well-being and DEFRA (2013) define well-being as existing of two dimensions. Firstly as subjective well-being in terms of how people think and feel about their own well-being, like life satisfaction, positive affect, and a judgement on whether life is meaningful. The other dimension is objective well-being, that's based on assumptions about basic human needs and rights, like physical health and how safe they feel. Mental well-being is a concept that is used to describe overall well-being and is more than just the absence of mental illness. It is a positive state of mind and body, underpinned by social and psychological well-being (DEFRA, 2013). Well-being and its connection to work indicate that job satisfaction is strongly positively associated with life satisfaction, even after controlling for satisfaction with other aspects of one's life (Rice et al., 1980).

Work-related stress on the other hand, has become an, increasingly problematic area. The Health and Safety Executive (HSE) defines work-related stress as a harmful reaction that people have to undue pressures and demands placed on them at work, and new statistics show that the prevalence of stress in 2011/12 was 428,000 cases (40 per cent) out of a total of 1,073,000 cases for all work-related illnesses in Great Britain (see HSE, 2013). It is not just absenteeism which can be problematic. The Sainsbury Centre for Mental Health (2007) suggests that most people suffering from stress continue to work, but may struggle with concentration and effective decision making, estimating that 'presenteeism' (functioning at less than optimum capacity while at work) costs UK businesses £15.1 billion per year in reduced productivity. Presenteeism accounts for 1.5 times as much working time lost as absenteeism and costs more to employers because it is more common among higher-paid staff (Sainsbury Centre for Mental Health, 2007). Effects of stress are not merely psychological in nature; stress can also affect physical and social health, innovation and productivity (e.g. Kawakami & Haratani, 1999; Kristensen, 1996; Stansfeld et al., 1999; Devereux et al., 1999).

Research on stress and its impact on an individual level is well founded. Although, the areas of how teams are affected by working under straining conditions or in relation to teams and well-being are less researched. It has been argued that, 'The limited research that has examined the association between teams and stress is not definitive regarding the relationship between the two' (Cruz & Pil, 2011, p.1266). The research on teams is mainly focused on team performance and team innovation in combination with well-being and stress. Results from a study researching the impact of team climate for innovation on well-being and stress shows that there was a positive relationship between perceived team climate that supports innovation and individual wellbeing, and that there was a negative relationship between team climate and stress as well as between well-being and stress, the author points out that well-being is a link between team climate for innovation and stress reactions (Dackert, 2010). Cruz and Pil (2011) concluded, focusing on the connection between team characteristics and stress, that team characteristics are significantly associated with team member perceptions of job control, job demands, and stress. In other words that team characteristics in itself, in this case, the level of autonomy and intra team interdependence, effect the level of stress in teams, and the authors suggests that teams with a low degree of autonomy and a high degree of intra team independence are associated with lower levels of stress. Another study about team coaching and innovation in 97 work teams indicated 'that the relationship between team coaching and team innovation is mediated by team goal commitment and support for innovation. Specifically, team coaching had a direct effect on support for innovation and an indirect effect on behavioural team process through team goal commitment' (Rousseau et al., 2013). The practical implications suggested in this study were that organisations may favour, by applying interventions aimed at developing team leaders' coaching skills, treating coaching as a core managerial responsibility (Rousseau et al., 2013, p.344).

TEAMS

Working in a team can be very rewarding and satisfying both for the individual and the organisation, and teams are a salient feature of modern organisations (Van Mierlo et al., 2007). The basic idea is that a team sharing and discussing ideas can solve problems or find solutions that require different specialties of knowledge, which are more effective than one person. The way we organise teams is changing and today team members can work in multiple teams, time zones, different cities and countries, and 'as electronic technologies for communication and co-ordination become more powerful and pervasive, teamwork-at-a-distance is becoming more the rule than the exception' (Hackman, 2011, p.5). One method that is used to develop teams, is team coaching. The term team coaching though is used for a variety of situations and is commonly associated with methods like facilitating in teams, coaching used together with different team assessments, team development and team building activities.

A team is not the same as a group of people. Historically the word group was first on the scene and used in the literature to describe a group of people belonging together in different ways. Later a need for a more specific definition emerged describing a more closely related work group and the word team was born. A work group can for example consist of individuals that do not necessarily work together to solve specific tasks or have mutual goals, where one person's performance has no real effect on another's. Work groups are used in organisations when performance relies on individual work products. One of the most commonly used definitions of a team is that of Katzenbach and Smith (1993) that states that '…a team is a small number of people with complementary skills who are committed to a common purpose, performance goals, and approach for which they hold themselves mutually accountable' (p.45). Another widely used definition is '…a group of people that are independent, with respect to information, resources and skills and who seek to combine their efforts to achieve a common goal' (Thompson, 2004, p.4). A team can also be organised in different ways for example virtual teams, 'small temporary groups of geographically, organisationally and/or time dispersed knowledge workers who co-ordinate their work predominantly with electronic information and communication technologies in order to accomplish one or more organisation tasks' (Ale Ebrahim et al., 2009, p.1578). This might include work teams that are responsible for creating tangible products and services (Devine, 2002) and project teams consisting of members usually belonging to different groups or teams, functions are assigned to activities for the same project and used for a defined period of time then disbanded. Another term used to describe a way of organising teams is cross – functional teaming, where a group of people are brought together across the organisation, with different functional expertise working toward a common goal (Krajewski & Ritzman, 2005). At the same time it is becoming more common to teamwork-at-a distance with the help of electronic tools (Hackman, 2011).

COGNITIVE BEHAVIOURAL COACHING

Cognitive behavioural coaching (CBC) has by tradition mostly been used in a one-to-one setting where it has been shown to have good effect on, for example, well-being and increased goal striving. Cognitive behavioural coaching (Neenan & Palmer, 2001; Neenan & Dryden, 2002; Palmer & Szymanska, 2007; Richard, 1999; Williams et al., 2010) is derived from the well-established principles and practice of cognitive-behavioural theory and therapy (e.g. Beck, 1976, 2005; Ellis, 1962). Palmer and Szymanska (2007) describe cognitive behavioural coaching as 'an integrative approach which combines the use of cognitive, behavioural, imaginal and problem solving techniques and strategies within a cognitive behavioural framework to enable coachees to achieve their realistic goals' (2007, p.86).

Research into cognitive behavioural coaching has found it to be effective for a range of issues including increasing goal striving, well-being and hope; reducing stress and depression; tackling perfectionism and self-handicapping (e.g. Grant, 2001, 2003, 2008; Grant, Curtayne & Burton, 2009; Green, Oades & Grant, 2006; Green, Grant & Rysaardt, 2007; Gyllensten et al., 2010; Grbcic & Palmer, 2006; Kearns, Forbes & Gardiner, 2007; Kearns, Gardiner & Marshall, 2008; Libri & Kemp, 2006).

Team coaching can be defined as 'a direct interaction with a team intended to help members make co-ordinated and task-appropriate use of their collective resources in accomplishing the team's work' (Hackman & Wageman, 2005, p.269). David Clutterbuck (2007) defines team coaching as a process of 'helping the team improve performance and the processes by which performance is achieved through reflection and dialog' (2007, p.77). Hackman and Wageman (2005) proposed a new theory for team coaching, a team coaching model focusing on three features, namely, the func-tions that coaching serves for a team, specific times in the process where coaching interventions are most likely to have effect, and thirdly, under what conditions team coaching is likely to have effect and when not. Some of the previous team coaching models were built on an interpsychological perspective focusing on the quality of the relationships in teams (Hackman & Wageman, 2005), what they proposed was a shift in perspective to what research had found was the factors or group interactions that enhance team performance and effectiveness. These factors were; the level of effort from team members collectively carrying out tasks, the importance of the tasks for the performance strategies the team uses at work and thirdly, knowledge and skills that the members bring into work (Hackman & Morris, 1975; Hackman & Walton, 1986).

To structure the team coaching process Clutterbuck (2007) describes seven important steps: Identify the need to improve/ change, observe and gather evidence, motivate to set and own personal improvements targets, help to plan how to achieve those targets, create opportunities to practice the desired skills, observe in action and give objective feedback and help the team to work through setbacks. Other important areas in need of consideration when working with team coaching include the 'readiness for coaching' (Hackman & Wageman, 2005, p.275), which means the degree to which the issues to be addressed are among those naturally on team members' minds at the time of the intervention. Further to this, the degree to which the team as a whole is not at that time preoccupied with more pressing matters and that coaching interventions are more effective when they address issues a team is ready for at the time they are made (Hackman & Wageman, 2005). There are three different time points in the life of a task-performing team when members are likely to be especially open to coaching interventions: the beginning, when a group is just starting its work, the midpoint, when half the work has been done and/or half the allotted time has passed (Gersick, 1988, 1989) and at the end, when a piece of work has been finished or a significant subtask has been accomplished (Kozlowski et al., 1996). Another important factor to take into account is the creation of the right climate for team coaching mainly by addressing factors like: unresolved matters or issues, creating psychological safety: building openness and trust by preparing the team for the team coaching and timing; making sure that the team has the time for team coaching and mastering time management issues (Clutterbuck, 2007).

A PROPOSED MODEL FOR CBTC

As suggested above, research into CBC suggests that it can be used to enhance wellbeing and prevent stress and to create a CBTC approach derived from individual coaching methods and practices. However, the method needs some revising and additional elements. Combining existing knowledge, models for CBC and important key areas concerning team coaching, as proposed by Hackman and Clutterbuck, could include different steps and a clear structure for working with goals and solving issues that are relevant to a particular team.

For example, it would include a planning process with the coach and team leader/leader to share information about the team coaching process and the elements it would include such as time management planning so that solutions for change that the team chooses to work with are prioritised between the coaching sessions. Another important area concerning planning is that the coaching sessions themselves are not moved too many times so time between meetings become prolonged, losing momentum and the created team process where team members might forget about what the previous sessions was all about. Questions relating to how management will handle issues that are brought forward by the team that are more organisational in essence, also needs to be addressed. Making sure that the team has the actual time to engage in team coaching and not at the finish line is also an important consideration.

Clutterbuck's (2007) model provides structured differenced steps much like the PRACTICE model of coaching developed by Palmer (2007) that integrates cognitive solution-focused strategies and techniques (e.g. Palmer, 2008; Williams, Palmer & Wallace, 2011). PRACTICE has been used for business, performance, executive, career, redundancy, health and life/personal coaching, and also to aid stress management, counseling and psychotherapy (Palmer, 2007).

The framework has been adapted to different languages and cultures (e.g. Dias et al., 2011) and includes seven steps in its solution-focused approach (Palmer, 2011):

1. **Presenting issues**

   What's the problem or issue or concern or topic you wish to discuss?

   What would you like to change?

   Any exceptions when it is not a problem, issue or concern?

   How will we know if the situation has improved?

   On a scale of 0 to 10 where '0' is nowhere and '10' is resolved, how near are you now today, to resolving the problem or issue?

   Any distortions or can the problem or issue be viewed differently?

   Can you imagine waking up tomorrow morning and this problem (or issue or concern) no longer existed. What would you notice that was different?

2. **Realistic, relevant goals developed**

   What do you want to achieve?

   Let's develop specific SMART goals (e.g. SMART goals).

3. **Alternative solutions generated**

   What are your options? Let's note them down.

4. **Consideration of consequences**

   What could happen?

   How useful is each possible solution?

   Let's use a rating 'usefulness' scale for each solution where '0' is not useful at all, and '10' is extremely useful.

5. **Target most feasible solution(s)**

   Now we have considered the possible solutions, what is the most feasible or practical solution(s)?

6. **Implementation of chosen solution(s)**

   Let's implement the chosen solution by breaking it down into manageable steps. Now go and do it!

7. **Evaluation**

   How successful was it?

   Rating 'success' scale 0 to 10.

   What can be learnt?

   Can we finish coaching now or do you want to address or discuss another issue or concern?

The PRACTICE model offers a structured solution-focused framework that could prove useful in an organisational and team setting. The inclusion of solution-focused techniques into the cognitive-behavioural framework helps orientate coaching towards personal strengths and solution construction, rather than problem analysis (Grant, 2003). Adapting PRACTICE to team coaching conditions would include planning for how to structure and balance the process of the individual team member and the team when it comes to, for example, presenting issues, goals and solutions generated. PRACTICE could provide the structure needed to clearly support goal attainment for a team. The coach would create possibility for all team members to have the opportunity to speak their mind but also to keep the structure and move the process forward. A clear communicated structure like PRACTICE could help the team focus on mutually decided goals and work towards not becoming overwhelmed by all issues that might be present. It would also have to include a team-based implementation process, dividing the team into smaller groups handling one or more prioritised goals. This could encourage different solutions to be communicated and addressed by all. Since PRACTICE is built on a cognitivebehavioural, solution-focused coaching framework goal attainment during the coaching process is best facilitated by understanding the consensual relationships that exist between thoughts, feelings, behaviour, and the environment. All issues are documented, so even though one area cannot be addressed or is not at that time prioritised in the CBTC, the team can address it at a later date. With built in focus on action, groups that focus on actual, 'here-and-now' issues that the team itself chooses, enable the CBTC approach to remain flexible to that specific teams agenda and a team-based solution-focused process can be obtained.

Before the team coaching starts, and taking into account Clutterbuck's (2007) points, there is need for preparations to inform about the process, build trust and a clear picture of what the team coaching will involve. Also clear guidelines are needed for how the documentation (with the team member's suggestions and results of their work) will be handled. If coaching is carried out at a time point with high work demands, the team coaching can be viewed as another demand, competing for time and attention. Figure 1 (overleaf) provides a summary of how the PRACTICE framework can be applied in CBTC programme with Whole team and Small team settings.

The difference between the suggested adapted PRACTICE CBTC model and the individual framework is that a team setting provides the possibility to focus on mutual issues the team may face together. To not lose the individual team members opinions due to the size of the team, it might be helpful using focus and action groups for some of the steps described in PRACTICE, creating a coaching process in both the smaller and whole team. The 'smaller' team setting will make it possible for everyone to speak their mind, discuss obstacles, for example, why some issues have been hard to address or solve, and eventually come up with different solutions for change discussing them together in a whole team setting. When you work with individuals, the work is generally focused on that particular person's process, and hopefully the structure in the suggested CBTC framework can provide the necessary means to both address the team and individual need for dialog around the issues and chosen solutions that can lead the team to mutual goal attainment.

PILOT STUDY

To investigate if the adapted PRACTICE framework can be used as a CBTC model and its usefulness, a pilot study will be carried out with focus on face-to-face teams working in a technology based global company. The teams are well established having worked together for a long period of time. Some of the teams may consist of team members that are based in other countries or are working in other countries as well. Most of the team members are civil engineers working with innovation, developing new technology products and are working within one or many projects and with other teams for longer or shorter periods.

The proposed pilot study aims to answer the question if cognitive behavioural team coaching can increase well-being and lessen strain. Team coaching will be carried out at three separate meetings lasting two hours each, for a period of three to four months, following the schedule presented in Figure 1. In total 40 participants will join the study from approximately 10 teams. The leader will participate in the team coaching and problems identified as connected to management or organisational issues and outside of the teams control are transferred to the leader, to be handled separately. Data will be collected with questionnaires from 20 per cent of the team members concerning, personal well-being and strain, for example, Scales of Psychological Well-Being (Ryff, 1989), HSE Stress Indicator Tool (HSE, 2004), Depression Anxiety Stress Scale (Lovibond & Lovibond, 1995) and the Personal Well-being Index (International Well-being Group, 2006; Lau, Cummins & McPherson, 2005). Stressors connected to the work environment are measured from 100 per cent of the team members with the Stress Indicator Tool (HSE, 2004). The reason that only 20 per cent of the team is measured concerning individual well-being and strain are that these data are more sensitive and participation in the study is voluntary to the individual, whilst the team coaching is a team choice. The data is collected pre-coaching, right after it ends and after three months at a follow-up. The individual team members will also be interviewed after three months by an independent rater, to follow-up on any change in well-being and stress.

Whole team setting	Small team setting

Coaching session 1

1. Presenting issues

   The team idea showers, identifies issues, collectively votes, and decides what areas that should be prioritised. Focus groups are created based on the vote. The individual team member choses what problem or focus group they want to join.

   - What's the issue or concern or topic you wish to discuss?
   - What would you like to change?
   - Any exceptions when it is not a problem, issue or concern?
   - How will we know if the situation has improved?
   - On a scale of 0 to 10 where '0' is nowhere and '10' is resolved, how near are you now today to resolving the problem or issue?
   - Any distortions or can the problem or issue be viewed differently?
   - Can you imagine waking up tomorrow morning and this problem (or issue or concern) no longer existed? what would you notice that was different?

   •

2. **Realistic goals** are set and decisions about what they want to achieve through developing SMART goals.
   - What do you want to achieve?
   - Let's develop specific SMART goals (e.g. SMART goals)

Coaching session 2

3-4. Alternative solutions generated and consideration of consequences

   The smaller group generate ideas for different solutions, consider different consequences and rate the usefulness of each solution.

   - What are your options? Let's note them down.
   - What could happen?
   - How useful is each possible solution?
   - Let's use a rating 'usefulness' scale for each solution where '0' is not useful at all, and '10' is extremely useful.

(Continued)

Figure 15.1   (*Continued*)

	5. Target most feasible solution(s)
	The fifth step includes working with and target the most practical solution.
	• Now we have considered the possible solutions, what is the most feasible or practical solution(s)?

Whole team setting	**Small team setting**

6. Implementation of chosen solution(s)
   (a) The smaller groups come together and report their findings and discuss it with the whole team.
   (b) Action groups are created based on the previous focus groups. Any team member can once again chose what group to work in.
   (c) The sixth step involves implementations of the chosen solutions and the action groups may try them out in the work environment, collecting their own data from any success or obstacles they might have encountered.
      • Let's implement the chosen solution by breaking it down into manageable steps.
      • Now go and do it!

Coaching session 3

7. Evaluation
   At the third and last coaching session, each action group reports or evaluates their findings
   to the whole team and discusses what can be learned from the team work.
   Decisions are made how to move forward and how to use the material in their future teamwork.
   • How successful was it?
   • Rating 'success' scale 0 to 10.
   • What can be learnt?
   • Can we finish coaching now or do you want to address or discuss another issue or concern?

Figure 15.1   *CBTC Programme for a Whole team setting and a Small team setting.*

Implications

The study will aim to provide insights as to whether CBTC can be a useful method to increase well-being in teams in an organisational context. It might also provide information about whether CBTC can help to solve different issues over time and furthermore what kind of areas a modern team of today views as important and needs attention.

CONCLUSION

Why develop a CBTC model for team coaching? In an organisational context coaching a team to increase well-being instead of separate individuals seems more effective. One of the few studies relating to team coaching showed that team coaching had an indirect effect on the behavioural team process through team goal commitment (Rousseau et al., 2013). Due to the lack of research on existing models on how to work with teams concerning well-being and strain it feels important to develop and investigate the effectiveness of a model that is based on previous well researched CBC practice and theories. Building a solution-focused CBTC model where a coach or a coaching psychologist can offer a structured method to create a problem solving process within the team (focusing on goal attainment facilitated by understanding the consensual relationships that exist between thoughts, feelings, behaviour, and the environment), might prove to be helpful for the team's well-being. The seven differentiated steps, might also provide a clear plan forward rather than getting stuck on a matter solely focusing on the problem side of the issue.

Although there is a lack of research concerning teams, well-being and stress, we do know that well-being is a key to psychological and physical health and that stress is becoming a problem at work that can affect the individual team member's well-being. It can be argued that the team, as we know it, now operates in a different environment where teamwork-at-a-distance is becoming more usual and teams are organised in new ways. So even if the team 'on paper' is based at one location, tools, relationships and meetings can be partly virtual.

Given these broader contextual changes to the team environment, CBTC could provide a structure for the team to clarify their roles and goals, examine support structures, and consider issues or concerns that affect the team at that moment in time. Building a coaching culture for team coaching could also prove to be valuable for the team even after the team coaching has ended. A CBTC approach might also provide a forum for encouraging a problem solving approach for issues relating to that specific team's situation, thus moving focus from the external demands to their own team environment and well-being.

REFERENCES

Ale Ebrahim, N., Ahmed, S. & Taha, Z. (2009). Virtual R & D teams in small and medium enterprises: A literature review. *Scientific Research and Essay*, 4(13), 1575–1590.

Beck, A.T. (1976). *Cognitive therapy and the emotional disorders*. New York: New American Library.

Beck, A.T. (2005). The current state of cognitive therapy: A 40-year retrospective. *Archives of General Psychiatry*, 62, 953–959.

Clutterbuck, D. (2007). *Coaching the team at work*. London: Nicholas Brealey.

Cruz, K.S. & Pil, F.K. (2011). Team design and stress: A multilevel analysis. *Human Relations*, 64, 1265–1289.

Dackert. I. (2010) The impact of team climate for innovation on well-being and stress in elderly care. *Journal of Nurses Management*, 18(3), 302–310.

DEFRA (2013). *Well-being and Health. Department of Health*. Retrieved 3 September 2013, from: https://www.gov.uk/government/uploads/system/uploads/attachment_data/file/225525/DH_well-being_health.pdf

Devereux J., Buckle, P. & Vlachonikolis I.G. (1999). Interactions between physical and psychosocial risk factors at work increase the risk of back disorders: An epidemiological approach. *Occupational and Environmental Medicine*, 56(5), 343–353.

Devine, D.J. (2002). A review and integration of classification systems relevant to teams in organisations. *Group Dynamics: Theory, Research, and Practice*, 6, 291–310.

Dias, G., Gandos, L., Nardi, A.E. & Palmer, S. (2011). Towards the practice of coaching and coaching psychology in Brazil: The adaptation of the PRACTICE model to the Portuguese language. *Coaching Psychology International*, 4(1), 10–14.

Ellis, A. (1962). *Reason and emotion in psychotherapy*. Secaucus, NJ: Citadel.

Gersick, C.J.G. (1988). Time and transition in work teams: Toward a new model of group development. *Academy of Management Journal*, 31, 9–41.

Gersick, C.J.G. (1989). Marking time: Predictable transitions in task groups. *Academy of Management Journal*, 31, 9–41.

Grant, A.M. (2001). *Coaching for enhancement performance: Comparing cognitive and behavioural approaches to coaching*. Paper presented at the 3rd International Spearman Seminar: Extending Intelligence: Enhancement and New Constructs: Sydney.

Grant, A.M. (2003). The impact of life coaching on goal attainment, metacognition and mental health. *Social Behaviour and Personality*, 31(3), 253–264.

Grant, A.M. (2008). Personal life coaching for coaches-in-training enhances goal attainment and insight, and deepens learning. *Coaching: An International Journal of Research, Theory and Practice*, 1(1), 47–52.

Grant, A.M. & Palmer, S. (2002). *Coaching psychology*. Meeting held at the British Psychological Society's Division of Counselling Psychology Annual Conference, Torquay, 18 May.

Grant, A.M., Curtayne, L. & Burton, G. (2009). Executive coaching enhances goal attainment, resilience and workplace well-being: A randomised controlled study. *The Journal of Positive Psychology*, 4(5), 396–407.

Green, L.S., Oades, L.G. & Grant, A.M (2006). Cognitive-behavioural, solution-focused life coaching: Enhancing goal striving, well-being, and hope. *The Journal of Positive Psychology*, 1(3), 142–149.

Green, S., Grant, A. & Rysaardt, J. (2007). Evidence-based life coaching for senior high school students: Building hardiness and hope. *International Coaching Psychology Review*, 2, 24–32.

Grbcic, S. & Palmer, S. (2006). *A cognitive-behavioural manualised self-coaching approach to stress management and prevention at work: A randomised controlled trial.* Paper given at the International Coaching Psychology Conference held on 18 December, at City University London.

Gyllensten, K., Palmer, S. Nilsson, E-K., Regnér, A.M. & Ann Frodi, A. (2010). Experiences of cognitive coaching: A qualitative study. *International Coaching Psychology Review*, 5(2), 98–108.

Hackman, J. R. (2011). *Collaborative intelligence: Using teams to solve hard problems.* San Francisco: Berrett-Koehler.

Hackman, J.R. & Morris, C.G. (1975). Group tasks, group interaction process, and group performance effectiveness: A review and proposed integration. In L. Berkowitz (Ed.), *Advances in experimental social psychology* (Vol. 8). New York: Academic Press.

Hackman, J.R. & Wageman, R. (2005). A theory of team coaching. *Academy of Management Review*, 2, 269–287.

Hackman, J.R. & Walton, R.E. (1986). Groups under contrasting management strategies. In P.S. Goodman (Ed.), *Designing effective work groups.* San Francisco: Jossey-Bass.

Health and Safety Executive (2004). *Stress Management Standards Indicator Tool.* Retrieved 27 September 2013, from: http://www.hse.gov.uk/stress/standards/pdfs/indicatortool.pdf.

Health and Safety Executive (2013). Stress and psychological disorders. Retrieved 3 September 2013, from: http://www.hse.gov.uk/statistics/causdis/stress/stress.pdf.

Katzenbach, J.R. & Smith, D.K. (1993). *The wisdom of teams: Creating the high-performance organisation.* New York: Harper Business.

Kawakami, N. & Haratani, T. (1999). Epidemiology of job stress and health in Japan: Review of current evidence and future direction. *Industrial Health*, 37(2), 174–186.

Kearns, H., Forbes, A. & Gardiner, M. (2007). Intervention for the treatment of perfectionism and self-handicapping in a non-clinical population. *Behaviour Change*, 24, 157–172.

Kearns, H, Gardiner, M. & Marshall, K. (2008). Innovation in PhD completion: The hardy shall succeed (and be happy!). *Higher Education Research & Development*, 27(1), 77–89.

Kozlowski, S.W.J., Gully, S.M., Salas, E. & Cannon-Bowers, J.A. (1996). Team leadership and development: Theory, principles, and guidelines for training leaders and teams. In M. Beyerlein, D. Johnson & S. Beyerlein (Eds.), *Advances in interdisciplinary studies of work teams: Team leadership, 3* (pp.251–289). Greenwich, CT: JAI Press.

Krajewski, L.J. & Ritzman, L.P. (2005). *Operations management: Processes and value chains.* Upper Saddle River, NJ: Pearson Education.

Kristensen, T.S. (1996). Job stress and cardiovascular disease: A theoretic critical review. *Journal of Occupational Health Psychology*, 1(3), 246–260.

Lau, A.L.D., Cummins, R.A. & McPherson, W. (2005). An investigation into the cross-cultural equivalence of the Personal Well-being Index. *Social Indicators Research*, 72(3), 403–430.

Libri, V. & Kemp, T. (2006). Assessing the efficacy of a cognitive behavioural executive coaching programme. *International Coaching Psychology Review*, 1(1), 9.

Lovibond, P.F. & Lovibond, S.H. (1995). *Manual for the Depression Anxiety Stress Scales.* Sydney: Psychology Foundation.

Neenan, M. & Palmer, S. (2001). Cognitive behavioural coaching. *Stress News*, 13(3), 15–18.

Neenan, M. & Dryden, W. (2002). *Life coaching: A cognitive behavioural approach.* London: Brunner-Routledge.

Palmer, S. (2008). The PRACTICE model of coaching: Towards a solution-focused approach. *Coaching Psychology International*, 1(1), 4–8.

Palmer, S. (2011). Revisiting the 'P' in the PRACTICE coaching model. *The Coaching Psychologist*, 7(2), 156–158.

Palmer, S. & Szymanska, K. (2007). Cognitive behavioural coaching: An integrative approach. In S. Palmer & A. Whybrow (Eds.), *Handbook of coaching psychology: A guide for practitioners*. London: Sage.

Rice, R.W., Near, J.P. & Hunt, R.G. (1980). The Job Satisfaction/Life Satisfaction relationship: A review of empirical research. *Basic and Applied Social Psychology*, 1, 37–64.

Richard, J.T. (1999). Multimodal therapy: A useful model for the executive coach. *Consulting Psychology Journal: Practice and Research*, 51(4), 30.

Rousseau, V., Aubé, C. & Tremblay, S. (2013). Team coaching and innovation in work teams. An examination of the motivational and behavioural intervening mechanisms. *Leadership & Organisation Development Journal*, 34(4), 21.

Sainsbury Centre for Mental Health (SCMH) (2007). Mental health at work: Developing the business case. London: SCMH. Retrieved 3 September 2013, from: http://www.centrefor mentalhealth.org.uk/pdfs/mh_at_work_summary.pdf

Stansfeld, S.A., Fuhrer, R., Shipley, M.J. & Marmot, M.G. (1999). Work characteristics predict psychiatric disorder: Prospective results from the Whitehall II study. *Occupational and Environmental Medicine*, 56, 302–307.

Thompson, L. (2004). *Making the team – a guide for managers* (4th ed.). Upper Saddle River, NJ: Prentice Hall.

Van Mierlo, H., Rutte, C.G., Vermunt, J.K., Kompier, M.A.J. & Doorewaard, J.A.C.M. (2007). A multilevel mediation model of the relationships between team autonomy, individual task design and psychological well-being. *Journal of Occupational and Organisational Psychology*, 80(4), 647–664.

Williams, H., Edgerton, N. & Palmer, S. (2010). Cognitive behavioural coaching. In E. Cox, T. Bachkirova & D. Clutterbuck (Eds.), *The complete handbook of coaching*. London: Sage.

Williams, H., Palmer, S. & Wallace, E. (2011). An integrative coaching approach for family business. In M. Shams & D.A. Lane (Eds.), *Coaching in the family-owned business: A path to growth* (pp.21–39).London: Karnac Books.

World Health Organisation (WHO) (2005). *Mental Health Declaration for Europe – Facing the challenges, building solutions*. Retrieved 3 September 2013, from: http://www.euro.who. int/__data/assets/pdf_file/0008/88595/E85445.pdf.

16 Coaching approaches for a lost sense of self – hunt it down or let it be?

Tessa Dodwell

Abstract

This article uses Stevens's (2002) five lenses (biological, experimentalist, social constructivist, psycho-dynamic and experiential) and Bachkirova's (2011) three stories of the self (self as an operator, an evolved self and no self) to describe different manifestations and interpretations of a lost sense of self. Using a developmental coaching approach, the article then explores three key considerations when coaching a lost sense of self. Firstly, the origin of the loss – how the loss was first sensed by the client. Secondly, the importance of understanding client self-concept is explored in two parts. Initially, understanding of their self-construction (unitary stable self, dynamic self, multiple selves and no self) and next their ego development stage (unformed, formed and reformed). Self-concept is likely to inform client response to their lost sense of self but also inform the type of coaching techniques that might be most appropriate. Finally, the coach perspective is considered. Coaches are encouraged to be aware of their own self-concept and how it might impact their approach. This article concludes that a blend of all these factors will determine whether a lost sense of self is hunted down or simply let be.

'The greatest hazard of all, losing one's self, can occur very quietly in the world, as if it were nothing at all. No other loss can occur so quietly; any other loss – an arm, a leg, five dollars, a wife, etc. – is sure to be noticed.' Kierkegaard (1957)

Keywords

lost sense of self; multiple self-perspectives; developmental coaching; self-concept; identity

Original publication details: Dodwell, T. (2020, June). Coaching approaches for a lost sense of self – hunt it down or let it be? *The Coaching Psychologist, 16*(1), 11–23. Reproduced with permission of The British Psychological Society.

There is widespread support for Kierkegaard's claim that losing one's self is indeed a great hazard: described as a feeling of paralysis (van Alphen, 1992), utter hopelessness (Wisdom et al., 2008) or walking off a cliff (Askew & Carnell, 2011). On the basis that pinpointing what we mean by 'the self' has proved an elusive unresolved puzzle (Bachkirova, 2011), then identifying what we mean by the lost sense of self, is likely to be equally as perplexing. This article initially explores a lost sense of self through Stevens' (2002) five perspectives (biological, experimentalist, social constructivist, psychodynamic and experiential), then reviews how differing theories about the self can influence how the client responds to the loss and the resultant coaching required.

1. The biological perspective of the self

The biological perspective concludes our physical configuration, our neurology determines our sense of self. Evidence of biological influence is highlighted through incidents of brain injury, chemical imbalance or dementia. In Nochi's (1998) qualitative review of subjects following traumatic brain injuries, three facets to a lost sense of self were reported: Loss of self-knowledge; loss of self by comparison to the past and loss of self in the eyes of others. Millière (2017) found ego dissolution, 'a dramatic breakdown of one's sense of self' when certain psychoactive drugs were administered to otherwise healthy subjects. Jetten et al. (2010) deemed that it was the effect of autobiographical memory loss on identity loss, amongst dementia patients, that compromised wellbeing.

2. The experimentalist perspective of the self

In Stevens' second perspective, the experimentalist self, cognition is inferred by interpreting observed behaviour. Two important historical experiments shed light on how cognition can be altered by your environment and potentially impact your sense of self – Milgram's obedience experiment and Seligman's learned helplessness. In Milgram's (1963) experiment, 65 per cent of subjects obeyed authority, administering maximum shock levels to another person. It is unclear if the subjects' sense of self was damaged by these experiments, but their inner conflict was observed by Milgram: 'It was clear from the remarks and outward behaviour that in punishing the victim they are often acting against their own values… one subject was reduced to the point of nervous collapse'.

Seligman's (1972) experiments on dogs showed how, over time, they became apathetic towards shocks. Once they realised there was no way of controlling the shocks, they withdrew, acted depressed and accepted their fate, a term called *learned helplessness*. Seligman extrapolated this work to humans and identified the importance of how negative uncontrollable events were explained internally. When the causation of negative uncontrollable events was attributed internally, this increased the risk of depression and damage to self-esteem (Abramson et al., 1978). Walker (1991) identified internal attribution amongst women who had unsuccessfully attempted to break free from violent relationships.

THE BIOLOGICAL AND EXPERIMENTALIST PERSPECTIVES: SELF AS AN OPERATOR

The above two perspectives suggest Bachkirova's (2011) first story of the self: that the 'self is an operator'. This story views the self as a continuous, self-contained, unique and autonomous agent acting on behalf of the whole organism. This appeals to our common sense and our experience of unity. The central criticism is that, if the operator controls the organism, who or what controls the operator? This would imply an impossible, infinite chain of homunculi. This hypothesised causal link between thought and action was disproved by Libet (1985) who demonstrated often our actions occur before our conscious thought. This story would assume we have privileged access to ourselves, controlling and predicting our outcomes, but as Claxton (1994) states we are better predictors of others behaviour than our own and tend to overestimate our capabilities (Dunning, 2006). Scientifically no physical part of the brain has been identified as representative of the self and the physical network of neurones suggest a more complex relationship than just operator and organism. So this first story – as Bachkirova asserts, 'there is no self in the sense of a homunculus in the brain – it is fiction' (2011, p.72).

3. The social constructivist perspective of the self

The next perspective is the distributed self, created through social interaction. The social constructivist view suggests that the self is not a self-contained entity but created through continual flux with its social environment. The people we interact with, and their relationship with us, will elicit differing responses. Understanding cultural, historical and social contexts is important; for example, differing local attitudes to race, gender and sexuality are likely to impact personal self-perception in terms of self-confidence, self-acceptance and self-esteem. In Stevens example, Kondo (1990, cited in Stevens, 2002, p.266) describes her new emergent Japanese self which metamorphosed depending on who was present, the situation or activity. Kondo was half-Japanese and half-American – she was born in the United States of America but went to live in Japan as a young adult. Kondo observed herself changing her thoughts, behaviour and even body to emanate the Japanese culture within which she was gradually embedding herself. Claxton (1994) views language as a critical part of cultural influence on self-development and notes language can carry subliminal cultural messages (e.g. in this example Japanese modesty bias and American self-promotion bias). Initially, Kondo describes more of a gap than a loss between what was expected of her (due to her Japanese appearance) and what she was capable of in her new role, but as she became more involved in the Japanese culture, there was a sense of losing her American self, so she vowed 'let me escape before I'm completely transformed'.

The importance of social connections is evident in statistics for attempted suicide (Milnes et al., 2002) as perceived unsolvable relationships are the most common cause of suicide, referred to by Baumeister (1990) as the 'ultimate escape from the self' (p.103). The social self builds multiple roles but when one of these roles ends a lost sense of self can be elicited. A lost sense of self is a common feature when a job role is lost on retirement (Kim & Moen, 2002) or a parental role lost when children leave home (Mitchell & Love-green, 2009). The stronger the initial attachment to the role, the harder detachment becomes. Broady (2017) found the more care-givers associate care-giving with their self-identity, the more disruptive they found the death of the care-receiver.

4. The psychodynamic perspective of the self

This psychodynamic view of the self suggests we may not be conscious of our self-hood in totality as much of it is hidden in our unconscious. The self is constructed of a multiplicity of sorts: the unconscious id, the moderating ego and the moral super-ego. The psychodynamic perspective believes much of our self-concept is crafted through internal representations of our relationships with others, especially childhood interactions with primary carers.

Psychodynamics believe that we structure our worlds defensively to avoid the psychological pain of anxiety and maintain a sense of unity. According to Stevens (2002, p.289), 'one of the most profound sources of anxiety is the sense of impending loss of identity, or fragmentation and loss of self'. To protect against this, to promote psychological survival, the mind creates defence mechanisms. These mechanisms are largely unconscious and can include projection, dissociation, and repression. Dissociation is depersonalisation, when someone's thoughts seem not to belong to themselves. This extreme loss of self, according to Chiu et al. (2017), is closely linked to stress, 71 per cent of patients who exhibited dissociation had experienced physical or sexual abuse as a child. Price (2007) suggests that post-traumatic stress disorder may result if trauma isn't processed instantly. To defend the organism from the trauma experienced, distressing material is segregated and blocked from the conscious to protect against self-disintegration.

THE SOCIAL CONSTRUCTIVIST AND PSYCHODYNAMIC PERSPECTIVES: AN EVOLVING SELF

Bachkirova's third story of the self is the most widely accepted current view of the self – 'an evolving self'. There are several developmental theories explaining how over time, or with experience, we are capable of change and different aspects of our selves evolve (e.g. Kegan's five orders of consciousness, Loevinger's ten and Bachkirova's three stages of ego development).

Wilber (1999) recognised the complexity of development, suggesting each line evolved 'relatively independently'; some lines or mini-selves co-existing harmoniously, others in conflict. Humphrey (2000) suggests the mini-selves collaborate to effectively steer the whole organism through life, most unconsciously, others knowingly. Developmental theories align with the widely accepted concept of multiplicity and are further supported by empirical evidence from Gazzaniga's (1985) split brain work, and Rowan's (2009) sub-personalities.

5. The experiential perspective of the self

Finally, the experiential perspective, by its very private nature, is not supported by extensive research, more philosophical musings. James (1890) suggested a man's self is the total of all that is his, but with this comes increased vulnerability, so a sudden loss of possessions can result in a 'partial conversion of ourselves to nothingness' (Csikszentmihalyi, 1993, p.79). In Lollar's (2010) autobiographical account, she concludes a loss of extended self when her home burnt down – 'the loss created a profound disruption of identity for me, leading to significant disorientation and confusion in normal functioning' (p.270).

Thus far, a lost sense of self has been regarded negatively but Csikszentmihalyi (1993) presents loss of self as being a positive experience. Csikszentmihalyi (1993) describes 'the illusion of self-hood' (p.76) as the side effect of being conscious and suggests a self is a figment of our imagination. Often the sense of 'no self' is articulated by religious scholars e.g. Mekur (2014) describes his experience as: '...an imageless experience in which there is no sense of personal identity. It is the experience that remains possible in a state of extremely deep trance when the ego-functions of reality-testing, sense-perception, memory, reason, fantasy and self-representation are repressed.' Buddhists encourage surrendering of possessions, goals and desires to give up the self, using tools like meditation, and paradoxically, intense self-analysis. This enables the self to be seen for what it is – a series of transient elements, often driven by external forces – thus the idea of a 'permanent "self" dies before our very eyes' (Giles, 1993). Csikszentmihalyi (1993) cites this ability to self-access as a rarity but describes a more accessible lost sense of self with his concept of 'flow experience' when we attend to, and enjoy, what we are doing in that moment. He recounts this sense of exhilaration experienced by a composer, 'you are in an ecstatic state to such a point that you feel as though you almost don't exist'.

EXPERIENTIAL PERSPECTIVE: NO SELF

This concept represents Bachkirova's second story of the self – there is no self. Philosopher Metzinger (2003) suggests the self is an illusion, it performs no function and only exists in our construction. Our actions are driven by multiple interactions with our environment, some rational and deliberate, others originating from underlying processes in our body or unconscious mind. Wegner (2005) welcomes this giving up of control and states: 'There are a whole lot of things that I don't have to worry about controlling because I know that I'm really just a little window on lovely machinery doing lots of things' (p.255). The self can be overcome momentarily with mindfulness or 'experience flow' or following prolonged deliberate spiritual practise. For many developmental theorists, this is the pinnacle of development; for example, Maslow's self-actualisation.

The first four of Stevens' perspectives are 'third-person' perspectives on the self which contribute to our understanding of the self-concept. However, in my opinion, the 'first-person' experiential perspective is most relevant for coaching. For the client, their subjective lived experience, their perception, is their reality. Although the 'self as an operator' is not a proven theory, it is the subjective sense of the majority. To maintain this illusion of a unitary self, our narrator strives to construct an overarching consistent and coherent 'self' that is plausible based on our personal history and cultural context. As Haidt (2006) suggests, our self-story is a work of historical fiction combining the socio-cultural aspects of language, our internal lens of interpretation and our distorted retrieved memories. It is my view that our sense of self is an illusory concept and we all hold differing but equally valid interpretations of its construction.

Having reviewed how Stevens' (2002) five lenses link to Bachkirova's (2011) three stories on the self, this next section looks at how this information can be used to inform coaching for the specific issue of a lost sense of self. Due to the complexity and depth of this 'self' topic, developmental coaching is a favoured approach.

Bachkirova (2016) identifies three mechanisms of developmental coaching that 'address the obstacles to organic change' (p.90).

The first mechanism is working with a client's quality of perception. As Simons and Chabris (1999) demonstrated, we see what we pay attention to. They asked people to watch a video and focus on counting the number of ball passes in a games hall and by focussing on this task, most people completely missed the presence of someone in a gorilla suit walk across the hall mid game. The second mechanism is working with our whole organism. Rather than relying on hard thinking to get results, 'looking for' an answer, Claxton (2006) recommends instead 'looking at', which he termed soft thinking. Recognising and listening to body signals or 'felt senses' termed 'focusing' by Gendlin (2003) can be enhanced through the use of imagery or mindfulness. The third mechanism of developmental coaching is working with multiplicity. Strawson (2009) describes two approaches to multiplicity – diachronics notice the multiplicity and attempt create a coherent narrative whereas for episodics, the self just happens. It is important to note that, as Carter (2008) suggests, different roles can be at different stages of development.

KEY CONSIDERATIONS WHEN COACHING A LOST SENSE OF SELF

Clients may present at coaching with a lost sense of self but typically this will emerge as coaching progresses. How to approach coaching a lost sense of self, depends on three key considerations – what triggered the sense of loss, the client's reaction to this loss and the coach approach taken.

A. Considering the trigger that prompted a lost sense of self

As the above examples demonstrate, there are a great variety of potential triggers which can prompt a lost sense of self in the client, some of which may even be hidden in the client's unconscious. The triggers might be brief (loss of job role) or enduring (loss of parental role), onset might be sudden (bereavement) or gradual (abusive relationship) and triggers may originate externally (social interaction), or internally (through conflict between mini-selves). Whatever the trigger, as Price (2009) warns, the therapy threshold must be carefully considered, and referrals made for severe responses, for example, attempted suicide or dissociation. Exploring the client trigger will offer a useful starting point for coaching and may provide insight into the priority of coaching needs. Self-awareness exercises may help identify triggers if origin is not explicitly known.

B. Considering the client response to a lost sense of self

The client's response to their lost sense of self is likely to be a deciding factor for the coach in how the coaching progresses (i.e. to hunt the loss or to let it be). Client response will vary with understanding of their self-construction (unitary stable self, dynamic self, multiple selves or no self), or their ego development (unformed, formed or reformed).

(a) The client's understanding of self-construction

(i) A unitary stable self

Clients who believe in a unitary, stable, 'self as operator' model might find a lost sense of self catastrophic – how are they to function at all without a self in charge? Clients may seek their one true authentic self – Hollis (1993) suggests a discrepancy between lived and authentic self can trigger a midlife crisis. In either case, clients will be compelled to find their lost self with some urgency. Coaching needs to appeal to their perceived operator, on the basis that by changing the operator, the belief is that the whole organism can be transformed. The operator may be accessed by building strong client trust or perhaps using neuro-linguistic programming.

(ii) A dynamic self

I have included a second understanding of self-construction – a dynamic 'story of the self' originating from my coaching practice. One client, Rachel described a self that was continually reinventing itself to suit the audi-ence or context, no consistent core self was detected. Clients may be comfortable with this seamless dynamism or, as in Rachel's case, feel unsettled and unable to articulate their 'true' self. In this situation the goal may be to work with articulation of the self, perhaps using narrative coaching (Drake, 2007) to enable the client to express their own 'self-story'.

(iii) Multiple selves

If the client believes in multiplicity, then loss of 'one' mini-self may feel unsettling, but is unlikely to feel catastrophic. Clients may choose to work on reconstruction of the lost mini-self, reinvention of a new mini-self or let the mini-self disappear. Conflict between the mini-selves can prompt a sense of fragmentation and the client may wish to resolve the conflict or synthesise the mini-selves to a cohesive whole. It is also possible that a lost sense of self is felt but not understood – perhaps if a lost mini-self is buried in the unconscious (e.g. post-traumatic stress disorder). This could prompt a desire for synthesis with unconscious mini-selves, so a hypnosis referral may help (Watkins, 1993).

(iv) No self

The client may believe in the notion of no self, viewing the self as an illusory concept or, via flow experience or spirituality, they have experienced the positive sensation of losing themselves. In these situations clients are likely to be comfortable with their lost selves and may attend coaching to increase its incidence. Clients wishing to work towards the notion of no self might welcome mindfulness as part of their coaching sessions.

(b) The clients' ego development
(i) Unformed

The unformed ego is dependent on others for social norms or guidance and tends to have a restricted self-view. Increasing self-awareness, encouraging independent thought and introducing differing perspectives (e.g. parent, adult and child of transactional analysis) can help them to understand their complexity and maybe even accept their multiplicity. To ensure the whole organism is engaged, dreams may be analysed, and soft thinking prompted to access a deeper voice.

A lost sense of self in an unformed ego prompts a hunt for cohesion and consistency. Cohesion might be achieved by resolving internal conflict between what they are capable of and what is expected of them (e.g. balancing work and motherhood, either increasing capability or reducing expectation). Alternatively, a new internal coach or mini-self (e.g. Mead's internalised generalised other, cited in Stevens, 2002, p.249) could provide resolution. Consistency could be achieved using narrative coaching, creating a coherent story to articulate a continually changing self, a historical self or a developing new self (Drake, 2007). According to Fingarette (2000), consistency is not a default, but needs work to be maintained, the narrator is continually synthesising stories to maintain unity.

Unformed egos often protect themselves by self-deception so elucidating discrepancies may overwhelm them. Self-deception by justification or avoidance is common when dissonant beliefs exist (Festinger, 1964). According to agency theory, individuals may justify themselves as acting on another's behalf to erase responsibility for their actions. Interestingly, Alexander (1949) observed within the concentration camps of World War II, that the SS remained guilt-free and, as Eichmann urged at his war crime trial, he was 'only following orders'. In terms of avoidance, it is possible unformed egos will avoid coaching for fear of what they might uncover. The client will benefit from a supportive, positive psychology approach focussing on optimism and anxiety reduction. Cognitive behavioural coach approaches (Williams et al., 2010) can be useful to uncover underlying fears or self-sabotage that might be maintaining dissonance.

(ii) Formed

The formed ego is commonplace amongst accomplished, busy executives. Multiplicity is readily accepted with regular juggling of many roles. Clients are likely to over-think, and believe hard thinking will resolve the issue. Coaching may initially focus on self-awareness and introduce multiple perspectives using tools like 360 degree feedback, or Johari window, or techniques that objectify the self (e.g. Gestalt chair technique or Kegan's subject–object interviews).

A lost sense of self in formed egos is commonly instigated by burnout when the body can no longer cope with the self-imposed stress. Challenging questions need to be carefully judged so stress isn't heightened. Coaching techniques should be broad to ensure that the coach is not just communicating with the client's conscious. In cases of burnout, the client needs to hold a greater respect for their body, so intuition must be heard and acted upon (Claxton & Lucas, 2007). Visual prompts can help access emotions, unlock free thinking and creativity. Gestalt techniques and Gendlin's (2003) focusing can help express emotions and encourage more feeling.

A lost sense of self in a formed ego is thought to be less painful (Bachkirova, 2011) yet could still prompt a hunt (for cohesion, consistency, reconstruction or reinvention) but, in cases of acceptance, a hunt may not be necessary. Conflict amongst formed egos could be self-instigated by a gap between their actual and ideal selves. This gap may manifest in the type of language used (e.g. 'should', which suggests expectations exist which have not been met). Setting ideal expectations could increase stress by setting yourself up to fail (Maxwell & Bachkirova, 2010). In Maxwell and Bachkirova's paper (2010) there are five methods suggested to promote cohesion of a self-concept, only three relevant for the formed ego: decrease the ideal, move towards the ideal, or do both. To encourage a consistent narrative, story construction might be aided with the voice dialogue method (Stone & Winkelman, 1985) where the motivation behind each mini-self is discovered. By synthesising the mini-selves and building an internal collaborative team, a coherent narrative may result. However, the client may not feel there is a need to synthesise – as Fingarette (2000) warns to synthesise is to misrepresent. Some encourage interventions to 're-establish, or …reconfirm the sense of self' (Pollack, 1994; i.e. building a new role, or working on a comprehensive, continuous, new narrative). Horowitz (2015) recounts the recovery of model Sophia following an accident which left her a blind amputee. Her rehabilitation included acceptance of her new body, establishing a new job role and clarifying a narrative to explain her continuity of self.

It is possible the stress of the formed ego is symptomatic of an underlying threat or self-deception. Hidden mini-selves in the unconscious should not be ignored (Lee, 2010), and their presence may be detected by metaphors, Freudian slips and non-verbal behaviour (Frosh 1991). Uncovering underlying threats can be addressed using techniques like Kegan and Lahey's (2009) immunity to change. Acceptance, using holistic techniques like visualisation, may be more appropriate for the formed ego once all mini-selves are identified. The client will benefit from coaching that raises challenging questions and encourages access to emotions.

(iii) Reformed

The reformed ego seeks meaning, often over-reflects and can instigate conflict between their lived experience and their preferred life full of meaning. Conflict can be resolved using techniques that focus on meaning and being, rather than doing. Transpersonal coaching helps normalise 'the crisis of meaning' and highlight the benefit and opportunities. Typically, reformed egos don't seek consistency as they already possess a versatile effective team of mini-selves. The biggest issue is likely to be interruptions from their confused narrator who is battling with reconciling authenticity and multiplicity. The key to development in this stage is improving perception and the client might be challenged to give up on the self altogether (Wade, 1996). Introducing clients to mindfulness or meditation might help them to focus more in the moment and quieten their narrator (Blackmore, 2003). Once conflict is resolved and the narrator silenced, the self can be truly seen. Another technique called psychosynthesis is promoted within transpersonal coaching. By working with the client's soul and spirituality, this tool encourages synthesis of the self, combining energy and pragmatism to establish client purpose, and evolve the client toward's self-actualisation (Whitmore & Einzig, 2007).

In Maxwell and Bachkirova's (2010) paper on self-concept and development strategies, the last two models are relevant for the reformed ego. Firstly, self-acceptance; for example, breaking the need to chase after ideals. Krishnamurti (1994) warns we should ignore truth-seeking and just *be*. This can be encouraged by 'thinking at the edge', mulling over issues on your metaphorical backburner (Claxton, 2006). Claxton advises order can be abandoned and whatever enters the consciousness is accepted as being on top of the whole organism's pile of needs. Secondly self-reduction, the reformed ego is seeking surrender, transcendence and elimination of the self in search of a higher meaning. Van Deurzen-Smith (2002) describes how existentialist coaches work well with the ambiguity of the reformed ego by just listening, being truly present, letting go of the need to diagnose and acting as a thought partner.

(c) Considering the coach approach

Kegan argues that 'amongst the many things from which a practitioner's clients need protection is the practitioner's hopes for the client's future, however benign and sympathetic these hopes may be'. (Kegan, 1982, p.295).

The coach needs to suspend their own self-view to gauge the client's lived experience of the self. It is important however that they understand their self-concept so they can be aware of how it might impact their coaching. Coaches with unformed egos might welcome a structured approach and will have a tendency to support rather than challenge their clients. Coaches with formed egos are more likely to challenge and will have crafted their own coach approach, which they will apply to empower the client achieve their own goals. Coaches with reformed egos are less likely to use structure, and more likely to rely on intuition. Coaching might be most effective when coach and client ideas on self-construction are aligned but, in terms of ego development, opinions differ. Laske (2006) suggests the coach should be at the same ego development stage as the client, or greater, whereas Bachkirova (2011) suggests your stage is less relevant and your presence and curiosity more valuable. If stages differ to your own, understanding the stage may not be necessary, as just listening and offering the client a space to explore their own theme can prompt creativity and self-resolution. At a time when I believed strongly in only one self-hood, I coached a client who claimed she had no self. I did not understand how it would feel to have 'no self' so found it difficult to relate to my client. This session was a steep but fascinating learning curve, but curiosity led us to an interesting conclusion, much more palatable in retrospect, than at the time.

Whichever ego stage, the coach must be self-aware, recognising their self-deception, their self-distorted story and prevent this frame of reference from restricting their client's experience. Equally the coach needs to recognise they are liaising with the client's narrator, which presents yet another layer of distortion. As Bachkirova suggests, your whole organism is your instrument, so you need to maximise your coach effectiveness by working on your self-awareness, ensuring self-care and monitoring for self-deception. Having a supervisor that identifies or challenges your self-awareness or self-deception can be an asset to your self-development.

Case study

Tom was a partner in a law firm. He sought coaching for remedial purposes at age 57, following an employee tribunal which caused him heightened stress and ultimately impacted his health. Tom really enjoyed the coaching process, so continued to attend coaching for several years. He had agreed to retire at age 60 (as part of his initial work contract with the law firm) and his transition to retirement occurred whilst still attending coaching. At the point of becoming retired he experienced a lost sense of self. As he explained, 'You lose your badge. For years, I'd been a partner in a law firm – if somebody had said, "What do you do?" I could say. I was worried I couldn't say who I was anymore… the transition (to retirement) was not easy at all.'

Tom had spent over 20 years at the same law firm and had played a key part in its growth. He had spent many hours working late and described himself as 'fully engaged in the firm' and 'absorbed' by his work.

In the run up to his retirement, the firm started treating him differently. Prior to his exit, when it was time for his annual appraisal, his HR department suggested he didn't need to complete his appraisal as he was soon leaving. He insisted on completing the appraisal as he wanted an opportunity to express how it felt being a departing partner.

At the point he turned 60, he was offered a role to continue working at the law firm but in the capacity of a part-time consultant. In an effort to sustain his identity as a lawyer, he accepted this offer but rather than helping, this hindered his transition. 'I found the experience unsettling… the hardest thing is accepting that where you were once fully involved and engaged in the central running of the practice and responsible for making decisions, you lose that, that stops and you feel as though you've become a bit of a supernumerary'.

Tom felt 'abandoned' by his firm – it was as if his value and worth had vanished overnight. That a change in age could have such an impact angered him, 'We still have tonnes to offer. We are a much healthier community of 60 year olds than previously. Why not look after us? We can be very, very productive – we can teach people, we are a great source of knowledge and experience, but we can also do stuff.'

The trigger: The transition to retirement.

Client self-concept: Tom presented as experiencing a unitary stable self. This self-concept was evidenced by his language where clearly his life revolved around his work. His identity and self-worth were synonymous with his job role. This strong role attachment meant he found the concept of losing his role as a lawyer catastrophic.

Client ego-development: Tom's ego-development stage was a formed ego. A law partner heavily invested in his work but experiencing health issues following burnout.

The coach: Initially chosen for her understanding of the law environment and experience of tribunals, after many years together, Tom's coach created an excellent bond founded on deep mutual trust. Tom felt his coaching sessions were a safe space where he talked openly, honestly and freely about himself. He valued her understanding of his work environment and felt they could 'exchange ideas at the appropriate sort of level'.

Coach approach: Tom's coach used techniques from Bachkirova's (2011) three mechanisms of developmental coaching to address Tom's lost sense of self.

1. Mechanism 1:
Working with the quality of perception
Tom's coach worked primarily on Tom's self-view. Tom had never previously used any self-awareness tools or psychometric testing like Myers-Briggs. He was astounded by what he discovered about himself. Tom alikened the exercises to 'black magic' finding them 'fascinating, …interesting, …helpful, important'. Tom explained these exercises 'shed light on things I didn't know about myself but should have known'. Coaching sessions prompted self-reflection and Tom valued the three-week gap between sessions, finding it 'really useful to ruminate' between self-discoveries.

There was evidence of some protective self-deception, especially surrounding the tribunal. This was explored sensitively with Tom and he recognised the importance of 'being honest with oneself'.

2. Mechanism 2:
Working with the whole body
Tom directly attributed his health issues to the stress of his job. Tom described his work environment as 'challenging… rigorous… it involved lots of long, long days and long evenings'. He recounted, 'I was always the idiot who was first in, last out…'. Tom's health suffered and the added stress of the tribunal tipped the balance, contributing to a stroke and depression, 'It was a real wake-up call'.

Through coaching, Tom learnt to have more respect for his body, to take better care of his health. Tom took up yoga and mindfulness. With hindsight, Tom reflected on how he wished he had previously 'been more selfish, taken more care of myself – both my physical health, and my mental wellbeing'.

Tom started to engage with other retired colleagues. Whereas previously his conversations had been work focussed, he chose to open-up about how he was feeling about his lost sense of self. He was delighted to discover he was not alone in his thinking and others were experiencing the same thoughts and feelings. He set up regular retiree meetings to share experiences, 'I found talking with my peers very helpful.'

3. Mechanism 3:
Working with multiplicity
The self-awareness exercises helped Tom realise he was much more than 'just a lawyer' and rediscovering skills and interests identified several mini-selves which had been

hidden, forgotten or suppressed. He enjoyed reacquainting himself with some of his core values and needs: 'I spent so many years indoors in an office, but actually I realised I'm more of an outdoorsy person'. With increased self-knowledge, and appreciation of his multifaceted post-retirement life, Tom became more comfortable with the concept of multiplicity.

When he was asked to write a CV and LinkedIn profile by a recruitment agency, he found it very difficult to articulate who he was 'creating your own brand, for somebody of my generation, is just anathema'. Tom didn't want to come across as 'Trumpesque... or boastful' so he used coaching to help him craft a new narrative he could feel comfortable with. As Tom's self-awareness improved, and his multiplicity became accepted, his profile was edited to synthesise his mini-selves and produce a more coherent articulation.

Tom has now found a balance postretirement that works for him. He continues to work part-time as a lawyer but mainly doing pro bono work. He values the time he spends with his clients, getting to know them and understand their world view. His clients are from diverse backgrounds and no longer just 'men in suits'. He finds his perceptions and expectations continually challenged which he finds enriching and invigorating in a way his previous work was not.

CONCLUSION

Most coaches, within the lifetime of their practice, are likely to come across clients who have experienced a lost sense of self. This article highlights three key considerations when this issue presents. Firstly, understanding the trigger can indicate whether the therapy threshold has been crossed and, if the client is deemed suitable for coaching, provides a useful starting point. Secondly, the client's response is shaped by their own self-concept and ego development. I believe the self is an illusory concept, but people's 'sense of self', however construed, is very real to them. Clients with a unitary self-concept are likely to find losing their sense of self catastrophic, whereas clients who support multiplicity, might find the loss easier to overcome. Client ego development stages prompt differing goals with unformed egos seeking self-consistency or coherence, whereas reformed egos seek self-acceptance or self-reduction. The final key consideration is the coach approach. Approaches will be tailored to the client's differing needs, but the ultimate aim will be the same – for clients to banish their sense of loss and be comfortable with themselves, whatever their self-perception. Developmental coaching is a helpful approach for coaching a lost sense of self and narrative coaching offers clients the chance to articulate their self-story, amend it or create new options. Most clients are likely to benefit from coaching for increased self-awareness, coaching the whole organism, identifying underlying self-deception and creating a coherent narrative. The coach needs to ignore their own self-concept, pay attention to their client's stance, adapt their questions to meet a unitary, multiple, dynamic or non-existent self. Coaches must also understand how their ego development might influence any resolution to a lost sense of self – whether to hunt it down or let it be.

REFERENCES

Abramson, L., Seligman, M. & Teasdale, J. (1978). Learned helplessness in humans: Critique and reformulation. *Journal of Abnormal Psychology*, *87*(1), 49–74. doi:10.1037/0021-843X.87.1.49

Alexander, L. (1949). The molding of personality under dictatorship. The importance of the destructive drives in the socio-psychological structure of Nazism. *Journal of Criminal Law and Criminology*, *40*(1), 3–27. doi:10.2307/1138348

Askew, S. & Carnell, E. (2011). *Transformative coaching: A learning theory for practice*. London, UK: Institute of Education Press.

Bachkirova, T. (2010). Dealing with issues of the self-concept and self-improvement strategies in coaching and mentoring. *International Journal of Evidence Based Coaching and Mentoring*, *2*(2), 29–40.

Bachkirova, T. (2011). *Developmental coaching: working with the self*. Maidenhead, UK: McGraw-Hill International.

Bachkirova, T. (2016). 'The Self of the coach: Conceptualisation, issues and opportunities for practitioner development'. *Consulting Psychology Journal: Practice and Research*, *68*(2), 143–156. doi:10.1037/cpb0000055

Baumeister, R. (1990). Suicide as escape from self. *Psychological Review*, *97*(1), 90–113. doi:10.1037/0033-295X.97.1.90

Blackmore, S.J. (2003). *Consciousness: An introduction*. New York, NY: Hodder & Stoughton.

Broady, T.R. (2017). Carers' experiences of end-oflife care: A scoping review and application of personal construct psychology. *Australian Psychologist*, *52*(5), 372–380. doi:10.1111/ap.12278

Carter, R. (2008). *Multiplicity: The new science of personality*. London, UK: Little, Brown.

Chiu, C.D., Tollenaar, M.S., Yang, C.T. et al. (2019). The loss of the self in memory: Self-referential memory, childhood relational trauma, and dissociation. *Clinical Psychological Science*, *7*(2), 265–282. doi:10.1177/2167702618804794

Claxton, G. (1994). *Noises from the darkroom: The science and mystery of the mind*. London, UK: Aquarian.

Claxton, G. (2006). Thinking at the edge: developing soft creativity. *Cambridge Journal of Education*, *36*(3), 351–362. doi:10.1080/03057640600865876

Claxton, G. & Lucas, B. (2007). *The creative thinking plan: How to generate ideas and Solve problems in your work and life*. London, UK: BBC books.

Csikszentmihalyi, M. (1993). *The evolving self: A psychology for the third millennium*. New York, NY: HarperCollins.

Drake, D.B. (2007). The art of thinking narratively: Implications for coaching psychology and practice. *Australian Psychologist*, *42*(4), 283–294. doi:10.1080/00050060701648159

Dunning, D. (2006). Strangers to ourselves. *The Psychologist*, *19*(10), 600–603.

Festinger, L. (1964). *Conflict, decision, and dissonance*. London, UK: Tavistock.

Fingarette, H. (2000). *Self-deception*. Berkeley, CA: University of California Press.

Frosh, S. (1991). *Identity crisis: Modernity, psychoanalysis and the self*. London, UK: Macmillan.

Gazzaniga, M. (1985). *The social brain*. New York, NY: Basic Books.

Gendlin, E. (2003). *Focusing*. London, UK: Rider.

Giles, J. (1993). The no-self theory: Hume, Buddhism, and personal identity. *Philosophy East and West*, *43*(2), 175–200. doi:10.2307/1399612

Haidt, J. (2006). *The happiness hypothesis: Putting ancient wisdom and philosophy to the test of modern science*. London, UK: Arrow Books.

Hollis, J. (1993). *The middle passage: From misery to meaning in midlife*. Toronto, Canada: Inner City Books.

Horowitz, M.J. (2015). Effects of trauma on sense of self. *Journal of loss and trauma, 20*(2), 189–193. doi:10.1080/15325024.2014.897578

Humphrey, N. (2000). One-self: A meditation on the unity of consciousness. *Social research*, 1059–1066.

James, W. (1890). *Principles of Psychology. Vol.1.* New York, NY: Henry Holt.

Jetten, J., Haslam, C., Pugliese, C. et al. (2010). Declining autobiographical memory and the loss of identity: Effects on wellbeing. *Journal of clinical and experimental neuropsychology, 32*(4), 408–416. doi:10.1080/13803390903140603

Kegan, R. (1982) *The evolving self: Problem and process in human development.* Cambridge, MA: Harvard University Press.

Kegan, R. & Lahey, L. (2009). *Immunity to change: How to overcome it and unlock potential in yourself and your organization.* Boston, MA: Harvard Business Press.

Kierkegaard, S. (1957). In S. Kierkegaard, H. Hong, & E. Hong (1980). *The sickness unto death: a Christian psychological exposition for upbuilding and awakening.* Princeton, NJ: Princeton University Press.

Kim, J.E. & Moen, P. (2002). Retirement transitions, gender, and psychological wellbeing: A life-course, ecological model. *The Journals of Gerontology Series B: Psychological Sciences and Social Sciences, 57*(3), 212–222. doi:10.1093/geronb/57.3.P212

Krishnamurti, J. (1994). *Commentaries on living, first series.* London, UK: The Theosophical Publishing House.

Laske, O. (2006). *Measuring hidden dimensions: The art and science of fully engaging adults.* Medford, MA: Interdevelopmental Institute Press.

Lee, G. (2010). The psychodynamic approach to counselling, in E. Cox, T. Bachkirova, & D. Clutterbuck (Eds). *The Complete Handbook of Coaching.* (pp.23–36). London, UK: Sage Publications Ltd.

Libet, B. (1985). Unconscious cerebral initiative and the role of conscious will in voluntary action. *Behavioral and brain sciences, 8*(4), 529–539. doi:10.1017/S0140525X00044903

Lollar, K. (2010). The liminal experience: Loss of extended self after the fire. *Qualitative Inquiry, 16*(4), 262–270. doi:10.1177/1077800409354066

Maxwell, A. & Bachkirova, T. (2010) Applying psychological theories of self-esteem in coaching practice. *International Coaching Psychology Review 5*(1), 18–28.

Merkur, D. (2014). The formation of hippie spirituality:1. Union with god. In: J. Harold Ellens (Ed), *Seeking the Sacred with Psychoactive Substances: Chemical Paths to Spirituality and to God.* California: ABC-CLIO.

Merkur, D. (2014). The formation of hippie spirituality 1: Union with God 2: Further and further. In: J. Harold Ellens (Ed.), *Seeking the Sacred with Psychoactive Substances: Chemical paths to spirituality and to God, Volume 1: History and Practices* (pp.207– 290). Santa Barbara, CA: Praeger.

Metzinger, T. (2003). *Being no one: The self-model theory of subjectivity.* Cambridge, MA: MIT Press.

Milgram, S. (1963). Behavioral study of obedience. *The Journal of abnormal and social psychology, 67*(4), 371–378. doi:10.1037/h0040525

Milliere, R. (2017). Looking for the self: Phenomenology, neurophysiology and philosophical significance of drug-induced ego dissolution. *Frontiers in human neuroscience, 11*, 1–22. doi:10.3389/fnhum.2017.00245

Milnes, D., Owens, D. & Blenkiron, P. (2002). Problems reported by self-harm patients: Perception, hopelessness, and suicidal intent. *Journal of psychosomatic research, 53*(3), 819–822. doi:10.1016/S0022-3999(02)00327-6

Mitchell, B.A. & Lovegreen, L.D. (2009). The empty nest syndrome in midlife families: A multimethod exploration of parental gender differences and cultural dynamics. *Journal of Family Issues, 30*(12), 1651–1670. doi:10.1177/0192513X09339020

Nochi, M. (1998). 'Loss of self' in the narratives of people with traumatic brain injuries: A qualitative analysis. *Social Science & medicine, 46*(7), 869–878. doi:10.1016/S0277-9536 (97)00211-6

Pollack, I. (1994). Individual psychotherapy. In J.Silver, S. Yudofsky, R. & Hales (Eds). *Neuropsychiatry of Traumatic Brain Injury*, (pp. 671–702). Washington, DC: American Psychiatric Press.

Price, J.P. (2007). Cognitive schemas, defence mechanisms and post-traumatic stress symptomatology. *Psychology and Psychotherapy: Theory, Research and Practice, 80*(3), 343–353. doi:10.1348/147608306X144178

Price, J. (2009). The coaching/therapy boundary in organizational coaching. *Coaching: An International Journal of Theory, Research and Practice, 2*(2), 135–148. doi:10.1080/1752 1880903085164

Rowan, J. (2009) *Subpersonalities – The people Inside Us*. London, UK: Brunner-Routledge.

Seligman, M.E. (1972). Learned helplessness. *Annual review of medicine, 23*(1), 407–412.

Simons, D.J. & Chabris, C.F. (1999). Gorillas in our midst: Sustained inattentional blindness for dynamic events. *Perception, 28*(9), 1059–1074. doi:10.1068/p281059

Stevens, R. (2002). *Understanding the self*. London, UK: Sage.

Stone, H. & Winkelman, S. (1985). *Embracing our selves*. Marina del Rey, CA: Devorss and Co.

Strawson, G. (2009). *Selves*. Oxford, UK: Clarendon Press.

Van Alphen, E. (1992). *Francis bacon and the loss of self*. London, UK: Reaktion Books.

Van Deurzen-Smith, E. (2002) *Existential Coaching and Psychotherapy in practice* (2nd edn). London, UK: Sage.

Wade, J. (1996). *Changes of mind: A holonomic theory of the evolution of consciousness*. Albany, NY: University of New York, NY Press.

Walker, L.E. (1991). Post-traumatic stress disorder in women: Diagnosis and treatment of battered woman syndrome. *Psychotherapy: Theory, Research, Practice, Training, 28*(1), 21–29. doi:10.1037/0033-3204.28.1.21

Watkins, H.H. (1993). Ego-state therapy: An overview. *American Journal of Clinical Hypnosis, 35*(4), 232–240. doi:10.1080/00029157.1993.10403014

Wegner, D (2005). 'Don't think about a white bear', In S. Blackmore (eEd) (2005), *Conversation on consciousness* (pp.245–257). New York, NY: Oxford University Press.

Whitmore, J. & Einzig, H. (2007). Transpersonal Coaching, in J. Passmore (Ed), *Excellence in coaching* (pp.119–134). London, UK: Kogan Page.

Wilber, K. (1999). *One taste: The journals of Ken Wilber*. Boston, MA: Shambhala.

Williams, H. Edgerton, N. & Palmer, S. (2010). Cognitive-behavioural coaching, in E. Cox, T. Bachkirova & D. Clutterbuck (Eds), *The complete handbook of coaching*, (pp.37–53). London, UK: Sage.

Wisdom, J.P., Bruce, K., Auzeen Saedi, G. et al. (2008). 'Stealing me from myself': Identity and recovery in personal accounts of mental illness. *Australian & New Zealand Journal of Psychiatry, 42*(6), 489–495. doi:10.1080/00048670802050579

Section 6
Cognitive Approaches

David Tee & Jonathan Passmore

INTRODUCTION

Western (2017) argues that coaching literature is dominated by applied psychotherapeutic models. Principles from behaviourism, such as repetitive task practice and the reinforcement of desired behaviour, can be seen to shape early workplace performance coaching. However, the practice of coaching evolved as the latter half of the twentieth century progressed.

One individual argued to influence this legitimising of focus beyond behaviourism's observable 'outer game' is Tim Gallwey. Working initially in a sports context with tennis players, Gallwey popularised the notion that more than physical skill and technical competence was required for success; that "… something else besides tennis is being played on the courts is obvious to the most casual observer" (Gallwey, 1974, p. 94). In essence, that there is a Self 1 whose thoughts are programming and controlling Self 2: the performer.

The potted histories of cognitive-behavioural coaching (CBC) one finds at the start of journal papers or book chapters on the subject typically point to creators of cognitive therapies, such as Albert Ellis and Aaron T. Beck as the foundation upon which CBC has been built. We argue that Gallwey's work had at least a partial influence too. Firstly, O'Broin and Palmer (2006) note that the appeal of sports to business people led to the migration of many sports psychology practices to occupational settings from the 1970s onwards. Peltier (2001) states that the association of coaching with successful athletes and sports teams aided its appeal as an intervention to business executives and also differentiated it from the related 'helping-by-talking' profession of counselling. He speculated that "Counselling is associated with weakness and inadequacy, while coaching is identified with successful sports figures and winning teams" (p. 170). Gallwey's background as captain of the Harvard tennis team and then as a successful sports coach helped spearhead this migrating of practices to the world of

Coaching Practiced, First Edition. Edited by David Tee and Jonathan Passmore.
© 2022 John Wiley & Sons Ltd. Published 2022 by John Wiley & Sons Ltd.
DOI: 10.1002/9781119835714.s06

work. Secondly, that within those practices, Gallwey legitimised 'diving below the surface': exploring the thoughts and feelings that might be aiding or hindering actual performance. As Sabat (2010, as cited in Wildflower, 2013, p. 40) stated, 'The book isn't really about tennis; it's how the human mind is meant to think and learn, and how far off we are in our preconceptions about those things'.

Gallwey (2000) confirmed this cross-pollination from sports to business with the publication of 'The Inner Game of Work'. With the positioning of coaching by this point as a badge of status and recognition within contemporary corporate settings (Wasylyshyn, 2008), it then became easy for CBC as an applied psychotherapeutic model to justify its relevance to executives. It became easy for coaches to promote "the idea of looking inwards instead of outwards" (Neenan, 2008, p. 3). The world of work was ready for CBC.

CBC places a strong emphasis on the beliefs, cognitions and perceptions a client may hold (Palmer, 2007). As such, CBC is argued to be a dual systems approach (Skews & Palmer, 2021), highlighting both the practical and the psychological aspects of dealing with issues or problems, often with the CBC coach finding that clients may need to first have a heightened awareness of and work through any emotional or psychological blocks prior to tackling the behavioural tasks.

Wildflower (2013) asserts that therapeutic practices from the cognitive-behavioural approach are particularly suited to coaching engagements: 'All forms of CBT, like coaching engagements, are time-limited. Both practices focus on the present. Both are oriented to changing thinking, behaviour and emotions. Finally, both practices are based on a relationship of collaboration between practitioner and client' (p. 96).

Many of the techniques involve encouraging the client to introduce flexibility to hitherto rigid attitudes or identifying cognitive distortions and replacing these with realistic and balanced alternatives (Dryden, 2018). This approach features largely in the papers contained in this section. In the opening paper, Stephen Palmer and Christine Dunkley discuss the client that states a keenness to progress towards a certain goal, but their actual behaviour, be it in session or in between sessions, is hijacking that goal attainment. With a clear, extended example, Palmer and Dunkley detail a four-step process and the considerations to be explored within each of those steps for tackling client 'Behaviour Incompatible with Goals' (BIG).

The second paper is an overview of rational coaching, which Stephen Palmer offers as an abbreviated term for 'Rational Emotive Behavioural Coaching' (derived from Albert Ellis's Rational Emotive Behavioural Therapy). The paper focuses strongly on the ABCDEF coaching model, with a worked example as Palmer explains each stage, as well as a description of how the client, through the use of forms, can apply this model to increasingly coach themselves.

Also featuring a case study example, the third paper has Sarah Corrie explore how we as coaches might work with clients that use polarised thinking. Containing a useful summary table of commonplace client cognitive distortions, the main focus of the paper is to detail continuum methods, with an eight-step process and some recommendations for best practice when using these with clients.

The fourth paper, concerning the 'Responsibility Pie', details a technique from CBT that can be used by coaches with clients that are reluctant to recognise their role in a given situation. Garret O'Moore (2011) explains how a coach initially asks the client to identify all people and factors that may have contributed to the current circumstances, and then to add their own name to the list. They are then asked to assign a percentage weighting to each listed person or factor and use this as a catalyst for insight about reattributing responsibility.

Finally, Stephen Palmer offers a detailed consideration of the connection between a client's beliefs and the consequences of those beliefs. The paper details the 'Deserted Island' technique, providing a script which uses the metaphor of a person stranded on a desert island without any friends to aid clients in raising self-awareness about the impact of 'mustabatory' thoughts: beliefs peppered with 'I must', 'I should' and other equivalent demands on self.

REFERENCES

Dryden, W. (2018). *Cognitive-Emotive-Behavioural Coaching*. Routledge.

Gallwey, W. T. (1974). *The Inner Game of Tennis*. Pan Books.

Gallwey, W. T. (2000). *The Inner Game of Work*. Random House.

Neenan, M. (2008). From cognitive-behaviour therapy (CBT) to cognitive-behaviour coaching (CBC). *Journal of Rational-Emotive & Cognitive-Behavior Therapy, 26*(1), 3–15.

O'Broin, A., & Palmer, S. (2006). Win-win situation? Learning from parallels and differences between coaching psychology and sport psychology. *The Coaching Psychologist, 2*(3), 17–23.

Palmer, S. (2007). PRACTICE: A model suitable for coaching, counselling, psychotherapy and stress management. *The Coaching Psychologist, 3*(2), 71–77.

Skews, R., & Palmer, S. (2021). Coaching psychology approaches and models: Solution-focused, behavioural and cognitive-behavioural. In S. O'Riordan, & S. Palmer (Eds.), *Introduction to coaching psychology*. Routledge.

Peltier, B. (2001). *The Psychology of Executive Coaching: Theory and application*. Brunner-Routledge.

Wasylyshyn, K. M. (2008). Behind the door: Keeping business leaders focused on how they lead. *Consulting Psychology Journal: Practice and Research, 60*(4), 314–330. http://dx.doi.org/10.1037/a0014041

Western, S. (2017). The Key Discourses of Coaching. In T. Bachkirova, G. Spence, & D. Drake (Eds.), *The SAGE Handbook of Coaching* (pp. 42–61). SAGE Publications Ltd.

Wildflower, L. (2013). *The hidden history of coaching*. Open University Press.

Palmer, S. & Dunkley, C. (2010). A behavioural approach to BIG problems encountered in coaching: Behaviour incompatible with goals. *The Coaching Psychologist, 6*(1), 32–37.

Corrie, S. (2018) Searching for shades of grey: Modifying polarised thinking with continuum methods. *The Coaching Psychologist, 14*(2).

Palmer, S. (2009a). Rational coaching: A cognitive behavioural approach. *The Coaching Psychologist, 5*(1), 12–18.

O'Moore, G. (2011). The application of the responsibility pie technique in coaching. *The Coaching Psychologist, 7*(2), 154.

Palmer, S. (2009b). Deserted Island technique: Demonstrating the difference between musturbatory and preferential beliefs in cognitive behavioural and rational coaching. *The Coaching Psychologist, 5*(2), 127 129.

17 A behavioural approach to BIG problems encountered in coaching: Behaviour Incompatible with Goals

Stephen Palmer & Christine Dunkley

Abstract

In this article a method of addressing Behaviour Incompatible with Goals (BIG) that can prevent coachees from making progress and achieving their goals will be covered. The methodology is derived from Dialectical Behaviour Therapy and adapted to coaching practice. Problems or issues that occur out-of-session are addressed.

Keywords

Behaviour Incompatible with Goals, BIG, DBT, Dialectical Behaviour Therapy and Coaching, chain-analysis, micro-analysis.

Original publication details: Palmer, S., & Dunkley, C. (2010, June). A behavioural approach to BIG problems encountered in coaching: Behaviour Incompatible with Goals. *The Coaching Psychologist, 6*(1), 34–39. Reproduced with permission of The British Psychological Society.

It is a quirk of human nature that people often behave in ways that appear contrary to their stated intention although theorists and researchers have attempted to explain the causal determinants for behaviour (e.g. see Ajzen, 1991; Armitage & Connor, 2001; Armitage, 2005; Ellam & Palmer, 2006). The phenomenon of 'Therapy Interfering Behaviour' (TIB) was identified by Marsha Linehan (1993a, 1993b) the originator of Dialectical Behaviour Therapy (DBT)[1], and addressing this behaviour is a central component of Linehan's treatment model (Linehan et al., 1991, 1994). Linehan (1993a) includes behaviours that reduce the therapist's motivation to treat the client, or that prevent the client from accessing or using the therapy, or that prevent the therapist from delivering the therapy. Linehan (1993a) points out that these behaviours can be on the part of the therapist as well as the client. Typical examples include behaviour such as cancelling appointments, being ill-prepared for sessions or avoiding certain topics can be seen as Therapy Interfering Behaviour on the part of the therapist.

This article considers how the concept of 'Therapy Interfering Behaviour' and principles from Dialectical Behaviour Therapy can be adapted to facilitate the coaching conversation and help the coachee to achieve their goals. The concept is widened out to encompass behaviours that are generally seen as incompatible with the goals of the coachee, and therefore with those of the coach and coaching psychologist. The acronym BIG – Behaviour Incompatible with Goals – can be a useful reminder to the coach and coachee to remain vigilant for signs of this unhelpful behaviour. This article specifically focuses on how to approach behaviours which are reported to the coach but occur outside of the session.

In Table 1 there are some examples of BIG problems that can occur in personal/life, health and career coaching.

Table 1   *BIG Problems.*

Out-of-session behaviour

I desperately want a career change but I still haven't written out my CV although I've committed to do it on four separate occasions.

I just want my husband to be supportive of my new venture, so I keep pointing out to him how useless and unhelpful he is.

I want to stop smoking but I just got a fantastic deal on a carton of 500 cigarettes.

In-session behaviour

I want you to help me but I 'yes – but' all your suggestions.

I pay to come to sessions then don't appear to be listening to anything you say.

I am committed to working with you but I keep telling you that coaching might not help me.

---

[1] Originally DBT was developed to treat women diagnosed with borderline personality disorder. The therapy attempts to reduce suicidal behaviour.

DEALING WITH BIG PROBLEMS

There are four key steps to take when dealing with 'BIG' problems:

1. Define the problem behaviourally.
2. Move from 'macro' to 'micro' chain-analysis of the problem behaviour.
3. Identify solutions.
4. Rehearse a more helpful (functional) behaviour.

STEP 1: DEFINE THE PROBLEM BEHAVIOURALLY

The first indication of a problem is often that the coach or coaching psychologist experiences a sense of annoyance or frustration, highlighting that coaching is not going to plan. It can be tempting at this point to define the coachee's behaviour in terms of the consequences. For example, 'He's sabotaging' or 'She's pushing all the responsibility onto me'. Sometimes this problem is shared with the supervisor in supervision and leads to a useful supervision conversation if the supervisor is prepared to explore the issues in more depth.

Linehan (1993a) points out the danger of assuming intent from looking at the consequences of the behaviour. In health coaching the consequence of the coachee buying 500 cigarettes is that the he or she will be more likely to smoke them. It is easy to conclude that buying the cigarettes indicates an ***intention*** to carry on smoking. This is a very simplistic assumption as the behaviour of ***buying*** the cigarettes may have been driven by a number of factors such as the high of getting a great bargain, the security of having loads of cigarettes in case you change your mind, the fear of being desperate for a cigarette and not having any, the thought that you are not allowed to buy them which may strengthen the urge or impulse to do so. Buying the cigarettes is therefore not necessarily an indication of a determination to carry on smoking. The aim of the coach or coaching psychologist is to understand the function of the behaviour.

STEP 2: MOVE FROM 'MACRO' TO 'MICRO' ANALYSIS OF THE PROBLEM BEHAVIOUR

A **macro**-analysis refers to noticing and highlighting the pattern of behaviour that occurs time and time again. For example, the careers or outplacement coach may say, 'I notice that on four occasions now you have made a commitment to write up your CV but each time there has been some reason that you didn't do it.'

Table 2   *Micro chain.*

Coach: So you were going to write up your CV this weekend, did you think about it at all?

Coachee: Well yes … once or twice.

Coach: What time did you think about it?

Coachee: Er … on Saturday afternoon, about two-thirty.

Coach: Where were you?

Coachee: Well, I popped into my study to check my e-mails and I thought, I guess I should do it.

Coach: What happened next?

Coachee: I don't know; I got distracted.

Coach: So it was literally just a 20 second thought?

Coachee: No, a bit more than that. I thought I'd have to spend at least an hour on it and there were so many other things to do – mow the lawn, clean the car.

Coach: So the hour you needed to spend, *at that point* did it seem impossible due to these other demands? Or was it more that it was unappealing in comparison?

Coachee: (Laughs) Yeah, I guess 'unappealing.'

Coach: What were your assumptions?

Coachee: Oh, that it will be tedious drawing all the stuff I need together, and that, you know, maybe it won't look so hot when it's all written up.

Coach: At that point, what was your feeling?

Coachee: maybe just a bit anxious …

Coach: Did you notice any urges?

Coachee: Yes, I really wanted to get outside.

Coach: What did you do?

Coachee: I started looking out of the window, and then I got up and went into the garden.

Coach: Did your anxiety go down when you went into the garden?

Coachee: I guess so; there was plenty that needed doing out there.

Behavioural Principle – stay as close (in time) as possible to the target behaviour

What often yields more useful information, though, is moving to a **micro**-analysis of one *particular episode* of the problem behaviour, moment-by-moment, looking for events, thoughts, emotions, urges and actions. A key principle here is that a micro-chain always revolves around a fixed point in time – and the closer the coach can stay to the time-fix, the more productive the chain is likely to be. Table 2 provides an illustrative example.

This micro-chain focuses on a crucial five-minute period in which the decision is made to abandon the task. The coach can now decide on a number of interventions to help.

STEP 3: IDENTIFY SOLUTIONS

A key question when analysing the chain is to establish the function of the behaviour. In the illustrative example in Table 2, the function of abandoning the task seems to be to reduce the anxiety, which in turn was related to thoughts about the quality of the

CV once it was written up. The coach might conceptualise the intervention options as related to each link in the chain. Examples are provided in Table 3.

The temptation would be to solve only the key links in the chain, based on an assumption that if the key link is discovered all the others will fall down like dominoes. Unfortunately this is not often the case as well-established behaviour is often resistant to change. This coachee may only realise when he gets into the garden that he has abandoned the task again, and needs a strategy to employ even at that point.

Behavioural Principle – a solution is required for every link in the chain

STEP 4: REHEARSE THE NEW BEHAVIOUR

With repeating patterns of behaviour insight alone is unlikely to solve the problem. The neural networks that support the problem behaviour are well established and new ones need to be strengthened. Behavioural rehearsal means encouraging the coachee to imagine being back in the scenario. Using props to mock up the scene can stimulate the coachee to remember the new behaviour.

The coachee needs to learn how to notice the unhelpful (dysfunctional) behaviour[2] cropping up and replace it with a behaviour compatible with his or her goals. For this reason linking the new behaviour to the coachee's goals is a crucial step in motivating

Table 3 *Conceptualising the intervention.*

Chain	Solution
Thought: It will be tedious drawing the stuff together	Preparation beforehand, 10 minutes per day gathering certificates, etc., together.
Thought: it might not look so hot when it's written up	Thought-challenging (look for contradictory evidence) or Mindfulness (noticing and unhooking from the thought).
Emotion: anxiety	Anxiety reduction, e.g. breathing techniques, or exposure to anxiety – going towards the thing you fear.
Urge: To get outside	Urge-surfing; notice the urge and experience it without acting on it.
Action: Looking out of the window	Motivational factors –visual reminders of reasons to continue the task.
Action: going outside	Going outside for 10 minutes then returning.

---

[2] In coaching it is best to avoid the use of terms such as 'dysfunctional behaviour'. Instead the term 'unhelpful behaviour' is preferable.

change. At the same time the coach has to be open about the difficulty of the task. If the coachee believes that the new technique will remove all discomfort then any discomfort that occurs will act as a signal to stop the new behaviour. Table 4 illustrates Step 4.

Table 4   *Step 4.*

Coach: It makes perfect sense that you were tempted away from your desk, and I've got to say that it is quite likely that the next time you sit down to do the CV, those same thoughts and feelings would come back. Given that there are always going to be other demands on your time, and that writing up the CV is going to be both tedious and a little anxiety-producing, why would you want to put yourself through that?

Coachee: Well, I guess if I don't do it sometime I'm going to be stuck in my current job, which I hate. I'm just not sure I can get anything else.

Coach: That's true, there's no way of knowing that you will get a new job. But we can be reasonably sure that you won't get one if you don't make any applications … What will be the best thing about changing jobs?

Coachee: I think I'm worth more than I'm currently paid, it would make a big difference to our family if I could get a decent pay-rise.

Coach: You sound really convinced right now, but we have to find a way of getting through that difficult time when you sit at your desk to do the CV. Let's mock-up how that might look (encourages coachee to sit at table). Imagine you're checking your e-mails and have the thought I should write up my CV. What do you need to do next?

Coachee: Open the folder on the PC where I keep my personal files.

Coach: Ok, can you picture yourself doing that in your mind's eye? So now imagine you have the thought; But maybe it won't look so hot …

Coachee: (Starts to shift on the chair) Yeah, I feel a bit anxious …

Coach: Ok, so this is an unhelpful thought. You could try labelling it as it occurs, saying 'that's an unhelpful thought.'

Coachee: It just comes back …

Coach: That is what thoughts do. Each time, just notice it. You can even count unhelpful thoughts, which is another way of avoiding getting caught up in them. Then bring your mind back to the task. Do you notice any urges?

Coachee: Yes – to look out of the window.

Coach: Maybe we need one of your payslips stuck up there?

Coachee: (laughs) Yes that would pull me up short!

Coach: Ok. Talk me through what you need to do to write the CV.

Coachee: Open the computer files, bring up the CV template …

Coach: Ok, now that thought will come back: what if it's not too hot? …

Coachee: (Still imagining himself in the scenario) That's an unhelpful thought. So I'm carrying on opening the files, I have the urge to get outside so I look at the window (glances to the right) I see my payslip propped up on the ledge … I have to let those unhelpful thoughts go and get back to the CV template.

Coach: What happens to the anxious feeling when you unhook from the thought and refocus on the practical task?

Coachee: It's starting to go down a bit, but it's still uncomfortable.

Coach: Yes, you could acknowledge to yourself that many people find it uncomfortable to do their CV as it can be very exposing. Would you be willing to tolerate some short-term stress and anxiety to get a better job?

Coachee: I guess so, I'm going to have to take a deep breath and get on with this.

As with other forms of coaching, an in-between session task or assignment is negotiated (e.g. Palmer, 2009; Palmer & Szymanska, 2007). The coachee is reminded of the links in the chain that are likely to occur, and the strategies to employ for each link. At the following coaching session the coach will obtain feedback to see how the task went. If the BIG problem occurred again another micro-analysis will be conducted to find out at what point in the proceedings the new plan was derailed. A new set of solutions can then be trialled.

CONCLUSION

This article has focused on an out-of-session Behaviours Incompatible with Goals and how the coach/coaching psychologist can assist the coachee increase their understanding of these behaviours and subsequently how to tackle them.

REFERENCES

Ajzen, I. (1991). The theory of planned behaviour. *Organisational Behaviour and Human Decision Processes*, *50*, 179–211.

Armitage, C.J. (2005). Can the theory of planned behaviour predict the maintenance of physical activity? *Health Psychology*, *24*, 235–245.

Armitage, C.J. & Conner, M. (2001). Efficacy of the theory of planned behaviour: A meta-analytic review. *British Journal of Social Psychology*, *40*, 471–499.

Ellam, V. & Palmer, S. (2006). To achieve or not to achieve the goal – that is the question: Does frustration tolerance influence goal achievement in coaching clients? *The Coaching Psychologist*, *2*(2), 27–32.

Linehan, M.M. (1993a). *Cognitive-behavioural treatment of borderline personality disorder*. New York: Guilford Press.

Linehan, M.M. (1993b). *Skills training manual for treating borderline personality disorder*. New York: Guilford Press.

Linehan, M.M., Armstrong, H.E., Suarez, A., Allmon, D. & Heard, H.L. (1991). Cognitive behavioural treatment of chronically suicidal borderline patients. *Archives of General Psychiatry*, *48*, 1060–1064.

Linehan, M.M., Tutek, D., Heard, H.L. & Armstrong, H.E. (1994). Interpersonal outcome of cognitivebehavioural treatment for chronically suicidal borderline patients. *American Journal of Psychiatry*, *51*, 1771–1776.

Palmer, S. (2009). Rational Coaching: A cognitive behavioural approach. *The Coaching Psychologist*, *5*(1), 12–18.

Palmer, S. & Szymanska, K. (2007). Cognitive Behavioural Coaching: An integrative approach. In S. Palmer & A. Whybrow (Eds.), *Handbook of coaching psychology: A guide for practitioners*. London: Sage.

18 Rational Coaching: A cognitive behavioural approach[1]

Stephen Palmer

Abstract

Rational Coaching is based on the Rational Emotive Behavioural Approach developed by Albert Ellis. It is suitable for personal/life, performance, executive and health coaching This paper covers the basic theory and practice of Rational Coaching and includes the ABCDEF coaching framework for assessment and intervention.

Keywords

Albert Ellis, Rational Coaching, Rational Emotive Behavioural Approach, ABCDEF model, inference chaining, B-C connection, bibliotherapy.

Rational coaching Is a shortened title for the full name: Rational Emotive Behavioural Coaching (REBC). Rational Coaching has been developed over the past two decades (see Neenan & Palmer, 2001a, b) and was influenced by a combination of Rational Emotive Behavioural Therapy (REBT) (Ellis, 1962, 1994), Rational Effectiveness Training (Ellis & Blum, 1967; DiMattia & Mennen, 1990) and other adaptations of

Original publication details: Palmer, S. (2009, June). Rational Coaching: A cognitive behavioural approach. *The Coaching Psychologist*, 5(1), 12–19. Reproduced with permission of The British Psychological Society.

1 This article is dedicated to Albert Ellis, the pioneer who developed the Rational Emotive Behavioural Approach.

REBT to the workplace (e.g. Ellis, 1972; Dryden & Gordon, 1993; Palmer & Burton, 1996; Palmer, 1995a, b; Richman, 1993). In the UK Cognitive Behavioural Coaching which has developed is based on an integration of the Rational Emotive Behavioural and the Cognitive Behavioural approaches, strategies and techniques (see Palmer & Szymanska, 2007). Theorists can readily recognise the Rational Emotive Behavioural Approach in the early cognitive behavioural coaching literature (e.g. Neenan & Palmer, 2001a; Neenan & Dryden, 2002) and the distinctions between them have been illustrated (Palmer & Gyllensten, 2008). This integration probably is due to the main developers of Cognitive Behavioural Coaching being trained and accredited practitioners in both approaches. However, like Cognitive Behavioural Coaching, the Rational Emotive Behavioural Approach can be used effectively without being integrated. Rational coaching is particularly useful for enhancing performance, reducing stress and increasing resilience.

BASIC THEORY AND PRACTICE

If the coachee presents with a practical issue or problem that does not necessitate a psychological intervention then a practical problem solving or solution focused model is used such as the PRACTICE framework (see Palmer, 2007, 2008). Otherwise, similar to Rational Emotive Behaviour Therapy, Rational Coaching focuses on the assessment and subsequent disputation and modification of four key types of irrational beliefs which Ellis (1994) asserts are based on rigid, absolutist, dogmatic, goal-blocking, unempirical, illogical and unhelpful thinking. These beliefs are at the core of poor psychological and behavioural performance in both personal and work life settings.

1. **Demands** are made upon ourselves, others and the world. They are absolutist and generally consist of 'must', 'should', 'ought', 'got to', 'have to' statements, e.g. 'I must perform well' or 'You've got to help me.'

And three major derivatives which Ellis (1994) hypothesised followed on from the demand:

2. **Awfulising** – events are defined as worse than bad, e.g. 'This is awful, really terrible.'
3. **Low frustration tolerance (LFT)** – the coachee believes that he or she can not tolerate discomfort or frustration, e.g. 'I can't stand it!' or 'I can't bear the situation any longer.' This derivative is also known as 'I can't stand it itis'.
4. **Depreciation or downing** of self, others or life which involves global negative ratings, e.g. 'As I've failed my exams therefore I'm a failure', 'He's totally stupid.' This derivative is often referred to as 'damnation'.

In Rational Coaching the four major 'irrational' or unhelpful types of belief are examined and disputed. Then rational or helpful (functional) beliefs are developed which are flexible, non-absolutist, empirical/realistic, logical and functional. For example:

1. **Non-demanding and preferential,** e.g. 'It's strongly preferable to perform well but realistically I don't have to.'
2. **De-awfulising,** e.g. 'The situation may be bad but hardly awful or the end of the world.'
3. **High Frustration Tolerance,** e.g. 'I don't like it but I can stand it.'
4. **Self- or other-acceptance,** e.g. 'If I fail it does not mean I'm a failure. I can still accept myself.' 'Just because he has acted stupidly does not make him stupid.'

Some theorists include all-or-nothing (all-or-never) thinking as a fourth derivative, e.g. 'I'm always going to fail' or 'He's never on time.' This contrasts with flexible thinking, e.g. 'Sometimes I may fail' or 'Occasionally he arrives late.' Ellis and associates (1997) included this fourth derivative in their book on stress counselling as so often in their practice, stressed clients expressed 'all-or-nothing' and overgeneralised thinking when discussing their problems.

Consequences and goals: Emotions, physiological and behavioural

Holding irrational beliefs can lead to unhelpful and goal-blocking, performance interfering emotional, physiological and behavioural consequences. For example, the belief, 'I must perform well and if I don't it would be awful', could trigger the emotion of anxiety prior to a performance related event such as giving a presentation. With performance anxiety there are the associated unhelpful physiological responses such as palpitations, butterflies in the stomach, dry mouth, sweaty and clammy hands. Behaviourally there is a tendency to avoid these situations and once in the situation, to talk quickly to finish the presentation as soon as possible and escape.

In Rational Coaching often emotional goals are developed. In this example, whereas *anxiety* can be performance interfering, a preferred emotional goal of coaching could be *concern* which may be more goal-focused. Other more functional alternatives are sadness instead of depression, annoyance instead of damning anger, disappointment instead of hurt, regret instead of shame/embarrassment, remorse instead of guilt (see Palmer & Burton, 1996; Ellis et al., 1997, for the taxonomy of negative emotions). Behavioural goals are developed, for example, in this case preparing the presentation and talking steadily without rushing. A physiological goal could be to reduce palpitations.

ABCDEF Rational Coaching Model Rational Coaching is based on the ABCDE model of emotional management, resilience and performance developed by Albert Ellis (1994, 1996). The acronym stands for Activating event or adversity, Beliefs, Consequences, Disputation and Effective new approach to the concern or problem.

The example below briefly demonstrates how the ABCDE model is used for assessment and intervention in Rational Coaching. In many ways, the approach takes Plato's (360 BC) words in *The Republic* very seriously, 'The beginning is the most important part of any work.' Careful early assessment helps to elicit the relevant hot cognitions that are performance interfering, goal-blocking and stress inducing.

A *Activating event*

Coach: What's the problem?

Coachee: Undertaking a difficult task. (Target problem.) Then an initial goal is developed and noted down.

C *Consequences*

This is a brief assessment to elicit the key negative emotion interfering with performance.

Coach: How do you feel about doing this task?

Coachee: Anxious.

A *Refining the problem or issue using Inference Chaining*

At this stage the coach assesses the critical aspect of the target problem (known as 'Critical A') that the coachee is disturbed about at '**C**'. In this case the coachee is anxious about doing the task. Assessment is undertaken by using an advanced technique known as inference chaining (see Palmer & Burton, 1996; Palmer, 1997). This technique will be described in more depth later.

A shortened version of inference chaining is illustrated below which is often used in brief coaching or in the first coaching session instead of the extended version:

Coach: What are you most anxious about when you imagine undertaking this difficult task?

Coachee: Not doing a perfect job

(The hypothesised Critical A). The initial goal may be refined or revised at this stage by discussion with the coachee. In this case the goals become: To start the task; to do an acceptable job.

B *Beliefs*

The Critical 'A' is used to elicit the key irrational and unhelpful beliefs:

Coach: Now imagine in your mind's eye that you are not doing a perfect job. Can you imagine it?

Coachee: Yes.

Coach: What thoughts are going through your mind now?

Coachee: I should do a perfect job *(Demand)*

Coach: And if you don't?

          (Coach asking the question to elicit a derivative)

Coachee: If I don't do a perfect job then I'm totally useless *(Self-downing)*

Coach: Do you find that situation bearable?

          (Coach asking the question to elicit another derivative)

Coachee: No! I can't stand it (LFT)

C *Consequences*

At this step the coach assesses other consequences, notes them down and the coachee develops additional relevant goals.

Emotion: Performance Anxiety – Goal: feel concerned.

Physiological: Butterflies in stomach – Goal: feel relatively relaxed.

D *Disputation*

At the next stage the unhelpful beliefs are disputed by the coach using empirical, logical and pragmatic (functional) questions. Examples of Socratic disputation of self-depreciation/self-downing beliefs are:

Empirical:	Where is the evidence that you are totally useless if you don't do a perfect job?
Logical:	Is it logical to conclude that if you don't do a perfect job, therefore you are totally useless?
Pragmatic (functional):	Where is it going to get you if you carry on believing that if you don't do a perfect job therefore you are totally useless?

In addition to questioning, a variety of cognitive, emotive, imaginal and behavioural techniques may have been used to help the coachee to modify their demanding beliefs to flexible beliefs, self-downing to self-acceptance, awfulising to deawfulising and low frustration tolerance to high frustration tolerance (see Palmer & Burton, 1996; Ellis et al., 1997; Neenan & Dryden, 2002). By tackling performance anxiety and developing performance concern instead, the procrastinating behaviour may be reduced or eliminated. The ABC assessment framework can be completed as below:

D *Disputation and restructuring unhelpful beliefs*

- It's strongly preferable to do a good job but realistically I don't have to.
- I can learn to accept myself if I don't do a perfect job.
- Although I don't like it I'm living proof that I can stand making mistakes.

E *Effective new approach*

- Stay focused on immediate task to achieve goals. Start the task and on completion reward myself with a large latte coffee and favourite cake once the task has been finished.

In Rational Coaching, the interventions focus on present and future goals and often coaches will focus on the last part of the framework as below (Palmer, 2002) so that coachees can learn to become their own self-coach:

F *Focus remains on personal or work goals and learning process may enhance future performance and reduce stress*

- Focus remains on tackling procrastination.
- Future focus – Learns not to rigidly demand a 'perfect' performance from self in future situations.

USE OF FORMS IN RATIONAL COACHING

In Rational Coaching the coachee is actively encouraged to become their own self-coach. As the approach provides an ABCDEF model and framework, coachees usually find it useful to complete forms in the coaching meeting that reflect this framework. This helps them to use the model outside of the coaching meeting. Figure 1 demonstrates how the previous example can be transferred to a five column Performance Enhancing Coaching Form. Note that the form is not completed in an obvious ABCDE order, but reflects the real order as described in the previous section. To make this process easier, the coach or coaching psychologist assists the coachee to complete the form and this can be undertaken at the first meeting especially if brief or time-limited coaching is being undertaken. It also provides a useful take-away from the meeting.

INFERENCE CHAINING

Inference chaining involves chaining together a set of inferences about a particular problem or issue to assess what aspect of the problem the coachee is most concerned about. Note that an inference is an interpretation which goes beyond observable reality but gives a personal meaning to it.

Sometimes a mini-inference chain described in the previous section is insufficient in eliciting the most Critical 'A' or aspect of an event. In their management book, Palmer and Burton (1996) illustrate how inference chaining can be used to discover why an employee was encountering difficulty cold-calling important customers. During this meeting the inferences are noted down on a whiteboard. The example is below (adapted 1996, 66-68)[2]:

Kaye: So you're finding you put off calls to important clients, and as you know, there have been a number of complaints.

Ron: Right.

Kaye: We spoke about this problem last week. It seems that you're still avoiding making the calls even though you agreed to make them.

Ron: I just seem incapable of making them.

Kaye: Hmm. We need to sort this out. I've got an idea how we can get to the root cause of the problem. Do you want to give it a go?

Ron: OK I've got nothing to lose.

---

2 @Palmer & Burton, 1996. Example reproduced with permission.

Kaye:	And perhaps all to gain. Just imagine for the moment that you're about to telephone an important client. (Kaye pauses for a few seconds to allow sufficient time for Ron to imagine ringing an important customer.) How do you feel?
Ron:	Anxious.
Kaye:	What is anxiety-provoking in your mind about actually speaking to an important customer?
Ron:	Well, I suppose I'm afraid of bad news. Kaye: Bad news?
Ron:	Yeah – maybe they'll say they've cancelled their order.
Kaye:	Well, let's suppose they have cancelled the order. Why do you get anxious about that?
Ron:	I get worried that I'll get no more commission and that would look bad.
Kaye:	And if that was true?
Ron:	I might lose my job and never get another good job again!
Kaye:	(Kaye now maps out the inference chain for Ron and refers to the whiteboard.) OK Ron. I want to recap. Which of these are you most anxious about: Speaking to a customer; Getting bad news; Being told that they have cancelled an order; Getting no more commission; Looking bad; Losing your job; Never getting a good job again?
Ron:	It's not so much the bad news. And frankly, it's unlikely that I'll lose my job. I reckon that I really get stressed about looking bad in front of my colleagues.

Note that in this example the true activating event or 'A' (from the ABC model) was not making telephone calls to his customers but 'looking bad in front of my colleagues'. Now this becomes the gateway into finding his self-defeating and irrational thinking. Kaye helps Ron to focus on the Critical 'A'.

Kaye:	Now really imagine that your colleagues are thinking badly of you.
Ron:	No trouble. I remember the last time it happened.
Kaye:	What are you telling yourself?
Ron:	I should always do well. They think I'm useless. And if that's true it would be really awful!
Kaye:	As long as you believe that you 'should always do well' and if you don't they would think you're 'useless' and it would be 'really awful', how will you feel?

(Kaye is hoping to show Ron the disadvantages of holding these self-defeating beliefs and thereby encouraging him to challenge them in a later meeting.)

Ron:	Anxious.
Kaye:	Would it be helpful to look at your thinking and attempt to deal with your anxiety?
Ron:	I'll give it a go.

Figure 1 *Performance Enhancing Form © 2001, Centre for Coaching (reproduced with permission).*

Target Problem (A)	Performance Interfering Thoughts (PITs) (B)	Emotional/ Behavioural Reaction (C)	Performance Enhancing Thoughts (PETs) (D)	Effective and New Approach to Problem (D)
Undertaking a difficult task *Mini inference chain*: *What are you most anxious about?* Not doing a perfect job Goals: Start task; to do an acceptable job; feel concerned instead of anxious	I should do a perfect job (Demand). If I don't do a perfect job then I'm totally useless (Self-downing). I can't stand making mistakes CLEF).	Performance Anxiety Procrastination Butterflies in stomach	It's strongly preferable to do a good job but realistically I don't have to. I can learn to accept myself if I don't do a perfect job. Although I don't like it I'm living proof that I can stand making mistakes.	Stay focused on immediate task to achieve goals. Start the task and on completion reward myself with a large latte coffee and favourite cake once a 'boring bit' has been finished.

© 2009, S. Palmer

MAKING THE B-C CONNECTION

In the first or second rational coaching meeting, it is important for the coachee to understand the connection between the Beliefs and the Consequences. This is often known as the B-C connection. In the example above, once Kaye had helped Ron to elicit the 'irrational beliefs', she clarified whether or not he understood the connection between his beliefs and the consequences:

> Kaye: As long as you believe that you 'should always do well' and if you don't they would think you're 'useless' and it would be 'really awful', how will you feel?
>
> Ron: Anxious.
>
> Kaye: Would it be helpful to look at your thinking and attempt to deal with your anxiety?
>
> Ron: I'll give it a go.

It was clear to Kaye that Ron understood the B-C connection. However, if he could not understand the link between the beliefs and the consequences, then it is likely he would not see the benefit of or understand the reason for her later examining and disputing his performance interfering and stress-inducing beliefs. If he had not understood this connection then Kaye would have spent additional time explaining the link, perhaps using an illustrative example (see Palmer, 1992). Often coachees hold an A-C theoretical stance i.e. the Activating Event directly triggers the Consequences. For example 'My manager (A) made me feel guilty (C)'. If this personal theoretical A-C model is not revised, then the coachee is unlikely to take responsibility for how he or she feels and not see the benefits of modifying their beliefs.

BIBLIOTHERAPY (BIBLIOTRAINING)

Rational emotive behavioural self-help books are used to assist the coachee in learning and applying the basic ABCDEFs of the approach outside of the coaching meetings. There are many books based on Albert Ellis' approach that are also suitable as bibliotherapy (sometimes known as bibliotraining) in coaching settings on a wide range of topics suitable for both personal and work contexts. For example, controlling anxiety (Ellis, 2000), enhancing happiness (Ellis, 1999; Froggatt, 1993), peak performance at work (Dryden & Gordon, 1993), people problems at work (Palmer & Burton, 1996), relationships (Ellis 2001; Ellis & Harper, 2004), stress management (Palmer & Cooper, 2007), self-acceptance and self-esteem (Ellis, 2005; Ellis & Powers, 2002; Wilding & Palmer, 2006), taking control (Froggatt, 2006).

CONCLUSION

This paper illustrated the basic theory and practice of Rational Coaching. Both Rational Coaching and Cognitive Behavioural Coaching are increasing in popularity as they go beyond behavioural coaching models and can tackle psychological blocks to performance. They provide an easy to understand theory which helps the coachee to rapidly become their own self-coach.

REFERENCES

DiMattia, D.J. with Mennen, S. (1990). *Rational effectiveness training: Increasing productivity at work*. New York: Institute for Rational-Emotive Therapy.

Dryden, W. & Gordon, J. (1993). *Peak Performance: Become more effective at work*. Didcot: Mercury Business Books.

Ellis, A. (1962). *Reason and emotion in psychotherapy*. New York: Lyle Stuart.

Ellis, A. (1972) *Executive leadership: A rational approach*. New York: Institute for RET.

Ellis, A. (1994). *Reason and emotion in psychotherapy, revised and updated*. New York: Birch Lane Press.

Ellis, A. (1996). *Better, deeper and more enduring brief therapy: The Rational Emotive Behaviour approach*. New York: Brunner/Mazel.

Ellis, A. (1999). *How to make yourself happy and remarkably less disturbable*. Atascadero, CA: Impact.

Ellis, A. (2000). *How to control your anxiety before it controls you*. New York: Citadel.

Ellis, A. (2001). *How to stop destroying your relationships*. New York: Citadel.

Ellis, A. (2005). *The myth of self-esteem*. Amherst, NY: Prometheus.

Ellis, A. & Blum, M.L. (1967) Rational Training: A new method of facilitating management labour relations. *Psychological Reports, 20*, 1267–1284.

Ellis, A. & Powers, M.G. (2002). *The secret of overcoming verbal abuse*. North Hollywood, CA: Wilshire.

Ellis, A. & Harper, R.A. (2004). *Dating, mating, and relating*. New York: Citadel Press.

Ellis, A., Gordon, J., Neenan, M. & Palmer, S. (1997). *Stress Counselling: A Rational Emotive Behaviour approach*. New York: Springer Publishing Company.

Froggatt, W. (1993). *Choose to be happy: Your step-by-step guide*. Auckland: HarperCollins Publishers.

Froggatt, W. (2006). *Taking control: Manage stress to get the most out of li f e*. Auckland: Harper Collins Publishers.

Neenan, M. & Palmer, S. (2001a). Cognitive Behavioural Coaching. *Stress News, 13(3)*, 15–18.

Neenan, M. & Palmer, S. (2001b). Rational Emotive Behaviour coaching. *The Rational Emotive Behaviour Therapist, 9(1)*, 34-41.

Neenan, M. & Dryden, W. (2002). *Life coaching: A cognitive behavioural approach*. Hove: BrunnerRoudedge.

Palmer, S. (1992). The Deserted Island Technique. *Counselling Psychology Review, 8(1)*, 47–48.

Palmer, S. (1995a). Occupational stress: Legal issues and possible new directions for rational emotive behaviour counsellors and trainers. *The Rational Emotive Behaviour Therapist, 3(2)*, 86-93.

Palmer, S. (1995b). A comprehensive approach to Industrial Rational Emotive Behaviour Stress Management Workshops. *The Rational Emotive Behaviour Therapist, 3(1)*, 45–55.

Palmer, S. (1997). Problem focused stress counselling and stress management training: An intrinsically brief integrative approach. Part 2. *Stress News, 9(3)*, 6–10.

Palmer, S. (2002). *Stress reduction and prevention at work: A cognitive behavioural approach to coaching, counselling and training*. Paper given at the ISMA, The Changing Face of Stress Management conference, London, 14 October.

Palmer, S. (2007). PRACTICE: A model suitable for coaching, counselling, psychotherapy and stress management. *The Coaching Psychologist, 3(2)*, 71–77.

Palmer, S. (2008). The PRACTICE model of coaching: Towards a solution-focused approach. *Coaching Psychology International, 1(1)*, 4–8.

Palmer, S. & Burton, T. (1996). *Dealing with people problems at work*. Maidenhead: McGraw-Hill.

Palmer, S. & Szymanska, K. (2007). Cognitive Behavioural Coaching: An integrative approach. In S. Palmer & A. Whybrow (Eds.), *Handbook of Coaching Psychology: A guide for practitioners*. London: Sage.

Palmer, S. & Cooper, C. (2007). *How to deal with stress*. London: Kogan Page.

Palmer, S. & Gyllensten, K. (2008). How cognitive behavioural, rational emotive behavioural or multimodal coaching could prevent mental health problems, enhance performance and reduce work related stress. *The Journal of Rational Emotive and Cognitive Behavioural Therapy, 26(1)*, 38–52.

Plato (360BC) (Version translated by B. Jowett, 2000). *The Republic*. Mineola, NY: Courier Dover Publication.

Richman, D.R. (1993). Cognitive career counselling: A rational emotive approach to career development. *Journal for Rational Emotive & Cognitive-Behaviour Therapy, 11(2)*, 91–108.

Wilding, C. & Palmer, S. (2006). *Zero to hero*. London: Hodder Arnold.

19 Searching for shades of grey: Modifying polarised thinking with continuum methods

Sarah Corrie

Abstract

This article introduces a set of techniques referred to collectively as continuum methods. Originating from a cognitive-behavioural perspective, continuum methods are a useful and potentially powerful means of helping clients develop greater cognitive flexibility, particularly in the context of polarised thinking. This paper gives a short description of these methods, provides a rationale for their use and offers a description of the process, using a fictitious case example to illustrate application.

Keywords

continuum methods, polarised thinking, dichotomous thinking, cognitive biases, cognitive-behavioural approaches.

Original publication details: Corrie, S. (2018, December). Searching for shades of grey: Modifying polarised thinking with continuum methods. *The Coaching Psychologist*, 14(2), 90–97. Reproduced with permission of The British Psychological Society.

INTRODUCTION

Theories of information-processing have highlighted how, given the limits of human cognitive capabilities, it is inevitable that we selectively attend to aspects of our environment, and process events through a series of cognitive filters. In particular, what we perceive, how we interpret events, and what we recall is strongly influenced by the mental templates we develop early in life as well as by the cognitive 'short cuts' we use to make sense of our everyday experiences in the present.

Our accounts of what happens in our lives cannot, therefore, be understood as 'factual' in any straightforward fashion but are rather the outputs of a system of information-processing that is idiosyncratic, selective and creative. This foundational assumption has spawned an entire literature in the field of cognitive psychology (the interested reader is referred to Eysenck & Keane, 2015, for an introduction) and has critical implications for professional practice. For example, understanding how our clients cognitively construct their worlds is critical to being able to empathise with their points of view (especially when their interpretations are profoundly different from our own) whilst the ability to help clients reflect upon and test out their interpretations of events is central to effective challenge. An appreciation of at least some aspects of information-processing theory is, therefore, a crucial component of the coaching practitioner's armoury.

Cognitive-behavioural approaches in particular have championed the importance of identifying and working with information-processing 'short cuts' and have argued strongly for how an understanding of these biases can aid practitioners in working with clients whose options may be limited by polarised thinking or who might otherwise benefit from greater cognitive flexibility (see Beck, 1995). Table 1 provides a list of commonly occurring cognitive biases which have been well-documented in the literature as negatively affecting wellbeing and functioning (for an application to coaching see Corrie, 2009).

It is important to note that we all engage in some of these cognitive biases at least some of the time, particularly when emotionally aroused. Dichotomous thinking, for example, has been shown to increase with stress levels (Kischka et al., 1996). Moreover, there may be occasions when information-processing biases confer a survival advantage. For example, seeing a dark shadow hovering at the end of an alleyway late at night may trigger a presumption of threat that leads an individual to retreat and take another route home. In this situation, the individual's safety is potentially enhanced by assuming the worst and interpreting the shadow in a 'catastrophic' way, rather than thinking optimistically or walking further down the alleyway to determine whether or not a threat is actually present. However, the ability to thrive requires the navigation of challenges that are more complex and ambiguous than shadows at the end of alleyways. Optimal functioning depends in part on the acquisition of sophisticated decision-making and problem-solving skills, and the ability to think in more flexible and creative ways than our cognitive short cuts permit. In such situations, cognitive biases work against us and become, therefore, a valid target of intervention in the coaching context.

Table 1 *Common cognitive biases*

Type of bias	Description and example
All-or-nothing (dichotomous) thinking	Viewing situations and events from extreme perspectives with no middle ground: e.g. 'If it's not perfect, it's useless.'
Over-generalising	Drawing sweeping, generalised conclusions that extend beyond the limits of the actual situation, facts or evidence: 'My boss wanted me to revise the document I drafted, which means I am doing badly in everything at work and am going to lose my job.'
Catastrophising	Exaggerating the significance of an event in an extreme and negative way. For example, 'If I don't achieve my goals, it will be the end of the world.'
Mind-reading	Assuming you know what others are thinking, typically believing that the other person has formed a negative impression without the evidence to support this conclusion. For example, 'She looked at her watch when we were talking just before the meeting began, which obviously meant she found me boring.'
Fortune telling	Predicting future events, usually in a catastrophic way, in the absence of any evidence (see example of catastrophising above).
Discounting positives	Discounting positive information about oneself or the situation and playing down one's strengths and accomplishments. For example, 'It's true I had a good appraisal, but everyone did; my line manager is new to her role and she's being gentle on everyone until she's settled in.'
Exaggerating negatives (also known as 'tunnel vision')	Focusing almost entirely on the negative aspects of a situation and failing to appreciate other, more positive aspects. For example, 'This member of my team can't do anything right – she upsets customers, her attention to detail is poor and she's late for work most days.'
Labelling	Summing up oneself or others with a single, fixed, global and usually critical or judgemental label: e.g. 'I am unlovable'; 'He is stupid'; 'They are useless.'
Personalising and blame	Blaming oneself for outcomes that are not directly under personal control: e.g. 'It's totally my fault my son failed his maths test, because I have been too busy at work lately to help him revise in the way he needed to.' (Sometimes this is also referred to as confusing influence with control).
Shoulds and musts	Focusing on how you think things ought to be, rather than how they actually are. This often involves imposing arbitrary rules or standards on oneself or others that become difficult to live up to. For example: 'I should excel in everything I do'; 'If you want to be in my life, you must do things my way.'
Unfair comparisons	Imposing unrealistic standards on oneself by focusing on others who appear more successful, and then judging oneself to be inferior in comparison. This is sometimes referred to as the 'compare and despair' trap.
Inability to disconfirm	Rejecting any evidence that contradicts our negative thoughts. This often appears in both thinking and speech in the form of a 'Yes, but…'
Emotional reasoning	Assuming something is true because it feels true. For example, a person assumes that they are failing at work because they are going through a phase of experiencing high levels of anxiety.

Cognitive-behavioural approaches use a variety of methods for modifying cognitive biases. These include recording and challenging negative automatic thoughts, evidence gathering, seeking alternative perspectives, positive tracking, cost-benefit analyses, pie charts, historical reviews, positive data logs and behavioural experiments, amongst others (see Leahy, 2017, for a comprehensive overview) all of which have the potential to support coaching clients in expanding the range of perspectives available to them. One such approach – and the focus of the current article – is the continuum method which seeks to introduce greater flexibility of thinking when a client perceives their circumstances or options in dichotomised (either/or) terms. Formerly colloquially referred to as 'black and white thinking' (with the coach's intention being, therefore, one of introducing 'shades of grey'), this bias reflects a tendency to see one's situation or choices in global and polarised terms with clients thinking in overly rigid terms.

What are continuum methods?

Continuum methods direct clients' attention to the range of possibilities that exist between two extreme points. In her review of continuum methods in the context of schema change, Padesky (1994) describes several approaches. These include the adaptive continuum (to support the development of a new, more adaptive belief, and illustrated in the case study below), criteria continua (using behavioural criteria to define the components of a specific belief, such as asking a client what they mean by the term success, failure, worth, lovability, etc.) and the two-dimensional continuum (to examine and revise two polarised ideas that are closely connected for the client, such as attractiveness and worth). For ease of introducing the approach, this article describes how to work with a continuum in its simplest form where, in broad terms, the steps are as follows:

1. The coach and client identify a belief that is extreme and, in some way, limiting for the client.
2. The client is then asked to rate how much they believe this idea to be true from 0 to 100 per cent (NB: the nature of dichotomous thinking is that it is extreme, so you would anticipate the client providing a very high rating at this point).
3. The coach draws a continuum (0 per cent at one end and 100 per cent at the other) and together, coach and client label either end of the continuum, creating a descriptor for both 0 per cent and 100 per cent. (NB: both 0 per cent and 100 per cent are the ultimate scores so each end needs to be described in extreme and absolute terms.)
4. Explore what might exist between the extreme end points of the scale, generating descriptors that illustrate different points on the continuum (e.g. how the client would describe 20 per cent, 50 per cent, 80 per cent, etc.).
5. Consider whether in light of steps 3 and 4, the client wishes to revise their initial self-rating.

6. To develop this further, ask the client to place on the scale individuals known to them (personally or by reputation) according to the client's evaluation of them on the dimension being considered (e.g. success, worth, failure, lovability, etc.) (NB: the aim is to help clients begin to recognise that no-one, however successful or highly regarded by the client's eyes, is capable of 0 per cent or 100 per cent).

7. Consider whether in light of step 6, the client wishes to revise their self-rating further.

8. Discuss any insights emerging from this process. How does the client now view themselves or their circumstances? What possibilities might now be available to the client from thinking about the situation / event / themselves in more graded terms?

Based on this process coach and client can then discuss any implications for next steps that the client might wish to take. This might include searching for evidence for a new, more adaptive belief, developing new behavioural repertoires or recruiting support from others to enable optimal problem-solving.

In the next section, this process is illustrated by the example of how a coach worked with Sally, a student at a prestigious music school, who was in the second year of her music degree and whose professional aspiration was a career as a classical soloist[1].

Case example

When her coach first met Sally, the agreed focus of the coaching contract was helping Sally address difficulties arising from 'stage fright'. The coach was aware that Sally had previously received therapy for depression and that she tended towards low self-esteem. Although Sally did not want further therapy, they agreed that they would monitor Sally's mood closely and recruit her GP if additional support was needed. The coach deemed this particularly important given that Sally had perfectionistic tendencies (which have been implicated in suicidal behaviour in individuals with comorbid psychopathology; Ranieri et al., 1987; Hewitt et al., 1992) and that the environment in which she was studying was demanding and highly competitive. As such, the coach identified at the outset that there were a number of factors that led Sally to have a complex relationship with notions of success and failure.

At their first coaching session, Sally advised her coach that she had just received the results of her latest set of exams. Affected by her stage fright, she had not performed at her best and her results had been disappointing. This had triggered a sense of herself as a 'total failure' and signs of low mood had begun to resurface. Rather than seeking help from those around her, she had withdrawn from the support of tutors and friends ('I feel so ashamed') and found it difficult to carry out her daily practice. As she explained it, 'It's down to me. I failed because I am no good as a musician.'

---

[1] Although this case study has been inspired by work conducted in the context of the author's professional practice, this is a fictitious case study used solely to illustrate the application of a continuum method.

On enquiring further, Sally's coach learned that three months before her exams, Sally's mother had been diagnosed with an aggressive form of cancer. In order to be at her mother's side whilst she underwent treatment, Sally had altered her practice schedule and had travelled across the country to stay with her mother whenever she could. She was also worrying about her mother which was disrupting her sleep. Significantly she had told no-one at college about her personal circumstances, nor had she enlisted the student support services on the grounds that, 'If you need help, you'll be seen as weak.' Sally began to ruminate on her exam results and concluded that because of this setback, she was 'a total failure'. When asked, Sally revealed her belief that she was a failure to be 100 per cent true. It was then that she and the coach agreed to examine her tendency towards polarised thinking.

At this stage there were a number of specific beliefs that the coach could have selected as the target of intervention. However, given the impact of the current, dominant belief around failure and the client's tendency to be organised around success, the coach began by asking Sally, 'If things had been different – if you had done really well in your exams as you had hoped, and things didn't unfold in the way that has led you to think of yourself as a failure, how would you have seen yourself?' Sally replied that she would have seen herself as 'a success'. The coach asked her to rate how much of a success she saw herself as being in the present moment and Sally gave a rating of 0 per cent.

Her coach then drew out a continuum of success and asked Sally to label 0 per cent and 100 per cent success. See Figure 1.

By labelling the extreme ends of the continuum, Sally recognised that in view of her successes to date (having achieved high grades in her music exams throughout childhood, securing a place at a highly prestigious and competitive music school, having been identified as having the talent for a solo career, amongst others) she couldn't truly rate herself as 0 per cent successful, so she modified her initial rating to 15 per cent. The beginnings of a less polarised and more flexible mindset had started to emerge.

Her coach then suggested that they identify a number of individuals whom Sally saw as supremely successful and others who had been less successful, and where she might place these on the success continuum. As she did so, Sally recognised that her role-models, whom she saw as having had the type of career to which she herself aspired, were no higher than 80 per cent on the continuum. She also recognised that other students at college whom she had scored more highly on the continuum than

0% |————————————————————————————————————| 100%

Never succeeds at anything, in any circumstances. Failed totally at everything they have ever tried. Unable to exert any positive influence on anything. Completely unable to make any positive decisions or solve any problems at any time, past or present.

Always succeeds at everything and at first attempt. Never experiences any difficulties or setbacks; never struggles, never has to work hard to achieve whatever they set their mind to; never experienced any challenges in life.

Figure 1 *Sally's Continuum of Success*

herself had actually performed less successfully in their academic studies than Sally had. Sally was unable to identify anyone who could score 0 to 10 per cent on the success continuum. She then re-rated herself at 40 per cent.

Her coach then asked Sally to describe (and later write down) the factors, experiences, qualities and successes that had led her to give herself a new rating of 40 per cent. What was she now able to see that she couldn't see before? What did this mean about her most recent set of exam results? What new options might emerge from a rating of 40 per cent rather than a rating of 0 per cent? Although she still felt emotionally fragile, Sally could engage with these questions and reported a greater sense of hope that she could navigate her way through the setback of her exam results.

Finally, the coach asked Sally where, ideally, she would like to be on the continuum. Sally initially found this difficult to answer. Prior to using the continuum, she was aware of wanting to rate herself as successful at 100 per cent, but she wondered now whether 100 per cent was such a good idea – even if it had been attainable. Seeing oneself as 100 per cent successful could, Sally surmised, lead to arrogance, complacency and a lack of ability to confront and deal with the realities of being a professional musician. Sally opted for the more modest rating of 60 per cent as her ideal – at least, at this stage in her career. Her coach congratulated her on having already attained 40 per cent and asked Sally to elaborate on what 60 per cent would look like, and what might need to happen for her to progress towards this new ideal rating. Their discussion continued. At this point, although still greatly shaken by her exam results, Sally's distress had diminished.

It is important to note that use of the continuum method was only the beginning of their work together, not the end of the coaching conversation. There were a number of issues arising from Sally's reaction to her personal circumstances and exam performance that warranted further exploration. Sally was a young adult attempting to navigate a complex and highly competitive professional world where the quest for exceptionality was a collective value. This environment would raise on-going challenges for a student who already held perfectionistic standards and tended towards low self-esteem. Furthermore, at the same time as undertaking her studies she was attempting to support a parent whom the coach suspected was terminally ill. Sally would need support from the college but was reluctant to seek this for fear of looking 'weak'. The coach realised that it would be necessary to look at how appropriate help-seeking might be incorporated into Sally's new definition of success. Related to this, as a very talented young musician, the coach was aware that success had historically come quite easily to Sally. She had not yet developed the type of resilience and emotional robustness that she would need to sustain her, and which comes from learning how to manage setbacks and challenges in life. This, too, would need to be a topic of future conversations. Finally, the coach remained acutely aware of Sally's background of mood disorder which would need careful monitoring in the weeks ahead and potentially require a conversation with Sally about seeking support from her GP – a resource of support that she had used effectively in the past.

In using the continuum method, therefore, the aim was not one of denying the realities with which Sally was confronted. Rather, the aim was to support Sally in identifying some 'middle ground' that could enable her and her coach to open up subsequent conversations with Sally about areas of growth and development. By helping Sally begin the process of developing a more nuanced definition of success, the aim was to help her gain a more accurate and adaptive view of her strengths and needs, take appropriate steps to improve her performance where this was needed, increase her ability for problem-solving and help her manage her self-care needs more effectively. The coach also hoped that developing a more adaptive belief about success would enable Sally to navigate the exceptional standards expected by her music school and which would be necessary if she were to fulfil her ambition of having a career as a classical musician.

Tips for using continuum methods

Continuum methods can be a powerful way of helping clients 'decentre' from firmly held beliefs, in order to contemplate a variety of alternative, more graded perspectives that may be helpful to them. These methods thus introduce a healthy doubt into painful ideas or unhelpful ways of viewing the world that obscure our clients' vision of themselves, their circumstances, and what might be possible for their lives.

Like a number of cognitive-behavioural techniques, continuum methods can have an illusory simplicity and are often more challenging to use effectively than they might first appear. In order to maximise their potential, the following points are useful to hold in mind:

- Remember to represent the continuum in visual terms when using this method with clients. Illustrating polarised thinking visually generally makes the process more impactful.
- Make sure that the points of the scale identified as 0 per cent and 100 per cent are extreme to the extent that they would be impossible for any human being to achieve. This immediately helps the client reconsider their initial rating. However…
- Make sure that the different points on the continuum, including 0 per cent and 100 per cent, are labelled in the client's own language. The aim is to illustrate the impossibility of the extremes, not to look for an objective definition of the construct under consideration.
- As a general principle, it is preferable to work with a continuum that is labelled in positive rather than negative terms.

For example, if there are beliefs about success and failure, it is often advisable to build a 'success continuum' rather than a 'failure continuum'. This is because, for most people, increasing a rating of success feels more meaningful and engenders greater hope and motivation than reducing a belief about failure.

- It is simplest and often most effective to include only one construct in any continuum. For example, it is typically easier to achieve an effective result using a success continuum from 0 to 100 per cent rather than a failure (–100 per cent) to success (+100 per cent) continuum.

- Clients with a tendency to engage in polarised or dichotomous thinking will often spontaneously refer to themselves as seeing the world in 'all-or-nothing terms'. Attend carefully to clients' use of language and if you notice a tendency to construe their choices in either/or terms, consider whether the continuum method might be helpful.

Self-practice task

Many methods drawn from cognitive-behavioural approaches are best mastered through a combination of self-practice and supervision. If you think that continuum methods might be useful to add to your armoury, try identifying a belief that you suspect currently impedes your own performance, wellbeing or some other aspect of your life. Give your belief a rating from 0 to 100 per cent and if the rating is extreme, follow the steps outlined in the article to see what you might learn and gain through applying this approach.

CONCLUSION

It is important to recognise that everyone engages in cognitive biases some of the time and that this is not inherently problematic. Cognitive biases only become problematic when the bias is too extreme, too frequent, or has a negative impact on the client's life or those around them. In searching out 'shades of grey' through use of the continuum method, the coach seeks to help the client identify new perspectives that might enable opportunities for both effective problem-solving and flourishing. This is rarely the end of the intervention but one that, as the case study has sought to illustrate, can lead to a greater degree of cognitive flexibility that ultimately liberates the client to consider options for their lives in new and more positive ways.

REFERENCES

Beck, J.S. (1995). *Cognitive therapy. Basics and beyond*. New York: The Guilford Press.

Corrie, S. (2009). *The art of inspired living. Coach yourself with positive psychology*. London: Karnac.

Eysenck, M.W. & Keane, M.T. (2015). *Cognitive psychology* (7th edn). Hove, East Sussex: Psychology Press.

Hewitt, P.L., Flett, G.L. & Turnbull-Donovan, W. (1992). Perfectionism and suicide potential. *British Journal of Clinical Psychology, 31*, 181–190.

Kischka, U., Kammer, T., Maier, S., Thimm, M. & Spitzer (1996). *Dopaminergic modulation of semantic network activation. Neuropsychologia, 34*(11), 1107–1113.

Leahy, R.L. (2017). *Cognitive therapy techniques. A practitioner's guide* (2nd edn). New York: The Guilford Press.

Padesky, C.A. (1994). Schema change processes in cognitive therapy. *Clinical Psychology and Psychotherapy*, 1(5), 267–278.

Ranieri, W.F., Steer, R.A., Lavrence, T.I., Rissmiller, D.J., Piper, G.E. & Beck, A.T. (1987). Relationships of depression, hopelessness, and dysfunctional attitudes to suicide ideation in psychiatric patients. *Psychological Reports*, 61, 967–975.

20 The application of the responsibility pie technique in coaching

Garret O'Moore

Abstract

This article focuses on the 'responsibility pie' technique which can help clients consider the degree to which they are personally responsible for a difficult situation or event and take appropriate action.

Keywords

Responsibility pie, Dennis Greenberger, Christine Padesky, reattribution of responsibility.

The 'responsibility pie' (Greenberger & Padesky, 1995) was developed for use within CBT to enable clients who felt guilty and ashamed about a situation or event to learn to reattribute an appropriate amount of responsibility between themselves and other causal factors.

The effectiveness of the technique has resulted in it being used with a range of client presentations including people diagnosed with OCD (Westbrook, Kennerly & Kirk, 2007) in which a core feature is an overdeveloped sense of responsibility (Veale, 2007).

Original publication details: O'Moore, G. (2011, December). The application of the responsibility pie technique in coaching. *The Coaching Psychologist,* *7*(2), 154–155. Reproduced with permission of The British Psychological Society.

Although initially developed for use in therapy it can be integrated into a range of coaching approaches where a coach finds themselves working with clients who have a tendency to attribute a disproportionate amount of blame to themselves or to others.

The following example illustrates how Sarah, who felt distressed after assuming that a missed customer deadline was 100 per cent her fault, constructed a responsibility pie to better attribute responsibility.

Sarah was encouraged by her coach to list all the people and factors that contributed to the missed deadline and when she was finished add her name to the end of the list. Although it took some prompting from her coach she came up with the following list:

1. My manager, who agreed an unrealistic deadline with our customers.
2. The fire at our supplier's factory that resulted in a shipment of key components arriving late.
3. The economic climate that has left us understaffed and our employees overworked.
4. My micro-managing that prevented me from seeing the bigger picture.

Although Sarah could see that there were a number of contributing factors she was asked to estimate out of 100 how much each item on her list contributed to the missed deadline and to convert it into a pie chart as shown in Figure 1.

After going through the list Sarah realised that she was only 20 per cent responsible for the missed deadline which helped alleviate some of her distress. As a secondary gain Sarah identified that in addition to reducing her micro-managing she could see the importance of taking action to contract with her manager about setting more achievable deadlines.

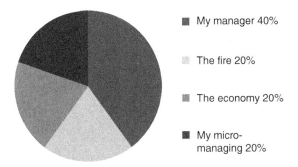

Responsibility for missed deadline

- My manager 40%
- The fire 20%
- The economy 20%
- My micro-managing 20%

Figure 1   *Sarah's Responsibility pie*

CONCLUSION

The responsibility pie is a useful technique that can be used to reattribute an appropriate amount of responsibility for a difficult situation or event and consequently enable a client to make a more informed decision about the most beneficial course of action to take.

REFERENCES

Greenberger, D. & Padesky, C. (1995). *Mind over mood*. New York: Guilford Press.

Veale, D. (2007). Cognitive behavioural therapy for obsessive compulsive disorder. *Advances in Psychiatric Treatment, 13*, 438–446.

Westbrook, D., Kennerly, H. & Kirk, J. (2007). *An introduction to cognitive behaviour therapy: Skills and applications*. London: Sage.

21 Deserted Island technique: Demonstrating the difference between musturbatory and preferential beliefs in cognitive behavioural and rational coaching

Stephen Palmer

Abstract

This article focuses on the Deserted Island technique which can be used in cognitive behavioural and rational coaching to teach the B-C connection and demonstrate the advantages of challenging and modifying musturbatory beliefs and subsequently how to develop preferential beliefs.

Keywords

Deserted Island technique; musturbatory beliefs; preferential beliefs; cognitive behavioural coaching; rational coaching; unhelpful and helpful negative emotions.

Original publication details: Palmer, S. (2009, December). Deserted Island technique: Demonstrating the difference between musturbatory and preferential beliefs in cognitive behavioural and rational coaching. *The Coaching Psychologist, 5*(2), 127–129. Reproduced with permission of The British Psychological Society.

Incognitive behavioural and rational coaching[1] (see Neenan & Palmer, 2001a, b; Palmer 2009a) sometimes it is useful to demonstrate to coachees the benefits of challenging and modifying demanding, absolutist and rigid beliefs. These beliefs often consist of 'musts', 'shoulds', 'have tos', 'got tos' and 'oughts' and are referred to as 'musturbatory' beliefs in the rational emotive behavioural literature and are considered 'irrational', unhelpful and goal-blocking (see Ellis et al., 1997). Once these beliefs are challenged, to ensure that the coachee is not left in a cognitive vacuum, the coachee is encouraged to develop non-demanding, flexible, realistic preferences, wants and desires instead such as 'I strongly prefer' as opposed to 'I must'. These are known as preferential beliefs in rational coaching and are considered as 'rational' (see Ellis et al, 1997; Palmer, 2009a).

Although many coachees quickly realise the advantages of modifying their unhelpful demanding beliefs, some do not. For example, coachees who hold strong perfectionistic beliefs are often reluctant to modify them in case it leads to underperformance and/or demotivation. They may believe that the coach is coaching for indifference (see Dryden & Gordon, 1993) and not high performance and disengage from the coaching process.

Palmer (1992, 1993) developed the 'Deserted Island' technique[2] to demonstrate that holding on to demanding beliefs, and not necessarily the situation itself or an activating event, can trigger unhelpful, performance and relationship interfering emotions. This helps to teach the B-C connection of the ABCDEF psychological model used in rational coaching (see Ellis et al., 1997; Palmer, 2009a, b). Within the work, family and social context unhelpful negative emotions include anxiety, damning anger, depression, guilt, morbid jealousy and shame. In contrast more helpful, although still negative emotions could be concern, annoyance, sadness, remorse, non-morbid jealousy and regret which may allow the person to function in a more constructive manner to deal with a particular situation or crisis (see Dryden, 1987, 1990, 1994; Ellis et al., 1997; Palmer 2009a). In rational coaching, emotional goals are also developed if necessary depending upon the issues the coachee wishes to address.

A typical dialogue of a coaching session using the Deserted Island technique follows (adapted Palmer, 1992, 1993):

Coach:	Let's say, for example, you've been left on a deserted island. You have all your needs such as accommodation and food met, but one thing you don't have on the island are any friends. Imagine being on the island and you hold the belief: I really would prefer to have a friend with me on the island but I don't have to have one. How would you feel about your situation?
Coachee:	I would be concerned I didn't have anybody to share it with.
Coach:	Now, let's say that you're still on the island but this time your belief is: I must, I must, I really must have a friend on the island. How would you feel this time?
Coachee:	Pretty anxious.

---

1 The term Rational Coaching is short for Rational Emotive Behavioural Coaching (see Palmer, 2009).

2 The Deserted Island technique is different to the Deserted Island fantasy developed by Lazarus (1971, 1989) which is used to assess interpersonal functioning in multimodal coaching and therapy.

Coach:	Let's just stay with this for the moment. Just imagine that an aeroplane flies over and a friend of yours jumps out and parachutes slowly towards the deserted island. Now imagine that you are still holding the beliefs: I must, I must, I really must have a friend on the island. Then your friend lands on the island. How do you feel now?
Coachee:	Very relieved.
Coach:	After a period of time, let's imagine that you are still holding the belief: I must, I must, I really must have a friend on the island. Don't forget, you've still got your friend on the island with you. Can you foresee anything that could happen that you could become upset about again?
Coachee:	The friend could be taken away. Coach: So even though you have your friend on the island, after a period of time your anxiety might return, especially if you feared that your friend could be taken away.
Coachee:	Yeah.
Coach:	Let's change it slightly again. You're still on the island and your friend is there and this time you're holding on to the belief: I really would prefer to have a friend with me on the island but I don't have to have one. Would you feel anxious this time?
Coachee:	No. I'd be much better. Coach: Can you see that in each example I've described similar situations? The only key difference has been your beliefs and the different beliefs evoked different emotions. The 'must' belief led to you feeling 'pretty anxious', while the preference belief led you to feeling just 'concerned'.
Coachee:	Yeah.

When demonstrating the Deserted Island technique coachees will often experience the unhealthy negative emotions of depression or anxiety when holding the demanding 'musturbatory' beliefs and the healthier negative emotions of sadness or concern when holding the flexible 'preferential' beliefs. Some may just state they would feel less depressed or anxious if they held onto the preferential beliefs. Note that when a person indicates they would feel relief after a situation then this is an indicator that they were probably feeling anxious previously and not concern.

It is important that the coach does not assume that the coachee has understood the message that the Deserted Island technique was attempting to convey. As with the application of any technique it is useful to ask the coachee whether or not they have understood it. If there is any doubt, it is usually good practice to ask the coachee to explain what the example demonstrated. Once the coachee has understood the technique then the coach can start to challenge and modify demanding beliefs or rules that the coachee may hold.

COMMENT

The Deserted Island technique has been used within coaching and stress management/ managing pressure workshops. In group work the coach or trainer can ask each participant in turn, at each stage of the demonstration, how they would feel in the given situation with the different beliefs. In group settings, the participants often become aware that their colleagues may experience different or slightly different emotions from them.

The Deserted Island technique can be used with most coachees to demonstrate how different beliefs may lead to different emotional and behavioural outcomes. However, if a coachee has just suffered a relationship breakup or a recent a bereavement then the technique can be adapted to describe a different scenario that does not relate to people or relationships. Other exercises or metaphors to teach the B-C connection include a money model which uses a loss of money as the activating event (Dryden, 1987).

REFERENCES

Dryden, W. (1987). *Counselling individuals: The rational-emotive approach*. London: Taylor and Francis.

Dryden, W. (1990). *Rational-emotive counselling in action*. London: Sage.

Dryden, W. (1994). *Invitation to rational emotive psychology*. London: Whurr.

Dryden, W. & Gordon, J. (1993). *Peak performance: Become more effective at work*. Didcot: Mercury.

Ellis, A., Gordon, J., Neenan, M. & Palmer, S. (1997). *Stress counselling: A rational-emotive behaviour approach*. London: Cassell.

Lazarus, A.A. (1971). *Behaviour therapy and beyond*. New York: McGraw-Hill.

Lazarus, A.A. (1989). *The practice of multimodal therapy*. Baltimore, MD: The Johns Hopkins University Press.

Neenan, M. & Palmer, S. (2001a). Cognitive behavioural coaching. *Stress News*, *13*(3), 15–18.

Neenan, M. & Palmer, S. (2001b). Rational-emotive behaviour coaching. *Rational-Emotive Behaviour Therapist*, *9*(1), 34–41.

Palmer, S. (1992). Editorial: What law of the universe states that you must …? *Stress News*, *4*(3), 1.

Palmer, S. (1993). The 'Deserted Island' technique: A method of demonstrating how preferential and musturbatory beliefs can lead to different emotions. *The Rational-Emotive Therapist*, *1*(1), 12–14.

Palmer, S. (2009a). Rational coaching: A cognitive behavioural approach. *The Coaching Psychologist*, *5*(1), 12–18.

Palmer, S. (2009b). Inference chaining: A rational coaching technique. *Coaching Psychology International*, *2*(1), 11–12.

Section 7
Motivational Interviewing

Introduction

David Tee & Jonathan Passmore

This section features a series of papers written by Jonathan Passmore exploring how motivational interviewing, an evidence-based therapy approach, can be translated to coaching psychology practice. Passmore has frequently argued that much value can be gained by coaching psychologists in drawing from the evidence-based well of counselling psychology and models of behavioural change. However, to take these concepts wholesale would be tantamount to ignoring the different nature of the presenting issues which are found in coaching, the different relational and contractual basis for the relationship and, finally, the differences in client expectations.

In this brief introduction, we will review the nature of Motivational Interview and its development before summarising the seven papers in this section. Let us start by exploring what we mean by the terms 'motivational interviewing' (PP) and 'MI coaching'.

Motivational interviewing is a counselling approach that helps people resolve ambivalent feelings and aims to help them find their internal motivation to make a change. The originators have defined MI in the following terms: "Motivational interviewing is a directive, client-centered counseling style for eliciting behavior change by helping clients to explore and resolve ambivalence" (Miller & Rollnick, 2002, p. 35).

MI draws heavily on the Transtheoretical model (DiClemente & Prochaska, 1998) of behaviour change. The Transtheoretical model describes how people prepare to change through a series of stages from pre-contemplation, through contemplation, planning, action and how successful change is maintained, or how relapse is managed.

MI has developed over the past three decades from a health-based intervention, focusing on addictive behaviours, to one which is now used in a wide range of contexts to help clients explore their ambivalence to a situation or challenge. This includes its

Coaching Practiced, First Edition. Edited by David Tee and Jonathan Passmore.
© 2022 John Wiley & Sons Ltd. Published 2022 by John Wiley & Sons Ltd.
DOI: 10.1002/9781119835714.s07

adaptation to use in helping managers deal with perceived poor performance and helping others managing redundancy.

The seven papers within this section include a brief review of MI, followed by six technique papers drawn from MI practice which are well suited to use with coaching clients. In the positioning paper for this collection, Jonathan Passmore explores the nature and origins of motivational interviewing as a therapeutic approach designed for working with clients experiencing habituated behavioural problems, such as alcohol or drug dependency. He notes the high levels of efficacy, from the robust studies undertaken during the early period of MI, and how MI can be a useful tool for working with coaching clients and some types of presenting issues, particularly in cases where clients are ambivalent about making a change. This idea of working with ambivalent clients is further developed in a case study (Passmore & Whybrow, 2019).

The first paper (Passmore, 2011a) in the series explores the nature of MI and how the approach may offer value to coaching psychologists, specifically through developing intrinsic motivation for clients who are stuck or are ambivalent about making a change. They want to, but continually struggle. An MI-informed coaching approach recognises that change is a complex and difficult process which is not linear and may involve slips and relapses and finally through putting in places plans for maintaining the new behaviour including drawing on a wider well of resources and supporters.

The second paper (Passmore, 2011b) in the series focuses on the skill of reflection within MI. It identifies three different types of reflection: 'simple reflection', 'overstated reflection' and 'under-stated reflection' and identifies when each has a role in an MI coaching conversation. While most coaches focus on simple reflections, the use of muted and amplified reflections adds to the coaches' repertoire, enabling them to more clearly explore clients' sometimes unspoken thoughts about an issue in more depth and, through this, more accurately align their behaviours with their values and beliefs.

In the third paper, Passmore (2011c) explores the use of decisional balance, which in an organisational context can be translated as the 'balance sheet technique'. Decisional balance (Miller & Rollnick, 2002) is a useful tool for helping the client to think through their ambivalence in an open and systematic way. It helps the client to deepen their self- understanding and reflect on their own behaviour by charging the arguments both for and against change, and contrasting these with the arguments for and against staying the same (or doing nothing). As a result of the exercise, the person's ambiguity is explored, and the individual is then able to better connect their choice with their core values.

The fourth paper in the set explores the 'typical day' technique (Passmore, 2012a). The exercise is a good way to start a session helping the client to reflect on their current situation (Miller & Rollnick, 2002). This exploration can follow on from the initial contracting and goal-setting segment of the session. While therapeutic in origin, the technique fits well in life coaching and in some organisational coaching conversations, providing the space for the client to talk, and specifically to break down the nature of the issue, moving away from their usually storytelling version, but to see the events through new eyes by taking each element step by step.

The fifth paper explores a technique known as *recognising change talk* (Passmore, 2012b). The technique goes to the heart of MI, which recognises the relationship between the words being used by clients and what this indicates in terms of their inner state, particularly their motivation to make a change or their ambivalence towards this change. The technique uses a framework, known as DARN CATS to inform the coach's judgements about how likely the client is to make a change and, subject to this language, for the coach to adapt their interventions to better reflect the client's current stage in the change cycle (Prochaska & DiClemente, 1983).

The sixth paper (Passmore, 2013a) explores the technique of agenda mapping, a simple process which helps the coaching to plan collaboratively with the client on the session, its focus and its expected outcomes. In this session, agenda setting is really a meta-conversation; it is a conversation about the conversation. When neglected, sessions are likely to lack focus; when done well, it can turbo charge the client and propel the session forward, like an arrow shot, initially, out of sight.

The final paper (Passmore, 2013b) explores the question of ethics, and whether, or in what circumstances, MI is an ethical application in coaching relationships. In traditional MI, the therapist has a view: drugs, alcohol or target-habited behaviour is considered undesirable, while it must be the client who comes to this view by exploring their behaviours and values. In contrast, within coaching, the coach has no such fixed view on the outcome: should the client leave or continue their job? Should they use their email less? In this way, we would argue, MI-based coaching is more collaborative and more egalitarian than its therapeutic cousin. However, as Passmore notes, using MI-informed coaching still raises some questions about the nature of coaching and what is acceptable and not acceptable within the contracted relationship with a client.

REFERENCES

DiClemente, C. C., & Prochaska, J. O. (1998). Toward a comprehensive, transtheoretical model of change: Stages of change and addictive behaviors. In W. R. Miller, & N. Heather (Eds.), *Treating addictive behaviors* (pp. 3–24). Applied clinical psychology.

Miller, W., & Rollnick, S. (2002). *Motivational Interviewing: Preparing people for change* (2nd ed.). Guilford Press.

Passmore, J. (2011a) Motivational interviewing – A model for coaching psychology. *The Coaching Psychologist*, 7(1), 36–41

Passmore, J. (2011b) Motivational interviewing: Reflective listening. *The Coaching Psychologist*, 7(1), 50–54.

Passmore, J. (2011c) Motivational interviewing: Balance sheet technique. *The Coaching Psychologist*, 7(2) 151–154

Passmore, J. (2012a) Motivational interviewing: Typical day. *The Coaching Psychologist*, 8(1), 50–52.

Passmore, J. (2012b) Motivational interviewing: Recognising change talk. *The Coaching Psychologist* 8(2), 107–111.

Passmore, J. (2013a) Motivational interviewing: Agenda Mapping. *The Coaching Psychologist*, *9*(1), 32–35.

Passmore, J. (2013b) Motivational interviewing: Reflecting on ethical decisions. *The Coaching Psychologist*, *9*(2), 112–116.

Passmore, J., & Whybrow, A. (2019). Motivational Interviewing. In S. Palmer, & A. Whybrow, *Handbook of Coaching Psychology: A guide for practitioners* (pp. 144–153). Routledge.

Prochaska, J. O., & DiClemente, C. C. (1983). Stages and processes of self-change of smoking: Toward an integrative model of change. *Journal of Consulting and Clinical Psychology*, *51*, 390–395.

22 Motivational Interviewing – a model for coaching psychology practice

Jonathan Passmore

Abstract

This is the first in a series of papers to look at Motivational Interviewing (MI) as an approach suitable for use with coaching clients. This paper presents a brief overview of MI for readers unfamiliar with MI and directs readers to other sources for a fuller account. The paper aims to set the scene from a practitioner perspective for subsequent papers in this section, rather than offer a detailed account of MI's application in coaching. Each of these subsequent papers will present a short description of a technique suitable for working with a coachee's ambivalence.

Keywords

coaching; motivational interviewing; coaching psychology; trans-theoretical model; behaviour change readiness for change.

Original publication details: Passmore, J. (2011, June). Motivational Interviewing – A model for coaching psychology practice. *The Coaching Psychologist, 7*(1), 36–40. Reproduced with permission of The British Psychological Society.

Coachee ambivalence to change can sometimes be an issue which coaches face in their work, in health as well as organisational coaching. Almost all of the coaching models, (for example GROW, Cognitive behavioural, solution focused) assume the client has mentally committed to make a change and that resistance is not a feature of the conversation. This is often the case, which is why skills in helping clients make links between their emotions, cognitions and behaviours, are useful, alongside skills in challenging irrational thoughts or developing personal action plans. However, from personal experience, I find a small proportion of clients are stuck and are unable to move forward through use of behavioural or cognitive behavioural models. They are stuck with behaviours which they do not see as problematical, but which others do. Or they may be stuck in ruminating on a problem without a clear commitment to take action. In these cases Motivational Interviewing (MI) is a useful evidenced-based approach which can be employed by the coaching psychologist to help the individual build sufficient motivation to take action.

THE DEVELOPMENT OF MI

MI was developed in clinical environments by counsellors working with drug and alcohol clients. They found that change processes inside counselling mirrored natural change processes outside of the counselling room. A key predictive factor whether people would change was the way they spoke about change during their sessions with the counsellor. Clients who made statements that signalled a high level of motivation and a strong commitment to change were more likely to make a change, than those demonstrating resistance to making a change.

Alongside this was a recognition by counsellors that the language used by the client could be influenced by the counsellor through the questions they asked. Specifically the counsellor could direct attention to specific aspects of behaviour through skilled reflections and summary and encourage the client to focus on talking about these aspects of their behaviour (Miller & Rollnick, 2002).

In addition, counsellors observed that changes in the words and language used by the client were a strong predictor of a future change in behaviour. However, getting this change in language through confrontation was less effective than using open questions, active listening, reflection and summaries (OARS).

MI evolved out of these observations through the work of Bill Miller and Steve Rollnick (Miller & Rollnick, 2002). Their focus was on enhancing intrinsic (internal) motivation towards behavioural change by helping the resolution of ambivalence to change in clients. Over the past decade a significant evidence base has demonstrated the efficacy of the approach for specific counselling client presenting issues. A full review of the evidence supporting MI is contained elsewhere (see Miller & Rollnick, 2002; Passmore, 2007; Passmore & Whybrow, 2007)

THE THEORY BASE OF MI – TRANSTHEORETICAL MODEL

MI draws heavily on the Transtheoretical model (DiClemente & Prochaska, 1998) of behaviour change. The Transtheoretical model describes how people prepare to change through a series of stages from pre-contemplation, through contemplation, planning, action and how successful change is maintained, or how relapse is managed.

In this section I will briefly describe the stages of the Transtheoretical model and the relationship between them. The Transtheoretical model itself is summarised in Figure 1.

The authors argue that people experience different thought patterns at different stages of change. This may start with consciousness raising, where a person learns new facts or ideas that highlight the existence of a problem (pre-contemplation). This leads to reflecting on the issue, the pro and cons of whether a change should or could be made (contemplation stage). This progresses to reflecting on what steps to make (planning), followed by the first steps of change (action stage) (Perz, DiClemente & Carbonari, 1996). A fuller account of the Transtheoretical model and MI's application in coaching is offered in Passmore and Whybrow (2007).

However, the movement through stages is not always a straight path from pre-contemplation to maintenance as suggested by the Transtheoretical model. Relapse is a common problem experienced by many of us when making a change. Relapse can occur at any stage. As a result, it is common for individuals to make progress and slip back. An example is when we commit to a new health plan. As part of this we may buy membership to a fitness gym at the start of a new year. However, we find out that other

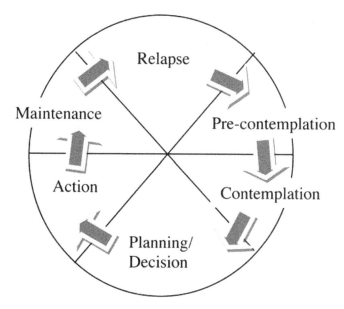

Figure 1 *Cycle of change*

Table 1   *Using MI and other interventions within a Model of Change*

Change Stage	Intervention model	Most useful interventions
Pre-contemplation	Humanistic/ Motivational Interviewing	Create relationship through empathy and rapport Use reflective listening If reluctant to change – encourage gathering of evidence/feedback If lack of belief that can change – offer belief encourage hope If giving reasons for not changing explore wider values, beliefs and impact of behaviour on others.
Contemplation	Motivational Interviewing/ Cognitive behavioural	Explore the reasons not to change and reasons to change Explore the 'problem' Explore the coachee's most important aspects/ goals of their life Reflect back discrepancy between goals/ values and current behaviour Explore confidence to change Explore barriers to change Reflect back desire to change and confidence statements
Planning	Motivational Interviewing/ Behavioural (GROW)/ Cognitive behavioural	Check for congruence in change communications Explore confidence to change Clarify and refine goals Review options and select chosen options Identify allies to support coachee Use visualisation to build confidence
Action	Motivational Interviewing and Behavioural (GROW)	Monitor and affirm small steps Explore next steps Explore barriers being encountered Plan actions to overcome barriers
Maintenance	Motivational Interviewing and Behavioural	Provide positive feedback on success Plan for coping if slip back Reinforce long term goals fit with values Encourage use of allies to continue positive progress
Relapse		Empathise and normalise Explore reasons for relapse Plan to prevent next time Explore successes and affirm Reflect back positive statements of desire for change Return to contemplation actions

priorities take over, and we slip back to our old ways. In reviewing our progress at the end of February we may find that we have stopped going to the gym and need to recommit to our fitness plan.

A key concept of MI is the importance of tailoring interventions to meet an individual's stage of change to help individuals from slipping back (Project MATCH, 1997). This includes selecting appropriate interventions including tools and techniques which are useful at specific stages of the change cycle.

Table 1 (overleaf) summarises each of the stages of change and highlights similarities with other approaches, such as humanistic and behavioural. It also suggests useful intentions which the coach could draw on at each stage to help the coachee move forward to the next step in the change cycle.

A common feature, and reason for drawing on MI, is that the coachee demonstrates ambivalence. Ambivalence is when the coachee asks *What's the point of changing?* It is this which can often keep the coachee stuck with old habits and not able to move forward.

A typical response to ambivalence is to offer advice, education or options of action (Rollnick, 1998). Such interventions from the coach are likely to result in resistance from the individual, rather than change. Coachees have usually had advice and instructions of what to do a hundred times before. Repeating these is likely to get the same result – no change.

To generate change the coaching psychologist needs to recognise and understand ambivalence as a natural part of the change process and to work with it (Passmore, Anstiss & Ward, 2009). In line with MI, a starting point is to recognise which stage of change the individual is at. One way of doing this is to ask the coachee to rate their perceived readiness to change on a scale of 0 to 10, with 10 being that they have already made change, and 0 being not at all interested in changing. A second is to listen closely to what the coachee has to say – do they know they have a problem, have they considered different options for what to do, do they have a plan, has the plan worked?

In MI the coaching psychologist uses their understanding of the stage of the change where the coachee is, to match their interventions (see Table 1). In successive techniques papers I will explore different techniques and tools which the coach can use to enhance the motivation to change.

CONCLUSION

One source of hope for coachees' from the MI approach, is that there is no 'right way' to change, and if one given plan for change does not work, a coachee is only limited by their creativity as to the number of other approaches that may be tried.

To accompany this hope described in the paragraph above, a word of caution. Human behaviour is difficult to change. The desire to change our behaviour and an actual change are two different things. To succeed the coach needs to be persistent, as does the coachee. However, if the coach is too persistent there is the danger they either become unethical in being overly manipulative in moving their coachee towards a predetermined outcome, or they move into persuasion which in turn leads to resistance. As coaching psychologists we need to understand our role is limited to one of encouraging personal responsibility and developing self awareness.

REFERENCES

DiClemente, C.C. & Prochaska, J.O. (1998). Toward a comprehensive, transtheoretical model of change: Stages of change and addictive behaviours. In W.R. Miller & N. Heather (Eds.), *Treating addictive behaviours* (2nd ed., pp.3–24). New York: Plenum Press.

Miller, W.R. & Rollnick, S. (2002). *Motivational Interviewing: Preparing people for change* (2nd ed.). New York: Guilford Press.

Passmore, J. (2007). Addressing deficit performance through coaching: using motivational interviewing for performance improvement in coaching. *International Coaching Psychology Review 2*(3), 265–279.

Passmore, J., Anstiss, T. & Ward, G. (2009) This way out: Motivational Interviewing. *Coaching at Work, 4*(2), 38–41.

Passmore, J. & Whybrow, A. (2007). Motivational Interviewing: A specific approach for coaching psychologists. In S. Palmer & A. Whybrow (Eds.), *The handbook of coaching psychology* (pp.160–173). London: Brunner-Routledge.

Perz, C.A., DiClemente, C.C. & Carbonari, J.P. (1996). Doing the right thing at the right time? The interaction of stages and processes of change in successful smoking cessation. *Health Psychology, 15*, 462–468.

Project MATCH Research Group (1997). Matching alcoholism treatments to client heterogeneity: Project MATCH post-treatment drinking outcomes. *Journal of Studies on Alcohol, 58*, 7–29.

Rollnick, S. (1998). Readiness and confidence: Critical conditions of change in treatment. In W.R. Miller & N. Heather (Eds.), *Treating addictive behaviours* (2nd ed.). New York: Plenum.

23 Motivational Interviewing techniques reflective listening

Jonathan Passmore

Abstract

This short article focuses on the skill of reflection within Motivational Interviewing (MI). It identifies three different types of reflection – 'simple reflection', 'over-stated reflection' and 'under-stated reflection' and identifies when each has a role in an MI coaching conversation.

Keywords

listening skills; reflection; motivational interviewing; reflective listening; motivational interviewing skills.

MOTIVATIONAL INTERVIEWING (MI)

As noted in Chapter 22 (Passmore, 2011), MI (Miller & Rollnick, 2002) is a sophisticated technique and one best used by advanced practitioners who are already skilled in using the core skills in coaching such as open questions, active listening, summary and basic reflection (Passmore, Anstiss & Ward, 2009). In this sense MI is well suited as

Original publication details: Passmore, J. (2011, June). Motivational Interviewing techniques reflective listening. *The Coaching Psychologist, 7*(1), 50–53. Reproduced with permission of The British Psychological Society.

a skill for coaching psychologists who already draw upon behavioural, cognitive behavioural and humanistic interventions within their coaching practice. It is, however, different from each of these approaches, while drawing on elements from all three (Anstiss & Passmore, in press).

REFLECTIVE LISTENING

Reflective listening is one of the key skills within MI. In popular language 'listening' often means just keeping quiet; waiting for our turn to talk. This level 1 style of listening is unhelpful in even basic coaching, although it is a frequent style of listening used in many every day conversations. Competent coaching psychologists should be aiming to listen at level 3 or 4, with excellent coaches occasionally stepping in to work at an interpretive level and sharing their insights where this is helpful to their coachee.

At level 1 and at level 2 the listener might be drawn into using an intervention which creates road blocks for the speaker, which stops the speaker moving forward (Gordon, 1970). These responses might include agreeing, reassuring cautioning or labelling, or even asking a question. For the coachee who is stuck in a dilemma and is seeking a way forward, but remains ambivalent about making a change a road block intervention is likely to maintain them in their current position.

Table 1   *Five levels of listening (adapted from Hawkins & Smith, 2006)*

Level 1: Waiting to speak – at this level we are simply waiting for our turn to talk.
Level 2: Basic listening – at this level the listener focuses on the words being said.
Level 3: Attentive listening – at this level the listener focuses on the words and tone of the communication to understand the true meaning.
Level 4: Active listening – at this level the listener listens to the words, tone and body language of the speaker and is aiming to understand what the speaker is intending to communicate.
Level 5: Interpretive listening – at this level the listener is seeking to move beyond the intended communication, they are interpreting meaning from the whole communication both intended meaning and unintended communications.

In Table 2 the coach uses both a affirming statement ('sounds really bad'), as well as a question to explore in further detail the nature of the behaviours which create the feelings.

Table 2   *Example of typical coach response*

Coachee: 'I am feeling fed up with my boss.' Coach: 'Sounds really bad, what are they doing?'

The coach, drawing on MI approaches, will try a different approach. The MI coach will try to leverage change through building change talk and thus helping the coachee to become unstuck.

Change talk is simply statements from the coachee which focus on desires or plans for making a change in their behaviour. We will focus on change talk itself in a later techniques paper.

If the coach is to avoid these road blocks what else can the coach say? MI evidence suggests that using a variety of reflection techniques at this stage is more likely to be effective in encouraging the coachee to develop change talk.

SIMPLE REFLECTION

In using 'simple reflection' the coach tries to understand the meaning of the coachee and reflect this back, capturing the words, phrases and critically the meaning of the coachee's communication. Using a reflective statement is less likely to provoke resistance. For example, if the coach asked about the meaning of the statement, this directs the coachee to step back and reflect on whether they really do mean what they have said. To illustrate this point, the coach could ask: 'You're feeling unsure?' This is done through an inflection, with the tone rising towards the end of the sentence. In contrast the coach could use reflective listening to reflect back 'You're feeling unsure'. This involves using a neutral tone throughout the sentence. The reflective statement communicates understanding and becomes a statement of fact. Such statements are more likely to encourage the coachee to talk more about this emotional state. As the coachee talks they think about this state and draw out for themselves the evidence of why they are feeling as they do. This deepens their understanding and the evidence suggests this leads into change talk – statements about wishing or planning to make a change.

Reflective statements can be quite simple and often can involve reflecting back a single word or pair of key words from the coachee's story. The coaches' skill is in listening and selecting the right word or words to reflect back which capture the heart of the message.

A more sophisticated series of options, however, are also available to the coach. These involve over-stating or under-stating the reflection. The use of these and the frequency of application will vary with the coach's skills. Inappropriate use can leave the coachee believing their coach is not listening to them and can undermine the coaching relationship. As a result caution is required along with skill in selecting the words to reflect back.

UNDER-STATED REFLECTION

This is best used when the coach wishes the coachee to continue exploring an issue and to confirm the strength of feeling they have about an issue. The coach may reflect back a lower level of emotion than that communicated by the coachee. For example, the coachee communicates 'anger', the coach may select to reflect back a lower intensity of 'anger', such as using the word' irritation' or 'annoyed'. This works well with British coachees where under-statement is a feature of British culture. The effect is the coachee is likely to speak further about the true emotion, possibly correcting their coach about the strength of feeling and to dwell on the true power of their feeling.

The key skill is to avoid under-stating to the extent that the coachee feels that the coach has not listened to what has been said. This takes both a high level of listening to the whole communication and a high level of skill in selecting the right word to reflect back – highly articulate coaches thus have less trouble in making word selections than those with a more limited emotional vocabulary.

OVER-STATED REFLECTION

In contrast if the coach selects to amplify the emotional content and over-state the emotion compared with the coachee's original communication, the likely effect is for the coachee to deny and minimise the emotion.

This is useful, for example, if the coachee was speaking about their dislike for their manager and faults in their manager's working style. The coach may reflect back an over-statement about the manager's 'total incompetence' or how the employee can't stand' their manager. This is likely to have the effect of getting the coachee to recognise some of the positive attributes of their manager and thus begin to build a more evidenced based perspective.

Once again the dangers of the coachee feeling they have not been heard are present and in a British cultural context this is further magnified. As a result the coach needs to be careful and limited in their use of over statement, to avoid danger to the coaching relationship.

DIFFERENCES BETWEEN COACHING AND COUNSELLING WITH MI

These responses can be useful when helping the coachee explore the two sides of an issue. In MI coaching, the coach wishes to help the coachee develop stronger arguments for change and to minimise the arguments in favour of indecision or inaction. This contrasts with MI counselling where a specific outcome is likely to be in the mind of the counsellor, such as helping the client to give up excessive alcohol consumption or illegal drugs. In coaching, there is less likely to be a vested interest (although this varies with the nature of the coaching assignment). The role of the MI coach is thus different and reflects the different circumstances of coaching work, ethical considerations, while also using the full repertoire of skills to encourage the coachee towards a deeper understanding of the issue and towards a decision for action.

CONCLUSION

Reflection, like coaching, is not a passive process. It is the coach who decides what to reflect on and what aspects to ignore. In this way the coach can direct the attention of the coachee and encourage them to focus on aspects which may help them to reframe the situation and to build a motivation for action.

REFERENCES

Anstiss, T. & Passmore, J. (in press). Motivational Interview. In M. Neenan & S. Palmer (Eds.), *Cognitive behavioural coaching*. London: Routledge.

Gordon, T. (1970). *Parent effective training*. New York: Wyden.

Hawkins, P. & Smith N. (2006). *Coaching, mentoring and organisational consultancy: Supervision and development*. Maidenhead: Open University Press/McGraw Hill.

Miller, W. & Rollnick, S. (2002). *Motivational Interviewing: Preparing people for change* (2nd ed.). New York: Guilford Press.

Passmore, J. (2011). Motivational Interviewing – a model for coaching psychology practice. *The Coaching Psychologist*, 7(1), 35–39.

Passmore, J., Anstiss, T. & Ward, G. (2009) This way out: Motivational Interviewing. *Coaching at Work*, 4(2), 38–41.

Passmore, J. & Whybrow, A. (2007). Motivational interviewing: A specific approach for coaching psychologists. In S. Palmer & A. Whybrow (Eds.), *The handbook of coaching psychology* (pp.160–173). London: Brunner-Routledge.

24 MI – Balance sheet techniques

Jonathan Passmore

Abstract

This article is the second paper drawing on the application of motivational interviewing within coaching. I previously summarised briefly the principles of Motivational Interviewing (Passmore, 2011a) and offered one technique – reflective listening (Passmore, 2011b). In this paper I will briefly review a technique called decisional balance or 'the balance sheet'.

BEHAVIOUR CHANGE

Making a change is hard for most of us. People often have views which both promote change and which get in their way. They see the potential advantages of changing, but also the advantages of their current behaviour. This type of thinking, arguing both sides of the argument for and against change, can lead to ambivalence. Ultimately this can lead to the coachee becoming stuck and being unable to make a change. This is natural, but for change to happen the coachee needs to overcome this log-jam of ambivalence and develop the motivation to make a change.

Original publication details: Passmore, J. (2011, December). MI balance sheet techniques. *The Coaching Psychologist, 7*(2), 151–153. Reproduced with permission of The British Psychological Society.

MI is a sophisticated approach to behaviour change which is suited to skilled practitioners such as coaching psychologists (Passmore & Whybrow, 2007). In using the approach the key task for the MI coach is to help their coachee explore and understand the coachee's own ambivalence – reluctance to change. By talking things through coachees have the opportunity to hear their thought processes aloud and to explore these from multiple perspectives with the aid of a coach.

THE TECHNIQUE EXPLAINED

The balance sheet technique, also known as 'decisional balance' (Miller & Rollnick, 2002) helps people think though their ambivalence in an open and systematic way. It helps the coachee to deepen their self-understanding and reflect on their own behaviour. As a result of the exercise the person's perceived importance for changing (or confidence about changing) is likely to increase and alongside this their motivation and readiness to change may also increase.

For the coach, the technique provides another opportunity to demonstrate good quality non-judgemental listening and to use the OARS (open questions, active listening, reflection and summary) discussed in previous papers, to understand the coachee, to roll with resistance (as opposed to offering arguments for change) and to notice and elicit change talk which comes directly from the coachee (these concepts are further explored in Anstiss & Passmore, 2011).

The technique works best with a sheet of paper (I have also used a flip chart or wipe board when these have been available – but be aware of removing the results at the end of the session to prevent others from reading the notes you have left behind). Divide the sheet into two main columns and two sub-columns (see Figure 1).

Using the responses from the coachee recorded on the balance sheet, the coach can direct the focus of the coachee to start talking about the current benefits of the behaviour, which they may want to change, through an open question such as *'Tell me a little more about how X can be exciting?'* Such behaviours are often maintained as the coachee derives some pleasure or positive affect from them. By starting with positives this reduces the chances of defensiveness from the coachee and the perception that the coach has a fixed agenda to 'make the coachee change their behaviour. In most

Benefits of activity	Costs of activity	Benefits of change	Costs of change

(Adapted from Miller & Rollnick, 2002)

Figure 1 *Coaching for change Balance Sheet*

applications of MI in coaching, I would suggest the role is not to lead the coachee towards selecting a specific behaviour (although MI is often used in clinical settings in this way to address offending or serious drug misuse behaviours) (Passmore, 2007).

The coach may specifically target aspects to encourage the coachee to talk more about the positive aspects of the desired behaviour. The coach may do this through directing attention to this aspect through a further question or by asking the coachee to give an example. Alternatively the coach may ask the coachee to talk about the feelings they have when they have made progress towards this new behavioural goal or when engaging in the desired behaviour.

As the coachee talks about each point in turn, the coach should invite the coachee to summarise the point in three or four words on the decision balance sheet. I have found it works best when the coachee writes down the points rather than the coach doing this.

Depending on the individual and their state, some coachees jump from one point to another and start talking about 'disadvantages' when they were asked about advantages of making a change, or vice versa. This is not a reflection of the coach, but a reflection of the coachee giving voice to their ambivalence and is natural and common. The coach may reflect back to let them know they have been heard and at the end of the point may direct attention back to the side of the equation which was the original focus of the question, by saying something like *'Well, we're going to talk about the disadvantages in a minute. But are there any other possible benefits to you?'*

As a result of these interventions change talk often emerges from the coachee. Coachees may say something like *'I'd really like to be home on time to put the children to bed'*, reflecting their desire to make a change to the time consuming nature of their role and the desire to break the pattern of behaviour.

The exercise can be completed more quickly, if time is a challenge. This can be done by just using two boxes as opposed to four columns. These two columns can be summarised under the heading: *'good things'* and *'less good things'*. By using a two as opposed to a four column approach repetition is avoided with items being repeated by the client in the disadvantages of one side of the balance sheet as well as the advantages of the other side of the other side. I have found however, that on occasions, coachees can miss items, when two rather than four columns are used.

At the end of the exercise the coachee has a sheet which they have completed which they can take away. The coach might ask them to spend some further time reflecting on this before the next session. Rather than leaving this free form, this works best when attention is directed towards the focus of change.

CONCLUSION

The decisional balance or balance sheet technique within MI can be used within other coaching models and is a simple but useful technique for coachee's to explore the consequences of their behaviour, to more fully understand the impact on their self and others and take personal responsibility for the consequences based on an informed choice about their behaviour.

REFERENCES

Anstiss, T. & Passmore, J. (in press). *Health coaching*. London: Karnac Press.

Miller, W. & Rollnick, S. (2002). *Motivational Interviewing: Preparing people for change* (2nd ed.). New York: Guilford Press.

Passmore, J. (2011a). Motivational Interviewing – a model for coaching psychology practice. *The Coaching Psychologist*, 7(1), 35–39.

Passmore, J. (2011b). MI techniques – Reflective listening. *The Coaching Psychologist*, 7(1), 49–52.

Passmore, J. & Whybrow, A. (2007). Motivational Interviewing: A specific approach for coaching psychologists. In S. Palmer & A. Whybrow (Eds.), *The handbook of coaching psychology* (pp.160–173). London: Brunner-Routledge.

25 MI techniques: The Typical Day

Jonathan Passmore

Abstract

This article is the third in the techniques series which are drawn from the motivational interviewing approach. In this paper I will briefly review a technique called 'A Typical Day'. Typical Day is a useful technique or more rightly an exercise, which is used at the start of a coaching conversation to encourage the coachee to talk about the key issue. It offers the coach the opportunity to demonstrate listening and empathy while also gaining a detailed understanding of the issue.

The 'typical day' exercise is a good way to start a coaching session and can follow on from the initial contracting and goal setting segment of the session which might dominate the first five to 10 minutes of the conversation. While this is a technique grounded in Motivational Interviewing (Miller & Rollnick, 2002), it is also a technique which can be used more widely in life coaching and for some organisational coaching conversations.

The technique offers the opportunity to the coach to demonstrate what coaching is all about and to get the coachee talking. The coach can use the technique to demonstrate that they are a good, non-judgmental, listener who really wants to understand. The coachee gets to talk about something they feel very comfortable with and know something about. Overall the technique builds empathy and rapport and increases the coachee's commitment to the process.

Original publication details: Passmore, J. (2012, June). MI techniques: The typical day. *The Coaching Psychologist*, 8(1), 50–51. Reproduced with permission of The British Psychological Society.

MI PRINCIPLES

As noted earlier (Passmore, 2011a) motivational interviewing is a set of principles as opposed to a set of techniques. The key aspect is to keep to the core principles rather than mechanically follow this or other MI techniques. When the technique is deployed well by the coach, the typical day exercise will have given the person a chance to talk naturally and comfortably for a several minutes about something they know well and to build the relationship with the coachee, thus providing a platform for further work later in the session or in future sessions.

THE TECHNIQUE

The coach may introduce the technique or exercise by saying, *'perhaps you could help me get a better understanding how your average day goes – starting from when you get up in the morning until when you go to bed? Would that be okay? How does your day start?'*

In response to this question some coachees will rush ahead and focus on the issue which they wish to discuss, for example, stress and work-life balance. They may say, *'Well nothing really happens until…'*. My suggestion is to slow these coachees down by asking them to tell you a little but more about how the day starts. Other coachees may take several minutes telling you about their thoughts even before they get out of bed. Good coaches will direct attention and manage the process through intervening, speeding up the slow coachees and helping those who are racing ahead to take the day in a step-by-step order.

During the description of their day, coachees will frequently use both 'sustain talk' (e.g. *'I just can't start stand the place, the bureaucracy drives me wild'*) and 'change talk' (e.g. *'I used to work in the private sector and had an enjoyable time working there'*). These will spontaneously emerge during the exercise without coach direction. Such responses provide the opportunity to 'go with the flow' while trying to develop more change talk by asking the coachee to elaborate. A further useful intervention from the coach is to make affirming statements or to reflect back what is being heard.

In using the technique in a MI spirit, the coach should try to avoid too many 'assessment' questions like *'On a scale of 1 to 10, just how stressed do you feel at that point of the day?'* Such interventions may have the affect of making the person feel judged or rated and may lead to them being less open later in the session.

The overall aim is to encourage the coachee to start talking and continue talking from an evidence based perspective about their day and how the issue which they wish to focus on manifests itself within their day (Anstiss & Passmore, in press). By directing attention through questions the coach gains a deep insight into the life of the coachee and a good sense of their current situation.

Towards the end of the exercise it will be helpful for the coachee if the coach summarises the key points which have emerged. This can demonstrate to the coachee they have been really listened to, as well as offering a chance to hear back and to further reflect on what they have been saying.

CONCLUSION

The technique offers a useful intervention for coaches using MI helping them start the coaching conversation, establish rapport, demonstrate empathy through active listening and offering an insight into the coachee's issue.

REFERENCES

Anstiss, T. & Passmore, J. (in press). *Health coaching*. London: Karnac Press.

Anstiss, T. & Passmore, J. (2011). Motivational Interview. In M. Neenan & S. Palmer (Eds.), *Cognitive behavioural coaching*. London: Routledge.

Miller, W. & Rollnick, S. (2002). *Motivational Interviewing: Preparing people for change* (2nd ed.). New York: Guilford Press.

Passmore, J. (2007). Addressing deficit performance through coaching: using motivational interviewing for performance improvement in coaching. *International Coaching Psychology Review*, 2(3), 265–279.

Passmore, J. (2011). Motivational Interviewing – a model for coaching psychology practice. *The Coaching Psychologist*, 7(1), 35–39.

Passmore, J. (2011b). MI techniques – Reflective listening. *The Coaching Psychologist*, 7(1), 49–52.

Passmore, J. (2011c). MI techniques – The balance sheet. *The Coaching Psychologist*, 7(2), 151–153.

26 MI techniques: Recognising change talk

Jonathan Passmore

Abstract

This article is the fourth in a series which is drawn from the motivational interviewing approach. In this paper I will briefly review a 'technique' which is at the centre of effective use of MI, 'Recognising change talk' (previously known as 'self-motivating statements'). The ability to recognise the type of change talk used by clients is a key skill of the MI practitioner and its content can usefully inform the practice of coaching psychologists.

Recognising the relationship between the words being used by clients and what this indicates, in terms of the inner statement, is an important aspect of MI. Research indicates there is a strong relation ship between client words and client deeds (for a fuller discussion of this see Anstiss & Passmore, 2013).

In previous articles I have explored basic techniques from MI, but ones which could be used by coaching psychologists within their own practice. Some may argue that these techniques, such as decisional balance (balance sheet) are not unique to MI. However, recognising, categorising and using this categorisation to inform the next intervention is a distinctive feature of MI. While many coaching psychologists may acknowledge that their interventions are informed by their coachee's previous statement, MI offers a way to categorise the coachee's statements and encourages the coach to listen for changes in the language used by the coachee particularly around goal commitment and goal mobilisation.

Original publication details: Passmore, J. (2012, December). MI techniques: Recognising change talk. *The Coaching Psychologist, 8*(2), 107–110. Reproduced with permission of The British Psychological Society.

MI PRINCIPLES

As noted earlier (Passmore, 2011a; Anstiss & Passmore, 2011) motivational interviewing is a set of principles as opposed to a set of techniques. The key aspect of MI is to keep to the core principles rather than mechanically follow this or another technique. When the MI principles are followed by the coach, Miller and Rollnick (2011) argue, an effective relationship will be built with the coachee. Further, the coach is making effective use of the OARS (open questions, affirming statements, reflections and summarises) as part of this relationship building and in doing so are helping the coachee to explore their issue. The coachee will be talking openly about their issue and the challenges they face in making a change and the coach will be actively and empathetically listening to the content of what is being said and unsaid by the coachee.

As the relationship develops the coach should pay particularly close attention to change talk. Sometimes people believe that because we suggest we may do things, we will do them. As an example I recently attended a coach training course as an external observer. The course trainer was a highly experienced coach. The trainer offered to demonstrate a technique drawn from NLP. The trainer asked for a volunteer from the group. She then coached the volunteer for around 10 minutes in a demonstration session. The coach concluded by encouraging the coachee to set a plan. The coachee was reluctant but after several questions they offered a possible action. Having got a plan the trainer was delighted with the outcome and suggested to the group that the session had demonstrated the power of the coaching technique. Sadly, what was missed was the detailed phrasing of the commitment, and the body language of the coachee, as they gave their commitment. What the coachee offered was preparatory change talk. The coachee's statements revealed recognition of the need to change and a wish to change. However, what was missing was a specific commitment that they would change. There is a danger for all of us that, unless we listen closely to what the coachee actually says, we can interpret desire as intention.

THE TECHNIQUE

So what are we looking for in the words and phrases used by the coachee?

Miller and Rollnick (2002, 2011) have suggested that change talk is like a hill. It comes in two parts; the uphill and downhill of change. The uphill side of the equation is the preparatory change talk. This is most likely to occur during the contemplation phase. The person is thinking about change and is weighing up whether change is really for them. In many cases the person is well aware of the advantages of making the change, but balanced against this are a series of barriers which have blocked their path to successfully making the change. It is this aspect which has created the ambivalence to making the change.

During this phase the coach needs to listen for what Miller and Rollnick (2011) have labelled DARNs. It is these statements which reveal an interest and consideration of

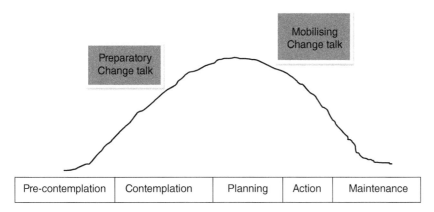

Figure 1 *Transpersonal model of change and change talk phases.*

change, but which lack a specific commitment to make the change. Such statements might express the individual's personal desires about making a change, the ability to make the change, their reasons for making the change and the need to change. Examples of these are summarised in Figure 2.

In general terms the coach should look out for statements which are conditional or hypothetical. These statements express desires (need to and want to), they may express ability (I can or I could), they express reasons for making the change and they may also express the need to make the change and the consequences of failing to do so. However, while such statements reveal the coachee has shifted from the pre-contemplation to contemplation phase of the stages of change model (Prochaska & DiClemente, 1983) there is no expressed commitment to make the change, or a specific plan as to how the change is going to be made, particularly how barriers and hurdles which have held the individual back will be overcome.

At this stage the role of the coach is to encourage this preparatory talk and continue to explore the ambivalence to change. The coach may use techniques such as the decisional balance sheet to explore the advantages or disadvantages of different choices, they may help the coachee think through the skills needed to make a change or the barriers which have got in the way before.

As this happens and the coach maintains effective listening and interventions, the coachee language is likely to change. In place of DARN statements will emerge what Miller and Rollnick (2011) have labelled CAT statements. These statements are likely to reflect a change in the coachee from commitment to mobilisation; from 'I want to'

Desire: *'I really want to do Y.'*
Ability: *'I think I could do Y if I really wanted to.'*
Reason: *'If they did X, then I think that would be enough and I would then do Y.'*
Need: *'I really need to do Y, or … will happen.'*

Figure 2 Examples of DARN statements.

Commitment: *'...next week I will do Y.'*

Action: *'I am really keen this time to make a success of it, I have thought about what went wrong last time and its going to be different on Tuesday.'*

Taking steps: *'...in advance of next Tuesday, have already done X. This will mean that went the meeting comes on Tuesday Y should be much easier this time.'*

Figure 3 *Examples of CAT statements.*

to 'I will'. Figure 3 provides examples of the three types of CAT statements which the coach should be looking for.

As Figure 3 shows commitment statements are concerned with intentions and promises. The coachee makes an unambiguous statement expressing their plans for the future. Keywords to look for as examples are 'will', 'promise' or 'guarantee'. Action statements reflect the individual's state of being willing, ready and prepared to act. Finally at the mobilisation stage the coachee may express statements reflecting their preparatory actions towards the goal.

CONCLUSION

Listening closely to the spoken and unspoken communications of the coachee is a central competence for coaching psychologists. What MI adds is the detail of what the coach should be listening for and by using this information to inform the next steps of the process, supporting the coachee to move from contemplation to action. Miller and Rollnick's DARN and CAT statements offer a handy heuristic to help the coaching psychologist in their practice of using a highly effective evidenced based model.

REFERENCES

Anstiss, T. & Passmore, J. (2011). Motivational Interview. In M. Neenan & S. Palmer (Eds.), *Cognitive behavioural coaching*. London: Routledge.

Anstiss, T. & Passmore, J. (2012). Motivational Interview approach. In J. Passmore, D. Peterson, & T. Freire (Eds.), *The Wiley-Blackwell Handbook of the Psychology of Coaching and Mentoring*. Chichester: Wiley–Blackwell.

Miller, W. & Rollnick, S. (2002). *Motivational Interviewing: Preparing people for change* (2nd ed.). New York: Guilford Press.

Miller, W. & Rollnick, S. (2011). *Motivational Interviewing masterclass, October*. Cardiff, UK.

Passmore, J. (2011a). Motivational Interviewing – A model for coaching psychology practice. *The Coaching Psychologist*, 7(1), 35–39.

Passmore J. (2011b). MI techniques – Reflective listening. *The Coaching Psychologist*, 7(1), 49–52.

Passmore, J. (2011c). MI techniques – The balance sheet. *The Coaching Psychologist*, 7(2), 151–153.

Passmore, J. (2012). MI techniques – A typical day. *The Coaching Psychologist*, 8(1), 50–51.

Prochaska, J.O. & DiClemente, C.C. (1983). Stages and processes of self-change of smoking: Toward an integrative model of change. *Journal of Consulting and Clinical Psychology*, 51, 390–395.

27 MI techniques: Agenda Mapping

Jonathan Passmore

Abstract

This article is the fifth in a series drawn from the Motivational Interviewing (MI) approach. In this paper I will briefly review a 'technique' which is at the start of the MI process and while not formalised in much of the coaching literature is a common practice among coaching psychologists when using Cognitive Behavioural Coaching and behavioural-based approaches such as GROW. This technique, Agenda Mapping, aims to help the coach and coachee to agree the focus for the coaching conversation.

In previous articles I have explored techniques from MI which could be used by coaching psychologists within their own practice. Some may argue that these techniques, such as recognising and working with change talk require a high level of sophistication in the skills of the coaching psychologist. This is true. But not all of the concepts used by MI are as complex or require such a high level of competence. Some of the methods used within MI share strong similarities with traditional coaching. What makes MI distinctive is that it offers a fresh way to conceptualise these approaches and a language to discuss them. Further, extensive research by practitioners has demonstrated that MI is a highly effective intervention. One example which has much in common with existing coaching practice is 'Agenda Mapping'. The approach itself is often used by coaching psychologists without detailed consideration. By highlighting these aspects I hope the paper will provide useful insights for both novice coaches in the development of their skill and for experienced practitioners reflecting on their own practice in more detail.

Original publication details: Passmore, J. (2013, June). MI techniques: Agenda mapping. *The Coaching Psychologist, 9*(1), 32–35. Reproduced with permission of The British Psychological Society.

MI PRINCIPLES

As noted in other papers (Anstiss & Passmore, 2011, 2013) MI is a set of principles as opposed to a set of techniques. The key aspect of MI is to keep to the core principles rather than mechanically follow this or another technique. When the MI principles are followed by the coach, an effective relationship will be built with the coachee. Further, the coach is making effective use of the OARS; open questions, affirming statements, reflections and summaries, as part of this relationship building and helping the coachee to explore their issue. When engaged, the coachee will be talking openly about their issue and the challenges they face in making a change. The coaching psychologist will be actively and empathetically listening to the content of what is being said, and what is unsaid by the coachee, summarising and reflecting to demonstrate listening and understanding, as well as providing the opportunity for reflection and thus deepening self-awareness for the coachee.

Early in the process, the coach will want to help the coachee to focus their discussion towards what the coachee would find most useful to focus on during the meeting. From personal experience I have found coachees may have one of three common responses to the question *'So what should be the focus of our conversation (today)?'*

Firstly, coachees may have a clear agenda which they wish to discuss. Secondly, coachees may have no clear plan or have not had time to think about the session and how they wish to use the coaching relationship (or individual session). Thirdly, they may have some idea but this has not been crystallised into a clearly articulated plan with priorities. It is in this third scenario that Agenda Mapping can offer a useful tool. The approach helps the coachee to plan the session, identifying and prioritising their issues and thus providing a clear focus to the conversation for the individual session.

Where the coachee has a clear agenda the coach is able to check this and confirm a joint understanding with the coachee before moving to the next stage; evoking change. Where the coachee has no plan or has not thought about the issue, the coach should continue to engage and seek to elicit the coachee's goal – *'How would you like the future to be different from today?'*

As readers may recall MI offers a four-part process (as reconfigured by Miller & Rollnick, 2011, 2012). This is summarised in Table 1.

Table 1   *Four stages of MI process.*

Engaging	The relational foundations
Focusing	The strategic focus
Evoking	Exploring collaboratively ambivalence
Planning	Developing a personal plan

(Adapted from Miller & Rollnick, 2011).

As Miller and Rollnick (2013, p.106) note: 'in essence Agenda Mapping is a metaconversation' – a conversation about the conversation. The technique is one used at the focusing stage, with the aim of helping the coachee to establish a key focus of the session or series of coaching sessions. When done well it helps those feeling stuck to see that there is a route map for travelling forward and exploring the challenges they face.

THE TECHNIQUE

Miller and Rollnick (2013) suggest the approach is like inviting the coachee to look at a map, seeing the places they might travel and planning a route for the next stage of their journey. Agenda Mapping offers an opportunity to help the coachee to establish for themselves the focus of the conversation and thus explain to themselves and the coach what they want to achieve from coaching. By offering a sequence of stages from generating alternative options to evaluating these choices to agreeing the focus, it offers a number of clear steps.

Where coachees are unable to establish a clear agenda, after using the approach, the coach may ask themselves (and the coachee) whether the coachee is ready to engage in coaching. The approach can thus also act as a tool to help inform the decision whether coaching is a helpful and useful approach for the coachee and whether they are ready to engage in coaching.

Agenda Mapping usually takes the form of a series of questions. The first is to gain agreement to move into a metaconversation. *'Is it ok if we spend a few minutes exploring what you want to get from our meeting today?'* or for those in mid-session, *'Can we stop for a few moments so we can take stock of where we are?'*

The second element is to help identify the objectives of the coachee. Once identified the coach can help the coachee to prioritise these objectives and settle on a specific focus. Finally the coach can help the coachee to refine and clarify the objective.

As an example I have included further possible questions which could be used in Table 2.

From personal experience it is not uncommon for the coachee to have a number of goals which they wish to achieve during the coaching assignment. In this case Agenda Mapping becomes a task of helping the coachee to prioritise which of the multiple goals they wish to focus on first. In many cases, particularly with more junior managers, long-term goals and short-term goals may be mixed up; *'I want to become a better*

Table 2   *Examples of useful agenda setting interventions*

- *What change shall we talk about?*
- *Why are we talking about x, and not y?*
- *I wonder about z, but what about you?*
- *Should we shift direction?*

leader of my team' alongside *'I want to get my manager's job when they move next year'*. In this instance the coach might help the coachee to focus on immediate short-term goals, working gradually towards long-term goals as the coaching assignment continues and shorter-term goals are achieved.

During Agenda Mapping it is important not to disappear into too much detail. The aim is instead to remain at a high level and move across a number of different issues before settling on the most important to the coachee.

So what are the outcomes that the coach should expect (seek) from Agenda Mapping? Firstly and most importantly the coachee should have a clear goal, which is understood and agreed with the coach Secondly, they have a series of sub-goals. These may be short-term or intermediate goals (milestones), which effectively enable the coachee to track their progress towards the longer-term goal. For each of these, both the long and intermediate goals, the coachee knows what success looks like at each stage. With an agreed set of goals the coach also helps the coachee to prioritise these goals, with one or more goal being the focus for each session.

The more clearly defined and personally held the goal, the more likely the coachee will be able to move forward to and achieve the goal.

CONCLUSION

Miller and Rollnick's Agenda Mapping approach captures what many skilled coaching psychologists do, but describes this in a useful way for coaching psychologists, as well as MI practitioners. It offers a handy heuristic to help the coaching psychologist in both recognising the importance of goal setting and thinking through when a conversation to clarify and refine goals is required.

REFERENCES

Anstiss, T. & Passmore, J. (2011). Motivational Interview. In M. Neenan & S. Palmer (Eds.), *Cognitive behavioural coaching*. London: Routledge.

Anstiss, T. & Passmore, J. (2013). Motivational Interview approach. In J. Passmore, D. Peterson & T. Freire (Eds.), *The Wiley-Blackwell handbook of the psychology of coaching and mentoring* (pp.339–364). Chichester: Wiley-Blackwell.

Miller, W. & Rollnick, S. (2002). *Motivational Interviewing: Preparing people for change* (2nd ed.). New York: Guilford Press.

Miller, W. & Rollnick, S. (2011). *Motivational Interviewing – Masterclass*. Cardiff, UK.

Miller, W. & Rollnick, S. (2013). *Motivational Interviewing: Helping people change* (3rd ed.). New York: Guilford Press.

Passmore, J. (2011a). Motivational Interviewing – a model for coaching psychology practice. *The Coaching Psychologist*, 7(1), 35–39.

Passmore, J. (2011b). MI techniques – Reflective listening. *The Coaching Psychologist*, 7(1), 49–52.

Passmore, J. (2011). MI techniques – The balance sheet technique. *The Coaching Psychologist*, 7(2), 151–153.

Passmore, J. (2012a). MI techniques – Typical day. *The Coaching Psychologist*, 8(1), 50–52.

Passmore, J. (2012b). MI techniques – Recognising change talk. *The Coaching Psychologist*, 8(2), 107–110.

Prochaska, J.O. & DiClemente, C.C. (1983). Stages and processes of self-change of smoking: Toward an integrative model of change. *Journal of Consulting and Clinical Psychology*, 51, 390–395.

28 Motivational Interviewing: Reflecting on ethical decisions in MI

Jonathan Passmore

Abstract

This article is the seventh and final one in this series drawn from the Motivational Interviewing (MI) approach. In this paper I will briefly return to reflecting on the MI process and specifically the question of ethics within the approach as we draw this series to a close.

Keywords

Motivational interviewing; coaching ethics; BPS ethical code; ethical guidelines; coaching supervision.

In previous articles I have explored techniques from MI which could be used by coaching psychologists within their own practice. Some may argue that these techniques, such as recognising and working with change talk, require a high level of sophistication in the skills of the coaching psychologist. This is true, but a number of concepts share strong similarities with traditional coaching, such as Agenda Setting.

Original publication details: Passmore, J. (2013, December). Motivational Interviewing: Reflecting on ethical decisions in MI. *The Coaching Psychologist*, 9(2), 112–116. Reproduced with permission of The British Psychological Society.

What makes MI distinctive is that it offers a fresh way to conceptualise these approaches through a systemised approach, which is grounded in extensive research. It is this aspect which in my view makes MI an obvious model for coaching psychologists to turn to, and enables them to differentiate themselves from other coaching practitioners offering interventions which are less informed by research, such as NLP.

One aspect which does draw frequent discussion is the ethical perspective of MI given its desire to evoke intrinsic motivation for change which may initially be counter to the current behaviour or attitudes of the individual. As a result some practitioners have considered this aspect of MI to be manipulative or unethical.

THE CORE OF MI PRACTICE

As previous readers of some of the earlier and more research focused work will be aware (see Anstiss & Passmore, 2011; Anstiss & Passmore, 2013; or Miller & Rollnick, 2013, for a fuller discussion of the research literature), MI has its roots in the work of counselling and specifically addiction counselling for drug and alcohol. Much of the research is based within these domains, where MI has built a strong evidence base with over 200 randomised controlled trials (see, for example, Groeneveld et al., 2008) and 18 meta-analyses studies (see, for example, Lundahl et al., 2010). More recently MI has been broadening its application as a methodology for supporting behavioural change in cases where clients are ambivalent about making future changes. MI, for example, is now being used to promote oral health practice (Almomani et al., 2009), educate diabetes patients (Bowen et al., 2002) and managing children's television viewing (Taveras et al., 2011). The evidence from each of these areas confirms MI as a highly effective methodology for supporting behavioural change.

EXTENDING MI TO THE WORK ARENA

A growing number of coaching psychologists too have seen the value of MI as an intervention which can play a valuable role in the workplace. These practitioners have been using MI to explore options and develop motivation for change, particularly in individuals who feel stuck. We (Tim Anstiss and I) have been using the intervention to explore career change, to assist individuals and organisations during periods of conflict, as well as using MI to help support organisational change. We have also been teaching practitioners MI skills to help them apply these tools with patients and when working with colleagues.

One question which emerges both as we critically reflect on our own application of MI in supervision and which also emerges as a common question during teaching MI, is the issue of ethics. Is it ethical to use MI if people's goals are different from the coach? Is MI ethical given the role of the coach is to evoke intrinsic motivation? I believe the answer to the use of MI is yes, but only where the coaching psychologist carefully navigates a route in the best interests of the client or clients. It is this final distinction which is particularly challenging for workplace coaches using MI given the nature of multiple clients within organisational settings and the difficulty of clearly identifying what is actually best for others.

ETHICAL GUIDANCE FROM MI COUNSELLING

Counselling psychologist's practice is rightfully underpinned by ethics. This is supported by the British Psychological Society's (BPS) own ethical code (BPS, 2009), by ethical decision making models (such as Carroll, 1996) and guided through counselling supervision where ethical dilemmas can be discussed with a supervisor.

Miller and Rollnick (2013) too recognised that the MI processes could benefit from guidance. The authors suggest that the ethical question needs to be asked of each of the processes within MI. Good listening, which includes tools such as reflective listening (Passmore, 2011b) they suggest is unlikely to do harm and in fact by itself may promote positive change. Focusing, which includes techniques such as Agenda Setting (Passmore, 2013), they note, involves the ethical guidance to review and establish goals. Evoking is also uncontroversial, they suggest, if the client has brought the goal. However, the authors note that 'ethical considerations arise when client and counsellor aspirations differ' (p129). Finally they argue that the planning stage presupposes a readiness to move forward and thus ethical considerations are less prevalent.

To help guide therapists in their reflections Miller and Rollnick have set out ethical guidance for the use of MI in clinical settings (see Table 1, oveleaf)).

Table 1   *Some ethical guidance for the practice of MI*

The use of MI component processes is inappropriate when:
1. Available evidence indicates that doing so would be ineffective **or harmful to clients**.
2. Clients experience (or appear to experience) discomfort.
3. Where client and counsellor perceived best interests differ.
4. When the counsellor's personal investment in achieving an outcome are high conflicts with the client's own perceived best interests.
5. When coercive power is combined with the personal investment of the counsellor.

Adapted from Miller & Rollnick, 2013.

ETHICAL GUIDANCE FOR MI COACHING

For coaching psychologists these ethical guidelines are both helpful but also require further consideration. One particular distinctive aspect of working in organisational settings is the issue of working with or to multiple clients. Most workplace coaching involves a commissioning manager, in the form of the line manager, an HR manager or chief executive, as well as the 'client'; the individual who is being referred for coaching. This 'multiple client' issue requires the coaching psychologist to consider the needs of all the clients involved and to act ethically towards all parties; the individual and the representatives of the organisation. One way which most psychologists try to manage this is through operating transparently in their dealings with both parties. For example, this might involve meeting both parties at an initial commissioning meeting and at a review meeting at the close of the relationship where there is an open discussion about the desired outcomes sought by both parties.

When coaching is focused on supporting managers in transitioning to new roles, preparing for or engaging in career development, in skills development or general reflective / sounding board conversations these tri-partite conversations are relatively simple and straightforward. The coaching psychologist can play the role of co-ordinator, encouraging both parties to set out their goals for the coaching relationship, which from experience are usually very similar. However, from my own experience in working on issues involving conflicts between the chief executive and a fellow director or in performance issues where the next step is potentially disciplinary action, such tri-partite conversations are often tense and guarded. The commissioning manager may need to communicate openly their concerns. During the tri-partite meeting the coach needs to listen to what is being said and what is unsaid, as well as to encourage the organisational client to fully and openly state their position. They also need to encourage the coachee to be equally transparent about their own position and their aspiration for the coaching relationship.

As a result Miller and Rollnick's table may benefit from adaption to the context of workplace coaching (Table 2).

Several of these aspects may be worth briefly discussing. For example, given the multiple client nature of coaching within organisations, consideration needs to be given to the needs of the individual as well as the organisation. Rarely in such circumstances can organisations come to physical harm, more frequently organisations are concerned about their reputation, which can itself be valued in millions. A second example where the framework is further developed is in point 2. In this item we have recognised that in coaching (certainly for senior managers) high challenge is often a key element (see, for example, Jones & Spooner, 2006). Thus one important aspect in coaching senior managers is to finely balance the level of challenge with that of empathy / support. An analogy is that of sailing a boat; the greatest speeds (gains) are achieved when the boat is sailing at full tilt, however, a single degree more and the boat can capsize.

Table 2   *Ethical guidance for the practice of MI in the workplace*

The use of MI component processes is inappropriate when:

1. Available evidence indicates that doing so would be ineffective or harmful to the coachee or have a detrimental impact on the organisation's reputation.
2. The coachee demonstrates continuing discomfort with the process, which the coach perceives to be beyond what the coachee can contain.
3. Where the understanding of the coachee and the organisational client differ as to the reasons for the coaching (for example, where a decision has already been made by the organisation to dismiss the coachee, and coaching is being used to make the decision more acceptable for an Employment Tribunal or for internal consumption).
4. When the coach is more concerned about delivering an outcome for the organisational client or for the coachee than in balancing these interests in an open and honest way.
5. When coercive power is used to achieve an outcome for one or either party (organisational client or coachee).
6. The coachee does not wish to engage in coaching.

From personal experience the central and most common issue which requires sensitive and direct management is where the initial organisational client brief varies from what the organisational client communicates in the room. Here the coach needs to act, without embarrassing the organisational client to ensure that the coachee fully understands the organisational client's perception of the issue rather than hearing a more socially acceptable version. Where openness cannot be achieved the coach is potentially placed in the situation of needing to deliver the news. In such cases I would advocate the coach should withdraw from the process until a shared understanding is achieved between the three parties as to the purpose of the coaching.

Finally, as in counselling, supervision can play a useful role to offer a space to explore and reflect on some of the ethical dilemmas which MI coaches work with. Rarely are these ethical questions clear cut. Instead the issue ebbs and flows as information emerges about a complex situation. As a result the coaches' own emotional responses and feelings are also likely to change and evolve during the process. Having an appreciation of these emotional responses, as well as a space to talk through actions and potential next steps is useful, if not essential in complex coaching cases, for the coaching psychologist in managing these ethical dilemmas.

CONCLUSION

MI is one of the most useful and evidence informed methodologies for stimulating and supporting behaviour change. Miller and Rollnick's contribution of MI is a significant addition to the coaching psychology field and should be recognised as such, given the wealth of research used to develop the approach over the past two decades.

MI, however, needs to be managed ethically in its application with vulnerable clients, as well as in its application with workplace coachees and their organisational client's. The responsibility to achieving this balance and manage these potential divergent issues rests with the coaching psychologist.

I hope this series, along with the original work and our attempts to translate the approach to the areas of work will help to establish MI as a key tool among the armoury of coaching psychologists.

REFERENCES

Almomani F., Williams, K., Catley, D. & Brown, C. (2009). Effects of an oral health programme, in people with mental health. *Journal of Dental Research*, 88(7), 684–652.

Anstiss, T. & Passmore, J. (2011). Motivational Interview. In M. Neenan & S. Palmer (Eds.), *Cognitive behavioural coaching*. London: Routledge.

Anstiss, T. & Passmore, J. (2013). Motivational Interview approach. In J. Passmore, D. Peterson, D. & T. Freire (Eds.), *The Wiley-Blackwell handbook of the psychology of coaching and mentoring* (pp.339–364). Chichester: Wiley-Blackwell.

Bowen, D. et al. (2002). Results of an adjunct dietary intervention programme in the womens' health initiative. *Journal of the American Dietetic Association*, 102(11), 1631–1637.

British Psychological Society (BPS) (2009). *Code of ethics and conduct*. Leicester: BPS.

Carroll, M. (1996). *Counselling supervision: Theory, skills and practice*. London: Cassell.

Groeneveld, I.F., Proper, K.I., van der Beek, A.J., van Duivenbooden, C. & van Mechelen, W. (2008). Design of a RCT evaluating the (cost-) effectiveness of a lifestyle intervention for male construction workers at risk for cardiovascular disease: The health under construction study. *BMC Public Health*, 8.

Jones, G. & Spooner, K. (2006). Coaching high achievers. *Consulting Psychology Journal: Practice and Research*, 58(1), 40–50.

Lundahl, B.W., Kunz, C., Brownell, C., Tollefson, D. & Burke, B.L. (2010). A meta-analysis of motivational interviewing: 25 years of empirical studies. *Research on Social Work Practice*, 20(2), 137–160.

Miller, W. & Rollnick, S. (2002). *Motivational Interviewing: Preparing people for change* (2nd ed.). New York: Guilford Press.

Miller, W. & Rollnick, S. (2013). *Motivational Interviewing: Helping people change* (3rd ed.). New York: Guilford Press.

Passmore, J. (2011a). Motivational Interviewing – a model for coaching psychology practice. *The Coaching Psychologist*, 7(1), 35–39.

Passmore, J. (2011b). MI techniques – Reflective listening. *The Coaching Psychologist*, 7(1), 49–52.

Passmore, J. (2011). MI techniques – Balance sheet. *The Coaching Psychologist*, 7(2), 151–153.

Passmore, J. (2012a). MI techniques – Typical day. *The Coaching Psychologist*, 8(1), 50–52.

Passmore, J. (2012b). MI techniques – Recognising change talk. *The Coaching Psychologist*, 8(2), 107–110.

Passmore, J. (2013). MI techniques – Agenda Mapping. *The Coaching Psychologist*, 9(1), 32–35.

Prochaska, J.O. & DiClemente, C.C. (1983). Stages and processes of self-change of smoking: Toward an integrative model of change. *Journal of Consulting and Clinical Psychology, 51*, 390–395.

Taveras, E., Gortmaker, S., Hohman, K., Leinman, K. & Mitchell, K. (2011). Randomised control trial to improve primary care to prevent and manage childhood obesity. The High Five for Kids Study. *Archive of Pediatric Adolescent Medicine, 165*(8), 714–722.

The Coaching Psychologist, Vol. 9, No. 2, December 2013

Section 8
Solution-Focused Coaching

Introduction

David Tee & Jonathan Passmore

This section features a series of papers based around the solution-focused approach written by several different writers including Mark Adams, Anthony Grant and Stephen Palmer. In this introduction, we will review the nature of brief solution-focused therapy, its adoption as an approach now commonly used in coaching and finally summarise the four papers in this section. Let us start by exploring the origins and nature of brief solution-focused therapy and its development into solution-focused coaching.

Solution-focused coaching draws on the work of Steve de Shazer and Insoo Kim Berg, two family therapists working at the Milwaukee Family Therapy Center. The two therapists noticed their practice centred around helping clients to move away from destructive or problematic behaviours. They wondered, what if they flipped this approach and started to work with what their clients wanted, that is moving towards a desired state as opposed to away from an undesired one. The second aspect they started to test out came from necessity. As a team, they were constantly overworked. What if, instead of working for months with a family, they refocused their work around a limited number of sessions? Out of these ideas was borne *brief solution-focused therapy*. As we think about these components, a solution-focused approach has much in common with coaching, with a fixed or limited number of sessions and a goal or aspiration focus which aims to inspire or motivate the client to move towards the goal.

Greene and Grant (2003) popularised the concept of solution-focused coaching, translating the ideas from therapy into a coherent and practical approach for coaches. Over the subsequent two decades, Anthony Grant continued to develop his thinking until his death in 2020 and, in so doing, set the key foundation stones for solution-focused work, and the evidence of its efficiency as an intervention with clients. As the

Coaching Practiced, First Edition. Edited by David Tee and Jonathan Passmore.
© 2022 John Wiley & Sons Ltd. Published 2022 by John Wiley & Sons Ltd.
DOI: 10.1002/9781119835691.s08

heart of solution-focused coaching are a series of principles which guide the coaching psychologist in their practice.

Firstly, the solution-focused approach avoids pathologising clients and their problems. It moves away from psychologist as expert and replaces the language of dysfunction with everyday language. By so doing, it aims to create an equal, collaborative partnership between the client and the coach.

Secondly, the focus of the conversation is towards constructing solutions (moving towards Solution Island), as opposed to time exploring, reflecting and analysing past problems or the current emotional state (exploring or trying to flee Problem Island).

Thirdly, the approach sees the client as the expert, being the individual best placed to identify a suitable solution for themselves. This recasts the coaching psychologist to a position of being a guide or a manager of the process, rather than the expert with special insight responsible for diagnosis or treatment.

Fourthly, the coach and client work together with a growth mindset, both learning from each other, further reinforcing the equality of the partnership.

Fifthly, each conversation is structured around a goal. The goal needs to be clearly defined, realistic and attainable by the client. The clarification and refinement of this goal rests with the client.

Finally, there is an expectation that the client will make positive change by undertaking actions agreed after each session. The combination of expectations and a clear plan contributes to enhanced outcomes, as we will see from the papers in the section.

In the first of these papers, Mark Adams (2016) offers a model for solution-focused coaching which can be applied in organisational settings with individuals and teams – ENABLE: Elicit preferred future, Notice exceptions, Activate strengths and resources, Build on what is working, Look for opportunities and Efficacy-supportive feedback.

Table   *ENABLE model – Questions*

Elicit preferred future	'Imagine a time in the future when you have achieved the goal you want to achieve…' 'What does that look like?'
Notice exceptions	'What are the signs now of your preferred future already happening?' 'On a scale from 0 to 10, where 10 is that your preferred future is already happening, where are things now? Why there and not any lower?'
Activate strengths and resources	'What helped to achieve those successes?'
Build on what is working	'What would a [n+1] on the scale look like?'; 'How can you build on your existing successes to move forward?'
Look for opportunities	'What are you going to do in the coming days or weeks?'
Efficacy-supportive feedback	'I've noticed that, as a team, you've previously been able to successfully embed a common approach to working'.

(Adapted from Adams, 2016)

Like GROW or other frameworks, the mnemonic provides an easy way to recall the essential ingredients of a solution-focused conversation.

In the second paper, Anthony Grant (2013) explores the translation of solution-focused approaches to the coaching environment. He notes that little attention has been paid to the process of teaching solution-focused coaching skills and, while solution-focused coaching is simple, it is not easy. In contrast, the transition for managers from instruction-led dialogues to reflective coaching dialogue is challenging, particularly for those with high levels of technical expertise. Grant sets out a series of principles to guide both tutors and learners in the process, helping to build a solution-focused coaching mindset, before the development of solution-focused skills. Grant offers a 'nine steps' pyramid which, if followed, can lead the coach and client to success.

The third paper in the series is also by Anthony Grant (2019), on this occasion further developing solution-focused approaches for the more advanced practitioner. In the paper, Grant explores the use of the 'cathartic wave': a model that tracks the emergence of emotional catharsis during the coaching conversation. The wave offers a guide for coaches, when listening to the client's 'problem talk', as to when to switch to solution mode, as opposed when to leave the client venting about their problem. Grant notes that a delay in switching can lead to a decline in energy and self-belief, making the switch to solutions more problematic.

The final paper in this set is from Stephen Palmer (2011). In this paper, Palmer reviews the PRACTICE model, originally drawn from the work of Wasik (1984): The model's seven steps are: **P**roblem identification; **R**ealistic, relevant goals developed; **A**lternative solutions generated; **C**onsideration of consequences; **T**arget most feasible solution(s); **I**mplementation of **C**hosen solution(s); **E**valuation. Palmer recasts the P of the model from Problem identification to **P**resentation of issue, acknowledging a shift in focus away from the 'problem' towards working on solutions.

While solution-focused therapy may have its roots in family work, its compatibility to coaching and its efficacy makes it a highly effective tool for the coaching psychologist.

REFERENCES

Adams, M. (2016) ENABLE: A solution-focused coaching model for individual and team coaching. *The Coaching Psychologist*, *12*(1), 17–23

Grant, A. M. (2013) Steps to solutions: A process for putting solution-focused principles into practice. *The Coaching Psychologist*, *9*(1), 36–44.

Grant, A. M. (2019) Solution-focused coaching: The basics for advanced practitioners. *The Coaching Psychologist*, *15*(2), 44–54.

Greene, S., & Grant, A. M. (2003). *Solution-Focused Coaching*. Pearson.

Palmer, S. (2011) Revisiting the P in the PRACTICE coaching model. *The Coaching Psychologist*, *7*(2), 156–158.

Wasik, B. (1984). *Teaching parents effective problem-solving: A handbook for professionals*. Unpublished Manuscript University of North Carolina.

29 ENABLE: A solution-focused coaching model for individual and team coaching

Mark Adams

Abstract

A number of coaching models exist that can add structure, direction and momentum to coaching conversations, including I-GROW, PRACTICE, SPACE and OSKAR (Whitmore, 2002; Palmer, 2007, 2008; Edgerton & Palmer, 2005; Jackson & McKergow, 2002). This paper introduces a new coaching model – ENABLE – which captures some of the key components of Solution-Focused Coaching (SFC) while reflecting a central underlying principle of a solution-focused orientation. The evidence base for the application of a solution-focused approach to coaching is explored, with specific reference to the impact of solution-focused practices on the coachee's sense of hope that change can be achieved. Possible applications for the ENABLE model are discussed, while caveats about its use are considered. It is suggested that the ENABLE model could represent a helpful tool for coaches and coaching psychologists, given the versatility of the solution-focused approach.

Keywords

Solution-focused coaching; coaching models; ENABLE model; hope.

Original publication details: Adams, M. (2016, June). ENABLE: A solution-focused coaching model for individual and team coaching. *The Coaching Psychologist*, *12*(1), 17–23. Reproduced with permission of The British Psychological Society.

INTRODUCTION

There are a number of well-known coaching models that can be used in coaching conversations or engagements. These include:

- I-GROW (**I**ssues, **G**oal, **R**eality, **O**ptions, **W**rap-Up; Whitmore, 2002);
- PRACTICE (**P**roblem Identification, **R**ealistic goals, **A**lternative actions, **C**onsidering consequences, **T**arget feasible solution, **I**mplement Chosen action, **E**valuation; Palmer, 2007, 2008).
- SPACE (**S**ocial context, **P**hysiology, **A**ctions, **C**ognitions, **E**motions; Edgerton & Palmer, 2005).

Models such as these can provide structure and momentum to a coaching conversation, while acting as an *aide-memoire* to both coach and coachee as to possible areas of inquiry. In some cases the acronym can also be useful as a reminder of specific components of a particular approach to coaching.

The solution-focused approach 'places primary emphasis on assisting the client to define a desired future state and to construct a pathway in both thinking and action that assists the client in achieving that state' (Cavanagh & Grant, 2014, p.51). From the solution-focused perspective, it is said to be counterproductive to spend too much time and energy on what could be described as 'problem talk' – for example, articulating the detail of 'the problem', exploring the history that led to the client's current state of affairs, and hypothesising about causal explanations (de Shazer & Dolan, 2007). Instead, the emphasis is on the construction of a preferred future, while supporting the client to harness their existing resources in the pursuit of their desired outcome (Berg & De Jong, 2002; de Shazer, 1985, 1988). The OSKAR coaching model (**O**utcome, **S**caling, **K**now-how, **A**ffirm and action, **R**eview) was developed by Jackson and McKergow (2002) to specifically capture some key components of a solution-focused approach to coaching, while O'Connell, Palmer and Williams (2012) have more recently introduced the SOLUTION coaching model to this end (**S**hare updates, **O**bserve interests, **L**isten to hopes and goals, **U**nderstand exceptions, **T**ap potential, **I**magine success, **O**wn outcomes, **N**ote contributions). This article introduces an additional solution-focused coaching model developed by the author – ENABLE – that can be applied in coaching work with individuals and teams.

SOLUTION-FOCUSED COACHING

A Solution-focused coaching (SFC) approach is underpinned by a number of core principles adapted from Solution-Focused Brief Therapy (Berg & De Jong, 2002; de Shazer, 1985, 1988). A guiding philosophy of solution-focused working is – to paraphrase the axiom of William of Occam – that it is vain to use more to do what can be achieved with less (see Iveson, George & Ratner, 2012; O'Connell & Palmer, 2007). In other words, if coaches can help coachees to achieve change with the application of a few simple principles, then the application of complex theoretical or therapeutic approaches/analysis is seen as an unnecessary self-indulgent luxury. Instead, the emphasis is on what might be described as a minimalist or parsimonious approach (in terms of the theoretical or therapeutic expertise brought to the relationship by the helper) that attempts to tap into and harness what is already working in the coachee's situation. Specific principles and techniques include:

- It is not necessary to understand the origin of a 'problem' in order to begin constructing a solution; instead, the coach can support the coachee to obtain clarity about the *preferred future* they would like to see happening.
- There are always *exceptions* in the coachee's life or experience – times when aspects of the preferred future are already happening (even if only in part). These represent valuable sources of learning, and the coach can actively guide a search for such exceptions.
- Coachees are resourceful people who bring *strengths*, *skills* and *qualities* to the engagement. The coach can attempt to elicit these and support the coachee to harness their resources as they begin to move towards their preferred future.
- Coaches can work with coachees to support them to build on what is already working in their life or situation, and to look for new opportunities to utilise their existing strengths and resources.
- Throughout the session, the coach can listen for examples of successes and strengths. At the end of a coaching session, the coach can provide the coachee with feedback about these in an attempt to enhance the coachee's sense of self-efficacy (Bandura, 1977; Maddux, 2005).

For further detail about each of these avenues of exploration, see Iveson, George and Ratner (2012), O'Connell and Palmer (2007) or O'Connell, Palmer and Williams (2012).

The above components of Solution-Focused Coaching can be represented using the acronym ENABLE, thus:

> Elicit preferred future;
> Notice exceptions;
> Activate strengths and resources;
> Build on what's working;
> Look for opportunities;
> Efficacy-supportive feedback.

The acronym itself reflects a fundamental principle of a solution-focused approach, specifically that of making change seem possible by igniting hope in the client (O'Connell, 2002). Indeed, with its emphasis on how coachees can harness and amplify their existing resources to take small steps towards their desired future, the solution-focused approach is truly enabling in its orientation.

The different stages of the ENABLE model will be described in further detail below. Before unpacking the model, however, it is important and instructive to consider the existing evidence-base for the solution-focused approach to working.

EVIDENCE OF THE IMPACT OF A SOLUTION-FOCUSED APPROACH

Studies in the therapeutic domain have indicated the positive impact of a solution-focused approach in areas such as child and adolescent counselling (Corcoran & Stephenson, 2000) and in working with depression (Dahl, Bathel & Carreon, 2000). O'Connell, Palmer and Williams (2012) summarise that studies of the impact of the solution-focused approach in therapeutic contexts have indicated comparable effectiveness to other therapies while being more efficient in terms of time and costs (see Macdonald, 2007, for more details). In therapeutic settings, then, the evidence base is strongly supportive of a solution-focused approach to practice.

The evidence base for SFC as specifically applied to coaching relationships is less well-developed, but nonetheless the indications are positive. For example, Green, Oades and Grant (2006) report that a 10-week cognitive-behavioural/solution-focused life coaching programme for adults was associated with 'significant increases in goal striving, wellbeing and hope, with gains maintained up to 30 weeks later on some variables' (p.142). Similarly, Green, Grant and Rynsaardt (2007) examined the impact of a combined cognitive-behavioural/solution-focused life coaching programme for senior female high school students, and found that participation in the programme was associated with 'significant increases in levels of cognitive hardiness and hope, and significant decreases in levels of depression' (p.24). In both of these examples the overall conclusions that can be drawn about the effectiveness of SFC are limited by the fact that the intervention comprised a combination of approaches; however, when discussing the findings from their studies both sets of authors specifically note that the use of solution-focused techniques seemed to enhance hope by helping participants to determine possible pathways towards their goals. At the very least, then, these two studies suggest that solution-focused practices represent a valuable component of coaching engagements for enhancing what might be termed as 'pathways thinking' (Green, Grant & Rynsaardt, ibid; c.f. Snyder, 1995).

In summary, then, the evidence base suggests that the solution-focused approach lends itself to a variety of applications in both clinical and coaching contexts, with the application of solution-focused techniques being specifically related to increased levels of hope in coachees. A solution-focused coaching model that draws upon such principles and practices could, therefore, represent a valuable component of the coach/coaching psychologist's toolbox if the aim is to leave coachees with the sense that change is both possible and practical. The detail of the ENABLE model will now be illustrated.

THE ENABLE MODEL OF SOLUTION-FOCUSED COACHING

The ENABLE model draws upon the previously described evidence-informed solution-focused principles and techniques, specifically the work of: Berg and De Jong (2002); de Shazer (1985, 1988); Iveson, George and Ratner (2012); O'Connell (2002); O'Connell and Palmer (2007); and O'Connell, Palmer and Williams (2012). Readers are referred to those texts for further details regarding the approach.

Elicit preferred future

Key question: 'Imagine a time in the future when you have achieved the goal you want to achieve… What does that look like?'

A *preferred future* description captures the coachee's vision of life when the hoped-for outcome has been achieved. Eliciting a description of the coachee's preferred future provides focus and direction to the engagement, and can also serve as a powerful motivator. The coach can support the coachee to describe a vision of their preferred future that is clear, specific and sufficiently detailed; for a summary of how coachee preferred future descriptions can be further shaped, see Iveson, George and Ratner (2012). The preferred future also serves as a benchmark against which future progress can be measured.

Notice exceptions

Key question: 'What are the signs now of your preferred future already happening?'

In solution-focused parlance, *exceptions* are either: (i) times when 'the problem' happens less; or (ii) times when the preferred future is already happening, even if only in part. At this stage the coach can support the individual or team to identify *specific examples* of times when their preferred future is already happening, or times when 'the problem' (if there is one) isn't quite as bad. *Scaling* questions can be used to good effect to support this exploration, for example:

'On a scale from 0 to 10, where 10 is that your preferred future is already happening, where are things now? Why there and not any lower?'

These exceptions then become a platform for the activation of the individual or team's resources, and a starting point from which further change can be considered (see below).

Activate strengths and resources

Key question: 'What helped to achieve those successes?'

A fundamental principle of the solution-focused approach is that coachees bring strengths, skills and experience to the engagement, and it is the role of the coach to help the coachee to tap into and harness such resources. Therefore, having brought exceptions to the coachee's attention, the coach can guide an exploration as to what helped to achieve them. The coach can listen for strengths and qualities shown by the coachee, and can ask questions to further probe for existing resources. It is here that it can be helpful for the coach to have a vocabulary of strengths and qualities so as to support the coachee in naming and recognising the nature of what it is they are doing well.

Build on what's working

Key questions: 'What would a [n+1] on the scale look like?'; 'How can you build on your existing successes to move forward?'.

Having identified where the coachee is 'at' on a scale, and having identified the resources that have taken the person to that point, the coach can support the coachee to identify what their reality might look like if they were to move a step closer to their desired future. Scaling questions can be returned to at this stage, with the coachee asked to imagine and describe how a small change in the direction of their preferred future would manifest (e.g. *'What would [n+1] on the scale look like?'*). The aim is to help the coachee to describe in detail the signs of this movement, in the hope that the answers will be informative.

At this stage the solution-focused coach is presented with a choice about whether or not to ask questions that are specifically focused on helping the coachee to plan actions that will take them in the direction of their desired future. Some writers suggest that a commitment to a concrete action plan is an essential component of the solution-focused coaching process (e.g. Greene & Grant, 2003); others suggest that implying the need for action may run the risk of limiting the coachee's freedom of thought or compounding any sense of hopelessness that the coachee may be experiencing (Iveson, George & Ratner, 2012). It is important to emphasise that the ENABLE model is more reflective of the former position, in that it explicitly incorporates action-planning questions / stages. However, the solution-focused coach must be aware of both positions and, crucially, be willing to change approach to suit the needs of the coachee before them.

To support the coachee in planning how to further build on their existing successes, the coach can ask the coachee to think of actions that could be taken to help make the step forward on the scale a reality *('What might help you to get to [n+1] on the scale?'; 'How can you further use your existing resources?')*. At this stage of the model, the emphasis is on diverging, that is, considering a range of possible alternatives in open exploration (Downey, 2003).

When coaching with teams, this stage can also support the cross-fertilisation of successful practices. In such circumstances, the key question can become: *'How can you learn from each other's successes to further develop your practice?'* For example, team members can each reflect on strategies used by their colleagues and then consider the extent to which they can take on such strategies themselves.

Look for opportunities

Key question: 'What are you going to do in the coming days or weeks?'

If the preceding stage of the model is about *possibilities*, then this stage is about converging on particular ideas and turning those possibilities into action (c.f. Downey, 2003). The coach can support the coachee to identify specific times or situations when the ideas generated at the previous stage can be made a reality. The emphasis is on identifying specific, concrete actions that the coachee can implement, in an attempt to enhance the likelihood that the coachee will take action in the direction of change.

Efficacy-supportive feedback Throughout the conversation, the coach can listen for strengths and qualities shown by the individual or team, and then provide specific feedback about these at the end of the session. The aim is to affirm aspects of the coachee's behaviour, and to strengthen the coachee's belief in their capacity to achieve success through their actions. For example: 'I've noticed that, as a team, you've previously been able to successfully embed a common approach to working' or 'In my view that seemed to take both courage and integrity'.

STRUCTURED COACHING MODELS: A CAUTION

While the ENABLE model is helpful in terms of delineating some of the key components of the solution-focused approach, it is important to emphasise a number of caveats about its application. Firstly, the model does not capture every solution-focused practice described in the literature, and there are other important aspects of solution-focused working (e.g. exploring pre-session change, engaging in problem-free talk, contracting as to the coachee's best hopes for the meeting, setting a 'noticing' task in which the coachee looks for signs of their preferred future happening) that are not reflected in the ENABLE model. Coaches will, therefore, need to ensure they are familiar with these other aspects of solution-focused working, and to then make their own decisions about if and when to integrate the ENABLE approach into their conversation. Moreover, application of the model needs to take place within the context of a sound *collaborative alliance* to enhance the likelihood of achieving positive outcomes; that is, coaching needs to take place within the context of a constructive interpersonal relationship, with agreement about the goals and tasks that will be explored (see Bordin, 1979; Murphy & Duncan, 2007). Application of the model should not distract the coach's attention away from these vital considerations. Finally, as is the case with any coaching model, the ENABLE structure should not be rigidly adhered to in the order described in this paper; rather, coaches should feel free to move fluidly around the components of the model as is relevant to the needs of the coachee and the conversation. In this way the ENABLE model is a guide rather than a prescription of a set sequence of conversational elements.

APPLICATIONS

O'Connell and Palmer (2007) draw upon the existing literature and research base to summarise multiple possible applications of the solution-focused approach, including:

- education;
- coaching;
- mental health;

- substance misuse;
- parent training;
- supervision;
- business and management;
- organisational change;
- team coaching and development.

The model described in this paper could, therefore, be applied in any of the aforementioned contexts. Readers who would like to see a more detailed description of a specific application of the ENABLE model are referred to Adams (2015), which reports on how the model was applied in an education setting to help a team of Early Years practitioners to develop their working practices for supporting children with Special Educational Needs and Disabilities.

CONCLUSIONS

The solution-focused approach has long been recognised as an optimistic and respectful way of working with clients to help them to move towards their desired futures. The ENABLE coaching model described in this paper captures some of the core components of the solution-focused approach, while the acronym itself reflects a central principle of this enabling way of working. It is hoped that the ENABLE model described in this paper will support coaches, coaching psychologists and other professionals in remembering and applying some of the key components of the solution-focused approach, which is sufficiently versatile to have applications in a broad range of contexts. If one of the aims of coaching is to enhance the coachee's strength of belief that change is both possible and practical, then the ENABLE model (either on its own in combination with other approaches) could represent a helpful tool in the coach's repertoire.

REFERENCES

Adams, M. (2015). *Coaching psychology in schools: Enhancing performance, development and wellbeing.* Oxon: Routledge.

Bandura, A. (1977). Self-efficacy: Toward a unifying theory of behavioural change. *Psychological Review, 84*(2), 191–215.

Berg, I.K. & De Jong, P. (2002). *Interviewing for solutions.* California: Brooks/Cole.

Bordin, E.S. (1979). The generalisability of the psychoanalytic concept of the working alliance. *Psychotherapy: Theory, Research & Practice, 16*(3), 252–260.

Cavanagh, M. & Grant, A. (2014). The solution-focused approach to coaching. In E. Cox, T. Bachkirova & D. Clutterbuck (Eds.), *The complete handbook of coaching* (2nd ed., pp.51–64). London: Sage.

Corcoran, J. & Stephenson, M. (2000). The effectiveness of solution-focused therapy with child behaviour problems: A preliminary report. *Families in Society, 81*(5), 468–474.

Dahl, R., Bathel, D. & Carreon, C. (2000). The use of solution-focused therapy with an elderly population. *Journal of Systemic Therapies, 19*(4), 45–55.

de Shazer, S. (1985). *Keys to solution in brief therapy.* New York: W.W. Norton.

de Shazer, S. (1988). *Clues: Investigating solutions in brief therapy.* New York: W.W. Norton.

de Shazer, S. & Dolan, Y. (2007). *More than miracles: The state of the art of solution-focused brief therapy.* Binghamton, NY: The Haworth Press.

Downey, M. (2003). *Effective coaching: Lessons from the coaches' coach.* Knutsford, Cheshire: Thomson-Texere.

Edgerton, N. & Palmer, S. (2005). SPACE: A psychological model for use within cognitive-behavioural coaching, therapy and stress management. *The Coaching Psychologist, 2*(2), 5–31.

Green, L.S., Grant, A.M. & Rynsaardt, J. (2007). Evidence-based life coaching for senior high-school students: Building hardiness and hope. *International Coaching Psychology Review, 2*(1), 24–32.

Green, L.S., Oades, L.G., & Grant, A.M. (2006). Cognitive-behavioral, solution-focused life coaching: Enhancing goal-striving, wellbeing and hope. *The Journal of Positive Psychology, 1*(3), 142–149.

Greene, J. & Grant, A. (2003). *Solution-focused coaching.* Harlow: Pearson.

Iveson, C., George, E., & Ratner, H. (2012). *Brief coaching: A solution-focused approach.* Hove: Routledge.

Jackson, P.Z. & McKergow, M. (2002). *The Solutions Focus: The SIMPLE way to positive change.* London: Nicholas Brealey.

Macdonald, A. (2007). *Solution-focused therapy: Theory, research and practice.* London: Sage.

Maddux, J. (2005). Self-efficacy: The power of believing you can. In C. Snyder & S. Lopez (Eds.), *Handbook of positive psychology.* New York: Oxford University Press.

Murphy, J.J. & Duncan, B.L. (2007). *Brief intervention for school problems: Outcome-informed strategies.* New York: The Guilford Press.

O'Connell, B. (2002). *Solution-focused therapy.* London: Sage.

O'Connell, B. & Palmer, S. (2007). Solution-focused coaching. In S. Palmer & A. Whybrow (Eds), *Handbook of coaching psychology: A guide for practitioners.* Hove: Routledge.

O'Connell, B., Palmer, S. & Williams, H. (2007). *Solution-focused coaching in practice.* Hove: Routledge.

Palmer, S. (2007). PRACTICE: A model suitable for coaching, counselling, psychotherapy and stress management. *The Coaching Psychologist, 3*(2), 71–77.

Palmer, S. (2008). The PRACTICE model of coaching: Towards a solution-focused approach. *Coaching Psychology International, 1*(1), 4–8.

Snyder, C.R. (1995). Conceptualising, measuring and nurturing hope. *Journal of Counselling and Development, 73,* 355–360.

Whitmore, J. (1992, 2002). *Coaching for performance: GROWing people, performance and purpose.* London: Nicholas Brealey Publishing.

30 Steps to Solutions: A process for putting solution-focused coaching principles into practice

Anthony M. Grant

Abstract

Solution-focused coaching is increasingly used by leaders, managers, and human resource professionals as well as professional coaches. Although the principles underpinning solution-focused coaching are simple, some people find it difficult to put those principles into practice in a systematic manner – simple is not the same as easy. Although there are a number of models designed to help guide solution-focused coaching conversations, to date little attention has been paid to the process of teaching solution-focused coaching skills. This is especially the case when teaching solution-focused coaching skills in organisational settings where time is limited and where individuals, particularly those with high levels of technical expertise may find it challenging to switch roles from manager to leader-as-coach. This article gives a short overview of key solution-focused principles, discusses some of the common challenges facing leaders, managers, consultants and other professionals as they learn solution-focused coaching approaches, and presents a simple step-by-step structured process for teaching, learning and practising solution-focused coaching

Keywords

Solution-focused coaching; executive coaching; coach education and training; leader as coach.

Original publication details: Grant, A. M. (2013, June). Steps to Solutions: A process for putting solution-focused coaching principles into practice. *The Coaching Psychologist,* 9(1), 36–44. Reproduced with permission of The British Psychological Society.

Solution construction sits at the very heart of the coaching process. Coaching, if nothing else, is about helping people find real-life solutions to real-life problems. This is the case regardless of whether you are coaching in a leadership or managerial role, or are a human resource professional seeking to develop others, or a professional coach working with clients on a wide range of developmental, performance or skills-related coaching issues.

At its simplest solution-focused coaching is about helping people identify preferred outcomes and specific goals so they have a clear idea about what they want to achieve. It is about helping them disengage from problem-focused or problem-saturated thinking so that they can spend more time thinking about possible solutions and pathways to success, rather than ruminating on the causes of the problem (de Shazer, 1988). Not least, it is about helping people acknowledge, identify, and then utilise a wide range of personal and contextual resources and personal strengths in the pursuit of their goals (Grant, 2011). Finally, this is all done within the context of a collaborative, mutually-respectful working alliance. This sounds easy, but the practice can be quite challenging.

Although there are a number of models to help guide solution-focused coaching conversations, to date little attention has been paid to the process of teaching solution-focused coaching skills (McKergow, 2011). This is despite the fact that solution-focused approaches to coaching are increasingly being used by leaders, managers, and human resource professionals as well as professional coaches. Hence, we need training methods that allow people to develop these coaching skills quickly and systematically. This is particularly the case when teaching solution-focused coaching skills in organisational settings where time is limited and where individuals may find it challenging to switch roles from manager to coach (Yukl & Mahsud, 2010).

This article draws on and extends past work (Grant, 2006; Greene & Grant, 2003), gives a short overview of key solution-focused principles, discusses some of the common challenges facing leaders, managers, consultants and other professionals as they learn solution-focused coaching approaches, and presents a simple step-by-step structured process for teaching, learning and practising solution-focused coaching.

KEY SOLUTION-FOCUSED PRINCIPLES

There can be few coaching modalities more straightforward than the solution-focused approach (de Shazer, 1988). In brief the key principles are:

A focus on solutions: The coach primarily facilitates the construction of solutions rather than trying to understand the aetiology of the problem. Allied to this is the use of a non-pathological framework. From this perspective problems are not indications of pathology or dysfunctionality, rather they stem from a limited repertoire of behaviour.

An assumption that positive change will occur: Change, particularly positive change, is viewed as inevitable. There is a fundamental expectation on the coach's part that positive change will occur, and an expectation that the client will engage in change-related activity outside of the coaching session.

The use of a collaborative working alliance: The coach does not take the position of the authoritarian expert who diagnoses the issues and then presents the solution or grandly solves the problem. Rather the coach treats the coachee as an equal, recognises that the coachee is the 'expert' in his/her own life, and works collaboratively with them to help them to develop solutions (Jackson & McKergow, 2002).

Changing the viewing to change the doing: Behaviour change is often facilitated by taking a different perspective. We can do this through reframing. Reframing is the process of looking at a situation from a different perspective in a way which fits the 'facts' of the same concrete situation equally well or even better. This new 'lens' or 'frame of reference' can foster a different understanding of the situation and often opens up new ways of thinking and new ways of behaving (Watzlawick, Weakland & Fisch, 1974).

Being pragmatic and flexible: Central to the solution-focused approach is the notion of being pragmatic and flexible in problem solving and solution-construction (O'Connell, 1998). The coaching process focuses on what works. The key notions are so simple it almost seems like cheating: (a) if it's not broken don't fix it; (b) find out what does works and do more of that; and (c) if that doesn't work, do something different.

USING SOLUTION-FOCUSED TOOLS: SIMPLE BUT NOT NECESSARILY EASY

As can be seen, the principles underpinning solution-focused coaching are very simple. However, it has been my observations, after teaching and practising solution-focused coaching for well over a decade-and-a-half, that some people find it quite difficult to put those simple principles into practice. To quote the renowned Reverend Robert (green)* 'just because it's simple, it don't mean it's easy'.

This is a non-exhaustive list of solution-focused tools and techniques that many coaches have found useful:

A refusal to purchase the problem: In every conversation, there is a buyer and a seller. One person 'sells' their explanatory story of the situation to the other, the other person 'buys' it. Successful solution-focused coaches don't buy into problem stories. Instead, they keep listening until they hear the glimmer of a solution. This is what they pay attention to. Holding an attitude of intelligent curiosity, service and facilitation allows the coach to respectfully, but firmly, focus the conversation on solution construction. It is almost as if the coach doesn't see the problem, the coach only sees the potential opportunity for a solution and he/she focuses the conversation on those possibilities.

Explicit goal-setting: Solution-focused coaching is outcome-focused (Grant, 2003), so it is important to identify preferred outcomes and specific goals so that the coachee can develop a clear idea about where they are going and articulate specific action steps in order to get them there.

Scaling: Scaling is a versatile way of subjectively measuring experience, and can be used in many different ways, for example asking the coachee to rate on a 1-to-10 scale how close to their goal they are, and then asking them what would take them to the next point on the scale. *Paying (genuine) compliments*: Appropriately praising the coachee and paying them genuine compliments in an authentic manner helps people recognise their achievements, builds self-confidence and often highlights additional personal resources that can be of use in the pursuit of their goals.

Exceptions to the problem: Not matter how bad the presenting problem, there is always a time when it is not quite so bad, or there is a time where the seeds of a solution are already present. The role of the coach is to highlight situations when the problem does not exist and use those times to gather clues as to what to do to make those exception times more frequent. This technique can be very empowering.

Doing more of what works: Once you have discovered when the problem does not exist, or when things are not quite as bad, the coach can help the coachee can plan to do more of what whatever it is that is making the difference.

Do less of what doesn't work: This sounds obvious, but we frequently keep trying to solve problems by using the same (failed) solutions. Insanity, as they say, is repeating the same mistake but expecting difference results!

Highlighting strengths and resources: Listen out for hidden and unacknowledged recourses. It is a cliché but it's true: every problem holds the seeds of its solution. It is amazing how often you can discover unrecognised strengths and resources within the problem itself.

Possibility language: This involves communicating with the coachee in a way that fosters discovery of potential solutions (de Shazer, 1984). One of the best-known techniques is the 'Magic Question' in which the coach asks (something like) *'Imagine that you went to bed tonight, and when you woke up the problem had somehow magically disappeared, and the solution was present… but you didn't know that the solution had arrived… what is the first thing that you'd notice that would tell you that the solution was present?'* Sometimes this kind of language is not congruent with the client, and this kind of linguistic mismatch can make it quite difficult for the client to answer the question. If this is the case, try re-phrasing. A useful variation is the 'What if question' – 'If things were going a bit better, what would be different?'

Using small steps to lead to big changes: The emphasis here is on doing small, easyto-achieve action steps and making small positive change rather than trying to make massive changes all at once.

Ask don't Tell: One of the most useful tools is the 'Ask–Tell' matrix (see Figure 1). The questions we ask as coaches lie on two intersecting dimensions: 'Telling to Asking', and 'Why to How to'. Observe yourself as you coach. Which quadrant do you spend most time in? Do you spend more time telling people what to do? Or maybe

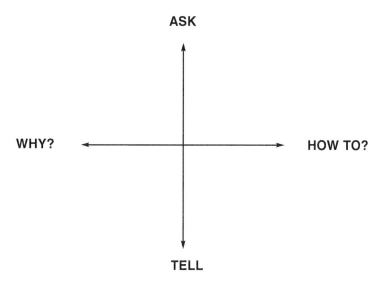

Figure 1   *The Ask-Tell Matrix.*

you spend a lot of time in diagnostic mode, telling them or asking them 'why'? Of course, it's not wrong to ask a 'why' question in coaching, or to give advice. A good coach will spend most of the time asking 'how to' questions that move the coachee forwards towards action planning and goal attainment.

A CHECKLIST FOR SOLUTION-FOCUSED QUESTIONS

It is important to note that solution-focused coaching is not just about asking a series of 'how-are-you-going-to-do-it' questions. That approach can too easily lead into an 'interrogation' style of coaching – the antitheses of the mutually-respectful collaborative approach we are seeking to develop.

Solution-focused coaching is about asking the kind of questions that raise awareness and help people develop actionable solutions that they themselves have a stake in completing.

Are your coaching questions solution-focused? Here is a three-point criteria checklist:

1. Solution-focused questions are questions that help people discover and articulate their specific *strengths* and their *ability* to build and enact solutions.
2. Solution-focused questions are questions that support and empower people in discovering their *own* solutions.
3. Solution-focused questions are questions that focus on those issues that people *have control over*.

THE SOLUTION-FOCUSED MINDSET: THE KEY CHALLENGE

Although these are all useful tools, it has been said that the solution-focused approach is less about the coach learning specific tech-niques, and more about the coach learning to adopt a mindset that is orientated towards facilitating solution-focused thinking in the coachee (or client or employee). The role of the coach is to help the coachee think through the issues, orientating their thinking towards solution construction (Szabo & Meier, 2009).

At its simplest level, focusing on solutions represents a shift of emphasis from problem analysis to solution construction. However, at a more profound level, it can mean a significant re-evaluation of the way that we look at events and circumstances.

Many people, particularly those with high levels of technical expertise and/or long-standing experience of positional power, find it hard to shift from being the man-agerial 'authoritative provider of solutions' to being the 'collaborative facilitator of solution-focused thinking'. As we all know, it is often difficult to stand back and simply ask questions that help the other person think through the issues, without jumping in to tell them what to do or offer suggestions, advice, or tips. This is particularly difficult to do where we have solid expert knowledge or personal experience of the issue or when there are time pressures at play.

Although most leaders, managers and change agents would agree that motivating people means working with them and asking them good questions that encourage and engage them, rather than simply telling them what to do (Barclay & Barclay, 2011), enacting the role of the 'guide on the side' rather than the 'sage on the stage' does not come easily to many. Hence, the principal challenge for the coach is taking on the mindset needed for effective solution-focused coaching.

One way to help people develop both a solution-focused mindset and the practical solution-focused skills is to give them a simple step-by-step structured process for learning and practising solution-focused coaching. The Steps to Solutions process aims to do just that.

THE STEPS TO SOLUTIONS PROCESS: USING THE STEPS

This is a simple step-by-step process designed to help people learn core solution-focused coaching skills in a structured, straightforward fashion (see Figure 2). It is designed to emulate the solution-focused coaching conversation. In coach training sit-uations, I ask people to simply follow the steps, one by one, starting at the bottom. Although some degree of flexibility is, of course, perfectly acceptable, I suggest that people try to work though the steps in a fairly linear fashion.

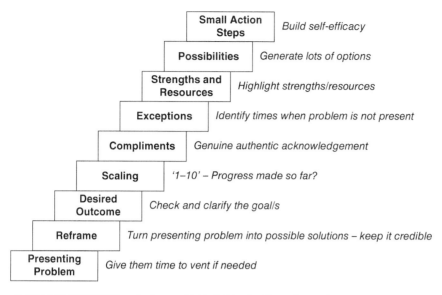

Figure 2 *The Steps to Solutions process.*

If they do have difficulties at any point as they move through the steps, it is often because they have not applied one or more of the key solution-focused principles. For example, they may be spending to much time in problem analysis – this often leads to feeling overwhelmed; or they may have chosen a goal over which the coachee has little or no control; or the coach may have slipped into the 'expert' mode; or they are talking about the goal in a way that is simply not engaging or energising for the coachee.

Whatever the reason, rather than rushing on to the next step, I typically suggest that they take the time to reflect on just how they are using the process and to try to use a different way of working with that particular step. Such challenges can indeed provide rich learning moments.

THE STEPS TO SOLUTIONS PROCESS

Here are some ideas and tips that people have found useful as they systematically learn to apply solution-focused coaching skills. Some of the example questions below might be helpful to you, but you might like to fine-tune and personalise the wording so that you feel conformable with how you express these ideas yourself.

The Steps To Solutions process is designed to be a helpful methodology to guide learning and skill development, not a rigid ideology to be slavishly adhered to, so some flexibility in its application is completely acceptable. Nevertheless, the step-by-step format is a useful and effective process.

STEP 1. LET THE COACHEE TALK ABOUT THE PRESENTING PROBLEM AND GIVE THEM TIME TO VENT IF NEEDED

The Steps to Solutions process can start with problem catharsis. Solution-focused coaching does not deny the existence of problems. As Insoo Kim Berg has said – just because we are solution-focused, it does not mean that we are problem-phobic! Many coachees want to talk about their problems, and stoping them from doing so can alienate them. Having the time and space to talk about problems can be cathartic. Indeed, in doing so people often develop significant clarity and insight and such conversation can build rapport between coach and coachee. Listen carefully to the problem. Don't object to problem talk, but don't 'buy into' or try to fix the problem. Just give them time to vent if needed, but if the coachee is content not to talk about the problem in depth, then move quickly on to Step 2.

STEP 2. REFRAME: TURN THE PRESENTING PROBLEM INTO POSSIBLE SOLUTIONS

The next step is to turn the presenting problem into a possible solution – but keep it credible. This must be realistic. As the coach you may have to be quite vague in your response at this stage until more solid ideas and goals develop as you move through the steps. For example: Coachee: *'I'm supposed to be the leader here, but I just can't relate to those people. They never seem to do what I ask of them.'* Coach's reframe: *'So, up till now in this leadership role you haven't found a way to connect with them in a way that motives and moves them into the right kind of action. I wonder what might help to begin to develop the right kind of motivating connection. What might be useful here?'*

STEP 3. ARTICULATE THE DESIRED OUTCOME

The next step is to ask the coachee to describe their goal or 'desired outcome' in fairly specific terms. Check and clarify. This step can take some time. Many people are not very good at articulating their goals. The coach needs to make sure that the goal is something that the coachee has direct control over. A common mistake is to set a goal that involves someone else doing something. Take time to check in with the coachee that this is something that they really do want to achieve. You may have to rephrase the goal a few times in order to make it attractive and energising for the coachee. Useful questions here include: *'What is your real goal here?'*, or *'Does this feel energising for you?'* or you could try *'If this works out, what would be different for you?'* This latter question is very useful in helping people articulate their desired outcome, but you may have to finetune their response to get at a more specific goal.

STEP 4. SCALING

Next, take a moment to help the coachee work out where they are at by using scaling. Scaling is a versatile way of subjectively measuring experience and can be used in many different ways. In essence, it invites people to perceive their problems, issues or goals as being on a continuum rather than being fixed or unchangeable. For example, the coachee might be asked to rate on a 1-to-10 scale how close they are to their goal right now. Once the coachee gives a number, the coach takes that rating and transforms it into talk about actions. For example, a coach might response to a rating of 3 out of 10 by complimenting the coachee (in an authentic and genuine manner) on the fact that they are 30 per cent of the way to their goal. The coach could ask about what has helped get the coachee to this point (thereby eliciting talk about personal strengths); or how is it that they are not at a 2; or they could ask what would it take to get to a 4 or 5 (eliciting talk about action-planning). The aim here is to foster small changes. This is not about rushing to a 10. Small steps (even 0.5 of a step increment) in the direction of goals and preferred outcome are the key to success.

STEP 5. COMPLIMENTS

This is a good place in the Steps to Solutions process to give some compliments, even if you have done so at previous points in the conversation. Praising the coachee and paying them compliments builds self-confidence. Of course, this must be done in an authentic and genuine fashion. As the work of Losada and Heaphy (2004) has shown, high performance teams tend to have a positivity-to-negativity ratio of at least 5 positive comments to 1 negative comment. So, go ahead – purposefully put some positivity into the conversation. Compliments play a vital role in coaching. They can be used to direct attention to, for example, personal strengths, they help develop collaborative relationships, and not least they make people feel valued and appreciated. Ideas for compliments include: progress made so far; personal resilience shown in the face of difficulty; willingness to discuss and address difficult issues; taking the time to be involved in the coaching conversation – the list is endless.

STEP 6. EXCEPTIONS

This is often a useful point in the process to explore exceptions. Exceptions are times when the presenting problem does not exist, or when things are going better than usual. The aim is to find out what is different at those times, and then to do more of that the difference that will make a difference (Bateson, 1972). The coach could say something like *'Well, from what we've talked about it certainly seems like you are making some progress, I wonder, are there any times when you have managed to deal successfully with this before?'* Or, *'Have you seen someone else deal with this? What's different about those times?'* The idea here is to gather clues as to what to do to make those exception times more frequent. The key to this, as in all solution-focused work, is to have good rapport, and a solid collaborative relationship in which the coachee feels respected and understood.

STEP 7. STRENGTHS AND RESOURCES

In order to build momentum and confidence before we start to explore new possi-bilities for action, it is often helpful to highlight the coachee's strengths and resources. Strengths can be a wide range of things including personal characteristics, past experiences, or personal resilience. Resources can also be about the person, but are often found in the social and physical environment. In every environment, there are individuals, networks, groups or institutions who can act as a support or a resource. Often these resources are already 'staring us in the face' – these are un-noticed and the role of the coach here is to help the coachee identify and use these. A useful question here is something like: *'What personal strengths do you bring to this?'* and/or *'How could you use your personal strengths here?'*

STEP 8. POSSIBILITIES

As we move towards the final stages of the process, we start to work with the coachee to develop options and possibilities. The key here is to brainstorm a wide range of options. Many ideas will have already emerged during the conversation and may have been written down already. A good tip here is to ask 'what else?' several times. Don't let the coachee come up with only one or two options. Push them a bit on this point – without being rude. Even if they seem to have exhausted all options, try diverting their attention for a moment by talking about something different, and then ask the question: *'…and what else comes to mind? What else could you do?'* –you may be surprised how often they come up with new ideas (Davis & Knowles, 1999).

STEP 9. SMALL ACTION STEPS

In the final stage, ask the coachee to describe (and write down) some specific action steps that will help him/her move towards his/her goal. I recommend small and specific action steps that will motivate them, create early wins and further build confidence and self-efficacy. Finally, ask them to rate on a scale of 1-to-10 how confident they are that they can complete these steps (with 10 being totally confident).

Ideally, they should rate themselves at least 8 out of 10. If their self-rating is below an 8 simply ask them what would move them up to an 8 or 9 and then incorporate those action steps or changes into the final action plan. This is an important final step as it helps both the coach and coachee finalise the coaching process. Make sure the coachee writes the action steps down. Writing down the action steps at the end of the conversation significantly increases the probability that the coachee will in fact do those things (Gollwitzer, 1999). Useful questions here include *'On a scale of 1-to-10, how confident are you that you can do all these action steps?'* and, *'How can you keep track of your progress over time?'*

SUMMARY

As solution-focused approaches to coaching are increasingly being used by leaders, managers, and human resource professionals as well as professional coaches, we need training methods that allow people to develop these coaching skills quickly and systematically. This is particularly the case when teaching solution-focused coaching skills in organisational settings where time is limited and where individuals may find it challenging to switch roles from manager to coach. Although there are a number of models to help guide solution-focused coaching conversations, little attention has been paid to date to the process of teaching solution-focused coaching skills (McKergow, 2011). The Steps to Solutions process is a theoretically-grounded step-by-step practical methodology for teaching and learning solution-focused coaching skills that has great potential in both professional coaching and organisational settings.

REFERENCES

Barclay, H.K. & Barclay, A.C. (2011). Recession compassion: Seven steps on how to treat employees to get the best performance during these global economic times. *Journal of Management*, 12(1), 21.

Bateson, G. (1972). *Steps to an ecology of mind: Collected essays in anthropology, psychiatry, evolution, and epistemology*. Chicago: University of Chicago Press.

Davis, B.P. & Knowles, E.S. (1999). A disrupt-thenreframe technique of social influence. *Journal of Personality & Social Psychology, 76*(2), 192–199.

de Shazer, S. (1984). The imaginary pill technique. *Journal of Strategic & Systemic Therapies, 3*(1), 30–34.

de Shazer, S. (1988). *Clues: Investigating solutions in brief therapy*. New York: Norton & Co.

Gollwitzer, P.M. (1999). Implementation intentions: Simple effects of simple plans. *American Psychologist, 54*(7), 493–503.

Grant, A.M. (2003). The impact of life coaching on goal attainment, metacognition and mental health. *Social Behaviour and Personality: An International Journal, 31*(3), 253–264.

Grant, A.M. (2006). Solution-focused coaching. In J. Passmore (Ed.), *Excellence in coaching: The industry guide* (pp.73–90). London: Kogan Page.

Grant, A.M. (2011). The Solution-Focused Inventory: A tripartite taxonomy for teaching, measuring and conceptualising solution-focused approaches to coaching. *The Coaching Psychologist, 7*(2), 98–106.

Greene, J. & Grant, A.M. (2003). *Solution-focused coaching: Managing people in a complex world*. London: Momentum Press.

Jackson, P.Z. & McKergow, M. (2002). *The Solutions Focus: The SIMPLE way to positive change*. London: Nicholas Brealey.

Losada, M. & Heaphy, E. (2004). The role of positivity and connectivity in the performance of business teams: A non-linear dynamics model. *American Behavioural Scientist, 47*(6), 740–765.

McKergow, M. (2011). Time to focus on SF training. *InterAction – The Journal of Solution Focus in Organisations, 3*(1), 5–7.

O'Connell, B. (1998). *Solution-focused therapy*. London: Sage.

Szabo, P. & Meier, D. (2009). *Coaching plain & simple: Solution-focused brief coaching essentials*. New York: W W Norton & Co.

Watzlawick, P., Weakland, J. & Fisch, R. (1974). *Change: Principles of problem formation and problem resolution*. New York: Norton.

Yukl, G. & Mahsud, R. (2010). Why flexible and adaptive leadership is essential. *Consulting Psychology Journal: Practice and Research, 62*(2), 81.

31 Solution-focused coaching: The basics for advanced practitioners

Anthony M. Grant

Abstract

The solution-focused approach has much to offer coaching both novice and advanced practitioners. The core solution-focused principles discussed in this paper can augment and extend all facets of coaching practice. This article outlines the central features of the solution-focused approach to coaching and extends the utility of those basic features for use and for reflection by novice and more advanced coaching practitioners. Practical models discussed in this article include the 'solution-focused cathartic wave' – a model that tracks the emergence of emotional catharsis during the coaching conversation; the 'probing for solutions model' which provides a simple structure for solution-focused coaching conversations; and also discussion on how a solution-focused approach can be used in a range of change-orientated settings.

Keywords

solution-focused coaching; cathartic wave; Ask-Tell matrix.

Coaching is intrinsically about helping individuals, groups, teams and organisational systems articulate and then move towards the attainment of desired goals, states and outcomes. In this sense all coaching is 'solution-focused' regardless of the theoretical framework that informs any specific person's coaching practice. For example, a

Original publication details: Grant, A. M. (2019, December). Solution-focused coaching: The basics for advanced practitioners. *The Coaching Psychologist, 15*(2), 44–53. Reproduced with permission of The British Psychological Society.

Coaching Practiced, First Edition. Edited by David Tee and Jonathan Passmore.
© 2022 John Wiley & Sons Ltd. Published 2022 by John Wiley & Sons Ltd.
DOI: 10.1002/9781119835714.ch31

coach who draws heavily on (say) psychodynamic family systems theory in order that the coachee can break free from dysfunctional behaviour patterns and move towards their desired goals or outcomes is in a sense 'solution-focused'. However, the use of the term 'solution-focused' implies some specific core philosophical assumptions and resultant boundaries that distinguish the 'solution-focused approach' from other philosophical and methodological approaches to delivering coaching services.

This article draws on a number of previously published issues relating to the solution-focused (SF) coaching including empirical research and practitioner-related tools and methodologies (e.g. Grant & Cavanagh, 2018; Grant & O'Connor, 2018). The aim of this article is to outline the central features as to what constitutes the solution-focused approach to coaching and to extend the utility of those basic SF features for both practical use and for reflection by novice and more advanced coaching practitioners. It should be noted that there are many different views on what constitutes a 'solution-focused approach' (for a detailed exposition of how SF approaches have changed over time see McKergow, 2016). However, there are a cluster of presuppositions and practice techniques that most SF practitioners would agree are essential defining characteristics of a solution-focused approach (identified from Grant, 2013; Greene & Grant, 2003; Neipp et al., 2015). Such philosophical assumptions would include:

CORE SF PHILOSOPHICAL ASSUMPTIONS

- *Use of a non-pathological model*: Problems are not indications of pathology or dysfunctionality; rather they stem from a limited repertoire of behaviour.
- *An assumption that focusing on constructing solutions will serve the client better than problem deconstruction*: The coach facilitates the construction of solutions rather than trying to understand the aetiology of the problem.
- *Use of existing client resources*: The coach helps the client recognise and utilise resources of which they were unaware.
- *An assumption that positive change will occur*: Change, particularly positive change, is viewed as inevitable. There is a fundamental expectation on the coach's part that positive change will occur, and an expectation that the coachee will engage in change-related activity outside of the coaching session.
- *An assumption that positive change can happen in a short period of time*: This stands in contrast to philosophical schools that assume that the problem must be worked on over a considerable period of time.

- *Each client is unique, and thus interventions should be strategic rather than 'cookbook'*:
- Coaching interventions are designed specifically for each client.
- *The future is where the future is; the present is where the future begins*: The emphasis is more on the future (what the client wants to have happen) than the past.

CORE SF TECHNIQUES AND METHODOLOGIES

Similarly, there are a group of core techniques and methodologies that most SF practitioners would agree are essential defining practical characteristics of a solution-focused applied methodologies or techniques. These include:

- *Reframing presenting problems as potential solutions*: Reframing is the process of looking at a situation from a different perspective in a way which fits the 'facts' of the same concrete situation equally well or even better. This new 'lens' or 'frame of reference' can foster a different understanding of the situation and often opens up new ways of thinking and new ways of behaving (Watzlawick et al., 1974).
- *The use of scaling*: Scaling is a versatile way of subjectively measuring experience, and can be used in many different ways; for example, asking the coachee to rate on a 1-to-10 scale how close to their goal they are, and then asking them what would take them to the next point on the scale.
- *The use of the 'what-if?' or 'magic question'*: This involves communicating with the coachee in a way that fosters discovery of potential solutions (de Shazer & Lipchik, 1984). One of the best-known techniques is the 'magic question', in which the coach asks (something like): 'Imagine that you went to bed tonight, and when you woke up the problem had somehow magically disappeared, and the solution was present… but you didn't know that the solution had arrived… What is the first thing that you'd notice that would tell you that the solution was present?' Sometimes this kind of language is not congruent with the client, and this kind of linguistic mismatch can make it quite difficult for the client to answer the question. If this is the case, try rephrasing. A useful variation is the 'what if question' – 'If things were going a bit better, what would be different?'
- *Highlighting exceptions*: From a SF perspective there is always an 'exception' to any problem state – a time or context where the presenting problem is not quite as bad. The technique here is to help the coachee identity those points and to find ways to do more of what is working and less of what is not; in brief, to find the difference that makes a difference.
- *The use of clear, specific goal setting*: Setting of attainable goals within a specific time-frame.

CAUTION: HIDDEN PHILOSOPHICAL TRAPS

Whilst the above points represent general points of agreement in the SF community (McKergow, 2016), there are also aspects that are points of dispute or difference. For example, Miller and de Shazer (1998) proudly ground their understanding of SF approaches in a postmodern Wittgenstein philosophy (where there is no 'objective truth'), whereas Gray (2011, p.7) decries the fact that 'the strengths perspective eschews professional expertise and scientific knowledge for common sense, tacit knowing, hunches and guesses. Its generative approach rejects the need for objective knowledge, the idea of objectivity, and an objective reality'. As Grey alludes, the problem here is that if we truly ground our work on a postmodern, subjective view of the world, we have no way of knowing if our work is effective. If all perspectives are equally valid, there are no grounds for claiming expertise or skill in any area of life. Yet those coaches subscribing to a postmodern approach typically undertake training to enhance their expertise and therapeutic skills.

Finally, if science is a fraud and there really is no means of conducting evaluations (in itself a self-refuting statement – how can we establish that science is a fraud unless we put it to the test?), coaches who rigidly adhere to a postmodern philosophical position cannot make claims as to the effectiveness of their coaching practice. According to this position the coachee would be just as well served by being coached by the garbage collector or the butcher. Accordingly, it would be ethically question-able to take payment for such services. This is clearly an unsatisfactory foundation for a truly professional practice! Clearly, coaches need to think about the philosophical and ontological constructs underpinning their coaching work and be aware of the implications of such philosophical positions.

ORIGINS OF SOLUTION-FOCUSED APPROACHES AND THE AVOIDANCE OF PROBLEM-SATURATION

As for many approaches to coaching, the SF approach has its roots in therapeutic modalities – in this case brief solution-focused therapy. The foundational work in brief therapy was conducted by Gregory Bateson, John Wicklund and others at the Mental Research Institute in Palo Alto, California, in the 1960s (Jackson & McKergow, 2007). This was further developed in the late 1970s and early 1980s by Steve de Shazer, Insoo Kim Berg and colleagues at the Brief Family Therapy Centre, in Milwaukee, Wisconsin, US. Since then, considerable work worldwide has been undertaken in articulating and developing the main tenets of the approach (Kim et al., 2019).

According to Berg and Szabo (2005), therapists and researchers at these therapeutic centres had become dissatisfied with traditional therapeutic approaches. They found (as have many contemporary coaching practitioners) that the more clients talked about their problems, the more entrenched in the problem they become. This sense of 'problem saturation' often leads to less clarity, with the coachee experiencing a sense of overwhelm, confusion and a feeling of disempowerment. Of course, one can continue ploughing on, talking through the problematic issues with the coachee or client until a moment of clarity or hope occurs and solutions start to somehow naturalistically emerge.

RIDING THE CATHARTIC WAVE

The 'cathartic wave' represented in Figure 1 is a simplistic representation of the conversational problem-saturation process. In the initial stages of talking about the problem (points A to B) feelings of relief arise, one feels unburdened, one feels listened to and acknowledged – positive affect increases. However, as one talks further about the problem the sense of relief begins to dissipate, one reaches the tip of the cathartic wave (e.g. at point B) and a sense of overwhelm and disempowerment then begins to

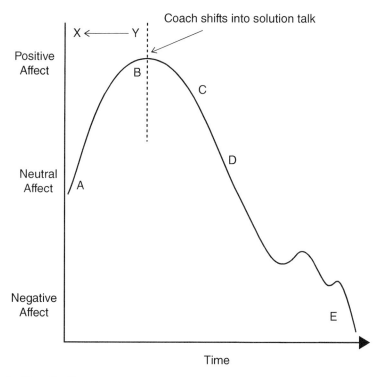

Figure 1   *The cathartic wave*

get stronger. If the coach continues to facilitate talk about the problem (problem-focused talk), then the sense of problem saturation builds, and negative affect increases.

Typically, coaches will try to turn the coaching conversation towards solution talk once the cathartic wave has been passed (point C). However, other coaches are less skilled at instigating solution-talk and may find themselves at point D, and some cannot make that turn until point E – where the coachee is almost screaming for help feeling crushed by a mountain of despair.

From this author's perspective, the skill of the solution-focused coach lies in keeping the time spent in the cathartic phase (points X to Y) to a minimum before moving into solution-talk. I like to think about this as 'riding the cathartic wave'. People need to feel heard. Problems need to be aired. Letting the conversation breach the peak of the cathartic wave invites problem saturation; jumping in with solution talk too early risks alienating the coachee, creating the feeling that they have not been heard. Some novice SF coaches seem almost afraid of any problem-focused talk. It often seems like a race to rush in and ask the 'magic question'. However, as Insoo Kim Berg said, being solution-focused does not mean being problem-phobic (Berg & Szabo, 2005). Indeed, research (e.g. Grant & O'Connor, 2010) shows that thinking about one's problem can in fact help people move towards their goals. Unsurprisingly however, solution-focused talk is far more effective in terms of facilitating goal progression, increasing positive affect and decreasing negative affect.

Although the cathartic wave diagram represented in Figure 1 is simplistic and does not purport to capture the complex dynamics of conversation-based solution-focused change, it is a useful tool that both novice and advanced practitioners can use to help them understand the relationship between problem-focused dialogue and positive/negative affect (or problem saturation). One practical idea is for coaches to keep the notion of the cathartic wave in mind as they coach their coachee through the process of uncovering exceptions or resources.

THE ASK-TELL MATRIX

The Ask-Tell matrix (Figure 2) provides another useful heuristic for delineating between problem-focused questions that explore causality, and solution-focused questions that are aimed at identifying goals and pathways to goal attainment. The Ask-Tell matrix, first popularised by Whitmore (1992), consists of two orthogonal dimensions: an Ask-Tell dimension and a How-Why dimension.

The solution-focused approach posits that agents of change, such as coaches, should aim to spend most of the time asking questions that elicit thoughts from the coachee about how to identify and best attain their goals, rather than asking 'why' questions that explore causality. This is the domain of the 'asking-how-to' quadrant.

In contrast, the underpinning assumption in a problem-focused approach is that the individual needs to explore the aetiology and development of the problem in order to gain the understanding deemed necessary for goal attainment. Typical 'problem-focused' approaches try to get to the bottom of a presenting problem; for example,

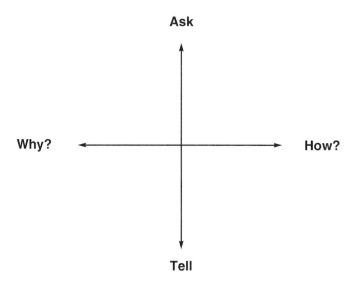

Figure 2   *The Ask-Tell Matrix*

'Why do you think it didn't last?'; 'What is it that you're most worried about?'; and 'Why do you find this much harder than others?'

From this perspective the conversation is more focused on the 'asking-why' quadrant. There are a number of different theoretical approaches that can be used in problem-focused interventions, including root cause analysis (e.g. Rooney & Heuvel, 2004; Wilson et al., 1993) and psychodynamic approaches (e.g. Buckley et al., 1984). However, regardless of specific theoretical orientation, the kinds of questions that stem from a problem-focused approach are questions that ask about the origin and causes of the problem, would seek to uncover details of the thoughts associated with the problem, and would explore the impact of those thoughts on the individual.

SOLUTIONS FOCUS VS. PROBLEM FOCUS: NOT A CLEAR-CUT DICHOTOMY

With typologies such as 'problem-focused' and 'solution-focused' it is all too easy to slip into simplistic dichotomous ways of 'us' versus 'them' thinking. As McKergow (2016) notes, the early pioneers of SF approaches such as Steve de Shazer (1988) and Insoo Kim Berg strongly encouraged completely problem-free talk, and the early work of Jackson and colleagues (e.g. Jackson & McKergow, 2007) and O'Hanlon and Beadle (1996) also emphasised a 'pure' approach to solution focused work.

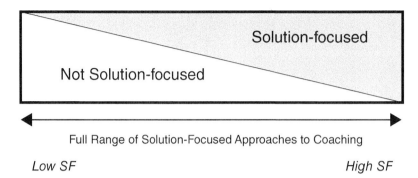

Figure 3   *Dimensions of solution-focused practice*

The clinging to the 'pure' core of any new or emerging methodology is understandable, as the new methodology emerges and its creators and early adopters seek to establish a unique identity in a tight marketplace where credibility and worthiness are tightly guarded, and newcomers actively excluded by those with established power and authority. However, in the long run an instance on maintaining a 'purest approach' ends up by establishing the puritanical. The puritanical in turn leads to rigidity, authoritarianism and exclusion – 'us' and 'them' – exclusion rather than inclusion. Consequently, over time, rather than join the 'pure' SF group, many practitioners from other theoretical or methodological approaches begin to absorb what they find useful in SF into their own practices – leading to a multiplicity of 'solution-focused' approaches. This has been very much evident with SF approaches to coaching, and from the present author's perspective, such diversity is a key strength.

The solution-focused approach is globally one of the most popular and widely used positive change methodologies (Trepper et al., 2006). Because at its core is a deep respect for client's resilience and previous client-generated solutions and exceptions to their own problems, one can apply SF approaches to a wide range of issues and problems. In addition, many techniques and methodologies can be incorporated into SF approaches (or vice versa), as long as such techniques and methodologies incorporate an abiding belief in clients' abilities to know what is best for them, develop self-concordant goals and to effectively plan how to get there (e.g. Trepper et al., 2006). It is this facet that makes the SF approach so applicable to the coaching genre – as long as the majority of one's coaching is about constructing solutions, I would argue that there is no one 'right' way to be a SF practitioner.

MULTIPLE APPLICATIONS OF THE SF APPROACH

It is now possible to find the SF approach incorporated into a vast range of positive change methodologies including Appreciative Inquiry (Cooperrider et al., 2000), complexity theory (Cavanagh & Grant, 2010), organisational change (Morgan, 2016),

Table 1 *Applications of the solution-focused approach*

Activity	Problem-focused	Solution-focused
Planning change	Emphasis on diagnosis Tell me about the problem Identity the blocks to change	Emphasises on desired outcome How would you like things to be? Identify progress made so far Highlight strengths & resources
Managing people	Sees people as source of dysfunction Who is the weakest link" How can we minimise risk?	Sees people as functional and source of solutions Where are our hidden strengths? How can we grow our people?
Monitoring progress	Identity weakness and failures What went wrong? How far have we got to go?	Emphasises on what works How did we cope so well? How can we build on progress made so far?
Trouble shooting	Uncover cause and effect Who's to blame? Is lack of progress a symptom of something deeper?	Emphasises on Desired Outcome How would you like things to be? Identify progress made so far Highlight strengths & resources

(Adapted from Cavanagh and Grant 2019)

general applications of coaching methodologies (Iveson et al., 2012), Positive psychology coaching (Biswas-Diener, 2010; Green & Palmer, 2019), cognitive-behavioural coaching (Willaims et al., 2010), and there are an increasing range of studies that attest to its effectiveness in a wide range of populations (Theeboom et al., 2013; Zhang et al., 2018). Indeed, SF philosophises, techniques and methodologies are now so widely used and have so frequently been incorporated into other helping modalities, that it is sometimes hard to see where 'solution' and 'non-solution' approaches begin. For a useful example of the fusion of acceptance and commitment therapy with SF approaches see Harris (2007).

The SF principles allow the SF approach to be used as a useful lens for a whole range of activities beyond the coaching conversation. Table 1 illustrates how the solution-focused approach could be used in a range of change-related processes.

INTO ACTION: THE PROBING FOR SOLUTIONS MODEL

It is often useful to have a simple step-by-step framework on which to model the coaching conversation. The 'probing for solutions model' (Greene & Grant, 2003) is a simple framework that can help the coach to stay on a solution-focused track. There are four

Figure 4 *The probing for solutions model*

very simple steps. These are not linear, rather they should act as guideposts to steer the conversation.

Step 1: Listen for solutions

In this section of the conversation the coachee is talking about his or her problem (or aspirations) and the coach's role here is to listen to the story, let the coachee know that they have been heard, and to look for solutions in the presenting story. The key skill here is in not 'buying the problem' but in reframing presenting problems in a way that allows the possibility of a range of solutions.

Step 2: Probe for solutions

At this point in the conversation the coach is asking questions that raise the coachee's awareness of potential solutions, by being curious and not taking the client's assumptions at face value.

Step 3: Talk about solutions

The coaching conversation here focuses on further developing potential or concrete solutions. The aim here is to develop a clear vision of a possible future, highlighting unrecognised strengths and resources and using those in the development of specific solutions.

Step 4: Plan for solutions

During the conversation, and particularly towards the end of the conversation, both the coach and the coachee should identify specific action steps. It's useful that the steps are written down by the coachee and that the steps are time-framed where possible. It is also useful to use scaling here and ask the coachee to rate their confidence of completing these steps on a 1 to 10 scale. This acts as a final reality check allowing the coach to gauge the effectiveness of the session and, if the confidence rating is not high (say 7 or below), to make modifications to any action plans.

CONCLUDING COMMENTS

The SF approach has been highly influential in coaching, consulting and many areas of personal and organisation change. Although it is often seen as being simple, it is not simplistic. Indeed, as is often said 'just because it's simple, it doesn't mean it's easy'. By focusing on solutions and using a solution-focused approach in one's coaching practice, coaches can bring hope, engagement and positivity into their client's lives. Even highly experienced coaches with a preference for analytical approaches to coaching can find utility and leverage from a solution-focused perspective if one keeps focusing because it works – 'if you work it'.

REFERENCES

Berg, I.K. & Szabo, P. (2005). *Brief coaching for lasting solutions*. New York: W.W. Norton.

Biswas-Diener, R. (2010). *Practicing positive psychology coaching: Assessment, activities and strategies for success*. London: Wiley.

Buckley, P., Conte, H.R., Plutchik, R., Wild, K.V. & Karasu, T. B. (1984). Psychodynamic variables as predictors of psychotherapy outcome. *American Journal of Psychiatry, 141*(6), 742–748. doi:10.1176.ajp.141.6.742

Cavanagh, M. & Grant, A.M. (2010). The Solution-focused coaching approach to coaching. In E. Cox, T. Bachkirova & D. Clutterbuck (Eds.) *Sage handbook of coaching* (pp.34–47). London: Sage.

Cooperrider, D.L., Sorensen, P.F., Whitney, D. & Yaeger, T.F. (2000). *Appreciative inquiry: Rethinking human organization toward a positive theory of change*. Champaign, IL: Stipes Publishing.

De Shazer, S. (1988). *Clues: Investigating solutions in brief therapy*. New York: Norton & Co.

De Shazer, S. & Lipchik, E. (1984). Frames and reframing. *Family Therapy Collections, 11*, 88–97.

Grant, A.M. (2013). Steps to solutions: A process for putting solution-focused coaching principles into practice. *The Coaching Psychologist, 9*(1), 36–44.

Grant, A.M. & Cavanagh, M. (2018). The Solution-focused approach to coaching. In E. Cox, T. Bachkirova & D.A. Clutterbuck (Eds.) *The complete handbook of coaching* (pp.35–51). London: Sage.

Grant, A.M. & O'Connor, S.A. (2010). The differential effects of solution-focused and problem-focused coaching questions: A pilot study with implications for practice. *Industrial and Commercial Training, 42*(2), 102–111. doi:10.1108/00197851011026090

Grant, A.M. & O'Connor, S.A. (2018). Broadening and building solution-focused coaching: Feeling good is not enough. *Coaching: An International Journal of Theory, Research and Practice, 11*(2), 165–185. doi:10.1080/17521882.2018.1489868

Gray, M. (2011). Back to basics: A critique of the strengths perspective in social work. *Families in Society*, *92*(1), 5–11. doi:10.1606/ 1044-3894.4054

Green, S. & Palmer, S. (2019). *Positive psychology coaching in practice*. New York: Routledge.

Greene, J. & Grant, A.M. (2003). *Solution-focused coaching: Managing people in a complex world*. London: Momentum Press.

Harris, R. (2007). *The happiness trap*. Auckland, NZ: Exisle Publishing.

Iveson, C., George, E. & Ratner, H. (2012). *Brief coaching: A solution focused approach new*. York: Routledge/ Taylor & Francis Group.

Jackson, P.Z. & McKergow, M. (2007). *Solutions focus*. London: Nicholas Brealey Publishing.

Kim, J., Jordan, S.S., Franklin, C., & Froerer, A. (2019). Is solution-focused brief therapy evidence-based? An update 10 years later. *Families in Society*, *100*(2), 127–138. doi:10.1606/1044-3894.4009

McKergow, M. (2016). Sfbt 2.0: The next generation of solution focused brief therapy has already arrived. *Journal of Solution Focused Brief Therapy*, *2*(2), 1–17.

Miller, G. & de Shazer, S. (1998). Have you heard the latest rumor about…? *Solution-Focused Therapy as a Rumor. Family Process*, *37*(3), 363–377.

Morgan, G. (2016). Organisational change: A solution-focused approach. *Educational Psychology in Practice*, *32*(2), 133–144. doi:10.1080/02667363.2015.1125855

Neipp, M.C., Beyebach, M., Nuñez, R.M. & Martínez-González, M.C. (2016). The effect of solution-focused versus problem-focused questions: A replication. *Journal of Marital and Family Therapy*, *42*(3), 525–535. doi:10.1111/jmft.12140

O'Hanlon, B. & Beadle, S. (1996). *A field guide to possibility land*. London: BT Press.

Rooney, J.J. & Heuvel, L.N.V. (2004). Root cause analysis for beginners. *Quality Progress*, *37*(7), 45–56.

Theeboom, T., Beersma, B. & van Vianen, A. (2013). Does coaching work? A meta-analysis on the effects of coaching on individual level outcomes in an organizational context. *Journal of Positive Psychology*, *9*(1), 1–18. doi:10.1080/17439760.2013.837499

Trepper, T.S., Dolan, Y., McCollum, E.E. & Nelson, T. (2006). Steve De Shazer and the future of solution-focused therapy. *Journal of Marital and Family Therapy*, *32*(2), 133–139. doi:10.1111/j.1752-0606.2006.tb01595.x

Watzlawick, P., Weakland, J. & Fisch, R. (1974). *Change: Principles of problem formation and problem resolution*. New York: Norton.

Whitmore, J. (1992). *Coaching for performance*. London: Nicholas Brealey.

Willaims, H., Edgerton, N. & Palmer, S. (2010). Cognitive behavioural coaching. In E. Cox, T. Bachkirova & D. Clutterbuck (Eds.) *The complete handbook of coaching* (pp.37–53). London: Sage.

Wilson, P.F., Dell, L.D. & Anderson, G.F. (1993). *Root cause analysis: A tool for total quality management*. New York: American Society for Quality Improvement.

Zhang, A., Franklin, C., Currin-McCulloch, J., Park, S. & Kim, J. (2018). The effectiveness of strength-based, solution-focused brief therapy in medical settings: A systematic review and meta-analysis of randomized controlled trials. *Journal of Behavioral Medicine*, *41*(2), 139–151. doi:10.1007/s10865-017-9888-1

32 Revisiting the 'P' in the PRACTICE coaching model

Stephen Palmer

Abstract

The PRACTICE model of coaching has been developing over time and adapted to the presenting issues arising during the initial stage of coaching. This paper will briefly highlight the options available.

Keywords

PRACTICE; problem-solving; cognitive-behavioural coaching; solution-focused coaching; Presenting issue; Purpose; Preferred outcome; Preferred option.

Over the past four decades various researchers and practitioners have developed problem-solving methods which have been applied to a wide range of issues such as decision making, stress and anxiety management, and settings such as coaching/coaching psychology, clinical, counselling, psychotherapy, training, human resources and management (see D'Zurilla & Goldfried, 1971; D'Zurilla, 1986; D'Zurilla & Nezu, 1999; Neenen & Palmer, 2001a, 2001b; Palmer & Burton, 1996; Palmer 1997a, 1997b; Palmer & Szymanska, 2007; Wasik, 1984). The steps in Wasik's (1984) seven-step problem-solving are: Problem identification; Goal selection; Generation of alternatives; Consideration of consequences; Decision making; Implementation; Evaluation.

Original publication details: Palmer, S. (2011, December). Revisiting the 'P' in the PRACTICE coaching model. *The Coaching Psychologist, 7*(2), 156–158. Reproduced with permission of The British Psychological Society.

Palmer (2007a, 2007b) developed the **PRACTICE** model of coaching which is an adaptation of Wasik's (1984) seven-step sequence. The acronym, PRACTICE, represents the seven steps: **P**roblem identification; **R**ealistic, relevant goals developed; **A**lternative solutions generated; **C**onsideration of consequences; **T**arget most feasible solution(s); **I**mplementation of **C**hosen solution(s); **E**valuation. The PRACTICE model has been used for performance, business, career, executive, stress, health, life and personal coaching in addition to being used within counselling, psychotherapy and stress management. Initially the PRACTICE model/framework was seen as a solution seeking, cognitive behavioural approach (see Palmer, 2007a, 2007b). However, PRACTICE has continued to evolve with a greater emphasis on the solution-focused approach to coaching (e.g. Palmer, 2008; Williams, Palmer & Wallace, 2011). Palmer (2008, p.4) highlighted a number of key items: *At the start of the first coaching meeting the coachee is given an opportunity to talk about him or herself without immediately focusing on their problem(s), issues or concerns thereby allowing the coach to learn more about them (O'Connell, 2003). During the coaching process the coach will draw attention to the coachee any relevant examples of their competence, strengths and qualities and also build on 'exceptions' when the presenting problem or issue is less of a problem. Throughout the whole process of the coaching meeting, scaling questions are used to monitor where the coachee currently is, if progress is being made and what the coachee would need to do to improve the rating.*

Table 1   *The revised PRACTICE sequence*

Steps	Possible questions, statements and actions
1. Problem identification	What's the problem or issue or concern or topic you wish to discuss? What would you like to change?
	Any exceptions when it is not a problem, issue or concern?
	How will we know if the situation has improved?
	On a scale of 0 to 10 where '0' is nowhere and '10' is resolved, how near are you now today, to resolving the problem or issue?
	Any distortions or can the problem or issue be viewed differently?
	Can you imagine waking up tomorrow morning and this problem (or issue or concern) no longer existed, what would you notice that was different?
2. Realistic, relevant goals developed (e.g. SMART goals)	What do you want to achieve?
	Let's develop specific SMART goals.
3. Alternative solutions generated	What are your options?
	Let's note them down.
4. Consideration of consequences	What could happen?
	How useful is each possible solution?
	Let's use a rating 'usefulness' scale for each solution where '0' is *not useful at all,* and '10' is extremely useful.
5. Target most feasible solution(s)	Now we have considered the possible solutions, what is the most feasible or practical solution(s)?
6. Implementation of Chosen solution(s)	Let's implement the chosen solution by breaking it down into manageable steps.
	Now go and do it!
7. Evaluation	How successful was it? Rating 'success' scale 0 to 10. What can be learnt? Can we finish coaching now or do you want to address or discuss another issue or concern?

The revised PRACTICE sequence is described in Table 1 and highlights additional solution-focused methods during step one, in particular (Palmer, 2008, p.5).

In purely solution-focused coaching, problem-talk is usually avoided and it may be preferable that the 'P' in the PRACTICE model represents another aspect of the coaching process such as 'Presenting issues' instead of 'Problem identification'.

Sometimes coachees come to coaching with fuzzy problems and unclear goals. For example, this can occur when a coachee is contemplating changing career but literally has no idea what direction to take. In this case 'P' can represent 'Purpose of coaching'. Usually more time is spent on exploration of the issues, concerns and strengths instead of overly focusing on developing coach-driven (and somewhat forced) goals prematurely. However, with other coachees it becomes clear in the first session that options and outcomes can be focused on. That is when the 'P' in PRACTICE can represent 'Preferred options' or 'Preferred Outcome' instead of 'Problem identification'.

For a fuller explanation of the solution-focused coaching approach, see Green and Grant (2003), Jackson and McKergow (2007), O'Connell and Palmer (2007), Palmer, Grant, and O'Connell (2007) and the cognitive behavioural approach, see Palmer and Burton (1996), Neenan and Dryden (2002), and Palmer and Szymanska (2007).

CONCLUSION

The PRACTICE model is continuing to develop often reflecting the needs of the coachee and sometimes the coaching orientation of the coach or coaching psychologist. More recently it has been adapted to different languages and cultures (e.g. Dias et al., 2011). In summary, the PRACTICE model is a solution-focused and cognitive behavioural approach depending upon how it is applied by the practitioner.

REFERENCES

Dias, G., Gandos, L., Nardi, A.E. & Palmer, S. (2011). Towards the practice of coaching and coaching psychology in Brazil: The adaptation of the PRACTICE model to the Portuguese language. *Coaching Psychology International*, 4(1), 10–14.

D'Zurilla, T.J. (1986). *Problem-solving therapy: A social competence approach to clinical intervention.* New York: Springer.

D'Zurilla, T.J. & Goldfried, M.R. (1971). Problem solving and behaviour modification. *Journal of Abnormal Psychology, 78,* 107–126.

D'Zurilla, T.J. & Nezu, A. (1999). *Problem-solving therapy* (2nd ed.). New York: Springer.

Greene, J. & Grant, A.M. (2003). *Solution-focused coaching.* Harlow, UK: Pearson Education.

Jackson, P.Z. & McKergow, M. (2007). *The solutions focus: Making coaching and change SIMPLE* (2nd ed.). London: Nicholas Brealey.

Libri, V. (2004). Beyond GROW: In search of acronyms and coaching models. *The International Journal of Mentoring and Coaching, II*(1), July.

Neenan, M. & Palmer, S. (2001a). Cognitive behavioural coaching. *Stress News, 13*(3), 15–18.

Neenan, M. & Palmer, S. (2001b). Rational emotive behaviour coaching. *Rational Emotive Behaviour Therapist, 9*(1), 34–41.

Neenan, M. & Dryden, W. (2002). *Life coaching: A cognitive-behavioural approach.* Hove: Brunner-Routledge.

O'Connell, B. (2003). Introduction to the solution-focused approach. In B. O'Connell & S. Palmer (Eds.), *Handbook of solution-focused therapy.* London: Sage.

O'Connell, B. & Palmer, S. (2007). Solution-focused coaching. In S. Palmer & A. Whybrow (Eds.), *Handbook of coaching psychology: A guide for practitioners.* London: Routledge.

Palmer, S. & Burton, T. (1996). *Dealing with people problems at work.* Maidenhead: McGraw-Hill.

Palmer, S. (1997a). Problem-focused stress counselling and stress management training: An intrinsically brief integrative approach. Part 1. *Stress News, 9*(2), 7–12.

Palmer, S. (1997b). Problem-focused stress counselling and stress management training: An intrinsically brief integrative approach. Part 2. *Stress News, 9*(3), 6–10.

Palmer, S. (2002). Cognitive and organisational models of stress that are suitable for use within workplace stress management/prevention coaching, training and counselling settings. *The Rational Emotive Behaviour Therapist, 10*(1), 15–21.

Palmer, S. (2007a). Cognitive coaching in the business world. Invited inaugural lecture of the Swedish Centre of Work-Based Learning, held in Gothenburg on 8 February.

Palmer, S. (2007b). PRACTICE: A model suitable for coaching, counselling, psychotherapy and stress management. *The Coaching Psychologist, 3*(2), 71–77.

Palmer, S. (2008). The PRACTICE model of coaching: Towards a solution-focused approach. *Coaching Psychology International, 1*(1), 4–8.

Palmer, S. & Szymanska, K. (2007). Cognitive behavioural coaching: An integrative approach. In S. Palmer & A. Whybrow (Eds.), *Handbook of coaching psychology: A guide for practitioners.* London: Routledge.

Palmer, S., Grant, A. & O'Connell, B. (2007). Solution-focused coaching: Lost and Found. *Coaching at Work, 2*(4), 22–29.

Wasik, B. (1984). *Teaching parents effective problem-solving: A handbook for professionals.* Unpublished manuscript. Chapel Hill, NC: University of North Carolina.

Williams, H., Palmer, S. & Wallace, E. (2011). An integrative coaching approach for family business. In M. Shams & D.A. Lane (Eds.), *Coaching in the family-owned business: A path to growth* (pp.21–39). London: Karnac Books.

Section 9
Mindfulness

Introduction

David Tee & Jonathan Passmore

In this section, we explore a series of papers based in the mindfulness tradition written by Jonathan Passmore. In this brief introduction, we will review the nature of mindfulness, its role in coaching and finally review the five papers in this section.

Let us start by exploring what we mean by the term 'mindfulness' (PP) and the development of 'mindfulness coaching' as a distinctive approach. The term 'mindfulness' is derived from a translation of the term "Sati". Sati combines aspects of "awareness", "attention" and "remembering", which are conducted with non-judgement, acceptance, kindness and friendliness to oneself and others. The practice dates back over 2500 years, with a long tradition of debate and discussion about the approach. The popularisation of mindfulness in the West since the 1990s has seen a growth in the academic debate about the nature and boundaries of the practice. Bhikkhu (1998) suggests that, at its most simple, mindfulness can be considered to be "reflective awareness" (p. 47). Michael Chaskalson (2014), a writer and practitioner, suggests mindfulness is "the quality of awareness that comes from paying attention to yourself, others and the world around you" (p. 6). However, possibly the most widely accepted definition has been offered by Jon Kabat-Zinn (1991), who suggests it is a way of paying attention on purpose in the present moment and non-judgementally: "Mindfulness is simply a practical way to be more in touch with the fullness of your being through a systematic process of self-observation, self-inquiry and mindful action. There is nothing cold, analytical or unfeeling about it. The overall tenor of mindfulness practices gentle, appreciative, and nurturing" (p. 13). The debate continues in academic circles and, while some attempts have been made to build an operational definition which could assist a more focused research into the practice, there remains a lack of agreed formal definition (Lutz et al., 2015).

Coaching Practiced, First Edition. Edited by David Tee and Jonathan Passmore.
© 2022 John Wiley & Sons Ltd. Published 2022 by John Wiley & Sons Ltd.
DOI: 10.1002/9781119835714.s09

When we start considering the application of mindfulness to coaching, we can trace this back to Passmore and Marianetti's paper (Passmore & Marianetti, 2007), which started to explore the potential for mindfulness as a tool to enhance their own coaching practice. Both writers were practising coaches, with separate mindfulness practices, and discussed four ways mindfulness could be used in service of their coaching clients. These included preparing for coaching sessions to centre oneself, maintaining focus in a session to manage the wandering mind, remaining emotionally detached during periods of high emotional content in a session and sharing this practice with clients to start developing their own mindfulness practice. These ideas were subsequently developed in a second conceptual paper (Passmore, 2016a).

Since then, a number of writers have taken up these ideas (Chaskalson & McMordie, 2019; Hall, 2013; Spence, 2017, 2019). Each has helped to both build the links between mindfulness research, which has exploded since 2010, and coaching research, which has seen a similar shift towards a greater interest in evidence-based practice, in part thanks to journals such as International Coaching Psychology Review and The Coaching Psychologist.

Unlike therapy, coaching has yet to adopt a specific manualised approach, such as Mindfulness-based cognitive therapy (MBCT). In some respects, this reflects the more eclectic and unregulated nature of coaching, with its diverse range of clients, presenting issues and challenges. In contrast, MBCT has become a popular and efficacious approach, suited to clients with depression and cognitive distortions.

This does not mean there is no place for mindfulness in coaching but, instead, coaching psychologists need to think more clearly as to why a specific approach or tool might be useful for their client and how this fits with their wider case conceptualisation. The provision of coaching tools drawn from mindfulness provides a flexibility, allowing coaches to select tools which may be helpful to their clients or a specific issue within a wider series of interventions.

The first tool concerns *identifying mindfulness distractions* (Passmore, 2016b). The technique involves encouraging the client to, as part of their homework, schedule a reminder on their phone or similar device. The reminder is a trigger to pause and engage in a short breathing mediation. During the three minutes of breathing, the aim is to bring the focus to the present moment and being, in contrast with the rush of always doing.

The second tool, *STOP* (Passmore, 2017), again is a homework task to share with clients which creates a break in the day, encouraging the client to refocus on priorities through making informed choices about what is important as opposed to what is simply urgent.

The third tool, *Choosing our attitude* (Passmore, 2018a), aims to encourage clients to create reflective moments in their day, to check in with themselves, how they are feeling and, from this, check in then choose an attitude which would facilitate the thoughts and emotions to enable them to more productively move forward.

The fourth tool in the MI set is entitled *Being the observer* (Passmore, 2018b), and has similarities with ACT and Meta-cognitive Therapy, in that it invites the client not to simply look at their thoughts and dispute them in a traditional CBC approach, but to move beyond the content and examine their thinking process from outside. The client seeks to recognise their thoughts as separate from them, disassociating from the thoughts in much the way one might do when using the techniques of 'Passengers on a bus', or 'Leaves on a stream' (Passmore et al., 2021). By drawing on mindfulness, the client is encouraged to step into the present moment and observe their thought processes from the outside, recognising they are not their thoughts, but these thoughts are transitory, passing and separate from who they are as an individual.

The final paper in this set is by Arthur Turner (2017) who explores the role walking can play in coaching practice, offering a reflective space for the client in a similar way to mindfulness. Turner notes the links between walking coaching and how other writers have used such experiences for deep reflection and the development of new insights both about themselves and about challenges they face. Turner's paper is possibly the first to have signalled the potential in this space which, in turn, has led to growing interest from both research and practice in eco-outdoors coaching and the potential contribution of blue-green spaces to wellbeing (Burn & Watson, 2021).

REFERENCES

Bhikkhu, B. (1998). *Mindfulness with breathing: A manual for serious beginners* Somerville, MA.

Burn, A., & Watson, A.(2021). Outdoor eco-coaching. In J. Passmore (Ed.), *The coaches handbook: The complete practitioners guide for professional coaches* (pp. 291–300). Routledge.

Chaskalson, M. (2014). *Mindfulness in eight weeks: The revolutionary 8 week plan to clear your mind and calm your life* London.

Chaskalson, M., & McMordie, M. (2019). *Mindfulness for coaching.* Routledge.

Kabat-Zinn, J. (1991). *Full Catastrophe Living: Using the Wisdom of your Body and Mind to Face Stress, Pain, and Illness, Delta Trade Paperbacks.*

Hall, L. (2013). *Mindful coaching: How mindfulness can transform coaching practice.* Kogan Page

Lutz, A., Jha, A. P., Dunne, J. D., & Saron, C. D. (2015). Investigating the phenomenological matrix of mindfulness-related practice from a neurocognitive perspective, *American Psychologist, 70*(7). 632–658.

Passmore, J., & Marianetti, O. (2007). The role of mindfulness in coaching, *The Coaching Psychologist, 3*(3), 131–138.

Passmore, J. (2016a). Mindfulness in coaching: A model for practice. *The Coaching Psychologist, 13*(1), 27–30.

Passmore, J. (2016b). Identifying mindfulness distractions. *The Coaching Psychologist, 13*(1), 31–33.

Passmore, J. (2017). Mindfulness in coaching: STOP. *The Coaching Psychologist, 13*(2), 86–88.

Passmore, J. (2018a). Choosing our attitude. *The Coaching Psychologist, 14*(1), 48–49

Passmore, J. (2018b). Being the observer, *The Coaching Psychologist, 13*(1).

Passmore, J., Day, C., Flower, J., Grieve, M., & Moon, J. (2021). *WeCoach: The complete handbook of tools, techniques, experiments and frameworks for personal and team development.* Libri Press.

Spence, G. B. (2017). Mindfulness at work, pp. 110–131. In: L. G. Oades, M. F. Steger, A. Delle Fave, and J. Passmore (Eds.), *The Wiley-Blackwell Handbook of the Psychology of Positivity and Strengths-Based Approaches at Work*. Wiley-Blackwell.

Spence, G. (2019). Mindfulness coaching: A self-determination theory perspective. In S. Palmer, & A. Whybrow, (Eds.), *Handbook of Coaching Psychology: A guide for practitioners* (2nd ed., pp. 195–205. Routledge.

Turner, A. (2017). Coaching through walking. *The Coaching Psychologist, 13*(2) 80–85

33 The role of mindfulness in coaching

Jonathan Passmore & Oberdan Marianetti

Abstract

In this article we explore the concept of mindfulness as a tool for helping both coaches and coachees. We argue that the coaching practice of the coach can be enhanced through using mindfulness as a preparation tool. We highlight research evidence on the impact of mindfulness in managing stress and contributing towards improved performance. We argue that coachees too can benefit when the coach shares these techniques with the coachee.

Keywords

Coaching psychology; Roger's necessary and sufficient conditions; mindfulness; meditation; emotional detachment; performance at work; focus; managing stress; managing emotions and breathing.

The challenge of developing and maintaining focus is one which has been raised in the coaching and counselling literature (Passmore, 2007a & 2007b). The coach can often see a number of coachees during the course of a day and need to balance these demands with the many other demands of a consultant psychologist. The recent BBC TV comedy series, *Help*, joked about the therapist thinking about his shopping list as he nodded and pretended to listen to his client. As this sketch suggests we often

Original publication details: Passmore, J., & Marianetti, O. (2007, December). The role of mindfulness in coaching. *The Coaching Psychologist, 3*(3), 131–137. Reproduced with permission of The British Psychological Society.

struggle to maintain the single-minded focus which our friends and clients deserve. So how do we improve our focused attention on our coachees during coaching meetings? How do we manage the emotions which we feel, left over from the day before or the meeting before? How do we try to manage the emotions aroused during our coaching session?

This article explores the role of mindfulness in coaching, as a tool to help the coach both develop and maintain focus within the coaching session, and as a technique to manage emotional detachment. It also suggests ways in which the coach could usefully teach mindfulness to coachees as a way of developing resilience and as a tool for managing stress.

WHAT IS MINDFULNESS?

It's not that mindfulness is the 'answer' to all life's problems. Rather, it is that all life's problems can be seen more clearly through the lens of a clear mind. (Kabat-Zinn, 1990, p.25)

Mindfulness is a practice that has long been proven to increase well-being among medical patients and healthy individuals (Shapiro et al., 1998; Kabat-Zinn, 1990). It is a practice with its roots in Buddhist and other meditative traditions, which teaches the art of 'nondoing' to facilitate absorbing reality 'as is' (Kabat-Zinn, 1990). Mindfulness cultivates conscious attention and awareness of the moment in a non-judgemental way.

We assume we know and understand the world that surrounds us. However, this is purely an illusion! On average we can process five to nine items of the several million stimuli that surround us at any one point in time (Miller, 1956). This creates a limited picture of the world that we mistake for reality. Mindfulness provides a break from the limitations of our mental models and promotes a form of pure exploration, a way of investigating reality that challenges our sense of safety derived by the illusion and the safety of 'knowing'. Mindfulness is a window on reality, a channel to the realisation and acceptance of the 'not-knowing', a lens that shows the world 'as is'.

Mindfulness can be learnt and cultivated by anybody through practice and dedication. Research shows that it is composed by at least four elements: awareness, attention (Brown & Ryan, 2003), time (Kabat-Zinn, 1990) and acceptance (Gunaratana, 1993). Awareness is the brain's ability to constantly monitor and recognise internal and external systems and stimuli. Attention is the brain's ability to focus the awareness to a specific phenomenon and so increasing the sensitivity to it. Time refers to 'the now'; the only place where we exist, experience and act. Acceptance represents our ability to let-go and to be non-judgemental; our ability to observe and absorb reality 'as is', without embarrassment, satisfaction or disappointment.

Mindfulness can contribute towards increasing our ability to live a fuller life by allowing us to own our lives moment by moment, as they unfold, in joy or in pain, in our relationships with others and ourselves, in our private and professional lives.

LINKS TO OTHER FRAMEWORKS AND APPROACHES

Coaching and counselling share a great overlap both in their underlying theories and the skills used, there are however some important distinctions. A number of approaches draw on the principles of mindfulness, including the work of Carl Rogers and Fritz Perls.

Central to Carl Rogers' humanistic approach were the concepts of Congruence and Empathic understanding (Rogers, 1961). Congruence is a way for the therapist (read: coach) to be true to themselves. Rogers suggests that during this state 'the feelings the therapist is experiencing are available to him, available to his awareness, and he is able to live these feelings, be them, and able to communicate them if appropriate' (p.61). It is apparent from this quote how central mindfulness is to this concept. Through congruence the coach facilitates psychological growth and provides the environment in which the client can flourish.

Empathy is often described as the ability to 'put oneself into somebody else's shoes'. This implies that a person who is empathic is able to 'step-out' of their own reality and match the one of their interlocutor. Mindfulness is yet again at the centre of this process. Being empathic creates a support structure necessary for the client to feel the presence, the support and the understanding of the coach. Being empathic also focuses the attention of the coach on the client's needs and away from their own perception of them. One of us (Passmore, 2007a) has argued that Rogers' necessary and sufficient conditions are central in developing an effective working relationship between the coach and coachee.

Gestalt is centred on the empathic, moment by moment exploration of the issues as they are raised by the coachee. Bentley has highlighted the value Presence, Phenomenology and Experiment have in developing the coaching relationship (Bentley, 2006). These concepts are key to a successful relationship and central to mindfulness. Presence, similar to Rogers' congruence, refers to the ability to focus attention on the client so to respond as authentically as possible to their needs. The 'Here and Now', and 'Next' refers to the exploration of the past and the future to inform us on ways to integrate learning in the present, the time when both are alive at the same time. 'Phenomenology' is about all that is happening in the session, the observable and the unobservable, both of which can prove very relevant to the development. Sharing what one sees may provide a fresh view and a learning opportunity for both parties. Finally, it is through 'Experiment' that the coachee is able to venture into unknown territory, away from their comfort zone and into their learning one. The coach at this stage can be creative and present novel ways to do things in a safe environment.

Presence, Here and Now, and Next, Phenomenology and Experiment all borrow and benefit from a mindful approach. Mindfulness liberates the mind from the constraint of our mental models, it fosters our ability to 'think out of the box' and of the 'not-knowing'; it stimulates creativity (Carrington et al., 1980) and allow us to pay attention 'on purpose, in the present moment and non-judgementally' (Kabat-Zinn, 1994, p.4).

Another central concept to the Gestalt approach to coaching is that of Context. Everything we are involved in as people and as coaches or coachees is heavily dependent and influenced by the context within which it happens. It is important that the coach approaches every session as a new session and not as a continuation of what has been. The coachee, the coach and their relationship constantly develop, it would be easy to become stuck in our perception of reality. Through mindfulness the coach is able to detach from what has taken place so far and enter the session with fresh eyes and a free mind. Only then the worlds of the coach and the coachee can meet and create a context that promotes change and development.

Mindfulness could be part of our daily lives and certainly of the coaching relationship. A state of mind that is present and non-judgemental shows the world as it actually is. This lessens the scope of the problem and increases the power of our resources, allowing for a path to growth and development.

MINDFULNESS RESEARCH

When you feel physically and mentally disturbed, the best thing you can do is to let go, relax, and still the wheels of your thought processes. Talk to your subconscious mind. Tell it to take over in peace, harmony, and divine order. You will find that all the functions of your body will become normal again. (Murphy, 2000, p.42)

Mindfulness research has focused broadly on the fields of health and well-being. Its application has proven very effective in the reduction of stress, pain, anxiety and depression, but its overall positive impact proves effective even for healthy individuals (Shapiro et al., 1998; Kabat-Zinn, 1990).

The following research-review presents some evidence about the positive influences that mindfulness brings at a psychological, physiological and behavioural level.

Stress can be defined in several ways. One widely-accepted model is the Lazarus and Folkman's Transactional Model (1984). Stress is seen in this model as the interaction between the environment and the individual as moderated by their appraisal, acceptance and coping strategies. As stated earlier, awareness and acceptance are also central concepts to mindfulness; this is what makes it so effective in reducing our perceived levels of stress. Mindfulness influences directly our ability to appraise the events and to interpret them for what they are. This allows us to gain a somewhat more objective view of the events and retain higher control of our response.

The concept of mindfulness can now be found in the corporate, medical, counselling and recreational worlds, with organisations training their staff in both the potential benefits and key techniques, as a way of managing conflict and stress in the workplace.

In a study with Motorola, Barrios-Choplin et al. (1997) found that in addition to physiological benefits, contentment, job satisfaction, and communication significantly increased after mindfulness training, while tension, anxiety, nervousness, and physical symptoms of stress significantly decreased.

Other constructs, such as control (Geer et al., 1970), creativity, burnout (Langer et al., 1988), productivity, attentional processes and learning (Langer & Piper, 1987) have all been shown to be positively influenced by mindfulness.

Research into individuals' health locus of control, state anxiety and mental adjustment found positive results in cancer sufferers who had been trained in the practice of mindfulness (Tacon et al., 2004). Other studies into the effects of cardiac coherence also provide supporting evidence for its positive effects on well being. Cardiac coherence is a technique aimed at regulating the heart beat and draws deeply from mindfulness practice.

It has been demonstrated to positively affect brain faculties (Watkins, 2002) and other physiological and psychological functions; blood pressure, cortisol levels and IgA levels are among some of them.

Blood pressure was significantly lowered in a study of 38 hypertensive employees within a large corporation, over a period of 3 months (McCraty, 2003) and in a study of 27 employees from Motorola, where a reduction in sympathetic nervous activity was also found (Barrios-Choplin et al., 1997). Cortisol levels and their relationship to stress were lowered by 23 per cent and confirmed in two other studies (McCraty et al., 1998; Kirschbaum et al., 1996); and IgA levels increased as a consequence of mindfulness practices, while recollecting positive memories (Rein & McCraty, 1995).

Brain structures and functioning seems to also be affected by mindfulness. In a mindfulness-based, randomised, controlled study within a high-stress biotechnology corporation, Davidson and colleagues (2003) demonstrated an increase of left-side, anterior activation in the brain, previously associated to feelings of happiness and dispositional positive affect (Davidson, 1992; Davidson et al., 1990). This study demonstrated a shift in brain activity from right to left hemisphere, which influenced the ability to feel happier, in contrast with previous beliefs that 'trying to be happier is like trying to be taller' (Lykken, 1999).

From a more general perspective, Rosenzweig and colleagues (2003) demonstrated that mindfulness can be an effective stress management intervention. They measured mood disturbance among medical students and assigned a group to mindfulness training and another to a wait-list control group. They found significantly lower mood disturbance scores in the experimental group as compared to the controls.

This evidence indicates some of the profound benefits that mindfulness practice can have on individuals. Research has shown that mindfulness can be developed through practice (Brown & Ryan, 2003).

Given the above, it would seem that mindfulness could be a useful element of coaching practice.

USING MINDFULNESS TECHNIQUES TO AID YOUR COACHING PRACTICE

Mindfulness can be applied to coaching in a variety of ways. The relationship between the two concepts can be explored from several angles: the coach, the coachee and their relationship.

As individuals, both the coach and the coachee can benefit from mindfulness by practicing it in their daily lives, which, given the research data, suggests that this will contribute to a less stressed and happier experience of life. There are, however, other areas to incorporate mindfulness in the coaching relationship.

Effective coaching requires the coach to offer each coachee their full focus and attention. This is not always easy when our personal and professional lives have blurred boundaries and the pressures of the two merge into a mix of worries and confusion. Mindfulness provides an answer; it focuses our attention to the only moment that 'is'. Here, a much narrower range of options are available and our resources all of a sudden look adequate to deal with the situation; we can 'be' with our coachee.

The experience for the coachee is not dissimilar. They too are caught in the vortex of their own pressures and anxieties and are likely to carry unhelpful baggage that holds back progress in the coaching session. Mindfulness can provide them the opportunity to focus their attention to the session and to their learning, effectively providing the ground for personal development and self-actualisation.

Whether the coach and the coachee choose to include mindfulness in their own individual benefits, their relationship can certainly become more effective because of it.

We suggest four specific uses: preparing for coaching, maintaining focus in the session, remaining emotionally detached, and teaching mindfulness techniques to the coachee.

(i) Preparing for coaching

From our personal experiences as coaches, we often rush from one meeting or coaching session to another. Our focus can sometimes be more on ensuring we get to the session on time, or arrive at the right place, without allowing enough time for ourselves to leave behind the thoughts, pressures and anxieties of the day. Mindfulness offers a technique to place these demands aside. One of us (Passmore) uses a four-minute mindfulness meditation to help centre themselves before each coaching session. This four-minute meditation involves a series of breathing exercises accompanied by a body-scan to check the bodily sensations being experienced. This is followed by a more practical review of the notes from the previous meeting and planning what the coming session might focus on.

(ii) Maintaining focus in the session

The second potential practical application is in helping the coach to remain focused during the session. We drew attention to the comedy sketch from Help in which the counsellor's mind wandered during his counselling sessions. As coaches we face the same challenge of a wandering mind. Mindfulness meditations when used between coaching sessions can help improve focus and concentration during two hour sessions. The concept can also be used during coaching sessions through maintaining watchfulness over the mind, and continually bringing it back to focus on the coachee, whenever the mind starts to wander.

(iii) Remaining emotionally detached

Mindfulness can be used to help us manage our changing moods and emotions during a coaching session. As a coach, remaining emotionally detached is a key skill. The coach needs to both experience the emotions being felt by their coachee, but not to be flooded by them to the point where these emotions prevent the coach helping the coachee to move forward. Flooding has occurred when the coach finds themselves crying at the news of their coachee's dismissal, or when the coach over identifies with the experiences of their coachee to the point where they feel anger towards the coachee's boss or another adversary.

Mindfulness can help the coach manage the conflicting emotions within coaching, for example, balancing empathy while simultaneously providing constructive challenge.

(iv) Teaching mindfulness to coachees

Mindfulness can be taught formally, as meditative practice, or informally, as an everyday tool. The coach may choose to engage in the formal or informal teaching depending on their clients' needs and experience, however, it is important that they have direct, on-going experience with mindfulness practice. While learning, clients will experience difficulties and addressing them from a logical, intellectual perspective is not possible. As Segal et al. (2002) say: 'A swimming instructor is not someone who knows the physics of how solids behave in liquids, but he or she knows how to swim'. Only through their own practice and understanding will the coach be able to guide their client.

Segal and colleagues also provide suggestions on the skills that should be included in mindfulness teachings:

– Concentration: this is central to mindfulness and represents the ability to focus one's full attention on one object or activity;
– Awareness: the conscious knowledge that life is 'as is';
– Acceptance: awareness of life is not sufficient, one must accept it and let go;

- Decentering: the client's ability to see thoughts just as thoughts and not as truths;
- 'being' rather than 'doing': 'doing' means eating the raisin; 'being' means eating the raisin and experiencing its taste and the feelings this elicits.

Mindfulness is not simply a skill, but becomes a way of being as it develops.

SUMMARY

In this paper we have shown the nature and research evidence behind a previously discussed but little published area of coaching practice. The evidence suggests that mindfulness can offer benefits both in terms of stress management but also in happiness and focus within our daily lives and in our coaching practice. We have also highlighted ways in which the coaching psychologist can draw on this research to begin to make use of the concept of mindfulness in their coaching practice to enhance their focused attention as well as to contribute towards overall performance improvement.

REFERENCES

Barrios-Choplin, B., McCarty, R. & Cryer, B. (1997). An inner quality approach to reducing stress and improving physical and emotional well-being at work. *Stress Medicine*, *13*(3), 193–201.

Bentley, T. (2006). *The art of executive coaching – A Gestalt approach*. Unpublished paper.

Brown, K.W. & Ryan, R.M. (2003). The benefits of being present: Mindfulness and its role in psychological well-being. *Journal of Personality and Social Psychology*, *84*(4), 822–848.

Carrington, P., Collings, G.H., Benson, H., Robinson, H., Wood, L.W., Lehrer, P.M., Woolfolk, R.L. & Cole, J. (1980). The use of meditation-relaxation techniques for the management of stress in a working population. *Journal of Occupational Medicine*, *22*(4), 221–231.

Davidson, R.J., Ekman, P., Sharon, C., Senulis, J. & Friesen, W.V. (1990). Approach withdrawal and cerebral symmetry: Emotional expression and brain physiology. *Journal of Personality and Social Psychology*, *58*, 330–341.

Davidson, R.J. (1992). Emotion and affective style: Hemispheric substrates. *Psychological Science*, *3*, 39–43.

Davidson, R.J. *et al.* (2003). Alterations in brain and immune function produced by mindfulness meditation. *Psychosomatic Medicine*, *65*(4), 564–570.

Geer, J.H., Davison, G.C. & Gatchel, R. (1970). Reduction of stress in humans through no-veridical perceived control of aversive stimuli. *Journal of Personality and Social Psychology*, *16*, 731–738.

Gunaratana, B.H. (2002). *Mindfulness in plain English*. Wisdom Publications.

Hawkins, P. & Smith, N. (2006). *Coaching, mentoring and organisational consulting*. Buckingham: Open University Press.

Kabat-Zinn, J. (1990). *Full catastrophe living. How to cope with stress, pain and illness using mindfulness meditation*. London: Piatkus.

Kabat-Zinn, J. (1994). *Wherever you go, there you are: Mindfulness meditation in everyday life*. New York: Hyperion.

Kirschbaum, C., Wolf, O.T. & May, M. (1996). Stress and treatment-induced elevations of cortisol levels associated with impaired declarative memory in healthy adults. *Life Sciences, 58*(17), 1475–1483.

Langer, E.J. & Piper, A. (1987). The prevention of mindlessness. *Journal of Personality and Social Psychology, 53*, 280–287.

Langer, E.J., Hefferman, D. & Kiester, M. (1988). *Reducing burnout in an institutional setting: An experimental investigation*. Unpublished manuscript. Cambridge, MA: Harvard University.

Lazarus, R.S. & Folkman, S. (1984). *Stress, appraisal and coping*. New York: Springer.

Lykken, D. (1999). *Happiness: What studies on twins show us about nature, nurture, and the happiness set-point*. New York: Golden Books.

McCraty, R.M., Barrios-Choplin, B., Rozman, D., Atkinson, M. & Watkins, A.D. (1998). The impact of a new emotional self-management programme on stress, emotions, heart rate variability, DHEA and cortisol. *Integrative Psychological and Behavioural Science, 33*(2), 151–170.

McCraty, R.M. (2003). Impact of a workplace stress reduction programme on blood pressure and emotional health in hypertensive employees. *Journal of Alternative and Complementary Medicine, 9*(3), 355–369.

Miller, G.A. (1956). The magical number seven, plus or minus two. *Psychology Review, 63*, 81–87.

Murphy, J. (2000). *The power of your subconscious mind*. London: Prentice Hall.

Passmore, J. (2007a). An integrative model for executive coaching. *Consulting Psychology Journal: Practice and Research, 59*(1), 68–78.

Passmore, J. (2007b). *Executive coaching*. Unpublished thesis. University of East London.

Rein, G. & McCraty, R.M. (1995). Effects of positive and negative emotions on salivary IgA. *Journal for the Advancement of Medicine, 8*(2), 87–105

Rogers, C.R. (1961). *On becoming a person. A therapist's view of psychology*. London: Constable.

Rosenzweig, S., Reibel, D.K., Greeson, J.M. & Brainard, G.C. (2003). Mindfulness-based stress reduction lowers psychological distress in medical students. *Teaching and Learning in Medicine, 15*(2), 88–92.

Segal, Z.V., Williams, J.M.G. & Teasdale, J.D. (2002). *Mindfulness-based cognitive therapy for depression*. London: The Guildford Press.

Shapiro, S.L., Schwartz, G.E. & Bonner, G. (1998). Effects of mindfulness-based stress reduction on medical and premedical students. *Journal of Behavioral Medicine, 21*(6), 581–599.

Tacon, A.M., Caldera, Y.M. & Ronaghan, C. (2004). Mindfulness-based stress reduction in women with breast cancer. *Families, Systems and Health, 22*(2), 193–203.

Watkins, A.D. (2002). *Corporate training in heart rate variability: Six weeks and six-months follow-up studies*. London: Hunter-Kane.

34 Mindfulness in coaching: A model for coaching practice

Jonathan Passmore

Abstract

This is the first in a series of papers to look at mindfulness coaching as an approach suitable for use with coaching clients. This paper presents a brief overview of mindfulness for readers who are less familiar with the approach and highlights other sources for a fuller account of mindfulness coaching. The paper sets the scene for a subsequent series of papers. Each of these subsequent techniques papers presents a short description of a technique grounded in mindfulness that can be used with clients or by coaching psychologists to enhance their own presence, resilience and empathy.

Keywords

Coaching, coaching psychology, mindfulness coaching, contemplation, reflection and meditation.

Original publication details: Passmore, J. (2017, June). Mindfulness in coaching: A model for coaching practice. *The Coaching Psychologist*, *13*(1), 27–30. Reproduced with permission of The British Psychological Society.

THE BACKGROUND – MINDFULNESS COACHING

The term mindfulness has its origins in the term 'Sati'. 'Sati' originally means to remember. The term combines remembering with a sense of non-judgemental acceptance, kindness and friendliness.

At a more formal level, a range of writers within the Buddhist tradition have offered definitions of mindfulness over the past 2500 years. Bhikkhu suggested that at its most simple, mindfulness could be considered to be *'reflective awareness'* (Bhikkhu, 1998, p.47).

More recently writers such has Jon Kabat-Zinn, who can be credited with polarising mindfulness in the West, has suggested it is a way of paying attention on purpose, in the present moment using a non-judgemental mind:

> *'Mindfulness is simply a practical way to be more in touch with the fullness of your being through a systematic process of self-observation, self-inquiry and mindful action. There is nothing cold, analytical or unfeeling about it. The overall tenor of mindfulness practices gentle, appreciative, and nurturing'* (Kabat-Zinn, 1991, p.13).

The core idea of awareness has links to other spiritual traditions including Islam, Judaism and Christianity. In Christianity this has been most commonly expressed through 'watching' within the Bible. A call for believers to watch is a theme present throughout Bible teachings. Watching was seen as a hallmark of being a disciple, but has become less talked about within modern Christian practice. Watchfulness involves being full present in the present moment. Through this awareness, Christians believe both the presence of the self and the presence of God becomes more real. For some practicing Christians this is expressed through the practice of contemplative prayer, which in other traditions may be considered to be meditation. This involves a greater focus on being in God's presence than of asking God for a specific outcome.

Lambert (2012) has offered one route for Christians to explore this through a 40-day meditative journey. Others, such as Langer (1997), Chaskalson (2015) and Bhikku (1988) have offered alternative routes within different traditions.

Ellen Langer came up with the term mindfulness independently of its Buddhist and wider spiritual traditions. She was exploring the concept of 'mindlessness' she felt had come to dominate modern life. She felt a switch to a more mindfulness state offered great benefits. In this approach Langer defined mindfulness as:

> *'...characterised by an entrapment in old categories; by automatic behaviour that precludes attending to new signals; and by action that operates from a single perspective'* (Langer, 1997, p.4).

For Langer, mindfulness is the opposite of this state of mindlessness. Mindfulness is the ordinary process of noticing, which involves three categories: *'the continuous creation of new categories; openness to new information and an implicit awareness of more than one perspective'* (Langer, 1997, p.4).

Having used mindfulness over the past decade or more within my coaching practice, I have come to use the following short-hand definition which I share with clients:

> 'Mindfulness is a state of mind that, when cultivated regularly, promotes an inclusive, accepted and authentic experience of the present moment.'

This definition's attraction is the experiential nature of the definition. While mindfulness writers have tended to focus on the process, for leaders and manager in organisations I have found an interest is in what the process can deliver.

Others, like writer Michael Chaskalson have suggested that mindfulness is nothing more than *'the quality of paying attention to yourself, others and the world around you in a certain way'* (Chaskalsen, 2014, p.6).

MINDFULNESS RESEARCH

The past 20 years has seen the quantity and quality of mindfulness research expand as a result of the development of MBSR and MBCT. Jon Kabat-Zinn is widely credited with popularising mindfulness and of the development of Mindfulness Based Stress Reduction (MBSR) course, which has been delivered across the world to thousands of participants, and with multiple RCT studies.

Mindfulness Based Cognitive Therapy (MBCT) was developed from MBSR by Mark Williams, who noticed that participants with depression who completed MBSR experienced significantly higher relapses than those from other groups.

As a result of these programmes multiple studies exist which show how mindfulness contributes to lower levels of stress, depression and burnout (Flook, et al, 2013), increased resilience (Aikens et al., 2014), improved work-life satisfaction (Michel et al., 2014), improved general health (Bazarko et al., 2013), greater self compassion (Flook, et al., 2013) while also helping in emotional detachment for workers in emotionally demanding roles (Krasner et al., 2009).

MINDFULNESS RESOURCES

From its origins more than 2000 years ago, through the work of Langer and Kabat-Zinn, and more recently the excellent work of Michael Chaskalson, there are a host of resources available for psychologists to draw upon. However there remains a gap in the coaching space with few papers exploring the coaching benefits or how coaches might develop their practice through applying mindfulness either for themselves or

Table 1   *Mindfulness coaching – books and chapters.*

Books	Book chapters and articles
Hall, L. (2013). *Mindful coaching: How mindfulness can transform coaching practice.* London: Kogan Page. Lambert, S. (2012). *A book full of spark: A study in Christian mindfulness.* Watford: First Apostle. Spence, G.B. (2008). *New directions in evidencebased coaching: Investigations into the impact of mindfulness training goal attainment and wellbeing.* Saarbrucken, Germany: VDM.	Marianetti, O. & Passmore, J. (2009). Mindfulness at work: Paying attention to enhance wellbeing and performance. In A. Lindley (Ed.) *Oxford handbook of positive psychology and work* (pp.189-200). Oxford: Oxford University Press. Passmore, J. & Marianetti, O. (2007). The role of mindfulness in coaching. *The Coaching Psychologist, 3*(3), 131-138. Spence, G.B. (2017). Mindfulness at work. In L. Oades, M.F. Steger, A. Delle Fave & J. Passmore. *The Wiley Blackwell handbook of the psychology of positivity and strengths-based approaches at work* (pp.110-131). Chichester: Wiley.

Table 2   *Four coaching benefits.*

Benefit for the coach	Benefits for clients
(i) Preparing for coaching for coaching A short body scan can be useful when preparing for a session as a tool to create the mind and create the appropriate mental space for the session to come. **(ii) Maintaining focus during the session** Mindfulness can help the coach observe and capture the wandering mind to remain fully focused through the session on the client and their experience. **(iii) Remaining emotionally detached** Mindfulness can help the coach be more conscious of their own emotional state, not only prior to the session but observing non-judgmentally changes during the session as the coach responses to the clients own changing emotions. Allowing the coach to respond empathetically while also observing these emotions to use these as useful material, where appropriate, for the conversation.	**(iv) Teaching the techniques to clients:** Coaches can draw on their own personal experience of using coaching for the benefits listed in column 1 and share their experiences with clients. What is important is to encourage clients to develop their mindfulness practice as a daily habit or routine, as opposed to a bandage to use in an emergency.

their coaches. Exceptions include Liz Hall's *Mindful Coaching* (2013) and Gordon Spence's work.

In Table 1 I have briefly summarised some of the papers and books available for coaching psychologists interested in this topic.

APPLYING MINDFULNESS TO COACHING PSYCHOLOGY PRACTICE

I have argued elsewhere (Passmore & Marianetti, 2007) that mindfulness can be useful for both the coach and coachee. I believe it offers four core benefits. These can be summarised as: preparing for coaching for coaching, maintaining focus during the session, remaining emotionally detached and sharing these practices with coaches for benefits at work and home. These are summarised in Table 2.

In the following series of technique papers I want to suggest some short prac-tical techniques which can turn the positive feeling many coaching psychologists have for mindfulness in to half a dozen practical tools to use with coaching clients. I hope colleagues will fi nd these useful and be inspired to share their own techniques in future editions of *The Coaching Psychologist*.

REFERENCES

Aikens, K.A., Astin, J., Pelletier, K.R. et al. (2014). Mindfulness goes to work: Impact of an online workplace intervention. *Journal of Occupational and Environmental Medicine, 56*(7), 721–731.

Bazarko, D., Cate, R.A., Azocar, F. & Kreitzer, M.J. (2013). The impact of an innovative mindfulness-based stress reduction program on the health and well-being of nurses employed in a corporate setting. *Journal of Workplace Behavioral Health, 28*(2), 107–133

Buddhadasa Bhikkhu. (1998). *Mindfulness with breathing: A manual for serious beginners*. Boston: Wisdom Publishing.

Chaskalsen, M. (2014). *Mindfulness in eight weeks*. London: Harper Collins.

Flook, L., Goldberg, S.B., Pinger, L., Bonus, K. & Davidson, R.J. (2013). Mindfulness for teachers: A pilot study to assess effects on stress, burnout, and teaching efficacy. *Mind, Brain, and Education, 7*(3), 182–195

Hall, L. (2013). *Mindful coaching: How mindfulness can transform coaching practice*. London: Kogan Page.

Kabat-Zinn, J. (1994). *Full catastrophe living: How to cope with stress, pain and illness using mindfulness meditations*. London, UK: Piatkus.

Krasner, M.S., Epstein, R.M., Beckman, H. et al. (2009). Association of an educational program in mindful communication with burnout, empathy, and attitudes among primary care physicians. *Journal of American Medical Association, 302*(12), 1284–1293.

Langer, E. (1997). *The power of mindful learning*. New York: Addison Wesley.

Lambert, S. (2012). *A book full of spark: A study in Christian mindfulness*. Watford, UK: First Apostle.

Marianetti, O. & Passmore, J. (2009). Mindfulness at work: Paying attention to enhance wellbeing and performance. In A. Lindley (Ed.) *Oxford handbook of positive psychology and work* (pp.189–200). Oxford: Oxford University Press.

Michel, A., Bosch, C. & Rexroth, M. (2014). Mindfulness as a cognitive-emotional segmentation strategy: An intervention promoting work-life balance. *Journal of Occupational and Organizational Psychology*, 87(4), 733–754.

Oades, L., Steger, M.F., Delle Fave, A. & Passmore J. (2017). *The Wiley Blackwell handbook of the psychology of positivity and strengths-based approaches at work*. Chichester: Wiley.

Passmore, J. & Marianetti, O. (2007). The role of mindfulness in coaching. *The Coaching Psychologist*, 3(3), 131–138.

Spence, G.B. (2008). *New directions in evidence-based coaching: investigations into the impact of mindfulness training goal attainment and wellbeing*. Saarbrucken, Germany: VDM.

Spence, G.B. (2017). Mindfulness at work. In L. Oades, M.F. Steger, A. Delle Fave & J. Pass-more. *The Wiley Blackwell handbook of the psychology of positivity and strengths-based approaches at work* (pp.110–131). Chichester: Wiley.

35 Mindfulness in coaching: Identifying environmental distractions

Jonathan Passmore

Abstract

This short article focuses on a specific technique, which can help us manage the environmental distractions that are a constant feature of modern life. The paper offers a short description of the process and when this technique may be helpful within a coaching conversation.

Keywords

Mindfulness coaching; meditation; coaching psychology.

INTRODUCTION

This paper is one of a series of papers focusing on mindfulness techniques that can be used by coaches with their clients. In previous papers we have discussed the nature of mindfulness and the benefits it can offer both coaches and their clients (Passmore &

Original publication details: Passmore, J. (2017, June). Mindfulness in coaching: Identifying environmental distractions. *The Coaching Psychologist, 13*(1), 31–33. Reproduced with permission of The British Psychological Society.

Marianetti, 2007; Marianetti & Passmore, 2007). In this paper the focus is a specific technique. The technique is highly experiential and requires coaches to practice it, as opposed to simply read it. This technique aims to help coachees become more conscious of environmental distractions from work colleagues to digital devices. The paper offers a short and simple mindfulness meditation accompanied by a short journal reflection for the coachee.

IDENTIFYING ENVIRONMENTAL DISTRACTIONS

We live in a world of constant distractions; interruptions from colleagues, mobile calls, emails, texts, tweets and social media sites pushing us the latest updates. Devices ring, ping and vibrate to grab our attention away from what we are doing to this latest communication. The popularity of these devices, and our constant engagement with them provides visible evidence of both their seductive power (Hertel et al., 2017); the nature of the human psychological condition is always seeking the new. A trip to any restaurant, coffee shop or a work meeting will reveal how we seem to prioritise communication with those who are not with us, over those we are with.

Given this challenge, how can we help coachees (and ourselves) to live more in the present moment? The following exercise is a means to help coachees to be more mindful of the environmental distractions. To help clients become more able to reflect on their impact on the present moment and how through this awareness they can become more choiceful (Passmore & Amit, 2017).

The technique involves encouraging the coachee to schedule a reminder, or on their phone, Fitbit or similar device. The reminder is a trigger to pause and engage in a short breathing mediation. Through three minutes of breathing bring the focus to the present. Finally, in closing the meditation to reflect on the environmental distractions which are negatively effecting the day.

Table 1 sets out a step by step guide to the process which could be used with a client or shared with them for use as a homework activity.

CONCLUSION

This technique is short and simple to use. It helps bring coachees' awareness to distraction and encourages a more considered engagement with such distractions. My suggestion, in both introducing the activity to clients and encouraging clients to repeat the activity as a new habit, is to focus on enhancing their personal productivity. When delivered in this way the feedback from coachees suggests this is a simple technique to add which offers real benefit in the same time it takes to walk to and from the water cooler or the washroom.

Table 1   *Exercise – identifying environmental distractions*

This exercise is a suggestion on how we can become clearer about what is disturbing our attention and how this impacts on our level of concentration and our productivity/personal relationships.

This is useful because it:
- Can help us be mindful of distractions that lead to us losing focus on the present
- Promotes self reflection
- Enhances self-awareness and offers the opportunity for self correction.

Here is what you do:
- Decide on a time of day you want to do this exercise
- Schedule this into your day
  ○ Use a smartphone app to remind you to do the exercise, or add a reminder to your calendar for a five minute meeting with yourself
- Set your timer on your phone to count down three minutes
- Take three breaths one after the other. For each breath, Breathe-in and out slowly. As you breath, focus on the sensation in your body created by the in-breath, and the separate sensation created by the out breath.
- Sit in silence for the remaining time
- As you sit in silence, reflect on the last few hours and ask yourself *"What external distractions did I encounter that drew my attention?"*
- Use the remaining two minutes to write some notes in a journal
  ○ You can write about anything you like; how it felt doing the activity, what you reflected on or your personal insights as to what you need to manage in the coming hour or afternoon.

Learning:
Ask yourself: *"Which of these distractions are in my control?"* (For example we can switch off our phones if we choose, or close our office door. However we may be unlikely to be able to stop the drilling from the building site across the street). Focus on what you can control and learn to accept what you can't.

Self-correcting
We cannot always prevent external noise and distractions. But we can bring our attention to our frustration or dis-ease as a result and attend to our inner self.

Is there any proactive action you would like to take to help you reduce distractions that are in your control? (Passmore & Amit, 2017)

REFERENCES

Hertel, G., Stone, D., Johnson, R. & Passmore, J. (2017). The psychology of the internet at work. In G. Hertel, D. Stone, R. Johnson & J. Passmore (eds.). *The Wiley Blackwell handbook of the psychology of the internet at work*. Chichester: Wiley–Blackwell.

Marianetti, O. & Passmore, J. (2009). Mindfulness at work: paying attention to enhance wellbeing and performance. In A. Lindley (ed.) *Oxford handbook of positive psychology and work* (pp.189–200). Oxford: Oxford University Press.

Passmore, J. & Marianetti, O. (2007). The role of mindfulness in coaching. *The Coaching Psychologist*, *3*(3), 131–138.

Passmore, J. & Amit, S. (2017). *Mindfulness at work the practice & science of mindfulness for leaders, coaches and facilitators*. Hauppauge NY: Nova Science Publishers.

36 'Mindfulness in Coaching': STOP

Jonathan Passmore

Abstract

This short article focuses on a specific technique, STOP, which is part of a wider series of papers on Mindfulness Coaching. The paper offers a short description of the process and when this technique may be most helpful within a coaching conversation.

Keywords

Mindfulness coaching; meditation; coaching psychology.

INTRODUCTION

This paper is one of a series of papers focusing on mindfulness techniques that can be used by coaches with their clients (Passmore, 2017). In this paper the focus is on helping coachees to STOP. The paper offers a short and simple mindfulness intervention to encourage coachees to be aware of their actions and refocus towards the most productive actions to complete the task in hand.

Original publication details: Passmore, J. (2017, December). 'Mindfulness in coaching': STOP. *The Coaching Psychologist, 13*(2), 86–87. Reproduced with permission of The British Psychological Society.

CATCHING THE WANDERING MIND

We live in turbulent times. Change is happening at the individual level in organisations, as we adapt to new technologies and cope with almost continuous restructures and reviews. It is also happening at the organisational level, as organisations and national economies try to respond to the forces of globalisation and disruptive technologies.

Technological advances have created a new challenge for managers. Email, Twitter, LinkedIn, Facebook, QQ, Instagram, Whatsapp and QZone create an entire new layer to manage. While social media and digital communications enhance our connection, they also place huge demands on individuals to respond. We can lose our focus, and become distracted by each new email, or flooded by the information from Twitter, our Facebook wall or newsfeeds.

The challenge of the wandering mind is one that has been highlighted by a number of writers including Kabat-Zinn (1994) and Lambert (2012). The wandering mind may

---

Exercise: STOP
This exercise is a suggestion to help us become more proactive by stopping and choosing mindfully how we want to continue with our day. The task takes less than five minutes.

This exercise is useful because it:
- Slows us down to stop and check in.
- Can stop us from being on autopilot
- Helps us be mindful of our present moment.
- Can help us to make informed choices.
- Supports us in holding the mindset we need to achieve the best results.

Here is what you do:
Set a trigger to STOP. This can be any time of day. You may choose to do this whenever you wish, but we often know when our performance declines: that may be a good time to select.
- **Stop** and be still.
- **Take** a few conscious breaths; watch your in-breath and out-breath. As you do this, notice what are you doing. Observe how you are feeling. Be conscious of what you are thinking. But in doing this try to avoid all judgment. Instead observe with acceptance.
- **Options:** Now reflect on your priorities. How will you best achieve this task? What options do you have?
- **Proceed:** Continue with your day. Perhaps this will involve making some changes to your schedule or your attitude.

Learning
Can we be more productive by occasionally 'stopping' and checking in with ourselves? By refocusing we can become more aware of when we are at our best and when to schedule our tasks. We can also become more aware and catch the wandering mind.

be considered a consequence of being human, with our ability to both reflect on past events and explore new possibilities or imagine future states and events. However distracted we become in these worlds, being triggered by external stimuli means we lose focus on the priorities of now. Mindfulness can be an ally in this balancing act, between a need to focus and the value of the curious, wandering mind.

The exercise in this short paper describes a technique to help us manage this balancing act. Like most of the techniques it is one we can use ourselves or share with our clients.

CONCLUSION

This technique is short and simple to use. Using STOP encourages the coachee to stop and be still, to take a few conscious breaths, notice what they are doing or how they are feeling, observe the options available to them and finally to proceed based on their priorities.

REFERENCES

Kabat-Zinn, J. (1994). *Full catastrophe living: How to cope with stress, pain and illness using mindfulness meditations*. London, UK: Piatkus.

Lambert, S. (2012). *A book full of spark: A study in Christian Mindfulness*. Watford, UK: First Apostle.

Passmore, J. (2017). Mindfulness coaching – A model for coaching practice. *The Coaching Psychologist, 13*(1), 27–30.

37 Mindfulness in coaching: Choosing our attitude

Jonathan Passmore

Abstract

This short article focuses on a specific technique: Attitude Choice. The paper offers a short description of the process and when this technique may be most helpful within a coaching conversation. It builds on the previous papers which have briefly reviewed the science and potential for mindfulness approaches in coaching and other techniques.

As a technique paper, I have deliberately kept the discussion short, but for those interested in the wider evidence behind the application of mindfulness, a more detailed review is included in earlier papers, as well as other techniques which can be used alongside attitude choice (Passmore, 20171a, 2017b and 2017c). For a comprehensive review, readers may wish to review Michael Cavanagh and Gordon Spence's critical review of the mindfulness literature (Cavanagh & Spence, 2013).

Keywords

Mindfulness coaching; meditation; coaching psychology.

This paper is one of a series of papers focusing on mindfulness techniques that can be used by coaching psychologists with their clients (Passmore, 2017b, 2017c). The focus in this paper is on helping clients to be more aware of their attitudes through being

Original publication details: Passmore, J. (2018, June). Mindfulness in coaching: Choosing our attitude. *The Coaching Psychologist*, 14(1), 48–49. Reproduced with permission of The British Psychological Society.

EXERCISE: MEDITATION TO ACTIVELY CHOOSE YOUR ATTITUDE

This exercise can be offered to clients as a meditation to help them connect with themselves and to refocus on what is most important to them, helping them reset their intention for their day, or the next part of their day.

We spend time planning our goals and action; what we want to achieve in a day. This exercise for a mindful meditation offers the opportunity for the individual to reflect and prepare how they want to be; their approach or their 'attitude' for the day (or the coming hour).

In undertaking the task it may be helpful for the client to start by making goals, objectives or task explicit, as part of their plan for the day.

The exercise is useful because it:
- Helps the client to prepare and select the appropriate attitude for their task.
- Builds consciousness around their being, helping them recognise that attitude, energy and outcomes are connected, and can be influenced.

Here is what you do:
- Invite the client to take a few slow breaths.
- Encourage them to focus on themselves, being aware of their body, any bodily sensations or tensions (a three-minute body scan can help at this point).
- Now invite the client to ask who they want to be:
  - What values will inform how they engage with others?
  - What assumptions do they wish to hold about others behaviour, or maybe about a specific persons' behaviour?
  - How would they like others to describe their attitude or approach?
  - What attitude can best serve the tasks they need to complete?

---

more mindful. Using this approach should allow the individual to be choiceful in selecting an alterative attitude that will facilitate them in the tasks they are facing during the day ahead.

ATTITUDES AND WORK PRODUCTIVITY

We can all think of a time, whether we are a psychologist, a professional coach or a passenger on the 'Clapham Omnibus', when our attitude has positively contributed to or adversely effected the performance of a demanding task.

The relationship between our cognitions, our behaviour and our emotions is the very essence of psychology, as well as sitting at the centre of cognitive behavioural approaches to behavioural change.

Some have suggested that mindfulness makes similar links between these three aspects of what it is to be human. However it does so by explicitly bringing these aspects in to the conscious awareness of the client. For this reason, mindfulness, and mindful coaching (Hall, 2015) are continuing the wider 'Cognitive Behavioural' tradition, alongside approaches such as Acceptance and Commitment Coaching (Anstiss & Blonna, 2015) and Compassionate Mind Coaching, (Anstiss & Gilbert, 2015). These are collectively creating what could be considered to be a third wave of CBT approaches. These new cognitive behavioural approaches have been shown to be equally effective as other CBT approaches (Hofmann & Asmundson, 2008).

The challenge for coaching psychologists is to help clients bring their awareness to the attitudes they hold. Secondly, to link this attitude to an awareness of how this influences their performance.

CONCLUSION

This technique is short and simple to use, and can be completed in less than five minutes in a coaching conversation. It helps to bring the client's awareness to the fore and invites them to make a conscious choice on the attitude which will enable them to best achieve their task or role. In using this practice with clients, I have found clients often find this technique liberating, allowing them to choose how they think about others or events, and that this choice is within their gift.

REFERENCES

Anstiss, T. & Blonna R. (2015). Acceptance and Commitment Coaching. In J. Passmore (Ed.), *Mastery in Coaching* (pp.253–276). London: Kogan Page.

Anstiss, T. & Gilbert, P. (2015). Compassionate Mind Coaching. In J. Passmore (Ed.), *Mastery in coaching* (pp.225–248). London: Kogan Page.

Cavanagh, M. & Spence, G. (2013). Mindfulness in coaching. In J. Passmore, D. Peterson & T. Freire, *The Wiley Blackwell handbook of the psychology of coaching and mentoring* (pp.112–134). Chichester: Wiley.

Hall, L. (2015). Mindful coaching. In J. Passmore (Ed.), *Mastery in coaching* (pp.191–220), London: Kogan Page.

Hofmann, S.G. & Asmundson, G.J. (2008). Acceptance and mindfulness-based therapy: New wave or old hat? *Clinical Psychology Review, 28*(1), 2–16.

Passmore, J. (2017a). Mindfulness coaching – A model for coaching practice. *The Coaching Psychologist, 13*(1), 27–30.

Passmore, J. (2017b). Mindfulness coaching – The STOP Model. *The Coaching Psychologist, 13*(2), 86–88.

Passmore, J. (2017c). Identifying environmental distractions. *The Coaching Psychologist. 13*(1), 31–33.

38 Mindfulness in coaching: Being the observer

Jonathan Passmore

Abstract

This short paper focuses on a specific technique: 'Being the observer'. The article offers a short description of the process and when this technique may be most helpful within a coaching conversation.

As a technique paper, I have deliberately kept the discussion short, but for those interested in the wider evidence behind the application of mindfulness, a more detailed review is included in earlier articles, as well as other techniques which can be used alongside attitude choice (Passmore, 20171a, 2017b, 2017c, 2018). For a comprehensive review, readers may wish to review Michael Cavanagh and Gordon Spence's critical review of the mindfulness literature (Cavanagh & Spence, 2013).

Keywords

Mindfulness coaching, meditation, coaching psychology.

INTRODUCTION

This article is one of a series of articles focusing on mindfulness techniques that can be used by coaches with their clients. The focus in this paper is on helping clients to observe themselves as they engage with others during their day.

Original publication details: Passmore, J. (2018, December). Mindfulness in coaching: Being the observer. *The Coaching Psychologist, 14*(2), 105–107. Reproduced with permission of The British Psychological Society.

EXERCISE: BE THE OBSERVER

Rumination is a common human trait. It can happen especially when the client is upset about something that has happened or a conversation that went wrong. When the client over identifies with their thinking they can become anxious and stressed. The exercise is aimed to help clients acknowledge that they are not their thoughts, and their thoughts are not the truth.

This is useful because:
- It can create some space between the clients' thoughts and their identity.
- It can help them to spot when and how often they are ruminating.
- It can help them learn a different approach to their thinking, thereby reducing criticism and increasing acceptance.

Here is what you do:
- If a client talks about an issue that has been troubling them, and the thought or anxiety is reoccurring, invite them to notice when this thought occurs.
- When it does occur, suggest they find a quiet space.
- Mute their phone and silence anything that may disturb them.
- Invite them to take 10 minutes for the mindfulness task.
- Invite them to take a few breaths and observe their body as they sit in the chair.
- Invite them to be aware of any sensations in their body, to observe them but not to judge such sensations.
- Next invite them to imagine they are in a movie theatre and are watching their thoughts as if they were viewing a movie.
- Help them to see their thoughts as separate – as opposed to being them – and to simply watch the 'movie'.
- If the movie gets too difficult for the client, they can turn their attention back to their breath.
- If not, after taking a few breaths they should return to the 'movie'.
- Invite them to watch the 'movie' without analysing or judging. If the thought itself is a judgment, to simply notice this and let it be.
- Ask the client whether the 'movie' changed as they have sat with it.
- Ask the client if these thoughts are them or, if there is an alternative 'movie' about the same story which they could 'play', what this alternative movie would be.
- Help them to recognise that our thoughts are not the truth, but a subjective experience.

BEING THE OBSERVER

Much of our life is spent rushing between one task and the next. We can be so engaged in the process that we may rarely take time to observe what is happening around us, or to observe our selves. When things become difficult we can find ourselves worrying about past or future events, ruminating about such events and how we currently are or might be dealing with them.

This exercise is designed to be used with coaching clients to help them observe their behaviour, their thoughts and their feelings. By doing so we are encouraging our clients to become more self-aware. The exercise is particularly useful for clients when they perceive something has gone wrong, or has gone not as they would have liked. By helping our clients to step out from their thought stream, of rumination about a past event, we can help them to take a more objective perspective of the events, observe their own thoughts and feelings, and make choices about thought, feelings and behaviours which may be more helpful.

As with most of these exercises, they can be taught or shared with clients quickly and used as homework or activities between sessions, with the following coaching session used to explore observations, insights and learning.

CONCLUSION

This technique helps to bring clients' awareness to their thoughts, to both gain greater distance from these ruminations and secondly to see that alternative thoughts or interpretations of events are possible. My experiences when using this technique in my own practice is that clients often find three or four different endings to their movies, and these multiple endings help clients develop more effective acceptance of stressful events.

REFERENCES

Cavanagh, M. & Spence, G. (2013). Mindfulness in coaching. In J. Passmore, D. Peterson & T. Freire *The Wiley Blackwell handbook of the psychology of coaching and mentoring* (pp.112–134). Chichester: Wiley.

Passmore, J. (2017a). Mindfulness coaching – A model for coaching practice. *The Coaching Psychologist, 13*(1), 27–30.

Passmore, J. (2017b). Mindfulness coaching – The STOP Model. *The Coaching Psychologist, 13*(2), 86–88.

Passmore, J. (2017c). Identifying environmental distractions. *The Coaching Psychologist, 13*(1), 31–33.

Passmore, J. (2018). Mindfulness coaching – Attitude Change. *The Coaching Psychologist, 15*(1).

39 Coaching through walking

Arthur Turner

Abstract

This article seeks to support innovation and creativity amongst the coaching fraternity.

Although walking-coaching is not entirely new as an approach (Read, 2016), coaching can too often be portrayed as a static event in closed offices or more informal spaces such as cafes. Such approaches can have a psychological dimension such as outlined in Bachkirova (2014) and Spinelli (2014), both of which highlight the ways in which learning can be considered as emergent as humans experience their own ways of being in the moment and in the environment.

Keywords

Walking body existential coaching place creative coaching approaches

INTRODUCTION

This article outlines some of the theoretical approaches to walking (such as the growth in interest in Psychogeography, Richardson, 2015) and the role of the body in leadership or leading (Sinclair, 2011), and the way in which coaching practice can be enhanced by considering embodiment and a different type of access to thinking and reflection through movement rather than a static, face-to-face, process. These ideas are based on the author's practical experience, some initial research and theoretical considerations. Thought is given to ways in which walking can be included in a coach's repertoire as a

Original publication details: Turner, A. (2017, December). Coaching through walking. *The Coaching Psychologist, 13*(2), 80–85. Reproduced with permission of The British Psychological Society.

further tool to develop affective coaching (Bloom, 2004) (as well as mentoring) interrelations and interactions.

Initial research with groups that had carried out this activity made the possibilities of making walking for paired use in development opportunities much clearer. One delegate (Leadership workshop through the University of the West of England, Bristol Council, September 2014) wrote, in feedback, after an hour's walk in pairs as part of a larger group:

> *'Worthwhile exercise, interesting approach to dealing with issues. Great tool for leaders, especially when dealing with contentious, confrontational or uneasy (sic). **Best suited to a one to one basis** [author's emphasis]. Allowed to consider outside my normal thinking in a safe, pragmatic way, whilst still rooted in work. Allows faster relationship building, as a wider range of topics than work were discussed'*

(Feedback was sought at the time of the research and quotation was given on the understanding that it would be used in a more open and wider forum).

The feedback encouraged me to look at walking as a coaching tool as well as one that enhances leadership development practice.

The principles of coaching through walking can be easily adapted for coaches and coachees who use wheelchairs and electric means of mobilising. More careful preparation of a suitable route and discussion with the coachee makes most routes, however short, quite feasible. Notwithstanding the acknowledgment that some people do have impaired mobility and can struggle to move easily from place to place, the technique of coaching through walking can be added to a set of coaching approaches that should be included in a more general programme of coaching.

Coaching, especially one-to-one coaching, is a deeply personal development tool and one that often takes place in a structured process bound by rules of engagement or organisational restraints (Whitmore, 1999). Approaches using just models, such as GROW, are argued to hold sway (Pardey, 2016), potentially giving rise to occasionally perfunctionary delivery by the coach in ways that might seem formulaic and routine. Yet building rapport is well recognised as an essential part of a coaching relationship (Hay, 2007; Rogers, 2012). However, a wide range of approaches (Peltier, 2010) have developed due to either theoretical considerations or to the context of the coaching itself. These approaches can, of course, have markedly different expressions depending on the purpose of the coaching or the internal cultures of the organisation within which the coaching takes place.

THE BENEFITS OF WALKING AS AN APPROACH

Movement and walking can be explained on many different levels. Walking can be seen to be a natural process for bipedal primates and one that takes into account the natural urge and necessity for humans to move between places (Ingold, 2000; Schein, 2010; Solnit, 2002) to be able to fulfil an active life. Walking encompasses a way in which this is easily done. Furthermore, Drake (2017) argues that bodily sensations can be used as a source of knowledge and that coaches could pay more heed to this, both within themselves (Drake, 2014) and their clients. Walking is inextricably linked to thinking and the psychological processes linked to the body and mind as being one (Wolever, 2012). In addition, finding landmarks and features of the landscape is argued to aid thought processes and the creation of ideas: Wattchow and Brown (2011) view this from the view of wildness areas whilst Maitland (2009) walks in the wilderness to experience and to achieve silence in her life. A wider range of professional thinkers (such as MacFarlane, 2007) and poets (such as John Donne, cited in Carey, 2011), link walking with observation and reflection. Furthermore, some philosophers, notably Heidigger (cited in Inwood, 2000), and other academics (Kahneman, 2011), have used walking as a perfect medium for building on ideas and providing opportunities for double-loop learning (Argyris & Schon, 1974). Kahneman (2011), writing from the field of behavioural economics, also advocates the value of walking with someone else in order to generate ideas or solve problems.

The first way in which walking and coaching came to my attention was during a leadership development programme held in the Brecon Beacons, where the outdoor environment was an important intervention design constituent for the client company, with an accompanying expectation that some of the learning would be undertaken outside of the classroom. This programme was also developed with action learning and coaching approaches as constituent parts of the learning, with the skills of listening and questioning being re-emphasised by delegates working in pairs outdoors. Often delegates were asked to walk in pairs for a specific amount of time – between 10 and 15 minutes commonly – with the resultant feedback from these relatively short activities seeming disproportionately detailed compared to the relative simplicity of the task undertaken.

What was noticed was that delegates seemed to enjoy the outdoors (whatever the weather) and that there were things 'going on' in that task that related to ways in which people engage with each other and with their moving and changing environment. In particular, people in pairs seemed to be naturally able to hold a conversation with one another despite the many distractions created by their environment. Hall's (1976) research into proximity helped explain the physical mechanisms in which many of the delegates in various ways managed a mobile conversation, remaining alert to the conversation despite the proximity of many environmental distractions. It struck me that this mobility is rarely considered for many coaching conversations.

Further experimentation occurred when working with groups that were learning about leadership and we were using walking more deliberately now to construct a backdrop to a questioning conversation. In this instance, coaching pairs would take it in turns to question or listening and then engage in some reflective processes whilst still sauntering through the – often wooded – environment.

Whilst suggesting that it is the walking itself that necessarily promotes more effective coaching, creating activity and momentum more generally does allow for an alternative approach on the more static typical coaching session that can lead to better insights into client topics. Using walking in a coaching context can provide a wide range of alternative approaches along the coaching spectrum (Peltier, 2011) which includes working with models or taking a more person-centred approach (Hedman, 2001).

There are a number of ways in which this seems to work:

Figure 1 *Walking and chatting*

Firstly, a walk can provide a small part of the coaching session that has more links to taking a break or a breather, helping to perhaps demarcate the working part of the session from the action or decision-making part.

Secondly, a walk might take the shape of a session that is interspersing movement with thoughtful reflection or deeper conversations between coach and coachee. City parks (Figure 1) are often suitable for this as they usually have safe areas to walk in, plenty of shelter and places to sit. Such variable venues often also have a café area which might lend itself to the more transactional part of the coaching, such as the end action planning or any initial contracting, where books or pens are needed to capture reflective text and formal documentation.

Thirdly, a coaching session might be more deliberately assigned to an outdoor walking scenario, particularly when the coachee is interested in walking, is fi t, or feels that the topics being touched upon need a more private or open space in which to develop the coaching conversation.

Fourthly, there can be a way in which a coaching programme can interspace a possibly more formal office-located coaching conversation with a more informal outdoor-located interaction: this can be articulated through the contracting process as part of the way in which coaching can have variety and difference.

A fifth way is to acknowledge that human conversation can be mediated by objects (Vygotsky, 1997) as the coaching pairs move through their environment (Figure 2). A passageway or journey that leads through varied environments can pick up environmental clues and incite emotions that help to enrich, advance or sustain conversations by fuelling vocabulary, jogging memories and often metaphorically shedding light upon an exposed issue or challenge (Fisher & Ashkanasy, 2000).

Walking attunes the mind to a rhythm, so that thought processes are strengthened: To achieve a state of competition... but not an intellectual. Not a tightening of the

Figure 2   *Paths that lead to undisclosed destinations*

mind but a participation with the whole body breathing and muttering, all senses attuned... Gros (2014, p. 213).

DISCUSSION AND POSSIBLE AREA FOR FUTURE RESEARCH

Coaching through the medium of walking is not meant to replace the more 'sit-down' approaches normally associated with workplace interventions designed to improve performance. My current 'take' on this is that there are strengths in both approaches, as illustrated in Table 1.

Table 1   *Some comparisons between walking and sitting coaching techniques.*

Walking	Sitting
Provides variety	Induces tight focus (no distractions)
Is healthy	Is time efficient
Delightful in good weather	Usually unaffected by weather
Conversation is more natural	Coaching conversation more professional
Note-taking can be restricted and therefore engagement improved	Access to note-taking materials and appropriate forms and written feedback easier on the spot!
Walking is interesting with lots of creative questioning possible as well as the stimulation of passing objects and 'things'.	Aids to creative thinking can become more straightforward to use and less random.

However, walking offers an alternative or complementary approach, even for coaches and coachees with restricted mobility. This approach utilises the role of space, place and pace in learning, as articulated in Heneberry and Turner's (2016) framework for the role of ritual and reflective space in critical action learning.

It is hoped this article will stimulate and encourage coaches to consider the urban and rural world outside closed doors with all its possibilities for encouraging deeper thought and more purposeful action. In addition, there is a recognition that formal research into walking whilst coaching is in its initial phase. Opportunities exist to generate greater understanding of the impact walking sessions may have on both the coachee and the coach; any specific approaches to coaching where this might most effectively be used and what 'best practice' considerations may exist for coaches seeking to integrate this approach into their craft.

REFERENCES

Argyris, C. & Schon, D.A. (1974). *Theory in practice: Increasing professional effectiveness.* San Francisco, CA: Jossey-Bass.

Bachkirova, T. (2014). Psychological development in adulthood and coaching. In E. Cox, T. Bachkirova & D. Clutterbuck (Eds), *The complete handbook of coaching* (pp.132–145). London: Sage Publications Ltd.

Bloom, G.S. (2004). Emotionally Intelligent Principals: Addressing the Affective Demands of Newcomers through One-on-One Coaching. *School Administrator, 61*(6), 14.

Carey, J. (2011). *John Donne: Life, mind and art.* London: Faber & Faber.

Cox, E., Bachkirova, T. & Clutterbuck, D.A. (Eds.). (2014). *The complete handbook of coaching.* London: Sage Publications Ltd.

Drake, D.B. (2014). Three windows of development: A postprofessional perspective on supervision. *International Coaching Psychology Review, 9*(1), 36–48.

Drake, D. (2017). Using the four gateways to tell new stories and make new choices. *The Coaching Psychologist, 13(*1), 22–30.

Fisher, C.D. & Ashkanasy, N.M. (2000). The emerging role of emotions in work life: An introduction. *Journal of Organizational Behavior*, 123–129.

Gros, F. (2014). *A philosophy of walking*. London: Verso Books.

Hall, E.T. (1976). *Beyond culture*. Garden City, CA: Anchor.

Hall, E.T. (1989). *Beyond culture*. Anchor Books.

Hay, J. (2007). *Reflective Practice and Supervision for Coaches*. Maidenhead, Berks: Open University Press.

Hedman, A. (2001). The Person-Centred Approach. In B. Peltier (Ed.) *The psychology of executive coaching: theory and application*. Ann Arbour, MI: Sheridan Books.

Heneberry, P. & Turner, A. (2016). Critical action learning–rituals and reflective spaces. *Action Learning: Research and Practice, 13*(1), 60–68.

Ingold, T. (2000). *The perception of the environment: essays on livelihood, dwelling and skill*. Abingdon, Oxon: Routledge.

Inwood, M.J. (2000). *Heidegger: A very short introduction*. Oxford: Oxford University Press.

Kahneman, D. (2011). *Thinking, fast and slow*. London: Penguin Books.

Macfarlane, R. (2007). *The wild places*. London: Penguin Books.

Macfarlane, R. (2012). *The old ways: A journey on foot*. London: Penguin Books.

Maitland, S. (2009). *A Book of Silence*. London: Granta Publications.

Pardey, D. (2016). *Introducing leadership*. Abingdon, Oxon: Routledge.

Peltier, B. (2011). *The psychology of executive coaching: Theory and application*. Hove, East Sussex: Routledge.

Read, S. (2016). An exploration of the 'walk and talk' coaching session format. *Coaching Psychology International 9*(1), 17–22.

Richardson, T. (2015). The New Psychogeography. In T. Richardon (Ed.), *Walking Inside Out: Contemporary British Psychogeography* (pp.241–254). London: Rowman & Littlefield Ltd.

Rogers, J. (2012). *Coaching skills: A handbook (3rd edn)*. Maidenhead, Berks: Open University Press.

Schein, E.H. (2010). *Organizational culture and leadership*. (4th edn). Jossey-Bass.

Sinclair, A. (2011). Leading with body. In E.L. Jeanes, D. Knights & P.Y. Martin (Eds), *Handbook of gender, work and organization* (pp.117–30). Chichester, West Sussex: John Wiley & Sons, Ltd.

Solnit, R. (2001). *Wanderlust: A History of Walking*. London: Verso.

Spinelli, E. (2014). Existential Coaching. In E. Cox, T. Bachkirova & D. Clutterbuck (Eds), *The complete handbook of coaching* (pp.132–145). London: Sage Publications Ltd.

Turner, Arthur. (2016). Coaching with puppets. *The Coaching Psychologist, 12*(2), 79–82.

Wattchow, B. & Brown, M. (2011). *A pedagogy of place: Outdoor education for a changing world*. Monash University Publishing.

Wolever, R.Q., Bobinet, K.J., McCabe, K., Mackenzie, E.R., Fekete, E., Kusnick, C.A. & Baime, M. (2012). Effective and viable mind-body stress reduction in the workplace: a randomized controlled trial. *Journal of occupational health psychology, 17*(2), 246

Whitmore, J. (1999). Performance coaching: In A. Landale (Ed.), *Gower Handbook of Training and Development* (3rd edn) (pp.252–260). Aldershot, Hants: Gower Publishing Ltd.

Vygotsky, L.S. (1997). *The collected works of LS Vygotsky: Problems of the theory and history of psychology* (Vol. *3*). Springer Science & Business Media.

Section 10
Narrative Coaching

Introduction

David Tee & Jonathan Passmore

If the variety of coaching approaches represented by the techniques and models in this volume are to be placed in a taxonomy, then Whybrow (2021) classifies narrative coaching as a constructivist approach, placing it alongside personal construct psychology and neuro-linguistic programming. Each of these approaches seeks to understand how we as human beings make sense of our own world; specifically, that how we find meaning is socially constructed, to a notable extent shaped by our own histories, families and cultures, and that meaning can therefore be reconstructed. For narrative coaching, Drake (2018) describes this as using a spiralling approach in partnership with the client as they "… release old stories that are no longer working for them and create new stories which enable them to make new decisions" (p. 111).

The specific scope for narrative coaching is a matter of debate amongst its leading contributors. Drake (2015) describes it as an open source, holistic methodology that draws from multiple disciplines beyond psychology, such as literary theory and the humanities. Law (2019a) and Stelter (2016) ask questions about Drake's inclusion of attachment theory, which Stelter states is psychodynamic-oriented and therefore represents essentialist thinking. That ongoing debate aside, there is much that unifies how these different writers conceptualise narrative coaching. Drake (2017), Stelter and Law (2010) have each described narrative coaching as the third generation coaching approach, with each generation being differentiated by the intentional orientation of the coach. They state the first generation featured a problem or goal orientation, the second generation featured a solution orientation and that this third generation was typified by a reflective perspective. Readers will note that Law uses the closing paper in this section to herald the advent of a fourth generation coaching approach.

Coaching Practiced, First Edition. Edited by David Tee and Jonathan Passmore.
© 2022 John Wiley & Sons Ltd. Published 2022 by John Wiley & Sons Ltd.
DOI: 10.1002/9781119835714.s10

Besides stating that storytelling has been a common theme across cultures for at least as long as our species has a recorded history, this approach is explicitly informed by narrative psychology and narrative therapy. For narrative psychology, Drake (2017, p. 295) states this offers insights on how people work with narratives at these four levels:

- *Intentions* (conscious and otherwise) for sharing this story this way in this moment.
- *Identities* (as constructed, lived and imagined) of the person telling the story.
- *Impacts* (on self and others, intended and unintended) of telling this story.
- *Interpretations* (spoken and unspoken) of the telling and impact of this story.

For narrative therapy, Law (2019b) acknowledges the foundational work of Michael White in particular but argues (Law, 2019a) that narrative coaching is more than a transportation of therapeutic techniques for a coaching clientele and that this may set it apart from other coaching approaches.

Narrative coaching is particularly suited to this volume, rather than its sister volume 'Coaching Researched' (Passmore & Tee, 2021), as its leading contributors acknowledge that there is a lack of published research or evidence to date. Only one randomised controlled study (Stelter et al., 2011) is known to have been conducted, with Stelter (2016) calling for further quantitative and qualitative research, particularly within the health and social sectors. Therefore, the current narrative coaching literature is dominated by writing on techniques and approaches, with this section bringing a sample of contemporary papers.

The section starts with a series of four papers from Ho Law, building from an introduction to Narrative Coaching and concluding with a call for the establishment of a new 'fourth generation' coaching practice. Law's first paper is entitled 'An introduction and the first step'. It particularly focuses upon externalising conversations, a core feature of coaching sessions as clients are invited to tell their stories about how they understand their recent experiences, which are then explored with the coach through stages of inquiry.

Law's second paper, 'Two forms of change structures: reauthoring and remembering', advise how we as coaches can develop the key skill of helping link the events of the client's story in sequences that unfold over time according to alternative possible plots. Specifically, the narrative coach may draw their client's attention to any neglected elements: exceptions or unique outcomes that may aid the client in reauthoring their storyline. Remembering moves the client from a passive recollection of the past to considering their life as a 'membered' club, where their life and life skills have been co-generated through the multiple voices of their significant memberships and that this remembering can lead to significant learnings and insights as they reshape their identity.

The third paper, 'Approaches for groups, teams, organisations and community', first details the 'outsider witness' technique. Here, a group member steps out of that group to act as witness to the story of a group participant. They honour and acknowledge the story then, working with the narrative coach's guidance, they re-tell the story, focusing on the elements that resonate with their own experiences. The 'definitional ceremony' technique builds upon this by then adding a second retelling by the initial storyteller and then a third retelling, possibly by the outsider witness or by others.

Law's final paper, 'Redesigning the GROW model as the fourth generation coaching for people and the planet', integrates GROW with narrative coaching. Law's motivation is to honour the legacy of Sir John Whitmore, who did much to popularise the GROW model and was keen to encourage coaching to play a role in addressing the eco-environmental crisis. Law therefore identifies the intentional orientation of the fourth generation coach as transpersonal: working with clients as they seek to find their higher self through the balancing of spiritual aspiration and material success. In doing so, Law's hope is that people will then be better placed to rise to the environmental challenges endangering our planet.

The fifth paper, 'Using the four gateways to tell new stories and make new choices', explores how clients can somatically learn by observing any tendency to focus solely on the rational dimensions of problem-solving, then countering these by speaking to each of the 'four gateways'. David Drake provides prompt questions that the client may wish to ask as they place their hands on Head, Heart, Hara and Hips respectively and enquire as to what these gateways have to say about the client's question. Through this technique, the client is able to make a more holistically informed choice.

The final paper, also from David Drake, focuses on working at thresholds with clients, proclaiming how this 'threshold crossing' may result in more lasting change than problem-solving. Drake explains four possible roles that narrative coaches can play during this process: the witness to the moment, the guardian at the threshold, the advocate for proximal development and the steward of the new narrative. This final role, Drake asserts, may well be our most under-rated value as coaches.

REFERENCES

Drake, D. (2015). *Narrative Coaching*. CNC Press.

Drake, D. (2017). Working with Narratives in Coaching. In T. Bachkirova, G. Spence, & D. Drake (Eds.), *The SAGE Handbook of Coaching* (pp. 291–309). SAGE Publications Ltd.

Drake, D. (2018). Narrative coaching. In E. Cox, T. Bachkirova, & D. Clutterbuck (Eds.), *The complete handbook of coaching* (3rd edn pp. 109–123). SAGE Publications Ltd.

Law, H. (2019a). Narrative Coaching – Part 1: An introduction and the first step. *The Coaching Psychologist*, 15(2), 39–43.

Law, H. (2019b). Narrative coaching for all (adults, children, groups and communities). In S. Palmer, & A. Whybrow (Eds.), *Handbook of Coaching Psychology* (3rd edn pp. 256–269). Routledge.

Stelter, R., & Law, H. (2010). Coaching–narrative–collaborative practice. *International Coaching Psychology Review*, 5(2), 152–164.

Passmore, J., & Tee, D. (Eds.). (2021). *Coaching Researched*. John Wiley & Sons Ltd.

Stelter, R. (2016). Narrative Approaches. In J. Passmore, D. B. Peterson, & T. Freire (Eds.), *The Wiley-Blackwell handbook of the Psychology of Coaching and Mentoring*. John Wiley & Sons Ltd.

Stelter, R., Nielsen, G., & Wikman, J. M. (2011). Narrative-collaborative group coaching develops social capital – A randomised control trial and further implications of the social impact of the intervention. *Coaching: An International Journal of Theory, Research and Practice*, 4(2), 123–137.

Whybrow, A. (2021). Coaching psychology approaches and models: Humanistic, integrative and constructivist. In S. O'Riordan, & S. Palmer (Eds.), *Introduction to Coaching Psychology* Routledge.

40 Narrative coaching – Part 1: An introduction and the first step

Ho Law

Abstract

This paper advocates narrative coaching as the most appropriate approach for the discipline of coaching psychology. It provides discussions on the epistemological lineage and theoretical foundations of the approach and describes a definition of narrative coaching followed by a step-by-step procedure of a narrative technique known as externalising conversation which is regarded as fundamental for all coaching conversation.

Keywords

coaching psychology; culture; externalising conversation; self-identity; learning; societal; positive psychology.

This is the first of four short 'techniques and approaches' articles on narrative coaching, in addition to the two papers from David Drake (Drake, 2017, 2018). In response to the invitation, I would like to make my contribution not only as a proponent of narrative coaching, but also as a response to Drake's papers as part of the unfolding conversation about narrative coaching, so that the reader would have a sense of

Original publication details: Law, H. (2019, December). Narrative coaching – Part 1: An introduction and the first step. *The Coaching Psychologist, 15*(2), 39–43. Reproduced with permission of The British Psychological Society.

continuity and coherence about the topic. After all, coaching is also about conversation amongst peers where understanding and knowledge of the issue are exchanged, transferred and learning takes place. As such, this paper aims to provide an overview on the topic, with an objective to describe the first key technique of the narrative coaching approach. It first provides a historical background and theoretical foundation on the development of narrative coaching followed by a definition and detailed description of the technique on externalising conversation.

WHY NARRATIVE COACHING? THEORETICAL FOUNDATION OF NARRATIVE COACHING

There are many techniques on coaching. Out of many, why do I advocate narrative coaching? It is not only because it is my long held belief that storying has power to transform life which is deep rooted since the dawn of human civilisation, but also because it has a long established psychological foundation which our discipline of coaching psychology is based – both in research and practice. In addition to the publication of the four classic texts: *Actual Minds, Possible Worlds* (Bruner, 1986), *Acts of Meaning* (Bruner, 1990), *Narrative Psychology: The storied nature of human conduct* (Sabin, 1986 edn) and *Narrative Knowing and the Human Sciences* (Polkinghorne, 1988), which was heralded as the narrative turn in the 1980s, Hiles and Čermák (2008, p.152) went further and boldly proclaimed that 'narrative psychology might represent a *third cognitive revolution*'. Hiles and colleagues (2009, p.56) further suggested that:

> *For psychology* [that includes coaching psychology], *this becomes something much more than a simple 'narrative turn', but entails the possibility of a third cognitive revolution, which will involve building much needed bridges across the human sciences, as well as within the discipline, offering a basis for integration between psychodynamic, cognitive, discursive, humanistic and even transpersonal approaches.* (Emphasis added)

It is therefore not surprising that my colleague Reinhard Stelter (2012) advocates the narrative approach as the third generation coaching and regards other approaches, including cognitive behavioural and solution-focused, as the second. Together we (with other colleagues) have laid down three theoretical foundations of coaching (Law, 2013a; Law, 2013b; Law et al., 2007; Stelter, 2012; Stelter & Law, 2010):

(i) The sociocultural foundation – Regards ethics, societal and socially constructed self-identity as central to its meaning-making frames.

(ii) The learning foundation (Kolb 1984; Vygotsky, 1962) – Emphasis on experiential learning, scaffolding changes to result in new actions known as proximal development (also see Drake, 2018 for coaching psychology).

(iii) Positive psychology (Seligman & Csikszentmihalyi, 2000) – Focused on individuals and communities; knowledge, skills, strengths, virtues, aspirations, hopes and dreams rather than weaknesses and despairs.

One can trace the lineage of the above foundations to various epistemological positions including realism, interpretivism and social constructionism with phenomenology as a key tradition that many coaching psychology practitioners adopt. This is because it focuses on individuals' lived experience and embodied in the present context. As we know, the presence (here and now) is a primacy in coaching, existentialistic and mindfulness practices.

None of the above epistemological foundations are concerned with clinical populations, which makes the narrative approach a key to coaching conversation and coaching psychology (rather than counselling and clinical psychology). It also marks its point of departure from other coaching techniques which tend to simply transport the established clinical approaches to the coaching context. For example, cognitive behavioural coaching was translated from cognitive behavioural therapy (CBT) and so on. I would go further to extend my observation of this coaching phenomenon (clinical transport) to include Drake's (2017) narrative approach which seems to place attachment theory as its foundation – a foundation on which many clinical practices are based.

DEFINITION

From the above development, Stelter (2012, p.8) proposed a definition of (narrative) coaching as:

> A developmental *conversation and dialogue, a* co-creative *process between coach and coachee with the purpose of giving (especially) the coachee a space and an opportunity for immersing him/ herself in reflection on and new understandings of: (i) his or her* own experiences *in the specific* context; *and (ii) his or her interactions, relations and negotiations with others in specific contexts and situations. This coaching conversation should enable* new possible ways of acting *in the contexts that are the topic of the conversation.* (Emphasis added)

From the above definition, we can regard narrative coaching as a co-creative process – a developmental conversation where the coach listens to the coachee's stories of lived experience and supports them to identify values, skills, meaning and strengths in order to redevelop those stories and re-author them, which opens new possibilities in the future. From this perspective, we can leverage coaching with a metaphor – a journey, as a process of storytelling where the coachee's stories are listened and analysed in relation to their own sense of identity.

The context specific aspect makes the approach especially sensitive to cultural aspects of the coachee and applicable across different cultures and community settings (Law, 2017; Rosinski, 2003). The approach is a social construct that is constantly evolving and dependant on the context: the coach, the co-actor, culture, values and anything that has an impact on the coachee's own universe (also see Stelter & Law, 2010)

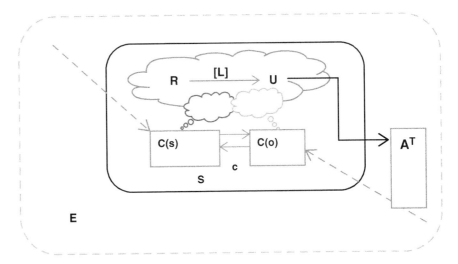

Figure 1 *Model of narrative coaching as a conversational space.*

Note: I use T as a superscript to denote A as a transform – To emphasise that it is a transformative process; Cs for coachee to remind me that the idea of narrative conversation is to discover the coachee's sense of self identity; and Co for the coach – reflecting that the coachees are in conversation with the other in that conversation (and vice versa) – a notion of outsider witness (I shall come back to this in a later issue). All these interactions are situated within a specific context/ environment (E).

So the role of a coach (Co) is to create a space (S) which allows the coachee (Cs) to reflect [R]; though the conversation [c] between the coach and coachee, they both develop a new understanding (U), which engenders the coachee to take new action (A^T) (Figure 1).

NARRATIVE COACHING TECHNIQUES

According to White (2005, 2007), the narrative approach may consist of the following techniques (I refer to them as stages, depending on the individual and context):

(i) externalising conversations
(ii) remembering/re-authoring
(iii) outsider witness re-telling (in group)
(iv) definitional ceremony (community) – re-tellings of re-tellings.

I would argue that all coaching conversations involve some form of externalising conversation, where the coachee makes the implicit explicit through coaching conversation by speaking out about their inner experiences. The difference in narrative coaching is that this *speaking out* is in the form of a story. Externalising conversation is an ontological starting point for a coach to learn what is out there that is possible to know about the coachee from their story. A key task of a narrative coach is to *listen with the third ear* to identify the coachee's *self-identity in context*. This could be hidden from the foreground of the story. In the next section of this paper, I shall describe the procedure of externalising conversation and the other techniques to be covered in the next three chapters respectively.

EXTERNALISING CONVERSATION STEP-BY-STEP

Externalising conversation may take the following steps:

Step 1: Storying/story description – Invite the coachee to tell a story about recent events and their experiences that has brought them to the meeting. Coaching tips: Focus on any unique outcome, learning, problem-solving skills, barrier and challenges that they had in the story.

Step 2: Identify various domains from the coachee's story in terms of the *background/ backdrop* (i.e. spaces and places (such as home, school, workplace); culture and context; *sequence of events* that took place *time*; *actors* (colleagues, peers, friends and the coachee's self as the key figure); self-identity (purposes, values, aspirations, hopes and dreams); and zone of proximal development (future possibilities, new plan and action)). Coaching tip: Do ask questions where there are information gaps in any significant domains. For example, about places and spaces: where did the event take place? (what, when, where, who and why?). Relation mapping/narrative plot: map the effects/influence of the barriers/problem identified through the various domains of the coachee's life story in which complications are identified, such as familiar relationships (e.g. colleague, peer, friendships and the self) that were most significant to the coachee's aspirations, beliefs, dreams, hopes, values and self-identity. Coaching tip: Metaphorically speaking we are trying to map the *landscape of events/action* onto the *landscape of consciousness/self-identity*.

Step 3: Evaluation/reflection – Invite the coachee to reflect and evaluate the impact (effects/influence) of the themes/plots that emerge from the stories within the given domains.

Step 4: Justification – Ask the coachee to justify their action and evaluation and make judgements about the agreed action in relation to their dreams, hopes, values and self-identity. Coaching tip: Ask the coachee, 'What will you do next?'

Step 5: Conclusion/recommendation – Invite the coachee to put into words valued conclusions about their lives and positional identities. These may be conclusions, wishes or pledges, about their preferred commitments, desires, longings, hopes and dreams that are congruent to their beliefs, values, purposes and self-identity. Finally, invite the coachee to formulate a plan of action.

Coaching tip: Ask the coachee to give their story a name/title in relation to the identified themes and plots (See Figure 2).

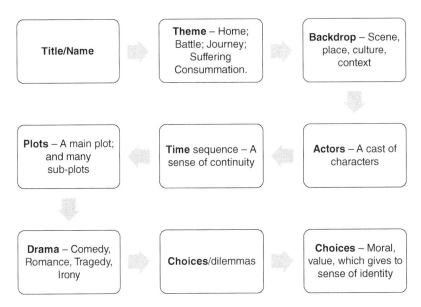

Figure 2 *Narrative elements in externalising conversation.*

SUMMARY AND CONCLUSION

In this paper I have advocated the use of narrative coaching as the most appropriate approach for the discipline of coaching psychology in terms of its epistemological lineage and psychological foundations. I have provided an up-to-date conceptual definition of narrative coaching and described the procedure of the fundamental narrative techniques known as externalising conversation. I hope that you (the reader) will be inspired by the beauty and the eloquence of the approach and start practising the technique in your coaching conversation. In the next chapter, I shall expand the power of storying by exploring further on the narrative conversation known as re-authoring.

REFERENCES

Bruner, J. (1986). *Actual minds, possible worlds.* Harvard, MA: Harvard University Press.

Bruner, J. (1990). *Acts of meaning.* Harvard, MA: Harvard College.

Drake, D. (2017). Using the four gateways to tell new stories and make new choices. *The Coaching Psychologist, 13*(1), 22–26.

Drake, D. (2018). Creating zones of proximal development in coaching: The power of working at Thresholds. *The Coaching Psychologist, 14*(1), 42–47.

Hiles, D.R. & Cermak, I. (2008). Narrative psychology. In C. Willig & W. Stainon-Rogers (Eds.) *Sage handbook of qualitative research in psychology* (pp.147–194). London: Sage.

Hiles, D.R., Cermak, I. & Chrz, V. (2009). Narrative oriented inquiry: A dynamic framework for good practice. In D. Robinson, P. Fisher, T. Yeadon-Lee et al. (Eds.) *Narrative, memory and identities* (pp.53–65). Huddersfield: University of Huddersfield Press.

Kolb, D.A. (1984). *Experiential learning: Experience as the source of learning and development.* Englewood Cliffs, NJ: Prentice Hall.

Law, H. (2013a). *Psychology of coaching, mentoring and learning* (2nd edn). Chichester: John Wiley & Sons.

Law, H. (2013b). *Coaching psychology – A practitioner's manual.* Chichester: John Wiley & Sons.

Law, H. (2017). The transpersonal power of stories: Creating a community of narrative practice. *Transpersonal Psychology Review, 19*(2), 3–11.

Law, H.C., Ireland, S. & Hussain, Z. (2007). *Psychology of coaching, mentoring & learning.* Chichester: John Wiley & Sons.

Polkinghorne, D.P. (1988). *Narrative knowing and the human sciences.* Albany, NY: SUNY Press.

Rosinski, P. (2003). *Coaching Across Cultures.* London: Nicholas Brealey.

Rosinski, P. (2003). *Coaching Across Cultures.* London: Nicholas Brealey.

Sarbin, T.R. (Ed) (1986). *Narrative psychology: The storied nature of human conduct.* Westport, CT: Praeger Publishers/Greenwood Publishing Group.

Seligman, M.E.P. & Csikszentmihalyi, M. (2000). Positive psychology: An introduction. *American Psychologist, 55*(1), 5–14.

Stelter, R. (2012). *A guide to third generation coaching: Narrative-collaborative theory and practice.* Dordrecht Heidelberg, Germany: Springer.

Stelter, R. & Law, H. (2010) Coaching – Narrative-collaborative practice. *International Coaching Psychology Review, 5*(2), 152–164.

Vygotsky, L.S. ([1926] 1962). *Thought and language.* Cambridge, MA: MIT Press.

White, M. (2005). Michael White workshop notes. Retrieved from www.dulwichcentre.com.au

White, M. (2007). *Maps of narrative practice.* New York, NY: Norton.

41 Narrative coaching – Part 2: Two forms of change structures: re-authoring and remembering

Ho Law

Abstract

This paper follows the introductory article by discussing the transformation function and forms of narrative coaching in comparison with other forms and types of coaching approaches in psychological interventions. It describes two forms of narrative techniques known as 're-authoring' and 'remembering'. The procedures show that the two techniques take different shapes or forms and are used in different contexts during a coaching conversation. Nevertheless, both techniques provide rites de passage for the coachee to achieve positive change and thus the same function of transformation. The narrative analysis and its implications are further discussed with a recommendation for further research.

Keywords

coaching psychology;change; coaching; narrative; practice; re-authoring; remembering; self-identity; learning; research; transformation.

Original publication details: Law, H. (2020, June). Narrative coaching – Part 2: Two forms of change structures: Re-authoring and remembering. *The Coaching Psychologist, 16*(1), 59–69. Reproduced with permission of The British Psychological Society.

As an introduction to this paper for those who are new to the narrative coaching approach, I will start with a recap. In Part 1, I advocated narrative coaching for coaching psychology and described the procedure of the externalising conversation as the first step for narrative coaching, which arguably is a foundation that is common in all psychological interventions (Law, 2019). Another common feature amongst all psychological interventions (be it coaching, counselling or psychotherapy) is that we would expect some changes to take place during or as a result of the conversation (hopefully the changes are positive in nature), otherwise who would want to engage in such a conversation? The question is – how do we generate change in the process?

We would also expect changes to occur in the externalising conversation and that the change should be positive. However, there are no guarantees that changes will happen. If there are any changes, there are also no guarantees that they are positive. For people who have suffered from post-traumatic stress disorder (PTSD), the very act of recounting the lived experience of the traumatic event might trigger the memory of the traumatic experience. The person might feel worse instead of better unless a proper formulation, procedure and preparation are in place within a therapeutic context; for example, see Schauer et al. (2011). The question 'How do we generate positive change in the process?' is the topic of this paper, which focuses on the technique known as re-authoring.

RE-AUTHORING

To achieve a positive change and outcome, let us examine a narrative conversation in more detail. As described in Part 1, a narrative process begins with an externalising conversation which consists of the following steps:

1. Storying/story description.
2. Narrative analysis.
3. Evaluation/reflection.
4. Justification.
5. Conclusion/recommendation.

It starts with an invitation for the coachee to talk about their lived experience of recent significant events that brought them to the meeting. The coach may make notes and write down the story being told in collaboration with the coachee in the conversation and, if necessary, ask questions such as what, when, where, who and why (story description).

NARRATIVE ANALYSIS

The coaching task begins with an analysis of the story by identifying various domains (sequences of events that happened in space, places and time with relevant actors). Based on the learning foundation mentioned in Part 1 (Law, 2019), it would be helpful to start preparing the analysis by sketching out an identity position map of all the stages/steps of the narrative process as the scaffolding for proximal development (Vygotsky, 1962). Coaches often refer to the Johari window in their coaching conversation, particularly when providing feedback (Jones & Pfeiffer, 1973). You may find it helpful to map out the Johari window within the structure of your coachee's identity position map (White, 2007) – see Figure 1.

For those who are familiar with the Johari window diagram from the earlier version of my publications (Law, 2013a, 2013b), note that here I effectively turn the Johari window upside down in embedding it within the map, as I did in the learning cycle (Kolb, 1984).

The task in hand here is to map out the sequence of events described by the coachee and identify their effects and influences on the coachee's life in which complications might have happened. These events may also contain action: when plotted along the horizontal time axis, it produces a visual landscape of events and action. This is a collaborative process. It requires both the coachee's input and the coach's facilitation with questions, clarification and further questions, and so on.

Very often the initial story line may be problem-saturated (e.g. about a challenging situation, personal failure, disappointment, embarrassment, weakness and/or shame – something that may already be in the public domain but it may be a hidden self-knowledge not many people know about it, but the coachee is aware of it). For example:

> *I am hopeless in making a speech in public…*
> *Making a presentation is not my strong point… I know that from the feedback…*
> *My mother told me that I was terrible at this…?*
> *People were just laughing at me…*
> *There was a window of opportunity that I could have helped, but I failed…*
> *I was such a fool!*

The problem situation dominates the foreground and may seem to be 'thickly' described in the story in a regressive (negative) tone. This would have left very little room to talk about the value and identity of the storyteller (the coachee); if these did occur, they might appear as thin traces in the background – We refer to this as a thin description (about the landscape of consciousness/self-identity), in contrast to the thick description. The two terms often get confused in the interpretation (see Ryle, 1949, and Geertz, 1973, for clarity).

We are mindful that there are many possible storylines that the coachee could have chosen to tell and disclose the information within the 'landscapes of the mind', to borrow Bruner's (1986) metaphor. We are curious about the cognition, the conscious decision that the coachee made. Why they are telling me this (choosing this storyline) instead of that…?

To assist the coachee to generate positive change, the coach would need to help them to change the problem-saturated storyline with a positive storyline (an alternative plot with more progressive tone). Help to identify:

- The more positive events of their lives (which might have been neglected, forgotten or hidden).
- Any unique outcomes or exceptions in those alternative storylines.

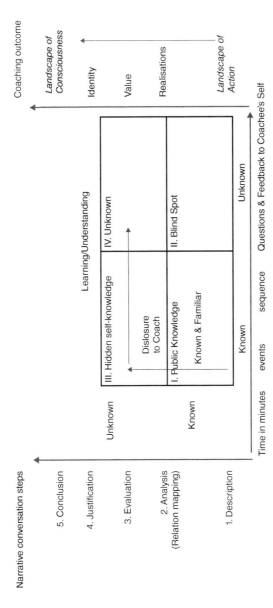

Figure 1 *Preparation for narrative analysis*

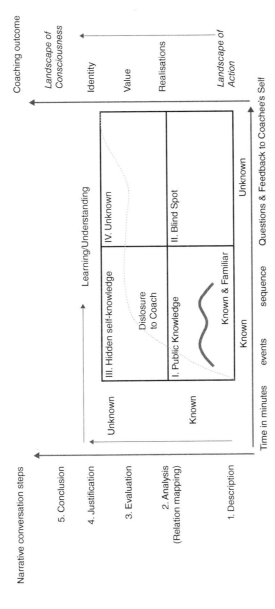

Figure 2 *Identity Position map 1: Relation mapping/narrative plot*

Coaching tips: If the above is absent from the story, you can ask directly, 'Have there been any exceptions?' and clarify and expand, if necessary. For example:

- Can you remember, was there a significant moment at which you felt that you had done something well that you were not good at?'
- … a situation that you were very good at (giving a presentation – or whatever task that you did)?'

Encourage the coachee to expand on this further (thicken the plot):

- 'Would you like to expand on this?' Q 'Please tell me more and help me to understand your intentions or purpose in that accomplishment?'
- 'Does this stem from any particular values or beliefs you hold in high regard? If so, what are they?'

These unique outcomes provide a *rite de passage* into the alternative storylines of the coachee's progressive life. The coach's questions at the critical point of conversation help the coachee to scaffold onto the alternative plot that could become a more positive and progressive development (see Figure 3).

I hope by now, if you have been following the narrative process step by step in our conversation, this moment of change (turning point) occurs during Step 3, after a detailed narrative inquiry and analyses have taken place. Both the coachee and coach reflect on what has been said and heard, reflect and re-evaluate the situation in relation to the coachee's self-identity (purpose, values, aspirations, hopes and dreams) so that further possibilities (zone of proximal development), a new plan and action can be possible. These steps were also regarded as motivation and anchoring (Stelter, 2012).

REMEMBERING

Remember as the story unfolds, the coachee may have referred to some figures who were significant to them in terms of their relationship, history, meaning-making and/or the conclusion of one's present life and identities. For example, the figure may be their parent, grandparent, uncle, aunt, any relative; or it could be their friend or teacher whom they admire. These figures do not have to be directly related or even known. For example, they may be a film star, authors of books, a character in a film or book or even an imaginary character in comics (say, a hero: superman or superwoman); or even an animal or object (e.g. cat, dog, pet or teddy bear; toy in childhood). The criteria are that the figure is identified by the coachee as important to their lives, history and identities.

In this case, we could use the significant figure as an agency for change (a rite de passage). Again, as in re-authoring, at the reflection/evaluation stage, ask the coachee

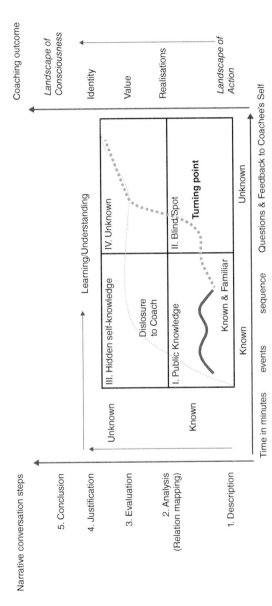

Figure 3 *Identity position map 2: Re-authoring an alternative plot*

to recount what the significant figure contributed to their life (R1); invite the coachee to imagine what/how they would be perceived in terms of their identity through the eyes of the figure (R2).

Coaching tips: Encourage the coachee to provide a description of the figure and a thick description of themselves from the figure's perspective, for example: Could you tell me a bit about this person (let's say X)?

- What does X look like?
- Could you tell me how your life has been influenced by X?
- What would X have done in this situation? Q Is there an example that comes to mind of the sorts of things you and X did together that captures something of what you both shared?
- Did it resonate with what is important to you?
- Are you honouring X's contribution to your life?
- What might X have appreciated in you that others might have failed to notice?
- If X were sitting/standing here now and witnessing you telling the story...? (If doing chair work with three chairs, pointing at the third empty chair, otherwise pointing at an appropriate empty space), What would X think about you?
- What would you say to X now?

Invite the coachee to recount what the person contributed to the life of this figure (R3), and encourage the coachee to enter the consciousness of this figure on matters of this figure's identity, initiating a thick description of the ways in which this connection shaped this figure's sense of who they were and what their life was about (R4) – see Figure 4.

Coaching tips: Encourage the coachee to provide a thick description of the person's belief, value and identity as a result of their relationship and interaction that they shared in their lives (again from the imagined figure's perspective). For example:

'Thinking back, what might you have done to receive X's appreciation?'
What do you think it contributed to X's life?
...in particular, that you, were appreciated?
What effect do you think your contribution has had on X's sense of purpose or sense of what life is about?
Did it reinforce X's purpose or did it take away from it?
Could you imagine how X would have felt if he/she were here now and hearing this conversation?
And what would X say to you now!

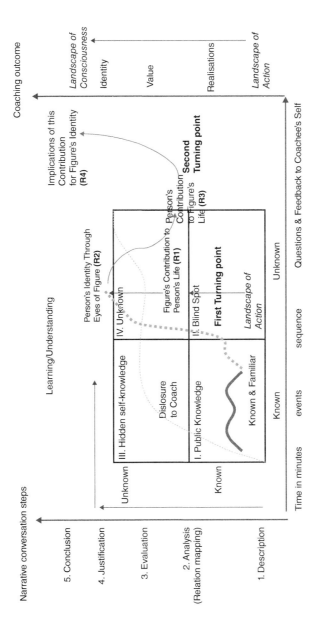

Figure 4 *Identity position map 3: Remembering a significant figure*

THE POWER OF METAPHOR AND STORY

We tell ourselves stories in order to live. (Joan Didion, 1979)

In Part 1, I argued the power of story, as it evokes our senses, embodies our emotions and is cumulative in our life, learning and history. One could argue that story itself can be a metaphor, as they share similar characteristics and have transformative powers (Berman & Brown, 2000). When we embed a metaphor within a story, the power becomes amplified manifold.

From the above description of both 're-authoring' and 'remembering' procedures, we can see that both achieve the transform function (A^T by definition) described in Part 1. However, we can also observe that the two techniques have different shapes or forms and are used in different contexts during a coaching conversation. Both techniques use the metaphor to leverage positive change in their alternative plot and amplify the positive embodied emotion (thickening the positive plot with a thick description).

In remembering conversation, the act of remembering itself is a metaphor (Myerhoff, 1982, 1986). It uses a significant figure to evoke 'life' as a 'membered' club, an 'association' of life. In doing so, it amplifies one's 'identity', value and strengths as they resonate and share in a multi-voiced story. I recall in Michael White's teaching, he emphasised this metaphor by insisting that remembering should be expressed as re-membering (White, 2005).

For me, whether it is remembering or re-membering, it does depend on the context of the story. Depending on the chosen significant figure in the story, especially when the figure is in a mythical form, it may take the narrative inquiry into the transpersonal realm (Law & Basil, 2016; Wade, 2019).

There are occasions that an awkward question could arise, 'What if the story contains a significant figure that has a negative rather than positive influence upon the coachee's life?' Or, for instance, what if the coachee answered the question – Did X's action reinforce your sense of purpose or did it take away from it? – with an answer, 'It took away from it'.

The possibilities for the revision of one's membership of life would enable the coachee to downgrade or revoke the membership of X. One can redraw the Coaching outcome club's boundary to exclude or disqualify other negative voices – map is not territory (Smith, 1993). The territory here represents a different meaning in the metaphor.

For a positive figure, remembering conversation could enrich the account of the preferred identity and knowledge of life and skills of living that have been co-generated in the significant membership of people's lives. This is another reason why having a role-model, mentor and/or coach is so important in one's life.

In general, remembering conversation within the narrative coaching context should not be confused with the theoretical phenomenon of transference (Übertragung) within the psychoanalytic therapeutic context where the client projects their unconscious feelings toward the therapist (Freud, 1991; Jung, 1983; Kapelovitz, 1987). However, when the significant figure in remembering is the coach/counsellor or psychotherapist, one needs to be mindful that such therapeutic phenomenon might also occur within the coaching and mentoring context. Transference and over reliance on the reference figure for behaviour modelling could have a negative impact, especially if that role model 'falls from grace' later. The concept of re-membering – re-drawing one's 'life club's boundary' to exclude the negative significant figure would seem useful, as referred to earlier (see Myerhoff, 1982, 1986; White, 2005; Smith, 1993).

CONCLUSION AND DISCUSSION

In this paper, I have described re-authoring and remembering narrative techniques within the context of externalising conversation procedure. Both techniques provide the *rites de passage* for the coachee to achieve positive change – the Transform Function (A^T) as defined in Part 1. I further argued that the two techniques take different shapes or forms and are used in different contexts during the narrative conversation. I have illustrated these differences with the use of position maps which show the scaffolding structure and process of re-authoring and the resonance nature of re-membering conversation that amplifies the power (P) of the transform function:

$$P = (A^T)^n,$$

where *n* is the number significant figure, $N = 1$ in re-authoring; and $N = 2$ in remembering conversation as both the coachee and the significant figures are counted as one.

Remembering conversation consists of an extra layer of collective identity which both the coachee and the significant figure share. The importance and implications of the above may not be obvious at this stage but imagine when the *n* increases manifold as application in groups and community (Law, 2017) the topic in part three.

On initiating the change process, I have emphasised the importance of narrative analysis. After all, narrative coaching (as in all coaching) is a process of inquiry during which the coachee is the participant of the research of their own life and identity. In re-examining the process of change in the narrative process, it has dawned on me that the process of narrative analysis is congruent with the qualitative research process – especially narrative research. It seems to me that the analysis can be regarded as a research method in its own right and therefore narrative research methods can be deployed and applied to this stage, for example narrative oriented inquiry (Hiles et al., 2009) and other general narrative research method (Murray,

2003). This comparison has profound implications on both ethical and philosophical levels.

A typical qualitative research consists of semi-structured interviews of participants. In general, the interaction between the researcher and participant stop at the end of the interview (Step 1 of narrative conversation – description of the participant's lived experience). The researcher would then be busy carrying on with further interviews and analyses and so on, drawing their own research conclusion without further engagement with the participant who contributed to the knowledge production. The ethics application stage usually requires them to ensure that the participants are not harmed and/or distressed at the end of the interview. This does not usually involve further intervention; in fact researchers are refrained from doing so, but simply providing the participants with information on a briefing sheet to seek further help if necessary. A golden opportunity – to help the participant to get better if distressed and/or if not, excel towards their aspirations at a critical juncture – could be missed.

Is this ethical and to whose benefit?

There are exceptions, for example, action research does involve intervention in the process, and the research results also generate further action and so on (dating back to 1946 by Kurt Lewin; see Law & Aquilina, 2013 for a more recent coaching example). I wonder if narrative conversation can be a process of the narrative research in practice; a new kind of action research. The proposal seems to be entirely congruent – both research and practice becomes one integral. This calls for further thinking and research. I would welcome colleagues who are interested in exploring the idea further to join me in collaboration with the innovative research and development (see correspondence for contact below).

REFERENCES

Berman, M. & Brown, D. (2000). *The Power of Metaphor – Story Telling & Guided Journeys for Teachers, Trainers & Therapists*. Carmarthen, UK: Crown House Publishing. Retrieved from www.crownhouse.co.uk.

Bruner (1986). *Actual minds, possible worlds*. Cambridge, MA: Harvard University Press.

Didion, J. (1979). *The white album*. New York, NY: Noonday.

Hiles, D.R., I. Cermak, & V. Chrz. (2009). Narrative oriented inquiry: A dynamic framework for good practice. In D. Robinson, P. Fisher, T. Yeadon-Lee, S.J. Robinson (Ed) *Woodcock, narrative, memory and identities* (pp.53–65). Huddersfield, UK: University of Huddersfield Press.

Jung, C.C. (1983) *The psychology of the transference* (1st edn). Abingdon, UK: Routledge.

Jones, J. & Pfeiffeer, J.W. (1973). *The 1973 annual handbook for facilitators*. San Diego, CA: Pfeiffeer & Co.

Freud, S. (1991). *The penguin freud library, Vol.1: Introductory lectures on psychoanalysis (Penguin Freud Library S.)* (new edn). London, UK: Penguin Random House.

Geertz, C. (1973). *The interpretation of cultures*. New York, NY: Basic Books.

Kapelovitz, L.H. (1987). *To love and to work – A demonstration and discussion of psychotherapy (1st edn)*. New York, NY: Jason Aronson.

Kolb, D.A. (1984). *Experiential learning: Experience as the source of learning and development*. Englewood Cliffs, NJ: Prentice Hall.

Law, H. & Aquilina, R. (2013). Developing a healthcare leadership coaching model using action research and systems approaches – a case study: Implementing an executive coaching programme to support nurse managers in achieving organisational objectives in Malta. *International Coaching Psychology Review*, 8(1) 54–71.

Law, H. (2013a). *Psychology of Coaching, Mentoring & Learning (2nd edn)*. Chichester, UK: John Wiley & Sons.

Law, H. (2013b). *Coaching Psychology – A practitioner's manual*. Chichester, UK: John Wiley & Sons.

Law, H. (2017). The transpersonal power of stories: Creating a community of narrative practice. *Transpersonal Psychology Review*, 19(2), 3–11.

Law, H. (2019). Narrative coaching – Part 1: An introduction and the first step. *The Coaching Psychologist*, 15(2), 36–40.

Law, H. & Basil, N. (2016). Reflections on Vera and Tree of Life: Multi-reflexivity, meta-narrative dialogue for transpersonal research. *Transpersonal Psychology Review*, 18(2), 32–57.

Lewin, K. (1946). Action research and minority problems. *Journal of Social Issues*, 2, 34–46. doi:10.1111/j.1540-4560.1946.tb02295.x

Murray, M. (2003). Narrative psychology. In J.A. Smith (Ed). *Qualitative psychology: A practical guide to research methods* (pp.111–132). London, UK: Sage.

Myerhoff, B. (1982) Life history among the elderly: Performance, visibility and re-membering. In J.Ruby (Ed.). *A Crack in the Mirror: reflexive perspectives in anthropology*. Philadelphia, PA: University of Pennsylvania Press.

Myerhoff, B. (1986). 'Life not death in Venice: Its second life'. In V. Turner, and E. Bruner (Eds.). *The Anthropology of Experience*. Chicago, IL: University of Illinois Press

Ryle, G. (1949). *The Concept of Mind*. London, UK: Hutchinson.

Stelter, R. (2012). *A guide to third generation coaching: Narrative-collaborative theory and practice*. Dordrecht Heidelberg, Germany: Springer.

Schauer M., Neuner F. & Elbert T. (2011). *Narrative exposure therapy: A short-term treatment for traumatic stress disorders*. Cambridge, MA: Hogrefe. Kindle Edition.

Smith, J.Z.Z. (1993). *Map is not Territory: Studies in the History of Religions*. Chicago, IL: University of Chicago Press.

Vygotsky, L.S. ([1926]; 1962) *Thought and language*. Cambridge, MA: MIT Press.

Wade, J. (2019). Get off the mountaintop and back in the marketplace: Leadership as transpersonal psychology's highest calling. *Transpersonal Psychology Review*, 21, 22–39.

White, M. (2005). *Michael White Workshop Notes*. Published on www.dulwichcentre.com.au

White, M. (2007). *Maps of Narrative Practice*. New York, NY: Norton.

42 Narrative coaching – Part 3: Approaches for groups, teams, organisations and community

Ho Law

Abstract

This paper explores how narrative coaching is applied for groups, teams, organisations and communities using techniques called outsider witness and definitional ceremony. It includes applications in the organisational context and discussions on their implications for research and practices. In Part 2, I called for action research as part of narrative coaching practice. This paper demonstrates how the process of action research can be embedded in narrative coaching. The procedures are powerful, effective, and an efficient way to widen access to training and psychological interventions especially in crisis situations e.g. the Grenfell Tower fire in 2017, Covid-19 pandemic and climate emergency.

Keywords

Climate emergency coaching psychology; Covid-19 pandemic; coaching; community; group; narrative; practice; self-identity; learning; action research.

Original publication details: Law, H. (2020, December). Narrative coaching – Part 3: Approaches for groups, teams, organisations and community. *The Coaching Psychologist, 16*(2), 59–70. Reproduced with permission of The British Psychological Society.

Coaching is…

'A one-to-one conversation focused on the enhancement of learning and development through increasing self-awareness and a sense of personal responsibility where the coach facilitates the self-directed learning of the coachee through questioning, active listening, and appropriate challenge in a supportive and encouraging climate.' (van Nieuwerburgh, 2012, p.17)

The above definition was devised by van Nieuwerburgh specifically for coaching in an educational context. I recall discussing this definition with a former colleague and asking, *'Has coaching to be one-to-one? What about coaching in groups?*. My colleague replied, *'That would be training, not coaching.'*

INTRODUCTION

Those who trained in psychology and psychotherapy would know that the practice would very often apply to a group setting. Indeed, experiential group practice is an essential part of training for most counselling and psychotherapy. If we follow our discussion in Part 1 (Law, 2019) on the phenomenon of 'clinical transport' that I observed in the development of coaching psychology, we expect that there would be similar applications for groups. For the non-clinical context, group coaching would most likely be in organisations, such as executive and team coaching. The application would not only be common, but also important for those organisations where cost effectiveness is a top priority. For example, in the National Health Services, a single session Cognitive Behaviour Therapy is routinely applied in groups (Clarke & Nicholis, 2018; Correir, 2020). In business and coaching contexts, Shams and Lane (2020, p.25) assert that team coaching is the most effective intervention for a family business, citing numerous literature references to support their argument (including Adkins, 2010; Hackman & Wageman, 2005; Mitsch & Mitsch, 2010; Peters & Carr, 2013; Thorton, 2010; Wageman et al., 2008). While highlighting the subtle differences between group and team coaching, Shams and Lane (2020) argued that both approaches could be integrated as a model of coaching in practice. The key differences between the two are the units of coaching focus and interactions: the group coaching focuses on individual member/ participant, the team or the whole group of participants as a single unit. They proposed the integrated team coaching model for family business (ITCMFB) for both group and team coaching and argued its effectiveness in delivering positive outcomes with a hypothetical example to illustrate the model. However, the example is too sketchy to substantiate the claim and the mechanism of how the model worked remains unclear. The context of the application was also too narrow in scope (only within a family business context) to enable wider practical use. This paper aims to explore how narrative coaching can be applied for groups, teams and organisations, as well as community, with the objective to describe the detailed process, procedure and structure of methods, namely: outsider witness and definitional ceremony. The following sections (2 & 6) describe these respectively. Each includes possible applications in the contexts of organisation and community (Sections 5 & 7 respectively). Section 8 concludes with discussions on their implications for research and practice.

OUTSIDER WITNESS RETELLING

As in Part 2 (Law, 2020), the procedure of externalising conversations described in Part 1 (Law, 2019) was used as a starting point. The principles can be applied in group or team situations, where one member from the group is asked to act as a storyteller; the rest of the group as outsider witnesses to the story.

The group/team members can assist the coach as they can provide extra support to the individual members beyond the tradition of acknowledgement (that is, in recognition of the importance of the story heard). After they have listened to the story, the coach can invite one of the members to re-tell the story. Here in the outsider witness retelling process, instead of simply reiterating what has been heard, they are guided by the coach's questions along the following steps:

1. Identify the expression of the storyteller – *What are the key expressions that you have identified from the story?*
2. Describe the image that the story has evoked – *Did the story evoke any images in your mind?*
3. Embody responses in their own life experiences – *Did the story strike a chord with you?*
4. Acknowledge any 'transport' of knowledge (learning) from the story to their own life – *How would you acknowledge your learning as a result? What would you say to him/her (the storyteller) who is standing/sitting here with us now in the group?*

As illustrated in the narrative analysis in Part 2, we can map the steps of the narrative process on an Identity Position Map as shown in Figure 1.

Note: For consistency, I have shown how each step of the *outsider witness retelling* maps onto externalising conversation steps and the *landscape of consciousness*, respectively; where the bottom line represents externalising conversation, reauthoring changes the line of externalising conversation into a dotted line. The top dotted line represents outsider witness retelling, which forms a mirror image of the story being told in the reauthoring conversation.

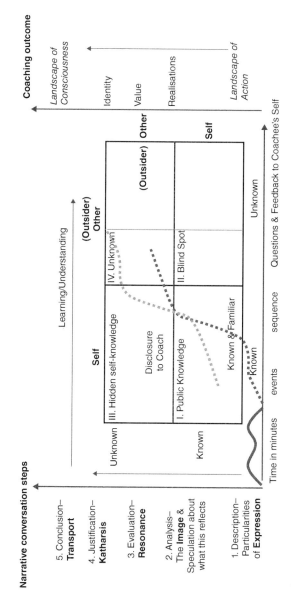

Figure 1   *Outsider Witness Identity Position Map 1+n: Retellings*

The role of participants as outsider witness

Participants in narrative practice perform the role of outsider witness. Their task is to listen to the story attentively. As they listen, they are invited to note down their reflections, paying attention to:

1. Any expressions that resonate with their own experience.
2. The image that the story may evoke.

After they have listened to the story, the outsider witnesses are invited to note down any acknowledgements that they would like to make to the storyteller. These should focus on what they have learned from the story that may be meaningful or helpful in their own life. When the outsider witnesses are invited to retell the story, they are not supposed to reiterate the story told nor to tell their own story; rather, they are expected to report on their reflection and acknowledge the storyteller's contributions to their learning.

Depending on the context of the space in which the outsider witness retellings take place, these activities may be shaped by the culture or tradition of the community, organisation, spaces and places. The following section illustrates some examples of various contexts of outsider witness retelling in group and team practices respectively.

OUTSIDER WITNESS IN REFLECTIVE PEER PRACTICE GROUPS

The narrative approach can be applied in reflective peer practice groups in coaching. As mentioned in the introduction, this kind of reflective practice is common in counselling and psychotherapy as well as in business organisation studies and was mandatory as part of some training programmes, for example, T group, (Lewin, 1948; Highhouse, 2002). For a more up-to-date review on group psychotherapy, see the recent Centenary Special Issue in *Psychotherapy Section Review* (Birchmore, 2019). The idea of reflective practice was also adopted in coaching and coaching psychology respectively. For instance, co-coaching practice advocated by the Association of Coaching and similar practice known as Peer Practice Group (PPG) was introduced in the SGCP by Dr Vicky Ellam-Dyson as part of her leadership (being the Chair in 2008-2009) to develop coaching psychology as a professional discipline. The PPG has become a regular group meeting among SGCP members, sharing coaching approaches as part of collaborative learning, continuing professional development (CPD) and communities of practice (Page, 2020; Shams & Law, 2012; Shams, 2013). A typical group coaching setting is shown in Plate 1.

Plate 1 *A typical group setting*

By geo pixel/CC BY 3.0, https://creativecommons.org/licenses/by/3.0

OUTSIDER WITNESS IN TEAM COACHING

A similar group coaching approach also applied in team coaching within the business and organisation context. This is usually used in leadership and organisation development as a reflective dialogue between manager and coach about their leadership practice. As observed by Stelter (2012), there are three aspects of this practice:

1. *Coaching as a reflective space for manager* – focus on value (trust, safe space, contract, equality,), action (to develop capacity) and commitment (meaning-making and long term goals). Ideally, the executive coach is an outsider of the company rather than an employee or employer. This can be used for managers from various departments or business units to meet and develop their personal leadership, alongside alignment with individuals, teams and organisation, for instance, with an aspiration to create a diverse senior management team (SMT).
2. *Coaching as a tool for staff development* – this may arise when employees approach mangers for advice. This is a good sign as an indication of trust, an opportunity for coaching, learning and development, or during annual performance review of staff (APR).

3. *The coaching-oriented manager as an organisational and team developer* – when managers act as a coach, they are

coaching-oriented in the team meeting, which aims to improve organisational and team performance with objectives to enhance individual wellbeing and business process within the organisation. However, the manager needs to be mindful of the power relationship.

Tip: the coaching-oriented manager needs to ensure that the two roles (coach/manager) are always clear; during conversation, when one is speaking as a coach, and when as a manager.

APPLICATIONS WITHIN ORGANISATIONAL CONTEXT

The narrative approach described above can be adapted in business processes, such as rapid prototyping *('sprint'* in Agile terms) in software development life cycles, for example within the context of the National Health

Service (NHS) digital project, by embedding user stories (their telling and retelling as an outsider) as part of the Agile coaching process (Davies & Sedley, 2009; Pioneer Network, 2015). This has been extremely vital, especially in crises such as the Covid-19 pandemic. Delivering a user-friendly intelligent interface in a virtual environment online is urgently required. The process of embedding the narrative approach in an Agile learning cycle is shown in Figure 2.

Figure 2 shows that the experiential learning cycle is central to the Agile iterative process within which the multidisciplinary team works in collaboration with a cross-functional team of stakeholders: the coach and end-users (as outsiders of the organisation). Each iteration starts with thinking/conception with a set of recommendations as its output for action planning (fed into the next stage), which is based on the user stories in the externalising conversation from the previous cycle. Note that the production cycle effectively is an action research process, with the raw experience of the narrative performance as a starting point; it recurses through a participative process with the following key stages (Change Management Coach, 2015; Kagan et al., 2011, p7; Lewin, 1946):

1. Thinking – defining and understanding the problem, planning and decision-making.
2. Doing action – implementing strategies for change.
3. Reflecting – evaluating progress and impact and reflecting on the skills and processes of change.

In the context of the NHS digital project, an Agile process usually closes with a demo and retrospective. As an example, a typical procedure of an Agile retrospective meeting is set in Table 1.

Tip: Challenges, Do's & Don'ts at each step

Preparation *Do*: arrive 15 minutes ahead of the rest of the team.

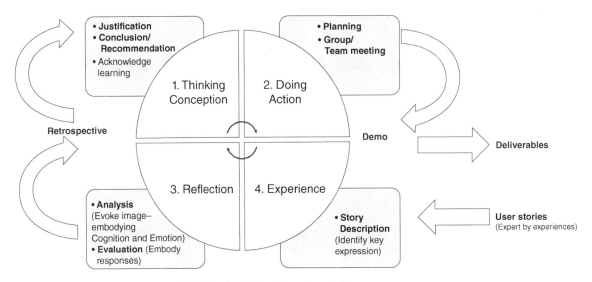

Figure 2   *Mapping narrative approach with Experiential Learning cycle on Agile process*

Table 1   *Procedure of an Agile retrospective meeting (60 minute)*

Steps	Activity	minutes
0	***Preparation*** - Book a meeting room for at least 45 minutes: 15 minutes to set up, and 30 minutes for the session. Bring all the necessary materials: whiteboard/flipchart, markers, sticky notes timer etc. Draw the headings "What did we do well?" and "What should have we done better?" up on the whiteboard.	15
1	***Setting and grounding*** - Facilitators briefly introduce themselves and invite participants to sit/stand in a circle if possible. Welcome everyone to the retrospective meeting and establish the rules of engagement. Apply positive psychology to continuous improvement. Share whatever you think will help the team improve.	5
2	***What went well?*** - Start the session on a positive note. Ask each team member to write down what they feel went well on green sticky notes (one idea per sticky). As people post their stickies on the whiteboard, the facilitator should group similar or duplicate ideas together. Discuss your ideas briefly as a team.	10
3	***What needs improvement?*** - Same as above but using pink stickies instead. Ask each team member to write down what they think needs improvement. Remind your team that this is about actions and outcomes - not about specific people.	10

(Continued)

Table 1   *(Continued)*

Steps	Activity	minutes
4	***What is the next step?*** - Identify concrete actions that the team can take to improve those items noted in Step 3. Ask your team to use blue sticky notes to place ideas on the board. Group them and then discuss as a team, agree to which actions you will take, assign owners and a due date to get them done.	5
5	***Acknowledgements*** - invite team members to acknowledge each other's accomplishments, learning, help and support received from other members. Thank everyone for their involvement and their honesty. Quickly run through the list of follow-up items, their owners and due dates.	5
Total		60

Step 1 Setting and grounding
Do:

1. Set the time boundary of your discussion / story telling – for example: *'We shall discuss our experience about using System X since the project started on [date / month / year]...';* *'Please tell us your story start since when... until... ?'*
2. Encourage the team to embrace a positive psychology mindset – for example: question 'What have we learnt?' What can we improve?' How can we be more constructive?'
3. Listen with an open mind.

Remember that everyone's experience is valid (even though you may not agree with it).
Don't:

1. Blame.
2. Make it personal.
3. Take it personally.

Step 2 Question – What went well?
Challenges: Discussions are dominated by one or two members of the team.

Tip: Step in and ask another member (especially quieter ones) to say something on the topic.

Step 3 Question – What needs improvement?
Do:
Emphasise the actions and outcomes – not about specific people.

Step 4 Question – What is the next step we can take?
Challenges: ideas raised do not seem to lead to improvements.

Tip: help translate ideas into tasks. Break them down into sub-tasks if easier.
Do:

1. Focus on real value.
2. On tasks.
3. Incorporated into your project plan
4. Allow room.
5. Provide resources.

Don't:

1. Compromise.
2. Cut corners.

Step 5 Acknowledgements
Do:

1. Be genuine.
2. Keep it brief.

DEFINITIONAL CEREMONY (COMMUNITY) – RETELLINGS OF RETELLINGS

Within the broader context of poststruc- turalism (onto-epistemological posi- tion that the narrative approach stands, as described in Part 1), we regard that a person's self-identity is not only governed by a private and individual achievement but also by the following social, historical and cultural forces:

1. One's own history.
2. One's own sense of authenticity.
3. Public and social achievements.
4. Acknowledgment of one's preferred claims about one's identity.

Let us focus on Point 4 – acknowledgement, as it is something that we can all do. The individual's self-identity is strengthened by the acknowledgment of one's own preferred claims about identity. *Definitional ceremony* is a powerful approach to provide social acknowledgement of the storyteller's self-identity. In narrative terms, a definitional ceremony thickens many alternative themes or counter-plots of the story and *amplifies* the empowerment that the storytellers receive that would not otherwise be available to them (Law, 2017).

A definitional ceremony may take the following steps (see Figure 3):

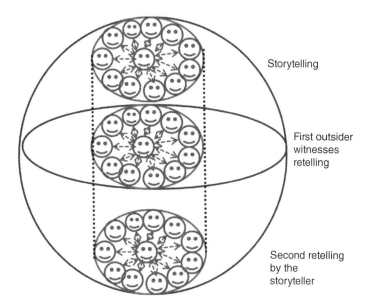

Storytelling

First outsider
witnesses
retelling

Second retelling
by the
storyteller

Figure 3 *The structure of a definitional ceremony*

1. Storytelling – the storyteller is at the centre of the ceremony. Other participants in the group act as outsider witnesses.
2. Retellings of tellings (first retelling) – the outsider witness retells the story that they have heard in relation to their own lived experience using the outsider witness retelling procedure described earlier.
3. Retellings of retellings (second retelling) – the initial storyteller retells the outsider witness's reflections and explores how these reflections help them to develop or take the next step.
4. Retellings of retellings of retellings (third retelling) – invite another participant to perform the role of outsider witness retelling based on what was heard in Step 3.
5. Repeat any of the above steps if the time allows.

Theoretically speaking, the above process could continue indefinitely. In practice, the layers of retelling depend on the physical and time constraints.

Metaphorically speaking, the storyteller is 'being moved/transported' from one place to another in life (here and now) as a direct consequence of the participation. The definitional ceremony is about 'moving' all participants and therefore is ideal for group or community work in community gatherings or in conference styles. For example, the format of an hour workshop for a group can be implemented as shown in Table 2.

Tip: It may be easier to ask the participants to spend a few minutes thinking about their recent experiences and write out a story first before telling it in the group. The instructions for writing a personal story may be:

Table 2   *Procedure of a definitional ceremony (60 minute workshop)*

Steps	Activity	minutes
1	**Setting and grounding** - Facilitators briefly introduce themselves and invite participants to sit in a circle if possible. It may be desirable to conduct a brief mindfulness exercise in the beginning of the workshop (e.g. see Chapman-Clark, 2015, exercise 2, p32)	5
2	**Introduction** - Facilitators introduce background/context of the workshop and the principles of the narrative approach.	10
3	**Story writing exercise** - Participants are given instructions to think/write about a short personal story about their recent experience.	10
4	The facilitator requests for a volunteer from the participants to share their story in the group. Ideally the volunteers should come out and stand at the centre of the group. Other participants are asked to act as the outsider witness and given instructions about their role as described in the previous section.	2
5	**Storytelling** The volunteer (storyteller) tells their story.	5
6	**1st outsider witnesses retelling** – the facilitator requests for a second volunteer from the participants (outsider witnesses) to re-tell the story that they have listened as outsider witnesses in the group.	5
7	**2nd retelling** -The facilitator asked the first volunteer (storyteller) to retell the outsider witness's retelling.	3
8	**Repeat** if time available.	10
9	**Plenary reflection** as a group.	10
Total		60

Think about a significant activity or event that occurred in the last three weeks (or three months if appropriate). Write a personal story about what happened and what you have learned because of the experience.

Acknowledgements of learning and appreciation are given to the participants at the end of the exercise.

The above process would need to be facilitated by a qualified/trained practitioner to ensure that the practice is in accordance with codes of ethics regarding confidentiality and principles of respect. The facilitators and participants should be familiar with the latest edition of the BPS Practice Guidelines as a reference. For example, relevant sections of the Practice Guidelines (BPS, 2017), such as working with different groups of people and safeguarding, can be highlighted as appropriate.

APPLICATIONS OF DEFINITIONAL CEREMONY

The procedure described in the previous section can easily be scaled up according to the time and space available. In addition to the conversation between coaches and members, other forms of communication can be used in this approach, such as writing via emails, diaries or letters and issuing certificates to honour the coachees' stories in a conference situation. The design can be rapidly implemented across the whole community in a network model (Figure 4).

The approach is more efficient and effective than the traditional care model and one-to-one interventions. The flexibility of the application means that the approach is applicable to diverse situations especially in crisis, as previously demonstrated at the aftermath of the Grenfell Tower fire (Law, 2017). A similar approach can be and is being adopted in response to the Covid-19 pandemic via online platforms with multiple meeting rooms/windows for the participants engagement, using video conferencing apps such as Microsoft Teams, Google Meet or Zoom (See Plate 2).

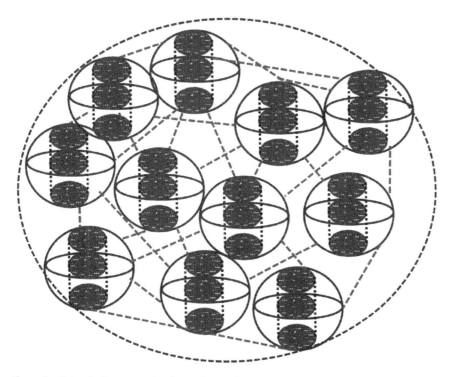

Figure 4   *Network of a community of narrative practice*

Plate 2 *example of online group meeting*

CONCLUSION AND DISCUSSION

In this paper, I have foregrounded a typical definition of coaching not simply as a pretext for introducing the topic of narrative coaching for groups but as a point of entry to open a wider debate on coaching, its principles, and practices in a wider context.

In Part 2 (Law, 2020), I described reauthoring and remembering narrative techniques within the context of externalising conversation procedure as the *rites de passage* for the coachee to achieve positive Transform Function (AT). I also highlighted the resonance nature of remembering conversation that *amp/ifies* the power (P) of the Transform Function (reproduced here in Equation 1):

$$\mathbf{P} = \left(A^{T}\right)^{n} \qquad \text{(Equation 1)}$$

where n is the number of participants.

n = 1 in reauthoring; and n = 2 in remembering conversation.

The power (n) increases manifold as the storyteller and the audiences share the collective identity and initiative actions in the group. Thus, narrative coaching for groups, teams, organisations and community would be more efficient and powerful as the number of participants (n) increases.

However, the number could not grow infinitely large in practice. There is an optimal number in human groups. As a rule of thumb, it is recommended to have up to five people in a group or team. This can be explained from the psychological perspective: we take the Miller's magical number $7(+/-2)$ to ensure the minimal optimal limits on our capacity for processing information without cognitive overload (Miller, 1956). This recommendation has been validated by more recent research in science and statics. For example, the evidence for a collective Intelligence factor in the performance of human groups. Science (Woolley et al., 2010) and designing small decision-making groups (Bramlett & Mosher, 2001).

Theoretically, there is no limit to the number of groups (N) within a community of practice or communities of the world, though n = 150 approximately was proposed by British anthropologist Robin Dunbar (1993). This would give N = 30 as an optimal number of groups within a community. Thus, the definitional ceremony approach for organisations and community is arguably the most powerful approach for creating a community of learning and practice (see Equation 2):

$$P = \left(A^T\right)^n \times N \qquad \text{(Equation 2)}$$

In Part 2 (Law, 2020), I called for using action research as part of narrative coaching practice. This paper has demonstrated how the process can be actualised and embedded in business, community, organisation, group and team contexts. The process embodies the experiential learning cycle (Kolb, 1984; Vygotsky, 1962) as one of our foundations in narrative approaches, as mentioned in our Part 1 Introduction (Law, 2019).

The procedure outlined in this paper also offers an efficient way to train more psychologists, counsellors, social workers, community leaders and trainers who may not be familiar in this approach, thereby widening access to psychological interventions (Law, 2017; 2020) — interventions that are very much needed in crisis situations such as the Grenfell Tower fire in 2017, Covid-19 pandemic and Climate Emergency which poses an existential threat to humanity.

The simplest form of the outsider witness retelling procedure has been described to provide a basic structure to scaffold a bigger platform for storytelling, retelling and sharing individual private spaces and identities in the definitional ceremony by *recursion* of the retelling itself. By *recursion*, I mean each iteration is subtly different from a simple repeat loop of performance. The story told and retold is being shaped and transformed into a new experience (from known to unknown and known again); each retelling is more powerful than the previous version through the learning process that amplifies the embodied emotion. The approaches involve and empower all participants in the process. The effect of the empowerment is transferred from one participant to another, but each transfer through the individual participant's retelling creates a renewal that is something that is larger than participants themselves individually. This enters the transpersonal realm – a topic of Part 4.

In Part 4, our final part of narrative coaching, we shall revisit the popular GROW model advocated by the late Sir John Whitmore (2017). I shall show you how the narrative process can map onto the GROW model in practice as part of our honouring the life of Sir John and our attempt to continue championing his eco-environmental concern through transpersonal coaching; that is coaching beyond the third wave. I regard this enquiry as his unfinished project to address the wider society, environment and the planet – the present and future challenges that we face in the 'new norm'.

REFERENCES

Adkins, L. (2010). *Coaching agile teams: A companion for scrumma.sters, agile coaches and project managers in transition.* Stoughton, MA: Pearson Education.

Birchmore, T. (2019 Ed). Centenary Issue: Special Issue on Group Psychotherapy. *Psychotherapy Section Review, 64.*

Bramlett, M.D. & Mosher, W.D. (2001). First marriage dissolution, divorce, and remarriage. *Advance Data Number, 323,* US Department of Health and Human Services.

Chapman-Clarke, M. (2015). *Mindfulness at work.* Alresford: Management Pocketbook.

Change Management Coach (2015). The Kurt Lewin Change Management Model. http://www.change-management-coach.com/kurt_lewin.html Retrieved on 7 August 2020

Clarke, I. & Nicholis, H. (2018). *Third wave CBT integration for individuals and teams - Comprehend, cope and connect.* London: Routledge - Taylor & Francis.

Correir, R. (2020). *Single-session group CBT post-sexual assault: An outcome study.* Professional Doctorate in Psychology Thesis. Middlesbrough: Teesside University.

Davies, R. & Sedley, L. (2009). *Agile coaching.* Dallas, TX: Pragmatic Bookshelf.

Dunbar, RIM. (1993). Coevoludon of neocortical size, group size and language in humans. *Behavioral and Brain Sciences, 16(4),* 681–735.

Hackman, J.R. & Wageman, R. (2005). A theory of team coaching. *Academy of Management Review. 30(2),* 269–287. doi:10.5465/amr.2005.16387885.

Highhouse, S. (2002). A history of the T-group and its early applications in management development. *Group Dynamics: Theory, Research, and Practice, 6(4),* 277–290. https://doi.org/10.1037/1089-2699.6.4.277

Kagan, C., Burton, M., Duckett, P., Lawthom, R. & Siddiquee, A. (2011). *Critical community psychology.* Chichester: Blackwell Wiley.

Kolb, D.A. (1984). *Experiential learning: Experience as the source of learning and development.* Englewood Cliffs, NJ: Prentice Hall.

Law, H. (2020). Narrative coaching – Part 2: Two forms of change structures: re-authoring and remembering. *The Coaching Psychologist, 16(1),* 59–69.

Law, H. (2019). Narrative coaching – Part 1: An introduction and the first step. *The Coaching Psychologist, 15(2),*36-40.

Law, H. (2017). The Transpersonal power of stories: Creating a community of narrative practice. *Transpersonal Psychology Review, 19(2),* 3–11.

Lewin, K. (1946). Action Research and Minority Problems. *Journal of Social Issues, 2,* 34–46. http://dx.doi.org/10.1111/j.1540-4560.1946.tb02295.x

Lewin, Kurt (June 1947). Frontiers in Group Dynamics: Concept, Method and Reality in Social Science; Social Equilibria and Social Change. *Human Relations, 1,* 5–41. doi:10.1177/001872674700100103.

Lewin, K. (1948). *Resolving social conflicts; selected papers on group dynamics.* Gertrude W. Lewin (Ed.). New York: Harper & Row, 1948.

Miller, GA. (1956). The magical number seven, plus or minus two: Some limits on our capacity for processing information. *Psychological Review, 63(2),* 81–97. CiteSeerX 10.1.1.308.8071. doi:10.1037/h0043158. PMID 13310704.

Mitsch, DJ. & Mitsch, B. (2010). *Team advantage: The complete guide for team transformation: Coach's facilitation guide set.* San Francisco, CA: John Wiley and Sons.

Shams, M. & Lane, D.A. (2020). Team coaching and family business. *The Coaching Psychologist, 16(1),* 25-33.

Shams, M. (2013). Communities of coaching practice: Developing a new approach. *International Coaching Psychology Review*, 8(2),89-91.

Shams, M. & Law, H. (2012). Peer coaching framework: An exploratory technique. *The Coaching Psychologist*, 8(1). 46-49.

Peters, J. & Carr, C. (2013). Team effectiveness and team coaching literature review. *Coaching: An International Journal of Theory, Research and Practice*, 6(2),116–136. doi:10.1080/17521882.2013 .798669.

Pioneer Network (2015). Changes in Health Care: Kurt Lewin Change Theory. https://www. pioneernetwork.net/wp-content/uploads/2018/02/2018-01-Kurt-Lewins-Change-Theory. pdf Retrieved on 7 August 2020

Stelter, R. (2012). *A guide to third Generation Coaching: Narrative-collaborative theory and practice.* Dordrecht Heidelberg, Germany: Springer.

Thorton, C. (2010). *Group and team coaching: The essential guide.* New York: Routledge.

Wageman, R., Nunes, D., Burruss, J. & Hackman, J.R. (2008). *Senior leadership teams: What it takes to make them great.* Boston, MA: Harvard Business School.

van Nieuwerburgh, C. (Ed.). (2012). *Coaching in education: Getting better results for students, educators and parents.* London: Karnac.

Vygotsky, L.S. ([1926] 1962). *Thought and language.* Cambridge, MA: MIT Press.

Whitmore, J. (2017). *Coaching for performance: The Principles and Practice of Coaching and Leadership fully revised 25th Anniversary Edition.* London: Nicholas Brealey.

Woolley, A.W., Chabris, C.F., Pentland, A., Hashmi, N., Malone, W.T. (2010). Evidence for a collective intelligence factor in the performance of human groups. *Science*, (*330*) 6004, 686–688. doi:10.1126/science.1193147

43 Narrative coaching – Part 4: Redesigning the GROW model as the 4th generation coaching for people and the planet

Ho Law

Abstract

This paper reflects and reviews the formulation of the GROW model in relation to narrative coaching in response to the climate change crisis, the socio-cultural and technological paradigms. It proposes a new coaching model by redesigning the GROW process and integrating it with the narrative coaching process. It argues that the new model called ROGWin can be regarded as the fourth generation coaching (4GC) in terms of the evolution of coaching psychology as a professional discipline. Its implications for future research and practice, including technological advances such as artificial intelligence (AI), and coaching's role in the wider world and its environment, are discussed.

Keywords

AI climate change; fourth generation coaching; 4GC; coaching psychology; GROW; environment.

Original publication details: Law, H. (2021, June). Narrative coaching – Part 4: Redesigning the GROW model as the 4th generation coaching for people and the planet. *The Coaching Psychologist*, *17*(1), 59–69. Reproduced with permission of The British Psychological Society.

INTRODUCTION

The story so far… In Part 3, I explained how narrative coaching could be applied for groups, teams, organisations and wider communities by embedding it in the action research process. I further argued that narrative coaching is more powerful, effective and efficient than conventional psychological interventions and more suitable for crisis situations, such as the 2017 Grenfell Tower fire disaster in the UK, the COVID-19 pandemic and the ongoing climate change crisis (Law, 2017; 2020b).

This paper, the final part of the series, aims to revisit the popular GROW model advocated by the late Sir John Whitmore (2017) as part of our honouring his life with an objective to continue championing his eco-environmental concern through transpersonal coaching. As said, I regard this as not only as Whitmore's unfinished project to address wider society, the environment and the planet, but also the 'big agenda' that we should all consider in terms of the present and future challenges that we face in the 'new norm'.

This paper first reviews other competing proposals as the best way to achieve the above objective (Section 2). Section 3 then describes how the narrative coaching process can map onto the GROW model in practice. The detail of its temporal dimension is discussed in Section 4 and consolidated in Section 5, giving the integration a new name: the acronym ROGWin. Section 6 proposes the new paradigm as 'fourth generation coaching' (4GC). Finally, Section 7 considers the implications for several fields, including future research and practice for coaching psychology as a professional discipline, technological advances such as artificial intelligence (AI) and our wider role in the world and environment.

PARADIGM SHIFT AND UNIVERSAL INTEGRATED FRAMEWORK (UIF)

Regarding climate change, Whybrow (2018, 2019) advocated redefining coaching as 'regenerative coaching' by including human concerns on the biosphere, planet, ecosystems, economics and regenerative design, based on Reed's (2007) Trajectory of Environmentally Responsible Design and Raworth's (2017) Doughnut Economics. However, these proposals were accepted uncritically without attention to the detail of the system integration to coaching which this paper aims to address.

Firstly, Reed's 'Trajectory' was oversimplistic and misrepresented the complexity of the *whole* system, which is dynamic (e.g., technologies could be part of the solution as well as the problem, as in conventional practice) and includes living and non-living systems, the planet, the cosmos *and* the universe (Law & Buckler, 2020); see Figure 1.

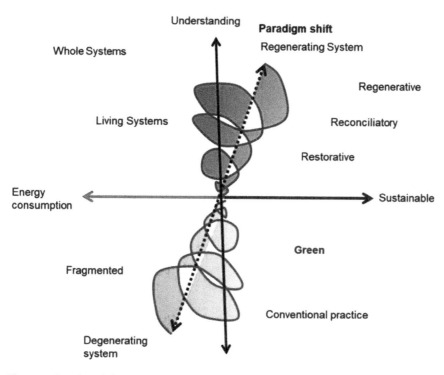

Figure 1 *Paradigm shift (adapted from Reed's Trajectory).*

Secondly, Raworth's 'Doughnut' metaphor for 'nested systems' was already addressed by the Universal Integrated Framework (UIF) of coaching (Law et al., 2007; Law & Buckler, 2020; Law et al., 2010); see Figure 2.

In Figure 2, the inner ring represents the social foundation (the bottom line) on which we build a sustainable, safe and just societal space. In this space, we can meet the needs of all within the means of the planet. Above and beyond that, we would hit the ecological ceiling (the outer boundary), leading to critical planetary degradation OR hit below, resulting in human deprivation (the hole at the centre). Law et al. (2010) advocated transpersonal coaching as a means to enable leaders in organisations to meet their Corporate Social Responsibility (CSR) for the wider socioenvironmental benefit. They called for organisations to operate within this fragile zone of sustainability – the so-called 'triple bottom line': for people, planet and profit.

While the paper at the time was meant to be a response to a similar call by Outhwaite and Bettridge (2009), it was equally applicable here to map onto Raworth's (2017) Doughnut Economics. Law and Buckler (2020) thus argue that redefining coaching further is unnecessary, as the climate change crisis has already been addressed with *transpersonal coaching*. This paper will expand this argument further and show in more detail how the model can be translated in practice by integrating the GROW model with the narrative coaching approach.

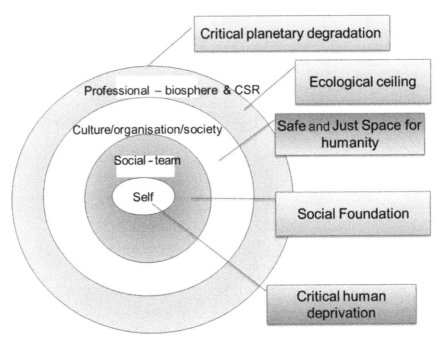

Figure 2 *Universal Integrated Framework (adapted from Law et al., 2010).*

RE-ENGINEERING THE GROW MODEL

While the GROW model has been popular and widely accepted in the coaching world (Whitmore, 2009), it has often been criticised by the coaching psychology community as 'no psychological theory or research is covered that underpins coaching practice' (Palmer, 2007, p. ix). Various attempts were made in recent years by coaching psychologists to underpin the model with psychological principles. For instance, the late Anthony Grant (2006) explored the psycho-mechanism of the multifaceted nature of goals in the goal-setting stage of executive coaching. Megginson and Clutterbuck (2004) suggested that the GROW model could be further improved by reviewing the coachee's current situation and agreeing on a *topic* (T) of discussion first, hence TGROW (see also Law, 2013a; Law, 2013b). As discussed in Part 1 of this series of articles (Law, 2019), a more natural flow for coaching would be:

Step 1. *Storying/Story Description* – Invite the coachee to tell a story about recent events and their experiences that has brought them to the meeting of here and now; that is, mindfulness in essence. So, the reality check should be the first stage of the model as a point of entry for context setting, followed by the Options stage with the possibility for transformation (reauthoring): see Figure 3.

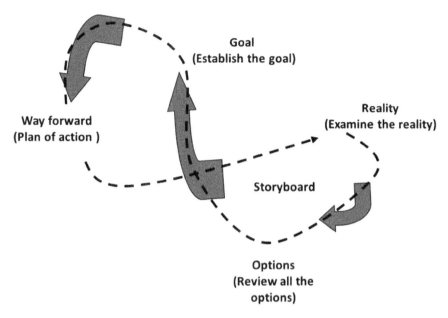

Figure 3   *GROW Model in narrative practice.*

Step 2. *Relation Mapping/Narrative Plot* with *possible options (O)* – Identify various domains and options from the coachee's story: the *background/backdrop* that is spaces and places (What, When, Where, Who and Why?); *self-identity* (purposes, values, aspirations, hopes and dreams); and the *zone of proximal development*. Map their effects/influence onto the coachee's *landscape of consciousness/self-identity* when selecting an option as a goal to move forward to Step 3 (Goal setting).

Step 3. *Identify the coachee's self-identity as a narrative goal (G)* – Invite the coachee to reflect and evaluate the impact (effects/influence) of the themes/plots and select an option that embodies and reflects the coachee's self-identity (purpose, values, aspirations, hopes and dreams). This may feature questions such as:

Why this Option/Goal (say A) instead of that (B, C, D, …, X, Y, Z)?

From the above, for the transformation (reauthoring) to take place, we are equating the chosen Option as a Goal:

IF T = TRUE OR T > 0
THEN
O = G
Where T is Transformation
O is option
G is goal

As such, the transformation is metaphorical and recursive in nature. I shall expand on this further in the next section. In Part 2 of this series of articles, we located this moment of change (*turning point*) that occurs during Step 3 after narrative analyses have taken place, so that further possibilities (*zone of proximal development*), a new plan and action can all be possible as a way forward (W): the next step (Law, 2020a).

THE TEMPORAL DIMENSION OF GROWING/DEVELOPMENT IN THE GROW MODEL

In practice, identifying a significant long-term goal is difficult by simply going through the GROW questions mechanically. It may not be accomplished within a single session. A significant long-term goal would be embedding the coachee's deep value, belief and self-identity. It is implicitly embedded in the context of the story: situational or positional identity (Hiles et al., 2009). The value-based goal is likely set at the evaluation stage of the narrative process. Once such a goal is evaluated and validated by the coachee, an action plan can easily be made at the Wrap-up stage. The outcome of implementing the action plan can then be reviewed in the next session. Hence the coaching process is dynamic and allows for forward and backward movement throughout each stage. It seems circular, but it should more accurately be described as spiralling upwards or forwards across time. Although we do not travel through time,

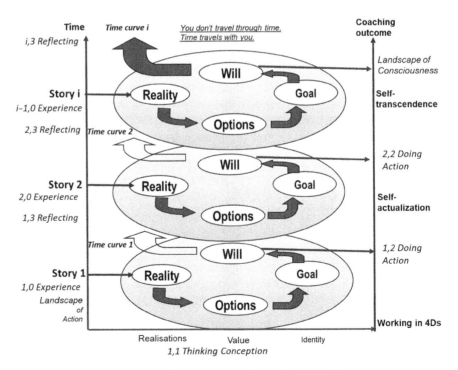

Figure 4 *Longitudinal GROW model integrative narrative practice (ROGWin).*

time travels with us in an unfolding process, whether travelling through space or in conversation. Longitudinally, the GROW process is recursive, as it spirals upwards over a number of sessions (i) through time (Figure 4).

INTEGRATING NARRATIVE PROCESS WITH THE GROW MODEL (ROGWIN)

Notice that, in Figure 4, by integrating narrative practice in the GROW process, it does not only embody Kolb's (1984) 'Experiential Learning Cycle' – a narrative foundation as indicated in Part 1 of this series (Law, 2019), but also works as an action research, as advocated in Parts 2 and 3 (Kagan et al., 2011; Law, 2020a, 2020b; Lewin, 1946). Thus, the new process can be redescribed as follows:

Stage 1: Start with the **Reality** (R) of here and now using storytelling as a point of entry to the narrative coaching process (Step 1. Description). The story embodies the coachee's lived experience that brought them to the coaching session. The process allows the coachee to richly describe what happened, alongside what and how they have been doing to get to this present point (the landscape of action). This marks the beginning of the first iteration of the action research, denoted by (1,0).

Stage 2: Explore all the possible **Options** (O) that emerge from each action. As mentioned earlier (Section 2), each option could potentially represent a *turning point* if it is selected by the coachee as their goal (G); it would guide the next course of action. This requires a lot of thinking in the conversation between the coachee and the coach. It represents the thinking (conception) stage of the action research, denoted by (1,1).

Stage 3: Formulate a **Goal** (G) that would call for action from the chosen option (when O = G). How do we know it is the right goal? One could feel that it is the right goal when it evokes emotions and excitement (hence a well-known coaching question – *What makes your heart sing?*), as it invokes the coachee's passion with a sense of meaning, purpose and responsibility, that is, it embodies the coachee's self-identity. This stage requires mapping the landscape of action from the story description upon the landscape of consciousness in the coachee's mind.

Stage 4: Agree a plan of action that the coachee has a determination (**Will**) to take forward at the Wrap-up stage. This represents the doing (Action) stage of the action research, denoted by (1,2).

The above four stage process is recursive in nature, as the outcome of implementing the action plan would generate a new experience (story 2) which, in turn, becomes the input to the next iteration. From a spatio-temporal perspective, the process could be described as a *time curve*, as the time/process spirals upwards into the next iteration (i + 1). The iteration is recursive in nature because each story at Stage 1 is another new (story 2), evolved from the previous story (story 1). In general, for i sessions, we have story (i) that is based on the experience of (i−1) iteration.

TRANSPERSONAL PARADIGM AS FOURTH GENERATION COACHING (4GC)

For the last two and half decades of his life, Whitmore continuously expressed his concerns on the climate change crisis and advocated transpersonal coaching as an intervention to help people rise to this challenge with a paradigm shift. The paradigm uses Assagioli's (1965) science of psychosynthesis to help coachees develop and recognise their personal responsibility, meaning, direction and wider purpose. Typically, Whitmore illustrated the concept with a traditional two-dimensional Cartesian Coordination System, as shown in Figure 5.

The vertical axis (y) represents spiritual aspiration with quantitative values; the horizontal axis (x) represents psychological attachment to material success, which are measurable quantitatively. Whitmore suggested that individual development tends to be biased towards one axis (either x or y) more than the other (represented by the dotted lines). As people progress along their developmental journey in such an imbalanced way, eventually they will reach a crisis point. This may be a 'crisis of meaning'

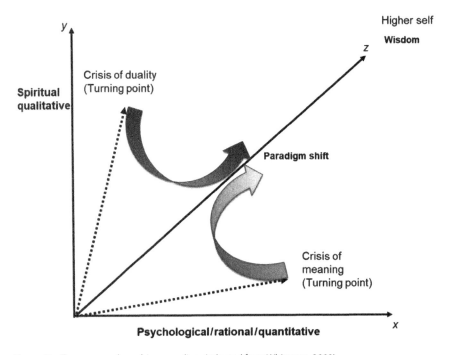

Figure 5   *Transpersonal coaching paradigm (adapted from Whitmore, 2009).*

if they focus too much on their materialistic achievement (biased towards x) OR a 'crisis of duality' if they are devoted too much to spiritual practice and lacking physical resources to sustain themselves (biased towards y). A balanced way is ideal: achieving the higher self, or 'the source of our wisdom and purpose' (Whitmore, 2009, p. 156), here represented by the 45 degree line (z).

While intellectually the concept makes sense to many coaches and coachees, especially those who were at a senior executive level (e.g., senior managers and directors), Whitmore had never explained how it could be put into practice with the GROW model which was continuously advocated by him and his associates (Hanley, 2011; Whitmore, 2017). By integrating the narrative process with the GROW model (ROGWin), as described in previous sections, we can map ROGWin and Reed's Trajectory in Figure 1 directly onto Whitmore's transpersonal coaching paradigm, as shown in Figure 6.

In Figure 6, The spirals represent the time curve; each upward spiral is a ROGWin cycle, as illustrated in Figure 4. Each iteration represents a recursion of ROGWin. As the coachee's storyline unfolds, the time curve progresses upwards along the z axis towards understanding, wisdom, the higher self or self-transcendence. The subtle but important difference between iteration and recursion was explained in Part 3 of this series. All the critical elements and moments (crisis, turning points, meaning and concepts of the self) are the core ingredients of narrative coaching, as was described in Parts 1 and 2 (Law, 2019; 2020a).

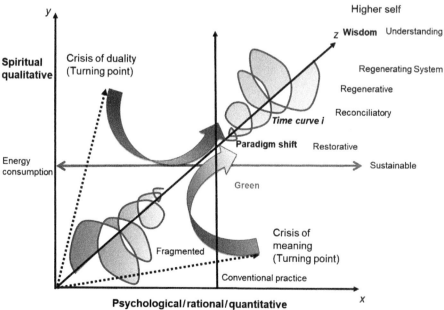

Figure 6 *Mapping transpersonal coaching paradigm shift onto Reed's Trajectory.*

CONCLUSION, DISCUSSION, REFLECTION AND REFLEXIVITY

To reflect and summarise the four-part story of narrative coaching, the Transform Function (A^T) was defined as the outcome action of the narrative coaching in Part 1 (Law, 2019). Narrative action research was advocated in Part 2 (Law, 2020a), and its applications for groups, teams, organisations and community was described in Part 3 (Law, 2020b). The function (A^T) was expanded in relation to its power (P), the number of participants (n), as in remembering conversation (Part 2, Law, 2020a) and Groups (N), as in outsider witness retelling for teams and community (Part 3, Law, 2020b). These are formulated in Equations 1 and 2, respectively (Law, 2020a, 2020b):

$$P = \left(A^T\right)^n \qquad \text{(Equation 1)}$$

It was suggested that n = 2 for reauthoring and remembering;

$$P = \left(A^T\right)^n \times N \qquad \text{(Equation 2)}$$

It was recommended that n = 5 and N = 30 are the maximum values for outsider witness retelling and definition ceremony respectively.

In this paper, I have continued our narrative dialogue amongst our colleagues and peers in coaching and psychology in response to their coaching and environmental concerns (e.g., Law & Buckler, 2020; Law et al., 2010; Outhwaite & Bettridge, 2009; Palmer, 2007; Whitmore, 2009; Whybrow, 2018, 2019). Storying is foregrounded again, not only as a point of entry to initiate the new GROW coaching process at its Reality stage (ROGWin), but also as a resource to address global challenges: in this case, the climate change crisis. The process of how to integrate narrative coaching with the GROW model has been described in detail in terms of its steps and stages. In doing so, a temporal dimension was added into the model; hence the Equations 1 and 2 can further be expanded to include t as the time function, as follows:

$$P = \left(A^T\right)^n t \qquad \text{for reauthoring and remembering;} \qquad \text{(Equation 3)}$$

$$P = \left(A^T\right)^n \times Nt \qquad \text{for groups, teams and community.} \qquad \text{(Equation 4)}$$

I hope this paper has done justice to honour the life of Sir John, celebrate his achievements in coaching and continue the unfinished project in championing eco-environmental concerns for people and the planet. This also provides an opportunity for us all to pause, reflect and consider the wider role of coaching and coaching psychology as well as our role and responsibility within the tapestry of this interconnected world.

Reflecting on the whole journey of this four-part series on narrative coaching, from the beginning we declared the narrative approach as third generation coaching and regarded other current coaching approaches, such as cognitive-behavioural and solution-focused, as the second (Stelter, 2012). The development of coaching and coaching psychology is like other disciplines. Considering coaching as an interdisciplinary branch of applied psychology, its practice is primarily linguistic-based ('clean language', for example). It would be a fair comparison with other disciplines, such as AI, cognitive psychology, computer science and programming in terms of its evolution and development. For example, programming languages developed rapidly as they evolved together with computer science and technology in parallel.

I remember, in the 1980s, when I worked as an applied psychologist (my first proper job) researching in AI (Boden, 1977) and developing knowledge-based systems, the so-called 'expert system' (Waterman, 1986), the key task then was eliciting knowledge from human experts and transferring their knowledge into computers (Diaper, 1989). We could not use natural language to communicate with computers. At the time, languages like c for the relational database and Unix operation system, the so-called fourth generation language (4GL), was considered as the 'cutting edge' in mainstream industries. For AI, we were using Lisp (List processing) and Prolog (Programming Logic), being described by observers as developing machine consciousness using sixth generation language on 4GL machines; frustrations were assured in the work – with a sense of being at the fringe. I was a dreamer; I thought that AI was our future; it would save the world from poverty and slavery.

It makes sense, therefore, to describe transpersonal coaching as fourth generation coaching (4GC); and I appreciate why it has not been in the mainstream of coaching and coaching psychology in accordance with the survey of our coaching psychology members (Palmer & Whybrow, 2004). But the time will come… as the discipline evolves.

I never thought that, more than 35 years later, coaching psychology has become a *professional discipline*; psychology has become one of the most popular subjects for young people to study (a subject of choice for university applications), the natural language recognition, learning machine and processing of big data has become a reality… And yet, we are still not training enough psychologists to meet the growing demand (Migration Advisory Committee, 2019). Globally, poverty and inequality are getting worse; more people could access a mobile phone than a psychologist (there were 5.11 billion unique mobile users worldwide in 2019 according to datareportal.com). We are told again by our leaders that AI will be a solution for our societal problems in the future. For instance, in her major speech on science, the former UK prime minister Theresa May was reported to 'pledge to revolutionise the health service by deploying AI in the NHS, aiming to prevent over 20,000 cancer-related deaths each year by 2033' (Cowburn, 2018).

A call for further research and development (R&D) of a coaching mobile app using AI technology sounds like a far cry as an endnote at a coaching psychology discussion. However, there are already antecedents of this trend. For instance, the success of cognitive-behavioural therapy (CBT), being regarded by the National institute for Health and Care Excellence (NICE) as a treatment of choice, has led to the development of CCBT: the computerised version of CBT. Despite its critiques from many psychologists and psychotherapists, CCBT has helped improve access to psychological therapies.

Like any process of automation, the essence of CCBT development is the algorithm that enables its procedure to be translated into a programming language for computer and mobile apps. This paper has explicated the procedure of a transpersonal coaching model (ROGWin) in a way that algorithms can be developed for automation using AI approach such as natural language recognition and qualitative algebra (Williams, 1988).

A professional discipline defines itself with its typical research agenda in terms of (1) its process, (2) competences and (3) contribution to the world, e.g., arts; philosophy; knowledge science and application or practices (Ormnerod, 2021). For coaching psychology, the first agenda item had been well covered by Whitmore's GROW model from the practitioner's experience at the early stage; the second agenda item by the formation of the special group of psychology practitioners (the forerunners and founding members of SGCP) grounding its ethics and core competence in line with psychology (Law, 2006). The third item on contribution still remains. *Can coaching psychology measure up as a discipline?* Hence Skews (2020) called for an evidence-based evaluation of coaching interventions. The potential impact of AI and new opportunities for coaching psychologists to engage in AI development and to supervise AI applications would help to facilitate self-coaching (Ellison, 2015), thereby increasing the impact of coaching psychology.

On reflection, I am somewhat surprised that the unfolding story of narrative coaching begins with its positioning firmly on the social constructivism and critical realism continuum – a qualitative paradigm within Postmodernism (Baudrillard, 1995) and ends with a call for a return to modernity – the unfinished project (Berman, 2010). This signifies another turning point: a new beginning. This time, hopefully, the transformation could achieve a harmony of discord (Ovid, 8 AD). That is another story.

On the reflexivity of 'telling' the narrative coaching story, I am mindful that 'the told' ultimately depends on and is limited by the author's own world view (*weltanschauung*), opinions, experience, knowledge, skills and self-identity. All these are situated within a particular period, time and spaces shaped by the forces of nature and culture, with this same human condition that I assume the reader, amongst peers and colleagues, shares. The value of my story could only be assessed by the trustworthiness of the content, its argument, coherency and source of references that I tried to cover with sincerity and good intention to help improve the profession, society and the wider world. I hope that you have enjoyed reading this series of narrative conversations, have been inspired by its eloquence and power of transformation and that you start applying the approach to your coaching agenda – be it for whom the people you care or for the planet as your wider concern. So, your next step: *What is your story?*

REFERENCES

Assagioli, R. (1965). *Psychosynthesis*. The Viking Press.

Baudrillard, J. (1995). *Simulacra and Simulation*. The University of Michigan Press.

Berman, M. 2010. *All that is Solid Melts into Air: The Experience of Modernity* ISBN 978-1-84467-644-6. Verso.

Boden, M. (1977). *Artificial intelligence and natural man*. Harvester Press.

Cowburn, A. (2018). *Theresa May says AI revolution will help NHS prevent thousands of cancer-related deaths by 2033*. The Independent. 21 May. https://www.independent.co.uk/news/uk/politics/nhs-artificial-intelligence-ai-cancer-deaths-2033-technology-promise-a8360451.html Accessed 21 March 2021.

Diaper, D. (Ed.). (1989). *Knowledge elicitation – Principles, techniques and applications*. Ellis Horwood (Wiley).

Ellison, R. (2015). Self-Coaching. L. Hall Ed., *Coaching in times of crisis and transformation – How to help individuals and organizations flourish*. Chapter 11 (222–244). Kogan Page.

Grant, A. M. (2006). An integrative goal-focused approach to executive coaching. In: D. Stober and A. M. Grant (Eds.), *Evidence-based coaching handbook* (pp. 153–192). Wiley.

Hanley, S. (2011) *From the grow model to transpersonal coaching – What is Sir John Whitmore on About?* Published Personal correspondence. https://coachworkssydney.files.wordpress.com/2011/09/from-the-grow-model-to-transpersonal-coaching-22.pdf Accessed 14/01/202011: 07.

Hiles, D. R., Cermak, I., & Chrz, V. (2009). Narrative oriented inquiry: A dynamic framework for good practice. In: D. Robinson, P. Fisher, T. Yeadon-Lee, S. J. Robinson, and P. Woodcock (Eds.), *Narrative, memory and identities* (pp. 53–65). University of Huddersfield Press.

Kagan, C., Burton, M., Duckett, P., Lawthom, R., & Siddiquee, A. (2011). *Critical community psychology*. Blackwell Wiley.

Kolb, D. A. (1984). *Experiential learning: Experience as the source of learning and development*. Prentice Hall.

Law, H. (2006). Ethical principles in coaching psychology. *The Coaching Psychologist*, 2(1), 13–16.

Law, H. (2013a). *Psychology of Coaching, Mentoring & Learning* (Second Edition.). John Wiley & Sons.

Law, H. (2013b). *Coaching Psychology – A Practitioner's Manual*. John Wiley & Sons.

Law, H. (2017). The Transpersonal power of stories: Creating a community of narrative practice. *Transpersonal Psychology Review*, 19(2), 3–11.

Law, H. (2019). Narrative coaching – Part 1: An introduction and the first step. *The Coaching Psychologist*, 15(2), 36–40.

Law, H. (2020a). Narrative coaching – Part 2: Two forms of change structures: Re-authoring and remembering. *The Coaching Psychologist*, 16(1), 59–69.

Law, H. (2020b). Narrative coaching – Part 3: Narrative coaching – Part 3: Approaches for groups, teams, organisations and community. *The Coaching Psychologist*, 16(2), 59–70.

Law, H., Lancaster, B. L., & DiGiovanni, N. (2010). A wider role of coaching psychology – Applying transpersonal coaching psychology. *The Coaching Psychologist*, 6(1), 30–38.

Law, H. C., Ireland, S., & Hussain, Z. (2007). *Psychology of coaching, mentoring and learning*. John Wiley & Sons.

Law, H., & Buckler, S. (2020). Transpersonal coaching as the fourth wave psychological intervention for people and the planet. *Transpersonal Psychology Review*, 19(2), 7–20.

Lewin, K. (1946). Action Research and Minority Problems. *Journal of Social Issues, 2(4)*, 34–46. http://dx.doi.org/10.1111/j.1540-4560.1946.tb02295.x

Megginson, D., & Clutterbuck, D. (2004). *Techniques for coaching and mentoring*. Routledge.

Migration Advisory Committee. (2019) *Full review of the Shortage Occupation List*. Gov.uk: Crown copyright. ISBN: 978-1-78655-811-4.

Ormnerod, R. (2021). The fitness and survival of the OR profession in the age of artificial intelligence. *Journal of the Operational Research Society, 72(1)*, 4–22. https://doi.org/10.1080/01605682.2019.1650619.

Outhwaite, A., & Bettridge, N. (2009). From the inside out: Coaching's role in transformation towards a sustainable society. *The Coaching Psychologist, 5 (2)*, 76–89.

Ovid, N. (8 AD 2008). E. J. Kenney Ed., A. D. Melville (Translator) *Metamorphoses (Oxford World's Classics)*. Open University Press.

Palmer, S., & Whybrow, A. (2004). Coaching psychology survey: Taking Stock. *Paper at the BPS SGCP Inaugural Conference*, on 15 December, held at City University, London.

Palmer, S. (2007). Foreword. In H. C. Law, S. Ireland, & Z. Hussain (Eds.), (2007). *Psychology of coaching, mentoring and learning*. John Wiley & Sons.

Raworth, K. (2017). *Doughnut Economics: Seven ways to think like a 21st Century economist*. Random House Books.

Reed, B. (2007). Shifting from 'sustainability' to regeneration. *Building Research & Information, 35(6)*, 674–680. https://doi.org/10.1080/09613210701475753

Skews, R. (2020). How to design and conduct quantitative coaching intervention research. *The Coaching Psychologist, 16(1)*, 41–52.

Stelter, R. (2012). *A guide to third generation coaching: Narrative-collaborative theory and practice*. Springer.

Waterman, D. A. (1986). *A guide to expert systems*. Addison-Wiley.

Whitmore, J. (2009). *Coaching for Performance: GROWing human potential and purpose. The principles and practice of coaching and leadership (Fourth Edition)*. Nicholas Brealey Publishing.

Whitmore, J. (2017). *Coaching for Performance: The principles and practice of coaching and Leadership fully revised 25th Anniversary Edition*. Nicholas Brealey.

Whybrow, A. (2018). Regenerative Coaching. *Presentation at the 8th International Congress of Coaching Psychology*, 11–12th October. International Society for Coaching Psychology. London.

Whybrow, A. (2019). Climate Criss. We are not OK. *Coaching at Work, 14(6)*, 43–47.

Williams, B. (1988). MINIMA: A Symbolic Approach to Qualitative Algebraic Reasoning. Published in *AAAI-88 Proceedings. Computer Science*, AAAI (www.aaai.org). pp. 264–269. https://doi.org/10.1016/B978-1-4832-1447-4.50026-2 Corpus ID: 17619152. Last accessed 26 March 2021.

44 Using the four gateways to tell new stories and make new choices

David Drake

Abstract

Coaches and clients can make more conscious and generative choices when they have greater somatic self-awareness.

Keywords

Attachment theory; choices; gateways; mutual regulation; narrative coaching; self-regulation; stories.

INTRODUCTION

Attachment theory provides an evidence-based source of guidance that both coaches and clients can use to make new choices in their sessions. While the theory was developed in relation to infants and caregivers, it reflects the same basic needs that adults have in coaching: creating healthy connections, being met appropriately and generatively, increasing the capacity for self-soothing and self-regulation, and exploring in

Original publication details: Drake, D. (2017, June). Using the four gateways to tell new stories and make new choices. *The Coaching Psychologist, 13*(1), 22–26. Reproduced with permission of The British Psychological Society.

Coaching Practiced, First Edition. Edited by David Tee and Jonathan Passmore.
© 2022 John Wiley & Sons Ltd. Published 2022 by John Wiley & Sons Ltd.
DOI: 10.1002/9781119835714.ch44

new directions to facilitate growth. As such, coaching can be seen as a process in which people develop new regulatory and narrative strategies (Drake, 2017). In so doing, they become more mature, resilient and agile in service of what they are seeking. This article connects self-regulation from an attachment perspective, self-awareness from a somatic perspective (four gateways), and the choices coaches make (formulations) and clients make (decisions).

Attachment theory is relevant here because any effort to assist clients in making decisions or new choices must address their underlying narrative patterns. Stories are perfect for this as they make visible people's largely invisible attachment and identity processes. Working somatically – as is done often in narrative coaching – enables clients to access aspects of their story that are hidden by their conscious mind but present in their body. As Paris (2007) observes, 'What the psyche refuses to acknowledge, the body always manifests' (p.xii). Questions such as, 'What do you notice in your body as you are telling this story? Where do you notice it?' 'What words or emotions come up for you there?' are commonly used for this reason. Inviting clients to slow down and access their somatic knowledge often yields powerful experiences in which they can access more of the truth in their story and make better decisions (Drake, 2015). The early phases in coaching are therefore less about moving toward the objective and more about shifting the person's presence and perspective to create a new starting point.

ATTACHMENT THEORY

As coaches, we routinely encounter vestiges of long-held patterns that continue to echo across our client's stories and lives. In tracking these patterns, we are looking for the ways in which clients are living the same story over and over again. Attachment theory offers a useful resource here because of its emphasis on the preverbal nature of our narrative patterns (Drake, 2009). In the context of coaching it is generally not a matter of exploring our client's past, but more about recognising, observing and working with the manifestations of these patterns in the present. For example, when speaking about a challenge at work, does the client adopt a posture which signals she may fault herself (slumping in her chair as if she is guilty) or a posture which may signal she faults the other person (sitting defiantly in her chair as if she is innocent). As a coach, you could use her body language as a way in to explore both the particulars of this story in the moment as well as the broader implications of the patterns in play (from the past and for the future). How might the awareness of her posture enable this client to gain access and then shift to what is going on in the moment – and by extension in her broader life? Through coaching, clients can develop an increased sense of attachment security through enriching their regulation, repertoire and resources in terms of how they meet their needs and relate to others. Many of the challenges our clients bring to coaching are remnants of the compromises we made as children, particularly when we had less than desirable attachment experiences.

This is based in the premise that attachment theory reflects an evolutionary imperative to keep vulnerable infants alive by instilling in them an instinctual drive to preserve safety and love. When children perceive a sign of threat, their attachment system is activated and they seek proximity to and care from attachment figure(s). If the result is satisfying, they develop greater security, engage in further exploration and build working models to suit. If it is not satisfying, they deploy insecure secondary strategies, engage in less (effective) exploration and build working models to suit. There are three primary outcomes from the attachment process for infants (Bowlby, 1969, 1988), each of which has a counterpart in adults. A sense of a *safe haven* results from the proximity of and access to a trusted caregiver when the child feels anxious or senses danger. This is analogous to the rapport and trust building that is required for clients to feel safe with their coach and the coaching process. The presence of a sufficient safe haven provides a child with a sense of a *secure base* from which to increasingly and confidently explore the world – and to which he or she can return as needed as part of ever-widening circles. This is analogous to our invitations to clients to try out new mindsets and behaviours during and after the sessions. As children grow, they begin to rely less on external figures for safety and more on the repeated experiences they have encoded in their implicit memory as *working models* they will increasingly carry within themselves. This is analogous to setting up scaffolding and other structures for success with clients, which they can use to be more proactive and less reactive in their responses and choices (Drake 2009).

Clients' working models can be seen as meta-narratives that inform how they see the world, relate with the world and act in the world. Since much of this is unconscious or tacit for them, they are best explored through working with their stories (particularly elements such as metaphors) and their bodies (postures, gestures, states, etc.). Metaphors work in this way because they often provide a shared linguistic shorthand and bridge the symbolic and literal, the emotive and logical, and the conscious and unconscious in a conversation. Working somatically enables clients to more easily access their emotional states, triggers and reactive responses. For example, when a client stands in a new way she notices a greater sense of confidence in herself. When a client lets go of his usual stance, it seems to make it easier for people to approach him. The aim in coaching is to help clients develop a greater sense of attachment security through our work with them.

FOUR GATEWAYS

The body is often overlooked by coaches, both in terms of their development and their practice. However, it is an important source of knowledge about what is happening within ourselves, with our clients and in the relational field between us. For example, a coach becomes aware of a knot in his stomach that leads him to pause and, in so doing, he realises that he has colluded with the client to keep the conversation at an abstract level rather than speak directly to what is actually going on in the client's stories. I developed the simple process below to help both coaches and clients to drop into their bodies as they work together. It is based in the system of chakras found in a number of philosophical traditions and modalities. These four gateways represent access points to the flow of energy (or lack thereof) in the body and each one can be associated with a different type of knowledge. The use of energy as a construct finds support in the neuroscience of attachment patterns and regulation, and it provides a way to ground intuition and increase self- and other-awareness. Coaches can use their gateways to better 'read' situations and to support their clients in making more informed and authentic choices. I primarily focus on these four gateways, but there are a number of others that can be used as needed (Drake, 2015).

Tool: Creating greater attachment security through coaching

Attachment need	Client need	Opening for change	Invitation by coach
Secure base	Gain support for his depressive state	Awareness of his triggers for stress	Shift his point of comparison to reduce judgment
Safe haven	Opportunity to be a results-oriented leader	Invitation from boss to step into a new role	Use his experience to offer a set of options rather than just accept what he was given
Working model	Develop a more strategic mindset	Need to talk with a key player impacted by decision	Increase his advocacy for his needs and awareness of impact on her if the strategy is to work

The premise is that people will be freer to make new choices and will make better decisions if they have access to knowledge in the fullest sense of that word. If not, they are often missing vital clues and energies, which will impede their processing and constrain their choices and actions. Working with the gateways and other somatic tools in coaching counters the bias toward rationality and cognition and enables the coach to address the whole person. The framework is most commonly used by placing a hand on each of the four spots on the body – one at a time – while focusing on a decision or issue at hand. With each of these gateways, the question is the same, 'What does this part of me, this way of knowing, have to say about my question? My current and desired state?' Coaches can do this for themselves and/or guide the client through the process. Either way, it is about moving up and down these four gateways as needed to gain new knowledge about the question or issue. This helps either of them to stand in the truth of his stories and open up to what can be learned there. For example, a client relaxes her habituated narrative when experiencing stress (head gateway) in order to pay closer attention to her values (heart gateway) and to explore the fear that blocks what is most true to her (hara gateway) such that her actions are avoidant (hips gateway).

Tool: The Four Gateways

Gateway	Focus	Association	Level of knowledge
Head	Thinking	Thoughts, mental models	Cognitive
Heart	Feeling	Values, emotions, relations	Emotive
Hara	Being	Gut instinct, primacy, power	Instinctive
Hips	Doing	Action, commitment	Active

Clients are asked to notice what comes up at each location, and the result often yields information that is useful for them in terms of the associated knowledge and energy. Many people find that how they hold their question or issue changes as new information emerges in moving through the four gateways. The person is encouraged to not pre-judge the sensations as good or bad because these labels tend to be oversimplified and non-generative. We are more interested in the acuity of their observations and articulations. For example, does the energy feel strong? Blocked? Unsettled? Peaceful? You can then work with the person to explore what is happening for him at that gateway, 'What do you notice? What words come up for you? What would it take to restore the flow here?' You can also use just one or two of the gateways: e.g., inviting the client to put her hand on her heart to name a feeling, put one hand on her heart and the other on her hara to ground her grief, or put one hand on her hara and the other on her hips to gather more strength to make a tough decision (and act on it). When clients feel complete and there is a restored sense of flow – or at least a sense of what is needed to restore flow – they are more informed and ready to do the work at hand.

One of the primary reasons clients struggle to make decisions or act in new ways is because they get stuck in their heads. Using the gateways helps people access more sources of knowledge they can then use to get unstuck and make better decisions. I find that clients can access more of their truth and make better decisions by using their head last rather than first. Otherwise, the executive function of their mind is often overwhelmed and not nearly as effective. However, I tend to start the gateways process with the head because that is where most people begin as they tell their stories in coaching, especially in organisations. Ultimately, it is about helping people to develop a greater sense of intimacy and agency through coming to trust that they have more resources within them than they may have once believed. As a result, they can access more energy and knowledge in support of their new choices and new actions (Drake, 2015). For coaches, it is a call to fine-tune our body as an instrument so that we can become a more masterful artisan of our craft (Drake, 2014).

Example of using the gateways in a client session:

1. Using the *head* gateway, the client notices that his story is jumbled as he tries to think about whether or not to stay in his current role.

2. Using the *heart* gateway, he feels a sense of sadness and loss he had not been aware of before, and he associates it with a realisation it may be time to move on.
3. Using the *hara* gateway, he first senses fear but then, as he breathes deeper into it, he discovers a sense of adventure he had been stifling.
4. Using the *hips* gateway, he becomes aware of a new energy as he imagines himself exploring other options.
5. Moving back through the gateways he feels the clarity and alignment he needs to start looking for a new role.

CLOSING

Our presence as coaches is critical and – as with the attachment process when we were young – much of that happens relationally and physiologically more than cognitively or linguistically. So, the more you can develop your somatic acuity the better you will coach. The more fully you can access your body as you coach, the more it opens up possibilities for clients to do the same through mutual regulation. The more that both parties can do this, the richer the material is to work with and the more deeply human the conversation can become. The better the working relationship and conversations in coaching, the greater the attachment security each person will gain. When our clients feel more secure, they are more able to:

- Distinguish between their experience and that of others.
- Sense and articulate their feelings and empathise with others.
- Self-soothe and mutually regulate so they can learn now.
- Break up their stories and reconfigure them in order to grow.

Working with the gateways in coaching enables both people to be more present as a whole person and to contribute to more of the whole story. It opens up more generative conversations and supports the somatic anchoring of new narratives, choices and actions. This is particularly important when the coach is confronted with a difficult task for which he is not necessarily prepared. If it is mutually recognised and fully engaged it can become a 'moment of meeting' (Stern, 1998). This requires that each person contributes something unique and authentic in response, and this is where growth happens. This means that formulating as we coach is less about figuring things out and more about paying attention to what is there (Drake, 2016). It is about staying present to the four questions in formulation as a dynamic and responsive process:

1. What story am I telling myself about what is going on?
2. What story am I telling myself about what caused it?
3. What story am I telling myself about what should be done?
4. What story am I telling myself about success?

This matters because 'most clients will not be able to travel farther in sessions than their coach is willing to go' (Drake, 2015, p.141). Where do your clients and their stories want to go? You can use these attachment tools to help them find the resolution that was there all along.

REFERENCES

Bowlby, J. (1969). *Attachment* (2nd edn, Vol. *1*). New York, NY: Basic Books.

Bowlby, J. (1988). *A secure base: Clinical applications of attachment theory*. London, UK: Routledge.

Drake, D.B. (2009). Using attachment theory in coaching leaders: The search for a coherent narrative *International Coaching Psychology Review, 4*(1), 49–58.

Drake, D.B. (2014). Three windows of development: A postprofessional perspective on supervision. *International Coaching Psychology Review, 9*(1), 36–48.

Drake, D.B. (2015). *Narrative coaching: Bringing our new stories to life*. Petaluma, CA: CNC Press.

Drake, D.B. (2017). *Using attachment theory to develop coaching capabilities in managers and leaders*. Paper presented at the Consulting psychology conference: The next wave of leadership, Seattle, WA.

Paris, G. (2007). *Wisdom of the psyche: Depth psychology after neuroscience*. London, UK: Routledge.

Stern, D.N. (1998). The process of therapeutic change involving implicit knowledge: Some implications of developmental observations for adult psychology. *Infant Mental Health Journal, 19*(3), 300–308.

45 Creating zones of proximal development in coaching: The power of working at thresholds

David Drake

Abstract

'The pattern that connects, as my dad [Gregory Bateson] called it, requires both process and form; it is part rigid and part imaginative. To study it, our first step is to remember that we are in fact part of the pattern, inside the ecology, and allow or encourage it to take another shape...' (N. Bateson, 2016)

This article looks at four roles coaches can play to accelerate client outcomes, the value of threshold moments as zones of proximal development, and the case for MVIs (Minimum Viable Interventions) in supporting change.

Keywords

advocate; attachment theory; change; guardian; problem-solving; steward; threshold; witness; zone of proximal development.

Original publication details: Drake, D. (2018, June). Creating zones of proximal development in coaching: The power of working at thresholds. *The Coaching Psychologist*, 14(1), 42–47. Reproduced with permission of The British Psychological Society.

In today's world, it seems increasingly difficult for many of our clients to chart clear paths amid ever-changing complexities. This presents an opportunity for coaching to evolve in order to come alongside your clients to help them see 'the patterns that connect' and make authentic choices. It is about helping them forge new connections, for example, between their stories and their behaviours, their leadership and their team's results, their purpose and their livelihood. Narratives are essential here because they enable us to make sense and meaning across time and space, the personal and the collective, the real and the imagined. The choices your clients make are profoundly shaped by the stories they tell themselves. As featured in the last article on attachment theory in coaching (Drake, 2017), we can work at many levels with these stories.

This article builds on the last one by offering four roles you can play in working with clients to meet their needs in the coaching process. Developing mastery as a coach requires not only proficiency in each role, but also the professional agility to move between them depending on the client's needs. I will explore why (1) threshold crossing generally leads to more lasting change than problem-solving; (2) clients need coaches to serve as guardians of this process; (3) thresholds serve as zones of proximal development; and (4) our most under-rated value as coaches may be as stewards of new narratives. This reflects the movement away from goal-based frameworks, problem-based formulations and coach-based methodologies to a view of coaching conversations as dynamic ecosystems. The difference is depicted in the two figures below.

In this view, the power in use is centered in coaches and their professional 'black boxes' even as the espoused power is professed to be with the client (see Argyris & Schön, 1974). It is based in the assumption that there is a direct connection between a problem and its solution, the need to thoroughly understand the problem in order for resolution to occur, and it is the coach's role to provide and lead the process. Unfortunately, when coaching is done this way, the mindset and behaviour changes made in sessions are less likely to be sustained because they are too dependent on the coach and the coaching process and less integrated in and for the client.

In contrast, a narrative view of coaching is seen as an integrative process of structured emergence in which coaches come alongside clients and processes that are already underway. Each of the four elements above – as well as the coach and the

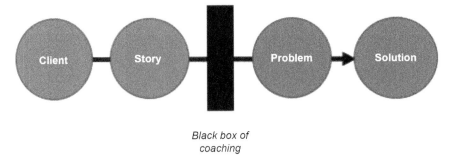

Black box of coaching

Figure 1 *Traditional view of coaching*

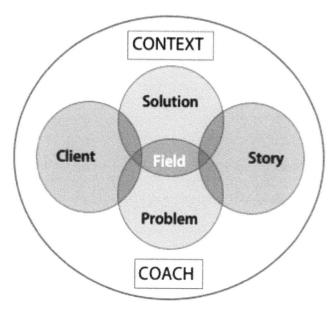

Figure 2   *Narrative view of coaching*

context – are part of the ecosystem and contribute to the desired outcome. In addition, it is truly centred in the client and in the 'field' in which the conversation takes place. It assumes that the resolution to whatever the client is seeking is already present in the conversation and in the narrative material that surfaces there. When coaching is done this way, there is much greater transference of the mindset and behaviour change because the client is fully involved in both the process and its outcome. This is reinforced by a more systemic view of the situation and its resolution.

The differences between these two views of coaching can be seen in the above diagram as well. In the first graphic, a solution (S) is seen as the missing puzzle piece which perfectly matches the problem (P) space. This assumes a mechanistic view of life and work that is often not the case and, even when it is the case, tends to only be a partial or short-term solution. This approach also fails to address the place of the presenting problem in the larger systemic ecology, the unintended consequences of the 'solution,' and the need for clients to develop better strategies and greater maturity for addressing similar situations in the future.

In the second graphic, the focus is getting to the crux (C) of their issue on and identifying what the client most needs to learn and/ or shift rather than finishing a puzzle. It typically comes down to a single moment in time when the issue becomes crystal clear as does the choice that is before them. These thresholds are opportunities for clients to step into new narratives and new actions (A) in which they are developing themselves and taking new actions. For example: (1) I will leave my father's empty shoes on this side of the threshold and, in crossing over, I will for the fi rst time walk my own path in life; (2) I will let go of putting myself between others to meet their

Figure 3   *Stepping into the coaching moment*

needs and, in crossing, I will allow myself to be visible so I can be seen and get my needs met.

Coaches need to have developed a sufficient level of personal maturity and professional agility to be able to work in these moments. I define *professional agility* as 'the ability to authentically, ably and appropriately move between roles in service of the best outcome – in the moment and over time.' Four roles are in coaching this way:

- Witness to the moment (to improve the client's sense of safe haven[1])
- Guardian at the threshold (to improve the client's sense of secure base)
- Advocate for proximal development (to improve the client's working model)
- Steward of the new narrative (to improve the client's 'family' systems)

I've integrated all four into a single model in Figure 4, but for now let's look in more depth at each of them.

WITNESS TO THE MOMENT

The first role involves observing when and where there are openings in the change process that is underway for a client. These often occur when there are what the attachment theorists call 'moments of meeting' (Drake, 2016; Stern, 2004) in which both parties are challenged to show up in a new way. In serving as a witness in these moments, you can help clients recognise the opening for change, 'see' them as they stand in it, and invite them to step into it fully with confidence and trust. The focus is on authentically engaging with the human being in front of you and strengthening the crucible for the real work that needs to be done. Your primary aim in these threshold moments is to support clients to be fully present to themselves, the moment, the choice and their wholehearted wish (Horney, 1945).

Anthropologist Arthur Van Gennep (1960) used territorial and spatial terms in developing his framework for rites of passage. It is from this perspective that the view of passages as crossing thresholds took hold, for example, the movement from the

---

1 See Drake, 2009; 2017; 2018 on attachment theory.

outer world to the inner world (and back) as people leave behind one role or status and prepare to take on a new one. Thresholds can be seen spatially as a doorway, a distinctive place of transition; and temporally as a movement, a more diffuse process of transition (Drake, 2018). They mark a shift in attention from:

- What is happening to what is required.
- Where one journey ends to where another begins.
- What is known to what is unknown.
- What is left behind to what is moved. toward

In these moments, a client can surrender her old story, engage more fully with reality, and emerge more quickly with a new story. Her pretenses and compromises fade away; she gains a greater clarity about herself, her situation and her needs; and she releases energy that was once trapped so she can channel it in new directions. This is big work that requires a witness to call out the moment, hold the space and intention for the process, and to invite the person to show up to what it represents and will make possible. This leads us to our second role, which is to act as a guardian at these gates, the thresholds these moments may offer.

GUARDIAN AT THE THRESHOLD

While thresholds are part of a longer process of transformation, they represent a singular point in space and time, a line to cross, a passage to make. Every threshold crossing takes you and the client into the Unknown. Your role as a coach is to help them distill their issue to its essence so they know exactly what the change entails. What is really the crux of the person's issue, the core distinction and/or choice? This is significant because, in many ways, a person cannot go back once they crossed over; they can never 'un-see' what they have now realised. That is why it is important to clearly sense if they are ready to move across the threshold it requires. In serving as a guardian at the threshold, the key question for you as the coach is, 'What does this person need most in order to be ready'?

Thresholds are not for the faint-hearted or the ill-prepared because they are where clients confront their most important choices, their most potent questions, and their deepest hopes and fears. That is why 'threshold guardians', as Joseph Campbell (1973) called them, are crucial. As a coach, you are there to remind your clients to not take their threshold lightly, to appreciate what is truly at stake, and to compassionately yet firmly challenge them to be present to what is calling them as they cross. Every guardian serves the same purpose: to lift the veil that has kept the person from seeing what was there all along and help him cross the threshold of his truth and choice. Guardians, whether allies or shadows, matter-of-factly stand at these doorways to ensure the person is taking seriously the power and the potential that reside there.

As a coach in this role, you can ask clients questions such as:

- What does this threshold represent?
- Why are you here?
- What do you most deeply want on the other side?
- What are you leaving behind?
- What do you need to confront to break through?

Clients will answer these questions and others at the level of clarity and truth telling they can manage at the time. Your role is to continue witnessing them and seeing them as a resourceful human being who is seeking to make a change in their life. As such, ask questions about their experience in the moment more than their expectations for the future. It is about healing and awareness in the present, not hunting and answers for the future. When coaches do their job well, clients can accelerate their learning and set themselves up for significant growth in a brief period of time. This is possible because the steps that are taken not only support new external choices but also shifts in their internal identities. It is as if their narrative DNA is reconfigured.

Tips on serving as a threshold guardian to support change in clients:

- Be fiercely compassionate and compassionately fierce.
- Be present to what is unfolding rather than thinking about what to do next.
- Be willing to sit with dissonance and move toward the unknown.
- Notice what they have brought with them and what they are leaving behind.
- Stay focused on the core commitment rather than the details of their stories.
- Stay focused on the felt experience; not the search for explanations.
- Preserve the integrity of the threshold, the space and the moment.

ADVOCATE FOR PROXIMAL DEVELOPMENT

When you do well as a guardian, clients are more able to cross the thresholds before them and at more significant levels. The coach, the coaching relationship and the coaching process must all be strong enough to transmute the existential experience of crossing a threshold into transformative learning, development and actions for clients. In many ways, we can think of threshold work as *serious play*, in that it is both improvisational and bounded by clear rules of engagement. This requires what I call *radical presence* in order to stay attuned to and leverage all of the dimensions of what is happening in those threshold moments. We can draw on the work of psychologist Lev Vygotsky (1934/1987, 1978) in understanding thresholds as places of serious play.

For Vygotsky, play was instrumental in children's learning and development because it enabled them to build on what they knew as they gained new capabilities.

Of particular interest is his notion of *zones of proximal development*, which he (1978) defined as 'the distance between the actual developmental level and the level of potential development under adult supervision or in collaboration with more capable peers' (p.86). According to Vygotsky, these zones are based in a symbiotic relation-ship between development and learning in which development, as an individually internalised process, generally lags behind learning as a culturally mediated process. The process of learning for children awakens a variety of internal developmental processes that only operate when they are interacting with people in their environ-ment and in cooperation with others, especially peers. Once those processes are internalised, they become part of a child's independent developmental achievement (Vygotsky, 1978).

The same is true in working with adults (see Day, Harrison & Halpin, 2009). Thresholds offer clients opportunities to have transformative learning experiences, from which a new pathway for development emerges. As such, thresholds can be seen as zones of proximal development in which clients move between what they can do now and what they can do with a coach's support to enable them to grow. As seen in fi gure 4 below, the threshold moment is defined by:

(1) the crux (C) of the client's issue; (2) the traversing of a zone of proximal development (white space); (3) the crossing of the threshold where the learning is owned; (4) the blue spaces representing the larger crucible for change and the specific scaffolding required; (5) the arrows that represent the fl ow of the process into and out of the zone; and (6) the zone that extends into the near future as the client takes new actions (A) based in his new narrative.

These liminal zones are important because people generally cannot go directly from an old state or story to a new one, but require an intermediary step that is nei-ther old nor new. People are more willing and able to make this step if they have sufficient scaffolding. It enables them to move between the 'known and familiar' of their current experience into the 'not yet known, but possible to know' territory of their preferred experience. This often takes the form of small steps to increase their awareness, focus, and resources. The good news is that most of the scaffolding they will need is already present in their stories, for example, current and desired state, preferred modalities of learning, pointers to allies and resources, related social nar-ratives, thresholds and key choices.

One of the tools I use in doing threshold work with my clients and students is what I call the MVI: Minimum Viable Intervention. What is the smallest possible

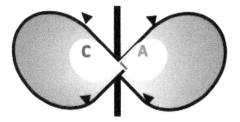

Figure 4 *Thresholds as zones of proximal development*

action you can take as a coach to support the client in moving to the next level of awareness or action? For example, you could call their attention to a character or perspective, invite them to adopt a new posture, place an object in front of them that is key to their next step. In so doing, keep in mind the narrative coaching principle to generate new experiences not more explanations. This minimalist approach is designed to maximise what clients can do on their own as they move forward. What they can do with you as their coach today, they can more independently and capably do on their own tomorrow (Vygotsky, 1934/1998). It is their journey, not yours.

STEWARD OF THE NEW NARRATIVE

Because of the integrative nature of crossing thresholds, the changes that clients make ripple through their lives at so many levels and with a much more lasting impact. As such, once the process is complete, clients need time and space to start metabolizing what they have learned and what has shifted in the process. Trust that the transformative process is already underway – as evidenced by the softer face, the more relaxed posture, the existential sigh of relief. When the time feels right, help them anchor the experience and identify where they will begin enacting their new narrative and new choices. This often involves important conversations they need to have. Invite them to talk through what they want to say so they can hear themselves speak from a new place and with new words. It gives them a taste of the real changes they have just made.

In working with clients' thresholds as a witness, guardian, advocate and steward, you are often called on to help them move through grief and be moved by joy. Each is central to the process of change and growth, and is therefore at the heart of what coaching can offer. Where are you feeling called to grow in terms of your professional agility and your ability to be present to your clients in this way?

REFERENCES

Argyris, C. & Schön, D. (1974). *Theory in practice: Increasing professional effectiveness*. San Francisco, CA: Jossey-Bass.
Bateson, Nora. (2016). *Small arcs of larger circles*. Axminster, UK: Triarchy Press.
Campbell, Joseph. (1973). *The hero with a thousand faces*. Princeton: Princeton University Press.
Day, D.D., Harrison, M.M. & Halpin, S.M. (2009). *An integrative approach to leader development: Connecting adult development, identity, and expertise*. New York: Psychology Press.
Drake, D.B. (2009). Using attachment theory in coaching leaders: The search for a coherent narrative *International Coaching Psychology Review*, 4(1), 49–58.
Drake, D.B. (2016). *Creating moments of meeting in coaching*. Paper presented at the Coaching in Leadership and Healthcare Conference, Boston, MA.

Drake, D.B. (2017). Using the four gateways to tell new stories and make new choices. *The Coaching Psychologist, 13*(1), 22–26.

Drake, D.B. (2018). *Narrative coaching: The definitive guide to bringing new stories to life* (2nd edn.). Petaluma, CA: CNC Press.

Horney, K. (1945). *Our inner conflicts: A constructive theory of neurosis*. New York: W.W. Norton.

Stern, D.N. (2004). *The present moment in psychotherapy and everyday life*. New York: W.W. Norton.

van Gennep, A. (1960). *The rites of passage*. M.B. Vizedom & G.L. Caffee (Trans.). Chicago: The University of Chicago Press.

Vygotsky, L.S. (1934/1987). Thinking and speech. N. Minick (Trans.). In R.W. Rieber & A.S. Carton (Eds.), *The collected works of L.S. Vygotsky (Vol. 1: Problems of general psychology* (pp. 39–285). New York: Plenum Press.

Vygotsky, L.S. (1978). Interaction between learning and development. In *Mind in society: The development of higher psychological processes* (pp.79–91). Cambridge, MA: Harvard University Press.

Section 11
Positive Psychology

Introduction

David Tee & Jonathan Passmore

In this section, we explore a series of papers based in the positive psychology tradition written by Jonathan Passmore and Lindsay Oades, two well-known writers in the field of positive psychology coaching. In this brief introduction, we will review the nature of positive psychology, its role in coaching and finally summarise the six chapters in this section.

Let us start by exploring what we mean by the terms 'positive psychology' (PP) and 'positive psychology coaching' (PPC). The term *positive psychology* is often associated with Martin Seligman, the president of the American Psychological Association (APA), in 1998. Seligman noted that the previous 100 years of psychology had been marked by a focus on dysfunction and deficit. Much had been written about clinical conditions, with classifications of dysfunction such as the Diagnostic and Statistical Manual of Mental Disorders (DSM). DSM IV, published in 1994, listed 410 clinical disorders in a manual stretching over 886 pages, and the majority of psychologists at that time focused on clinical, counselling and health-related topics.

Seligman argued for a change in focus to acknowledge the importance of optimum function and peak performance. While the previous balance had been strongly towards deficit models, many other writers over the previous decades had drawn attention to these issues, from Albert Maslow's (1943) hierarchy of needs, the person-centred therapy of Carl Rogers (1961) and Mihaly Csikszentmihályi's (1990) flow states. What all of these writers had in common was a belief that human performance and wellbeing could be enhanced, and the potential to achieve this rested inside each person. The role of the psychologist or therapist was to create the correct conditions for the individual to flourish.

In returning to PP, while the ideas of PP remained connected with the central ideas within what became known as the human potential movement, the methods diverged,

Coaching Practiced, First Edition. Edited by David Tee and Jonathan Passmore.
© 2022 John Wiley & Sons Ltd. Published 2022 by John Wiley & Sons Ltd.
DOI: 10.1002/9781119835714.s11

with a shift towards a greater use of statistical analysis, in contrast with the theoretical and qualitative studies which typified the human potential movement. A range of definitions of PP have been offered by writers from Seligman to Gable.

Seligman and Csikszentmihalyi (2000, p. 6) offered the following definition "the scientific study of positive human functioning and flourishing on multiple levels that include the biological, personal, relational, institutional, cultural, and global dimensions of life". In contrast Gable and Haidt suggested that PP is "the science of the conditions and processes that lead to optimal human function" (2005, p. 103).

Turning to positive psychology coaching (PPC), the application of positive psychology research to coaching emerged more slowly. One of the first published titles was Biswas-Diener and Dean (2007) in their book of the same title. The book explored the application of emerging ideas from PP research to the world of coaching. This first title was followed by a number of book chapters and papers, including Kauffman et al. (2018), who defined PPC as a "scientifically-rooted approach to helping clients increase wellbeing, enhance and apply strengths, improve performance and achieve valued goals" (p. 153). Green and Palmer (2014) defined it as "evidence-based coaching practice informed by the theories and research of positive psychology for the enhancement of resilience, achievement and wellbeing" and Oades and Passmore (2014, p. 15) who define PPC as "coaching approaches that seek to improve short-term wellbeing (i.e. hedonic wellbeing) and sustainable wellbeing (i.e. eudaimonic wellbeing) using evidence-based approaches from positive psychology and the science of wellbeing and enable the person to do this in an ongoing manner after the coaching has completed".

What is consistent across each of these definitions is the focus on science or evidence, and the pursuit of wellbeing and improved performance through enhanced goal-focused actions. However, in reviewing definitions of coaching across the piece, the reader will quickly realise that these aspects are common features in coaching approaches. This begs the question, 'Is all coaching psychology an application of PP?' Or is PP a theorisation of coaching psychology practice? Which came first, the chicken or the egg? In reality, both have their origins in the human potential movement of the 1960s and thus share a common view that optimal functioning should be an aspiration for all. While coaching has developed from practice led by practitioners such as John Whitmore and Laura Whitworth, PP has emerged from academia with a focus towards theory and evidence.

This series of six papers, originally published in *The Coaching Psychologist* (Passmore & Oades, 2014a, 2014b, 2015a, 2015b, 2016a, 2016b), aimed to provide a short insight into the nature of PPC and its manifestation through five tools available for coaches to use with their clients in individual sessions.

In the first of these papers, Passmore and Oades (2014a) explored the definitions of positive psychology coaching and the underlying psychological theories. They identify four theories: strengths theory (Proctor et al., 2011), broaden and build theory (Frederickson, 2009), self-determination theory (Spence & Oades, 2011) and wellbeing theory (Seligman, 2002) which they argue are foundational for PPC. They concluded that PP offers a theoretical, conceptual and an evidenced basis for coaching: "coaching psychology is where the rubber of positive psychology theory, hits the road of organisational and health practice" (Passmore & Oades, 2014a, p. 69).

In the subsequent papers, Passmore and Oades explore specific tools from PPC. The first, active constructive responding, explores the use of a PP technique which many may know as affirmations or reflections (Oades & Passmore, 2014). The authors note the technique can help the coach enhance client-coach relationships, through encouraging the coach to respond more actively and constructively, observing and reflecting back when things go right for the client. To be applied well, the coach needs to deeply listen and capture the meaning of the client, not just the words; playing this back, allowing the client to develop both insight from the response, but also reinforcing the client's self-belief.

The second technique is positive case conceptualisation (Passmore & Oades, 2015a). This reframes the traditional case conceptualisation work within coaching psychology (Lane & Corrie, 2009). A traditional case conceptualisation is the formation of a rationale and framework, underpinned by an evidence base, to summarise the therapists thinking and inform their future work with the client. Within PPC, the case is orientated towards the positive: What is it that is good, positive and enhancing that the client does, and which coaching can reinforce?

In the third technique, the authors explore random acts of kindness, which they reframe as Consistent Acts of Kindness (CAKE) and activity or tasks that coaches can invite clients to undertake as homework. They note the technique can be "an antidote to this culture and the isolation that the focus on the self creates. RAK fits within Positive Psychology Coaching (PPC) and offers benefits if practiced by the coaching psychologist or coach" (Passmore & Oades, 2015b, p. 90).

The last two techniques in the series explore Gratitude and Three good things (Passmore & Oades, 2016a, 2016b). How can coaches help their clients to experience more gratitude and happiness in their lives? Again, set as homework techniques, the writers set PPC as a way coaches can draw on the theory of the underpinning theories at the heart of positive psychology such as 'broaden and build' theory to develop practical tools to share with clients.

REFERENCES

Biswas-Diener, R., & Dean, B. (2007). *Positive psychology coaching: Putting the science of happiness to work for your clients*. John Wiley and Sons.

Csikszentmihályi, M. (1990). *Flow: The psychology of optimal experience*. Harper & Row.

Gable, S. L. & Haidt, J. (2005). What (and Why) Is Positive Psychology? *Review of General Psychology*, 9, 103–110.

Frederickson, B. (2009). *Positivity: ground-breaking research reveals how to release the hidden strength of positive emotions, overcome negativity and thrive*. New York: Random House.

Green, S., & Palmer, S. (2014). *Positive psychology coaching*. Workshop 4th International Congress of Coaching Psychology. 15 November 2014.

Kauffman, C., Boniwell, I., & Silberman, J. (2018). The Positive Psychology Approach to Coaching. In E. Cox, T. Bachkirova, & D. Clutterbuck (Eds.), *The Complete Handbook of Coaching* (3rd Edn.). London, UK: SAGE Publications Ltd.

Lane, D., & Corrie, S. (2009). Does coaching psychology need the concept of formulation? *International Coaching Psychology Review, 4*(2), 193–206.

Maslow, A. H. (1943) A theory of human motivation. *Psychological Review, 50*(4), 370–396.

Oades, L., & Passmore, J. (2014). Positive psychology coaching: A complete psychological toolkit for advanced coaches. In J. Passmore (Ed.), *Mastery in coaching: A complete psychological toolkit for advanced coaches.* Kogan Page

Passmore, J., & Oades, L. (2014a). Positive Psychology Coaching: A model for coaching practice. *The Coaching Psychologist 10*(2), 68–70

Passmore, J., & Oades, L. (2014b). Active Constructive Responding. *The Coaching Psychologist 10*(2), 71–73. Passmore

Passmore, J., & Oades, L. (2015a). Positive Case Conceptualisation. *The Coaching Psychologist 11*(1), 43–45.

Passmore, J., & Oades, L. (2015b). Consistent Acts of Kindness & Empathy. *The Coaching Psychologist 11*(2), 91–93.

Passmore, J., & Oades, L. (2016a). Gratitude. *The Coaching Psychologist 12*(1).

Passmore, J., & Oades, L. (2016b). Three Good Things. *The Coaching Psychologist 12*(2).

Proctor, C., J. Maltby, and P. A. Linley (2011). Strengths Use as a Predictor of Well-Being and Health-Related Quality of Life. *Journal of Happiness Studies 12*(1): 153–169.

Rogers, C. (1961). *On Becoming a Person: A Therapist's View of Psychotherapy.* Constable

Seligman, M. E. P. (2002). *Authentic Happiness: Using the new positive psychology to realize your potential for lasting fulfillment.* Free Press

Seligman, M. E. P., & Csikszentmihályi, M. (2000). Positive psychology: An Introduction. *American Psychologist. 55*(1): 5–14.

Spence, G.B. & Oades, L.G. (2011). Coaching with self-determination theory in mind: Using theory to advance evidence-based coaching practice. *International Journal of Evidence Based Coaching and Mentoring, 9*(2), 37–55.

46 Positive Psychology Coaching – a model for coaching practice

Jonathan Passmore & Lindsay G. Oades

Abstract

This is the first in a series of papers to look at Positive Psychology Coaching (PPC) as an approach suitable for use with coaching clients. This paper presents a brief overview of PPC for readers who are less familiar with the approach and highlights other sources for a fuller account of PPC. The paper sets the scene for a subsequent series of papers. Each of these subsequent techniques papers presents a short description of a technique grounded in PPC and which are suitable for use with coachees.

Keywords

Coaching; coaching psychology; positive psychology coaching model and applied positive psychology.

THE BACKGROUND – POSITIVE PSYCHOLOGY COACHING

Positive psychology has been referred to as the science at the heart of coaching (Kaufmann et al., 2010). While other approaches in active use by coaching

Original publication details: Passmore, J., & Oades, L. G. (2014, December). Positive psychology coaching – A model for coaching practice. *The Coaching Psychologist, 10*(2), 68–70. Reproduced with permission of The British Psychological Society.

psychologists, including motivational interviewing, (referred to in a set of earlier papers in this journal) have a strong evidence base, Positive Psychology Coaching (PPC) is becoming an increasingly popular coaching methods used by coaching psychologists, and other alike, under a range of titles including PPC, evidence-based coaching (Grant & Cavanagh, 2007) or strengths coaching (Govindji & Linley, 2007).

Whilst these approaches overlap, our specific focus is on PCC. What is PPC? We have defined PPC as:

> *'coaching approaches that seek to improve short term well-being (i.e. hedonic well-being) and sustainable well-being (i.e. eudaimonic wellbeing) using evidence-based approaches from positive psychology and the science of well-being and enable the person to do this in an ongoing manner after coaching has completed'*

(Oades & Passmore, 2014).

Short-term (hedonic) well-being can be seen as similar to cash flow; something great to have, but which is short-term and can easily be gone if there is not a longer-term supply.

In contrast Sustainable (eudaimonic) wellbeing can be viewed as an asset; it can be built or lost, and also impacts upon cash-flow. These analogies may also be useful to coachee and clients when collaboratively discussing aspects of well-being, which are often outside of the language and understanding of the average manager.

Underlying PPC are four key positive psychological theories; strengths theory (Proctor, Maltby et al., 2011), broaden and build theory (Frederickson, 2009), self-determination theory (Spence & Oades, 2012) and well-being theory (Seligman, 2011).

Strengths theory (ST) is perhaps better considered a family of theories, or a unifying proposition, as opposed to a single theory. The central proposition is that people will perform, feel and function better if they are using their strengths. For this reason, strengths researchers and practitioners have developed strengths assessment tools, to assist people to gain knowledge of their strengths, and then use their own strengths and spot strengths in others.

Broaden-and-build theory (BBT) was primarily developed to seek answers to the question 'What is the function of positive emotion?' (Frederickson, 1998, 2001). The broaden-and-build theory proposes that experiences of positive emotions broadens people's momentary thought-action repertoires – that is the menu of choices of thinking and acting is broader when a person is experiencing positive emotions. In turn, the theory holds that the aim should be to build enduring personal resources including physical, intellectual, social and psychological resources. Fredrickson's (2009) has suggested one route to doing this is through providing positive feedback in a ratio equal or higher than three positives to one negative.

Self-determination theory (SDT), sometimes referred to as meta-theory, is a set of theories that examine the effects of different types of motivation (Deci & Ryan, 2000). The sub-theories are Basic Needs Theory, Cognitive Evaluation Theory, Organismic Integration Theory, Causality Orientations Theory, Relationships Motivation Theory and Goal Contents Theory. SDT is a needs theory that argues that there are three universal psychological needs: (a) autonomy; (b) relatedness; and (c) competency. As a result, people need to make their own choices, connect with others and feel competent as they exercise and grow their capacities. The theory proposes that if these three needs are met, a person will have increased autonomous motivation, leading to greater perseverance at tasks, particularly at tasks set or imposed on them, such as at work.

The fourth and final theory of the set is Well-being Theory (WT). WT is sometimes referred to simply as PERMA theory. It suggests that there are five domains of life that both constitute and which may be instruments in developing well-being. The five components are **P**ositive Emotions, **E**ngagement, (Positive) **R**elationships, **M**eaning and **A**ccomplishment.

EXPLORING PPC

The increasing popularity of PPC has seen a number of excellent texts emerge including books and individual short chapters aimed at practitioners and advanced practitioners from writers such as Kate Hefferon (Hefferon, 2011), Ilona Boniwell and Carol Kaufman (Kauffman, Boniwell & Silberman, 2010), Teresa Freire (Freire, 2013) and Ed Biswas-Diener (Biswas-Diener, 2010).

APPLYING POSITIVE PSYCHOLOGY THEORY TO COACHING PSYCHOLOGY PRACTICE

Some may argue, however, that positive psychology has been dominated by theory, and insights into psychological make-up, but has been harder to apply when compared to other approaches such as Cognitive Behavioural Coaching or even Motivational Interviewing. We would suggest that coaching psychology is in fact applied positive psychology theory. In short, coaching psychology is where the rubber of positive psychology theory hits the road of organisational and health practice. Positive psychology theories come together with practical techniques that can be used in organisational, as well as well-being coaching. In the following papers we have taken a selection of techniques and illustrated how these techniques can be used by coaching psychologists in their day-to-day coaching sessions.

Table 1 *PPC books and chapters*

Books	Book chapters
Driver, M. (2011). *Coaching Positively.*	Hefferon, K. (2011). Positive psychology.
Biswas-Diener, R. (2010). *Practicing positive psychology coaching.*	Kauffman, C., I. Boniwell, & Silberman, J. (2010). The positive psychology approach to coaching.
Biswas-Diener, R. & Dean, B. (2007). *Positive psychology coaching: Putting the science of happiness to work for your clients.*	Oades, L. & Passmore, J. (2014). Positive Psychology Coaching.
	Freire, T. (2013). Positive Psychology Approaches.

REFERENCES

Biswas-Diener, R. (2010). *Practicing positive psychology coaching.* New Jersey: Wiley.

Biswas-Diener, R & Dean, B. (2007). *Positive psychology coaching: Putting the science of happiness to work for your clients.* New Jersey: Wiley.

Deci, E.L. & Ryan, R.M. (2000). The 'what' and 'why' of goal pursuits: Human needs and the self-determination of behaviour. *Psychological Inquiry, 11*(4), 227–268.

Driver, M. (2011). *Coaching Positively: Lessons for coaches from positive psychology.* Maidenhead: Oxford University Press.

Fredrickson, B.L. (1998). What good are positive emotions? *Review of General Psychology, 2,* 300–319.

Frederickson, B.L. (2001). The role of positive emotions in positive psychology. The broaden-and-build theory of positive emotions. *American Psychologist, 56,* 218–226.

Frederickson, B. (2009). *Positivity: Groundbreaking research reveals how to release the hidden strength of positive emotions, overcome negativity and thrive.* New York: Random House.

Freire, T. (2013). Positive psychology approaches. In J. Passmore, D. Peterson & T. Freire (Eds.), *Wiley-Blackwell handbook of the psychology of coaching and mentoring* (pp. 426–442). Chichester: Wiley.

Govindji, R. & Linley, P.A. (2007). Strengths use, self-concordance and well-being: Implications for strengths coaching and coaching psychologists. *International Coaching Psychology Review, 2*(2), 143–153.

Grant, A.M. & Cavanagh, M.J. (2007). Evidence-based coaching: Flourishing or languishing? *Australian Psychologist, 42*(4), 239–254.

Hefferon, K. (2011). Positive psychology. In L. Wildflower & D. Brennan, *The handbook of knowledge-based coaching.* San Francisco: Jossey-Bass:

Kauffman, C., Boniwell, I. & Silberman, J. (2010). The positive psychology approach to coaching. In E. Cox, T. Bachkirova & D. Clutterbuck (Eds.), *The complete handbook of coaching* (pp. 158–171). Los Angeles: Sage.

Oades, L. & Passmore, J. (2014). Positive psychology coaching. In J. Passmore (Ed.), *Mastery in coaching.* London: Kogan Page.

Proctor, C., Maltby, J. et al. (2011). Strengths use as a predictor of well-being and health-related quality of life. *Journal of Happiness Studies*, *12*(1), 153–169.

Seligman, M.E.P. (2011). *Flourish*. New York: Simon & Schuster.

Spence, G.B. & Oades, L.G. (2011). Coaching with self-determination thoery in mind: Using theory to advance evidence-based coaching practice. *International Journal of Evidence Based Coaching and Mentoring*, *9*(2), 37–55.

47 Positive Psychology Techniques – Active Constructive Responding

Jonathan Passmore & Lindsay G. Oades

Abstract

This short article focuses on the skill of Active Constructive Responding, a technique used when working within a positive psychology coaching framework. The paper offers a table that describes the behaviours, cognitions and emotions at six levels of listening. It offers a way to combine active listening with positive feedback responses to help demonstrate empathy and foster positive self-regard.

Keywords

Levels of listening; active listening; listening; active constructive responding; questioning and positive psychology coaching.

Active constructive responding (ACR) (Gable et al, 2004; Gable, Gonzaga & Strachman, 2006; Magyar-Moe, 2009) is a simple and understandable technique that can assist people improve their close relationships, by enabling (for example) coaches to respond more actively and constructively, observing and reflecting back when things go right for their coachees (Oades & Passmore, 2014).

Original publication details: Passmore, J., & Oades, L. G. (2014, December). Positive psychology techniques – Active constructive responding. *The Coaching Psychologist, 10*(2), 71–73. Reproduced with permission of The British Psychological Society.

The technique starts with the coach being focused and actively listening to the coachee's communcations at both the verbal and non-verbal level. The coach is specifically attuned to positive success, or moments of pride, which the coachee is seeking to share.

While listening is acknowledged as one of the key skills required of the coach, there has been relatively little written about active listening, when compared with the volume of work written about alternative coaching models. There are notable exceptions, for example, Gerald Egan (Egan, 2009), Bill Miller and Steve Rollnick (Miller & Rollnick, 2013) and Nancy Klein (Klein, 1999). We suggest that when using ACR, the coach needs to listen at a deeper level, compared with traditionally listen in a normal conversation. We have tried to categorise listening into six levels. These styles of listening are illustrated in Table 1. We recognise this is just one way of categorising listening and the behaviours, emotions and cognitions described are typical rather than universal. As a result, not all individuals display all of the behaviours, cognitions or emotions described in the table.

Table 1   *Six Levels of Listening*

Level	Typical coach behaviour	Typical coach cognition and emotions
1. Ignoring	The coach does not maintain eye contact, but engages with their phone, looks out of the window or engages in another task. They may interrupt the speaker with the question they have formed.	The coach's thoughts are engaged on the other task.
2. Waiting my turn to talk	The coach may appear to be listening by making eye contact, nodding occasionally or give verbal attentions. They may interrupt the speaker with the question they have formed.	The coach's thoughts are focused onsomething other than what the coachee is saying for example they may be preparing the words to use for their next question. The coach's emotions may be anxiety, in trying to get the words of their next question right or other emotions which are centred on their experience rather than the coachee.
3. Listening to the words	The coach makes eye contact, nods and gives verbal attentions to demonstrate listening. The coach may summarise what the coachee has said.	The coach's thoughts are focused on the content of the words being used by the coachee.

4. Listening to words and body language (Active listening)	The coach is focused on the coachee. They use their eyes and ears to listen to what is being said in words and actions. The coach may summarise and reflect back their understanding of what they hear and see.	The coach's thoughts are on words and body language. The focus is still on the coach's emotional response rather than on the emotional experience of the coachee.
5. Empathetic listening	The coach is wholly focused on the coachee – is listening with their eyes and ears. Based on the cognitions the coach may reflect back what they see or imagine is being felt in a sensitive appropriate way, avoiding labelling.	The coach is drawing on both their understanding of body language and emotions to make sense of what the coachee may be feeling and to image what feelings the coachee may be experiencing.
6. Active Constructive Listening (ACL)	In addition to actions in 4, the coach will be seeking to also constructively respond, by focusing on positive aspects to enhance pride, joy and self-regard.	The coach is maintaining a positive mind frame of the individual and while using cognitions and emotions in 5, is actively seeking to particularly focus on the positive emotions.

Table 2 offers an illustration of ACR within a coaching conversation.

In the short example in Table 2 the coach, having listened to John's news, recognises the importance of the message. Rather than simply acknowledging what has been said, the coach, using ACR, responds to the excitement in the voice tone and body language by providing positive feedback (*'I'm so pleased'*). This response is grounded, (supported by evidence), explaining why the coach shares this excitement (coachee's *'hard work'*). Thirdly, the coach's intervention is supported with attaching emotional content to the statement (*pride*). This makes the feedback sound more authentic and more affirming for the coachee. It allows the coachee to rest for a moment in that success. This contrasts with the more traditional approach, taught within coaching, which is for the coach to respond by trying to move the coachee back towards the focus of the session. This common happens by the coach asking the follow-up question; *'What does this mean to you?'* The emotion of sharing this experience is then lost, as the coachee returns to the work of the session, without having an opportunity, for a short moment, to dwell in their success.

The impact of this technique, when delivered well, is that it displays empathy towards the coachee, supporting the development of the coaching relationship, and secondly it fosters positive self-regard within the coachee.

Table 2 *Active Constructive Responding: When coachee shares with their coach they have been promoted*

Within five minutes into the coaching conversation John (coachee) tells Sue (coach) 'he has been promoted, he is very proud and excited of the opportunities it will bring'.	Active Constructive	A common coach responses
	'I'm so pleased John. I am, really pleased because you have worked so hard over the past months, and you deserve this... well done... I'm so proud of you'.	*'Good – you have been promoted...' And/or 'What might this mean for you?'*

CONCLUSION

This style of responding encourages the coach to adapt an explicitly positive stance towards their coachee through active listening and responding to what they have heard at the verbal and non-verbal level.

REFERENCES

Egan, G. (2009). *The skilled helper*. London: Waddesworth.

Gable, S.L., Reis, H.T., Impett, E.A. & Asher, E.R. (2004). What do you do when things go right? The intrapersonal and interpersonal benefits of sharing positive events. *Journal of Personality and Social Psychology*, 87, 228–245.

Gable, S.L., Gonzaga, G.C., & Strachman, A. (2006). Will you be there for me when things go right? Supportive responses to positive event disclosures. *Journal of Personality and Social Psychology*, 91, 904–917.

Klein, N. (1999). *Time to think*. London: Hachett.

Miller, W.R. & Rollnick, S. (2012). *Motivational Interview: Helping people change* (3rd ed.). New York: Guilford Press.

Oades, L. & Passmore, J. (2014). Positive psychology coaching. In J. Passmore (Ed.), *Mastery in coaching*. Kogan Page: London.

Magyar-Moe, J.L. (2009). *Positive psychological interventions. Therapist's guide to positive psychological interventions*. San Diego, CA: Academic Press.

48 Positive psychology techniques – Positive case conceptualisation

Jonathan Passmore & Lindsay G. Oades

Abstract

This short techniques article is part of a series of papers and builds on the initial outline paper which explored the potential of positive psychology approaches within coaching (Passmore & Oades, 2014). This paper focuses on the skill of positive case conceptualisation, which allows coach and coachee to work collaboratively on building a shared understanding of the positive issues under discussion.

Keywords

case conceptualisation; positive case conceptualisation; positive diagnosis; coaching mind maps; positive psychology; positive psychology coaching.

CASE CONCEPTUALISATION (CC)

The concept of case conceptualisation has derived from work within therapy, and is commonly used in cognitive behavioural therapy. Counselling psychologists have defined the term as:

Original publication details: Passmore, J., & Oades, L. G. (2015, June). Positive psychology techniques – Positive case conceptualization. *The Coaching Psychologist, 11*(1), 43–45. Reproduced with permission of The British Psychological Society.

Coaching Practiced, First Edition. Edited by David Tee and Jonathan Passmore.
© 2022 John Wiley & Sons Ltd. Published 2022 by John Wiley & Sons Ltd.
DOI: 10.1002/9781119835714.ch48

'Case formulation aims to describe a person's presenting problems and a theory to make explanatory inferences about causes and maintaining factors that can inform interventions. First, there is a top-down process of cognitive behavioural theory providing clinically useful descriptive frameworks. Second the formulation enables practitioners and clients to make explanatory inferences about what caused and maintains the presenting issues. Thirdly case formulation explicitly and centrally informs intervention. Case formulation is a cornerstone of evidence-based CBT practice. For any particular case of CBT practice, formulation is the bridge between practice and theory and research. It is the crucible, where the individual particularities of a given case relevant theory and research synthesise into an understanding of the persons presenting issues in CBT'(Kuyken et al., 2009, p.42).

In short, case conceptualisation is the formation of a rationale and framework, underpinned by an evidence base, to summarise the therapists thinking and inform their future work with the client.

POSITIVE CASE CONCEPTUALISATION (PCC)

Lane and Corrie (2009) importantly identified the issue of case conceptualisation in coaching psychology practice, and suggested there was value in coaches reflecting on the presenting evidence and formulating an evidenced-based approach to address the issue.

Others (Biswas-Diener & Ebooks, 2010) have used slightly different language, such as Positive Diagnosis, to consider similar issues. The concept has also been used in solution-focused approaches (Green, Oades & Grant, 2006). Drawing on these writers and the application of CC in CBT, we have developed the ideas into a positive psychological based approach (Oades & Passmore, 2014).

In Figure 1, we have used a real life example from a personal coaching assignment on which one of the authors was engaged.

This illustration shows how the coach and coachee make sense of the relationships between key aspects of the person's psychological and social world, using key concepts within positive psychology, such as strengths, positive emotions and meaning. The aim here is not to 'diagnose', by finding deficits or causes of the coachees' perceived problems, but rather to reconfigure possibilities and look for opportunities. The positive case conceptualisation examines what the solution looks like. The conceptualisation is of a possible preferred situation and how it relates. In this example, new opportunities came from exploring the new work and new house possibilities. The coachee started to see several opportunities once those two changes were conceptualised as part of a bigger solution including living closer to work, being closer to the airport for her husband and greater involvement of the coachee's mum in looking after children. These possibilities arose iteratively as the case was conceptualised through a positive and solution-based lens.

Figure 1   *Diagrammatic representation of positive case conceptualisation developed during coaching.*

A key guiding question is *'If things are functioning really well, and people in the system are feeling good, what does it look like?'* Hence, whilst the coaching may be triggered by a problem, difficulty or transition, the PCC itself seeks to identify what things functioning well look like, using the language of positive psychology and the science of wellbeing applied to the context.

What we have found works well is to draw this as a mind map, rather than a linear list, which allows for the opportunity to show relationships/links between the different aspects identified. By using different colours the mindmap can be further enhanced.

Biswas-Diener and Ebooks (2010) describe three core areas of PCC as: (a) a positive focus; (b) benefits of positive emotion; and (c) the science of strengths. Whilst this is appropriate, the conceptualisation expands these three areas to include a greater emphasis on the sustainable well-being (eudaimonic well-being) components, which emphasises the importance of meaning in life, a sense of purpose and striving towards one's perceived full potential.

CONCLUSION

The technique offers an opportunity to apply creativity in the coaching conversation and for the coach and coachee to work together to build a shared understanding of the positive aspects of the issue under discussion.

REFERENCES

Biswas-Diener, R. & Ebooks, C. (2010). *Practicing positive psychology coaching: Assessment, activities, and strategies for success*. Hoboken, NJ: Wiley.

Green, L.S., Oades, L.G. & Grant, A.M. (2006). Cognitive-behavioural, solution-focused life coaching: Enhancing goal striving, well-being and hope. *Journal of Positive Psychology, 1*(3), 142–149.

Kuyken, W. Padesky, C.A. & Dudley, R. (2009). *Collaborative case conceptualisation: Working effectively with clients*. New York: Guilford Press.

Lane, D & Corrie, S. (2009). Does coaching psychology need the concept of formulation? *International Coaching Psychology Review, 4*(2), 193–206.

Oades, L. & Passmore, J. (2014). Positive psychology coaching. In J. Passmore (Ed.), *Mastery in coaching*. London: Kogan Page.

Passmore, J. & Oades, L.G. (2014). Positive psychology coaching, *The Coaching Psychologist, 10*(2), 68–70.

49 Positive psychology techniques – Random Acts of Kindness and Consistent Acts of Kindness and Empathy

Jonathan Passmore & Lindsay G. Oades

Abstract

In this techniques paper we explain how using random acts of kindness can be built into consistent acts of kindness and empathy, helping clients build, hope, self-regard as well as long-term physical health.

Keywords

Random Acts of Kindness; RAK; Consistent Acts of Kindness; CAKE empathy; Positive Psychology Coaching (PPC).

Original publication details: Passmore, J., & Oades, L. G. (2015, December). Positive psychology techniques – Random acts of kindness and consistent acts of kindness and empathy. *The Coaching Psychologist*, 11(2), 90–92. Reproduced with permission of The British Psychological Society.

Random acts of kindness are selfless acts performed by a person wishing to either help or positively affect the emotional state (mood) of another person. Anne Herbert, a journalist, claims to have invented the phrase in a call to others to 'Practice random kindness and senseless acts of beauty', back in 1982 while sitting in a restaurant in Sausalito, California. Whether this is truth or myth, the idea certainly pre-dates positive psychology. It may be argued that kindness has its roots in religion. Jesus preached the idea of showing kindness not just to friends, but to those we don't like, those who have different values or lifestyles to us, and our enemies; 'If you love those who love you, what credit is that to you? Even sinners love those who love them' (Luke 6:32). Judaism too places a focus on kindness to others; 'the world is built on kindness,' while Buddhism talks of the importance of 'loving kindness'.

Psychological research evidence overwhelmingly confirms that RAK brings positive benefits to the individual giver, in terms of both mental and physical health gains (see Post, 2005, for a discussion of the research).

However, our experience in an individualistic world, where time is money, and the dominant culture is 'i-think', is that these elements are too often forgotten. The focus at work is often targets, outcomes and financial return, in contrast with employee wellbeing, customer experience, creating optimum shared value and Gross Domestic Happiness.

We suggest the random acts of kindness technique can be an antidote to this culture and the isolation that the focus on the self creates. RAK fits within Positive Psychology Coaching (PPC) and offers benefits if practiced by the coaching psychologist or coach, as well offering a technique that the coach can invite the coachee to undertake as homework exercises.

We might encourage the coachee to slow their pace, and to both savour each experience and to show appreciation to those they encounter – these are aspects of gratitude and savoring. These are a starting point for creating the right mind to undertaking acts for other people.

The nature of RAK is that their specific content cannot be prescribed, and the list of possible actions is limitless. One example is the viral video a few years ago of an on-duty US police officer who went into a store to buy socks and shoes for a homeless man he had just met on the street and who was barefoot. There are many other examples, you can check out the following three examples in Table 1.

In Table 2 we have set out a one-week plan to help further develop RAK. Of course these need to be adapted to reflect the individual and their personal circumstances.

Table 1   *Make Yourself smile – some examples of RAKs*

Random Acts of Flowers	https://www.youtube.com/watch?v=YuMSpKpiHLQ
40 Acts for Lent	http://www.40acts.org.uk
Random Acts	https://www.youtube.com/watch?v=uge8sMTrzx0

Table 2 *Random Acts of Kindness – a one-week plan*

Monday: Compliment one thing which you like on/about three people you meet during the day.

Tuesday: Write a hand-written card to a boss or colleague to thank them for something they have done.

Wednesday: Say good morning to each person you meet in the lift at work or the reception staff when you arrive at the building/s you are visiting that day.

Thursday: Pick up some litter and put it in the bin on your way to work.

Friday: Use people's names (read their name badge) when talking to the staff in the canteen, café or coffee house and ask about their day.

Saturday: Place an uplifting note in library books or in a second hand book you are donating to a charity bookshop.

Sunday: Take flowers to a parent or a friend.

Using RAKs over a one-week period, as illustrated in Table 2, will provide psychological benefits to the giver, as well as benefits to the receiver. Much of the literature has focused on the random nature of these acts, which of course is useful.

However, we have suggested in this article and in our wider practice as coaching psychologists, the adoption of CAKE. This is a consistent approach to displaying acts of kindness to others through holding an empathetic stance towards all we meet, be they friends or those trying to do harm to us; from the person who cuts us up in traffic, to the colleague we see shouting at his staff.

CAKE encourages the individual to adopt this mind set, not just when the mood takes them, but as a permanent way of being. What we are really seeking is for the individual to think and act in this way in a more consistent basis. The aim in doing so is to build empathy towards others, why are they acting as they are, and to respond with empathy and kindness. One question we might ask ourself is 'what situation would cause me to behave in that way or to hold that opinion?'. By aiming to hold a more positive stance towards others, we can try to recognise, respect and celebrate others humanity and vulnerability, while at the same time cultivating humility in ourselves.

This attitudinal change requires the development of an adjustment from being i-centric towards a more 'we-centric' view of our relationships at home and work and adopting a similar view of all those we see and encourage.

CONCLUSION

This technique paper offers a simple approach, which can be used by the coach to foster empathy and loving kindness in themselves, as well as homework tasks to offer to the coachee for them to apply

REFERENCES

Oades, L. & Passmore, J. (2014). Positive Psychology Coaching. In J. Passmore (Ed.), *Mastery in coaching*. London: Kogan Page.

Post, S. (2005). Altruism, happiness, and health: It's good to be good. *International Journal of Behavioural Medicine, 12*(2), 66–77.

50 Positive psychology techniques – gratitude

Jonathan Passmore & Lindsay G. Oades

Abstract

This article builds on a descriptive paper on positive psychology coaching and several previous techniques papers. This paper explores the application of gratitude, with its associated benefits, as a part of positive psychology coaching practice.

Keywords

gratitude; positive psychology coaching.

Gratitude is a concept which has become diminished in Western society, almost in parallel with the increasing wealth which most of its members enjoy. For many, wealth, possessions and health have become expected norms rather than personal 'blessings' that are appreciated. As expectations have changed, so gratitude has diminished. Gratitude has, for many, been replaced by disappointment, anger and resentment when expected 'blessings' either do not appear or they disappear.

This view contrasts with many religious traditions. Jews may start the day with Modeh Ani, a short Hebrew blessing in which God is thanked for life. The Christian tradition too shows gratitude to God for blessings, for example, with a short prayer of Grace before food, or thanks for family, life and the many blessings which life bestows. Gratitude in the Buddhist tradition can be linked to the concept of dependent origin, in which all things originate from other things; hence existence itself implying a form of gratitude.

Original publication details: Passmore, J., & Oades, L. G. (2016, June). Positive psychology techniques – gratitude. *The Coaching Psychologist, 12*(1), 34–35. Reproduced with permission of The British Psychological Society.

Some writers (cf. Emmons, 2008) have suggested that gratitude serves a social function in helping build and maintain relationships between family members and the wider kinship group. More importantly, gratitude encourages individuals to focus their attention on the positive aspects of their life, in contrast with dwelling on negative issues and events.

Research too (cf. McCullough, Emmons & Tsang, 2002) has linked gratitude with hope, life satisfaction and more proactive behaviours towards others.

By applying these insights through simple exercises for coachees, similar positive effects have been found (see Emmons, 2008). For coachees who are Christians, as well as those with other religious beliefs, the exercise can be set around finding a time of day to reflect on the good things in the coachee's life. The coachee can say a short two minute prayer expressing gratitude for these blessings: a convenient time is at the end of a day. For coachees without a faith, a reflective exercise can be set where the coachee is asked to spend a similar short period reflecting on the things which they most appreciate during their day.

This technique can be adapted for conflict situations, with the coachee asked to reflect on the individual with whom they are in conflict. Similarly, where a relationship is less strong, the coachee is invited to reflect and identify one (or – even better – two or three) characteristics they admire or appreciate in the other person. By expressing gratitude for these aspects of the person, and by focusing attention on these aspects, an anchor can be provided which may allow the relationship to develop.

This technique can form a regular routine that the coachee can develop and which can be used to help build positivity and manage workplace stress, challenging times or difficult situations. This can be done through using a 'gratitude diary' or letters. Which of these tools to use will depend on the individual and their situation, with Emmons (2008) suggesting that we need to be cautious in offering only one 'gratitude' technique.

Research by Seligman et al. (2005) found individuals who did this task daily become bored, whilst those asked to write down their gratitude felt anxious about their writing becoming public (Emmons, 2008). This echoes our own personal experiences of using these techniques. If overdone, this exercise can become boring and repetitive, so it may be better undertaken as a weekly task or as a felt expression of thanks rather than merely expressing an obligation or task to be fullfilled. Further meditation, as opposed to a written note, may make this activity less demanding whilst producing the same benefits.

In short, when selecting gratitude tasks for coachees, discuss the task with the individual, offering them a selection of activities. This allows the coachee to tailor the task to their individual situation and preferences. In addition, provide them with space to talk about any anxieties or feelings concerning the task and periodically review the coachee's progress.

CONCLUSION

This short technique of gratitude can help both coaches and coachees in the development of positivity, potentially leading to enhanced wellbeing.

REFERENCES

Emmons, R. (2008). *Thanks. How practicing gratitude can make you happier.* New York: Houghton Mifflin.

McCullough, M.E., Emmons, R. & Tsang, J. (2002). The grateful disposition: A conceptual and empirical topography. *Journal of Personality & Social Psychology, 82,* 112–127.

Oades, L. & Passmore, J. (2014). Positive Psychology Coaching. In J. Passmore (Ed.), *Mastery in coaching.* London: Kogan Page.

Seligman, M.E.P. (2002). *Authentic Happiness: Using the new positive psychology to realise your potential for lasting fulfilment.* New York: Free Press.

51 Positive psychology techniques – Three Good Things

Jonathan Passmore & Lindsay G. Oades

Abstract

This short article is the last in a series of six papers exploring positive psychology coaching techniques. The previous papers have explored the concept of positive coaching psychology and how it may be applied. The focus of this paper is a technique that encourages the mind to pay more attention to good things and develop a mind more observant of the positive in life.

Keywords

Three good things; positivity; positive psychology coaching.

THREE GOOD THINGS

Three good things', like 'active constructive responding' (Passmore & Oades, 2014b) and the other techniques in this series, is a technique which can be used both in coaching conversation and, more generally, in one-to-one conversation where the coach, manager or facilitator of the conversation wishes to encourage

Original publication details: Passmore, J., & Oades, L. G. (2016, December). Positive psychology techniques – Three good things. *The Coaching Psychologist, 12*(2), 77–78. Reproduced with permission of The British Psychological Society.

more positive responses from their coachee (team member). It forms part of the wider approach to positive psychology coaching we discussed earlier in this series (Passmore & Oades, 2014a) and in other papers (Passmore & Oades, 2014c)

This technique starts with the use of a question: 'What are the best three things about working here?' (or 'What are the three best things about today?'). Some individuals are able to repond by listing three aspects without further prompts. This opens up a conversation about the three 'good things', with the coachee encouraged to expand or provide specific details. By talking about a recent experience, or by explaining why these are the top three items the coachee has selected, the coach is encouraging the coachee to focus on the positive aspects of an issue, day or relationship, rather than being drawn to the negative.

Other individuals find it hard to start with a positive statement or complete the description with three positives without moving onto negative features. If the coachee mentions a negative aspect, the coach intervenes; 'We can look at some of the downsides later, but what have you enjoyed most?'. The interventions bring the focus back to the positive. Such an approach of reframing to the positive links back to Fredrickson's 'Broaden and Build' theory (Fredrickson, 2001) .

The repeated use of this technique (for example, daily practice over several months or — even better — a year or more) may strengthen the neural pathways which look for the positive aspects or issues which the individual encounters. As a result, the negative (downsides) focus and thinking is reduced (Seligman, 2016).

One of us has used coaching extensively with his children. To our surprise, children respond positvely to coaching as a learning aid that helps them think about their reasons for doing or not doing things (like running in the road or standing on their chair while at the table). This raises self-awareness. By exploring potential outcomes, coaching can also enhance personal responsibility for future actions.

By adapting general coaching techniques, the use of three good things has become part of one of the authors regular night time routines with his two daughters: Florence and Beatrice. Having used the technique for several years, the author now regularly receives coaching back from his four-year-old daughter. After asking her for her three good things, her reply is often followed up by; 'Dad, what were your three best things about today?'

Table 1 illustrates two real exchanges with Florence, when she was aged three. These were used on two consecutive days to reflect on her experiences from that day. The first example used standard open questions to encourage reflection on the day. The second placed a positive focus on the reflection with the specific aim of encouraging Florence to talk about her positive experiences and, in doing so, think about these experiences as she was getting ready for bed. What was interesting was that this exchange lead to Florence acting out her own positive experience with her doll as she thought and described the experience. While she was less able to articulate the experience than an adult, she was able to re-experience the emotion and then, having reflected on it, to act it out with her dolls.

The power of the technique is built through repeated use. We would typically invite adult coachees to take the intervention away as a homework task and to repeat it for seven days, including writing down the details of the event and emotion. What we have found is that having tried it for a week, just like our children,

Table 1   *Three good things — Example*

Day 1: Example using Typical coaching questions	Day 2: Example using 'Three good things' questions
Coach: 'So Florence, how was your day?' Florence: 'Okay' Coach: 'What did you do?' Florence 'I played dollies' Coach: 'What else? Florence 'I played with Tabatha' Coach: 'It sounds you had a lovely time'.	Coach: 'Florence what were the best three things you did today?' Florence: 'Going to Valerie's house' Coach: 'What did you like about going to Valerie's?' Florence: 'Getting a present from Valerie.......baby' Coach: 'What did you like about the baby' Florence: 'Cuddling baby...........playing with baby Coach: 'What else did you enjoy?' Florence: 'Pasta and ice cream tea....chocolate ice cream '(Florence had eaten ice cream and pasta at Valerie's House. A few moments later, Florence picked up her new doll and starts feeding pretend food to it. Florence (to her dolls): You like ice cream....... more ice cream?......... it's nice....'

many choose to make it a regular part of their routine. Coachees report that they find it pleasurable, useful, stimulating and an effective counter to negative ruminations at the close of the day.

CONCLUSION

As with many of the other techniques, 'three good things' is a technique the coach can use themselves, as well as offer to coachees' as a homework exercise, helping them to develop a more positive thinking style and enhance satisfaction with life and work.

REFERENCES

Fredrickson, B. (2001). The role of positive emotions in positive psychology: The broaden-and-build theory of positive emotions. *American Psychologist, 56 (3)*, March, 218–226.

Passmore, J. & Oades, L.G. (2014a). Positive Psychology Coaching. *The Coaching Psychologist. 10(2)*, 68–70.

Passmore, J. & Oades, L.G. (2014b). Positive Psychology Coaching Techniques: Active Constructive Responding. *The Coaching Psychologist, 10(2)*, 71–73.

Oades, L. & Passmore, J. (2014c). Positive Psychology Coaching. In J. Passmore (Ed). *Mastery in coaching*. London: Kogan Page.

Seligman, M. (2016). *Three good things*. Retrieved 2 February 2016 from https://www.youtube.com/watch?v=ZOGAp9dw8Ac.

Index

Note: Page numbers followed by "*f*" refers to figures and "*t*" refers to tables.

Coaching Practiced, First Edition. Edited by David Tee and Jonathan Passmore.
© 2022 John Wiley & Sons Ltd. Published 2022 by John Wiley & Sons Ltd.
DOI: 10.1002/9781119835714.bindex